ANNUAL REVIEW OF Global Peace Operations

2012

This volume is a product of the Center on International Cooperation's (CIC) Global Peace Operations program. CIC is an independent institution housed at New York University.

Project Team

VOLUME EDITOR AND LEAD RESEARCHER
Megan M. Gleason

SERIES EDITOR
Bruce D. Jones

CONTRIBUTING EDITOR
Jake Sherman

PROGRAM OFFICER
Morgan A. Hughes

CONTRIBUTORS
Tatiana Carayannis, Matthew Carrieri, Angus Clarkson, Tristan Dreisbach, Richard Gowan, Alischa Kugel, Yanikk Lewis, Laurie Mincieli, Nathaniel Olin, Aaron Pangburn, Sofia Sebastian, Elizabeth Sellwood, Keith Stanski, Lyla Sultan, and Erin Weir

The project's advisory board is composed of Lakhdar Brahimi, Jayantha Dhanapala, Rosario Green, 'Funmi Olonisakin, John Ruggie, Sir Rupert Smith, and Stephen J. Stedman. CIC is grateful for their advice and support.

The Center on International Cooperation is solely responsible for the content of this publication. Any errors of fact or analysis, and any and all judgments and interpretations about missions and operations discussed herein, are those of CIC alone.

This project was undertaken at the request of and with the support of the Best Practices Section of the UN Department of Peacekeeping Operations.

ANNUAL REVIEW OF
Global Peace Operations
2012

A PROJECT OF THE
Center on International Cooperation

LYNNE
RIENNER
PUBLISHERS

BOULDER
LONDON

Published in the United States of America in 2012 by
Lynne Rienner Publishers, Inc.
1800 30th Street, Boulder, Colorado 80301
www.rienner.com

and in the United Kingdom by
Lynne Rienner Publishers, Inc.
3 Henrietta Street, Covent Garden, London WC2E 8LU

ISBN: 978-1-58826-839-6 (pbk)
       978-1-58826-814-3 (hc)

ISSN: 1932-5819

Printed and bound in Canada

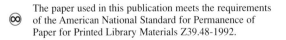 The paper used in this publication meets the requirements
of the American National Standard for Permanence of
Paper for Printed Library Materials Z39.48-1992.

5 4 3 2 1

Contents

Foreword, *Hervé Ladsous*   vii
Preface, *Jake Sherman*   ix
Mission Acronyms   xi
List of Boxes   xiii
Map of Global Peace Operations, 2011   xiv

Director's Comment   1
    Bruce D. Jones

Strategic Summary 2011   3
    Jake Sherman and Megan M. Gleason

1 Peacekeeping and Support for State Sovereignty   11
    Jake Sherman

2 Mission Reviews   27
  Alphabetical order by location

  2.1 Afghanistan (ISAF, EUPOL Afghanistan)   28
  2.2 Côte d'Ivoire (UNOCI, Operation Licorne)   36
  2.3 Democratic Republic of Congo
       (MONUSCO, EUSEC RD Congo, EUPOL RD Congo) 45
  2.4 Haiti (MINUSTAH)   53
  2.5 Liberia (UNMIL)   61
  2.6 Sudan and South Sudan (UNMIS, UNMISS, UNISFA, UNAMID) 69

3 Mission Notes   79
  Alphabetical order by location

  3.1 Bosnia and Herzegovina (EUFOR Althea, EUPM, OSCE BiH) 80
  3.2 Cyprus (UNFICYP)   83
  3.3 Georgia (EUMM)   87
  3.4 Kosovo (UNMIK, EULEX, KFOR, OMIK)   90
  3.5 Middle East (UNIFIL, UNDOF, UNTSO, EUBAM Rafah,
       EUPOL COPPS, TIPH, MFO Sinai, NTM-I) 96
  3.6 Solomon Islands (RAMSI)   106
  3.7 Somalia (AMISOM)   109
  3.8 Timor-Leste (UNMIT, ISF)   117
  3.9 Western Sahara (MINURSO)   123

4 Global Statistics on UN-Commanded Missions   127

5 Global Statistics on Non-UN-Commanded Missions   165

6 UN Mission-by-Mission Statistics   193
   Alphabetical order by mission acronym

   6.1   MINURSO (UN Mission for the Referendum in Western Sahara)   198
   6.2   MINUSTAH (UN Stabilization Mission in Haiti)   207
   6.3   MONUSCO (UN Organization Stabilization Mission in the
         Democratic Republic of Congo)   216
   6.4   UNAMID (UN-AU Hybrid Mission in Darfur)   225
   6.5   UNDOF (UN Disengagement Observer Force)   234
   6.6   UNFICYP (UN Peacekeeping Force in Cyprus)   243
   6.7   UNIFIL (UN Interim Force in Lebanon)   252
   6.8   UNISFA (UN Interim Security Force for Abyei)   262
   6.9   UNMIK (UN Interim Administration Mission in Kosovo)   269
   6.10 UNMIL (UN Mission in Liberia)   277
   6.11 UNMIS (UN Mission in Sudan)/
         UNMISS (UN Mission in South Sudan)   287
   6.12 UNMIT (UN Integrated Mission in Timor-Leste)   297
   6.13 UNMOGIP (UN Military Observer Group in India and Pakistan)   306
   6.14 UNOCI (UN Operation in Côte d'Ivoire)   312
   6.15 UNTSO (UN Truce Supervision Organization)   322

Index   329
About the Book   343

Foreword

United Nations peacekeeping continues to be a critical instrument for the maintenance of international peace and security. The diverse mandates provided by the Security Council to peacekeepers cover a broad spectrum of tasks, reflecting the reality that, in the postconflict environment, so much must be accomplished to rebuild and sustain peace. Peacekeepers help to provide security and assist national actors to re-establish legitimate governance through elections and constitutional reform, to disarm and demobilize ex-combatants, to reform the security sector and justice systems, to protect human rights, and to build peace, thereby contributing to help kick-start economic recovery and development.

Where conflict has disrupted or destroyed the institutions of the state, peace often cannot be secured simply through the establishment of a new postconflict government by a single cycle of elections. Where postconflict governments face severe challenges to re-establish basic institutions, we see a number of peace operations engaged in efforts to help extend state authority. In the absence of a functioning and accountable military, police, judiciary, or civil service, or where a government has limited access to the entirety of its territory, a meaningful extension of state sovereignty (such as a significant presence or the provision of basic services to which its citizenry will be entitled if the state is to retain legitimacy) is a challenge.

In such circumstances, peacekeeping operations often provide support to extend state authority in both functional and geographic terms. Peacekeepers assist national authorities in strengthening key institutions of government and help to support governance beyond the capital, where lack of logistics, transport, and security can mean that local authorities look to peacekeepers for essential help. Extending state authority is often critical if fragile peace is to be solidified and if investments and assistance made earlier in peace processes are to be realized. Yet, where government authority may still be contested, close association with the institutions of state can raise issues of partiality for UN operations. Equally, supporting nascent state security institutions in their efforts to secure territory while promoting human rights compliance can prove to be extremely challenging. Chapter 1 in this edition of the Center on International Cooperation's *Annual Review,* which focuses on the extension of state authority and the experience of missions with this complex set of tasks, provides an important contribution to policy dialogue on these challenges.

Whereas the year-on-year growth in scale of peacekeeping that was seen over the past decade has slowed, a vast enterprise remains, and the complexity of tasks and the stakes for peacekeeping operations remain very high. The extension of state authority is but one of numerous complex mandates provided by the Security Council to peacekeeping operations.

The range of tasks undertaken and the accomplishments of peacekeepers are noteworthy, a testament to their remarkable flexibility and versatility, and 2011 proved no exception. A few examples of the challenges faced and met by peacekeepers in 2011: Peacekeepers supported elections held in Haiti, Côte d'Ivoire, Liberia, and the Democratic Republic of Congo, as well as the referendum on the status of South Sudan. In Côte d'Ivoire, the mission was called upon to protect itself and the outcome of the electoral process. The UNMIS operation was drawn down in Sudan, even as UNMISS was established to support the new state of South Sudan and also UNISFA to assist in the resolution of the situation in Abyei and related issues.

The scale and complexity of the challenges that peacekeeping continues to face mean that efforts to strengthen and reform the instrument remain absolutely necessary. The overall cost of deploying peacekeepers also demands that we seek the utmost efficiency from our operations. After being appointed by the Secretary-General to lead the Department of Peacekeeping Operations (DPKO), I have reaffirmed the need to continue peacekeeping reforms, in particular efforts to strengthen the partnership among the Security Council, member state troop, police, and financial contributors, and the Secretariat—a partnership that is critical to successful peacekeeping. With this partnership strong, ongoing efforts to build and expand peacekeeping capacities (both uniformed and civilian) and to address policy gaps and strengthen field support mechanisms are all the more likely to succeed. The need to continue to further strengthen UN partnerships with regional and other organizations is also essential, including, but not limited to, partnerships with the African Union and European Union.

Our goal must be to ensure that global peacekeeping capacity overall is enhanced. Our effectiveness and impact on the ground are also inextricably linked to the safety and security of peacekeeping personnel, to which we must give top priority.

We have before us a full agenda for peacekeeping reform, all the more reason that the *Annual Review* continues to be an indispensable publication for all those involved in peacekeeping. It analyzes and comments ably on the rich and varied operations deployed around the world. It also helps to place United Nations peacekeeping operations within a broader array of peace and security instruments.

Looking ahead, I welcome CIC's intent to bring together its various reviews to present a coherent picture of a complex and rapidly evolving operational environment of peace operations. Whereas the presence of troops is a distinguishing characteristic of multidimensional peacekeeping operations, it is hardly a defining one. Peacekeeping missions share with other political and peacebuilding missions many elements based on the common quest to provide a wide range of support to countries making the transition to peace. In this context, viewing comprehensively the full spectrum of peace missions will be informative and help collective efforts to strengthen the partnerships needed for them to succeed.

Today and for the foreseeable future, we will continue to face the challenge of building and strengthening peacekeeping, as part of a range of instruments at the disposal of the international community to support the maintenance of international peace and security.

—*Hervé Ladsous*
Under-Secretary-General for Peacekeeping Operations
United Nations

Preface

The 2012 edition of the *Annual Review of Global Peace Operations,* the seventh in the series by the Center on International Cooperation (CIC) at New York University, comes amid intense debates around the role of peacekeeping and its financing. While the impact of the global financial crisis continues to constrain the resources available for multilateral peace operations, 2011 saw the authorization of two new United Nations peacekeeping operations in Sudan and South Sudan and the strengthening of the African Union's peacekeeping mission in Somalia. Events this year have also demonstrated the continued need for peacekeepers to respond to a broad range of needs in-country, including ushering in a newly independent South Sudan, protecting civilians in Libya and Côte d'Ivoire, supporting elections in multiple missions, and supporting ongoing recovery in Haiti. These events highlight the role that peace operations play in supporting the extension and consolidation of state authority, the thematic focus for this year's volume of the *Annual Review.*

This edition of the *Annual Review* would not be possible without the financial support of the Norwegian Ministry of Foreign Affairs, the German Foreign Office, and Australian Departments of Defense and of Foreign Affairs and Trade, as well as the Compton Foundation. Their generosity funds not only the production of the *Annual Review,* but also much of the vital outreach that helps us reach this volume's intended audience and inform global policy discussions.

While retaining its editorial independence, the *Annual Review* is the result of our close, ongoing partnership with the UN's Department of Peacekeeping Operations (DPKO) and Department of Field Support and the Peace and Security Department of the African Union (AU). CIC is grateful for the support from Susana Malcorra, UN Under-Secretary-General for the Department of Field Support, and Ramtane Lamamra, AU Commissioner for Peace and Security.

CIC also wishes to express its appreciation for the cooperation and encouragement of Hervé Ladsous, UN Under-Secretary-General for Peacekeeping Operations, who wrote the foreword to this volume. We are grateful that he could share his vision of the future of peace operations as he takes the helm of the Department of Peacekeeping Operations.

The *Annual Review* is the product of CIC's Global Peace Operations program, a small group of talented and industrious individuals who provided much of the editorial and research work behind the volume. Megan Gleason deftly oversaw the project, coordinating a complex network of contributors and tight deadlines. In her first year as lead editor, she expertly managed the process and displayed the attention to detail needed to coordinate this publication. Morgan Hughes took on the daunting task of collecting, organizing, and presenting the tremendous set of data that is a pillar of the *Annual Review,* while also providing invaluable help in its production and editing. Alischa Kugel provided much appreciated support throughout the production process, and Tristan Dreisbach's assistance throughout all stages was critical.

Our core team depended greatly on the

tremendous assistance of CIC staff members Yvonne Alonzo, Shiri Avnery, Lynn Denesopolis, Molly Elgin-Cossart, Jane Esberg, Antonie Evans, Noah Gall, Richard Gowan, Tom Gregg, Marc Jacquand, Camino Kavanagh, Parnian Nazary, Emily O'Brien, Barnett Rubin, W. P. S. Sidhu, Keith Stanski, Teresa Whitfield, and Constance Wilhelm. We are especially grateful for the help provided by Francisca Aas, Matthew Carrieri, Yanikk Lewis, Laurie Mincieli, and Aaron Pangburn. This year's volume also benefited from the expertise of Tatiana Carayannis, Angus Clarkson, Nathaniel Olin, Sofia Sebastian, Elizabeth Sellwood, and Erin Weir, all of whom provided valuable contributions. Former CIC staff members Victoria DiDomenico, Andrew Sinclair, and Benjamin Tortolani—all veterans of the *Annual Review*—also provided guidance and support.

We owe a debt of thanks to the many individuals at the United Nations who make this volume possible. There is not sufficient space to thank all who provided their assistance, but David Haeri of DPKO's Best Practices Section, as always, was a tremendous help, as were Leanne Smith and Cris Stephen. We would also like to thank Lin Bai, Vladamir Bessarabov, Adam Day, Raphaëlle Guillon, Megh Gurung, Patrick Hein, Clare Hutchinson, Kathryn Jones, Amin Mohsen, Gloria Ntegeye, Rafael Peralta, Amy Scott Hill, Kristina Segulja, Bojan Stefanovic, and the many desk officers who reviewed drafts of the mission reviews and notes. A special mention must go to Ayako Kagawa and Geraldine Velandria of the UN's Cartographic Section, who worked closely with us to prepare the many detailed maps that appear in the book. CIC alone is responsible for all errors, omissions, and mistaken statements of fact or analysis contained herein.

As in years past, this volume would not be possible without the support of the Stockholm International Peace Research Institute (SIPRI). We are tremendously grateful to Claire Fanchini at SIPRI, who collected and provided us with the non-UN data.

Last but certainly not least, we must also thank everyone at Lynne Rienner Publishers who assisted in the production of this year's *Annual Review*. Special mention must be made of the tireless efforts of Steve Barr and Lesli Brooks Athanasoulis. We are grateful for their patience and accommodation throughout the process.

—*Jake Sherman*
Deputy Director for Programs (Conflict), and
Contributing Editor, *Annual Review,*
Center on International Cooperation

Mission Acronyms

AMISOM	AU Mission in Somalia
EUBAM Rafah	EU Border Assistance Mission at Rafah
EUFOR Althea	EU Force in Bosnia and Herzegovina
EULEX	EU Rule of Law Mission in Kosovo
EUMM	EU Monitoring Mission in Georgia
EUPM	EU Police Mission in Bosnia and Herzegovina
EUPOL Afghanistan	EU Police Mission in Afghanistan
EUPOL COPPS	EU Coordinating Office for Palestinian Police Support
EUPOL RD Congo	EU Police Mission in the Democratic Republic of Congo
EUSEC RD Congo	EU Advisory and Assistance Mission for Security Reform in the Democratic Republic of Congo
IMT	International Monitoring Team
ISAF	International Security Assistance Force
ISF	International Security Forces
JCC	Joint Control Commission Peacekeeping Force
KFOR	NATO Kosovo Force
MFO Sinai	Multinational Force and Observers in Sinai
MICOPAX	Mission for the Consolidation of Peace in the Central African Republic
MINURSO	UN Mission for the Referendum in Western Sahara
MINUSTAH	UN Stabilization Mission in Haiti
MONUSCO	UN Organization Stabilization Mission in the Democratic Republic of Congo
NTM-I	NATO Training Mission in Iraq
OMIK	OSCE Mission in Kosovo
RAMSI	Regional Assistance Mission in the Solomon Islands
TIPH	Temporary International Presence in Hebron
UNAMID	UN-AU Hybrid Mission in Darfur
UNDOF	UN Disengagement Observer Force
UNFICYP	UN Peacekeeping Force in Cyprus
UNIFIL	UN Interim Force in Lebanon
UNISFA	UN Interim Security Force for Abyei
UNMIK	UN Interim Administration Mission in Kosovo
UNMIL	UN Mission in Liberia
UNMIS	UN Mission in Sudan
UNMISS	UN Mission in South Sudan

UNMIT	UN Integrated Mission in Timor-Leste
UNMOGIP	UN Military Observer Group in India and Pakistan
UNOCI	UN Operation in Côte d'Ivoire
UNTSO	UN Truce Supervision Organization

Boxes

The 2011 *World Development Report: Conflict, Security, and Development*   8

The Review of International Civilian Capacities   16

India-Pakistan (UNMOGIP)   32

Peace Operations and Electoral Violence   40

Central African Republic (MICOPAX)   48

UN Peacekeeping Troop Reimbursement   56

Helicopters in Peacekeeping Operations   64

Safety and Security   72

Moldova-Transdniestria (JCC)   82

Women, Peace, and Security   85

HIV/AIDS and UN Peacekeeping   93

Libya (NATO Operation Unified Protector)   99

Regional Organizations: ASEAN and the CSTO   107

Piracy off the Coast of Somalia   115

From Host Nation to Troop Contributor   116

Mindanao, Philippines (IMT)   120

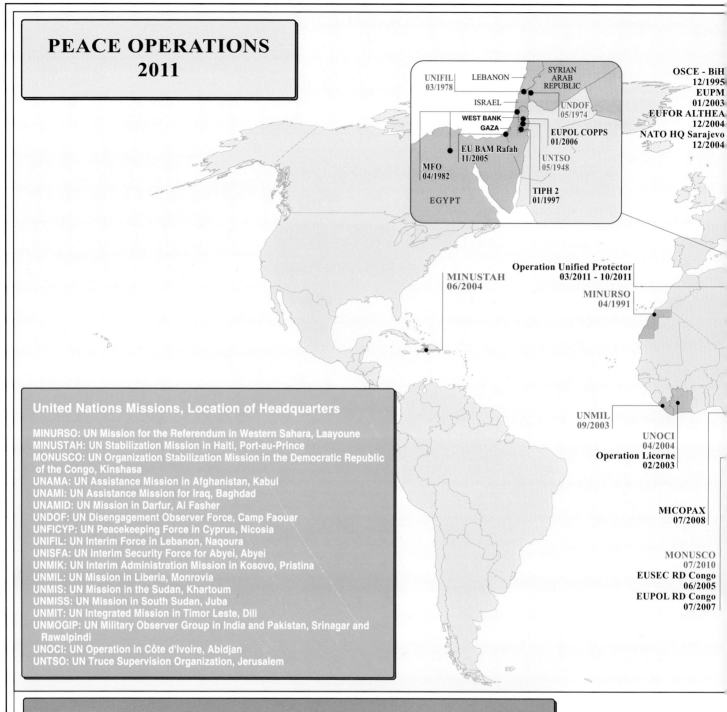

PEACE OPERATIONS 2011

UNIFIL
03/1978

LEBANON

SYRIAN
ARAB
REPUBLIC

OSCE - BiH
12/1995
EUPM
01/2003
EUFOR ALTHEA
12/2004
NATO HQ Sarajevo
12/2004

ISRAEL

UNDOF
05/1974

WEST BANK
GAZA

EUPOL COPPS
01/2006

EU BAM Rafah
11/2005

UNTSO
05/1948

MFO
04/1982

TIPH 2
01/1997

EGYPT

MINUSTAH
06/2004

Operation Unified Protector
03/2011 - 10/2011

MINURSO
04/1991

UNMIL
09/2003

UNOCI
04/2004
Operation Licorne
02/2003

MICOPAX
07/2008

MONUSCO
07/2010
EUSEC RD Congo
06/2005
EUPOL RD Congo
07/2007

United Nations Missions, Location of Headquarters

MINURSO: UN Mission for the Referendum in Western Sahara, Laayoune
MINUSTAH: UN Stabilization Mission in Haiti, Port-au-Prince
MONUSCO: UN Organization Stabilization Mission in the Democratic Republic of the Congo, Kinshasa
UNAMA: UN Assistance Mission in Afghanistan, Kabul
UNAMI: UN Assistance Mission for Iraq, Baghdad
UNAMID: UN Mission in Darfur, Al Fasher
UNDOF: UN Disengagement Observer Force, Camp Faouar
UNFICYP: UN Peacekeeping Force in Cyprus, Nicosia
UNIFIL: UN Interim Force in Lebanon, Naqoura
UNISFA: UN Interim Security Force for Abyei, Abyei
UNMIK: UN Interim Administration Mission in Kosovo, Pristina
UNMIL: UN Mission in Liberia, Monrovia
UNMIS: UN Mission in the Sudan, Khartoum
UNMISS: UN Mission in South Sudan, Juba
UNMIT: UN Integrated Mission in Timor Leste, Dili
UNMOGIP: UN Military Observer Group in India and Pakistan, Srinagar and Rawalpindi
UNOCI: UN Operation in Côte d'Ivoire, Abidjan
UNTSO: UN Truce Supervision Organization, Jerusalem

Non-UN Missions, Location of Headquarters

AMISOM: African Union Mission in Somalia, Mogadishu
EU BAM Rafah: EU Border Assistance Mission at Rafah, Rafah
EULEX KOSOVO: EU Rule of Law Mission, Pristina
EUFOR ALTHEA: EU Military Operation in Bosnia and Herzegovina, Sarajevo
EUMM: EU Monitoring Mission in Georgia, Tbilisi
EUPM: EU Police Mission in Bosnia and Herzegovina, Sarajevo
EUPOL Afghanistan: EU Police Mission in Afghanistan, Kabul
EUPOL COPPS: EU Police Mission for the Palestinian Territories, Ramallah
EUPOL RD Congo: EU Police Mission in the Democratic Republic of the Congo, Kinshasa
EUSEC RD Congo: EU Security Reform Mission in the Democratic Republic of the Congo, Kinshasa
IMT: International Monitoring Team, Cotabato
ISF: International Security Forces, Dili
ISAF: International Security Assistance Force, Kabul - NATO

Dates following the abbreviated mission names represent dates of effect (for UN missions), and start dates (for non-UN missions).

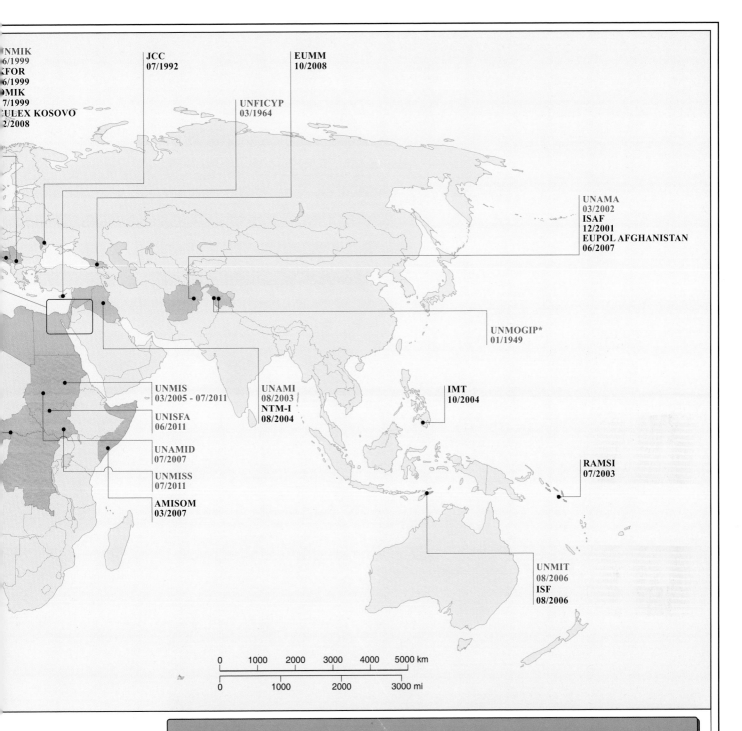

NMIK
6/1999
KFOR
6/1999
OMIK
7/1999
ULEX KOSOVO
2/2008

JCC
07/1992

UNFICYP
03/1964

EUMM
10/2008

UNAMA
03/2002
ISAF
12/2001
EUPOL AFGHANISTAN
06/2007

UNMOGIP*
01/1949

UNMIS
03/2005 - 07/2011

UNISFA
06/2011

UNAMID
07/2007

UNMISS
07/2011

AMISOM
03/2007

UNAMI
08/2003
NTM-I
08/2004

IMT
10/2004

RAMSI
07/2003

UNMIT
08/2006
ISF
08/2006

```
0    1000  2000  3000  4000  5000 km
0         1000        2000        3000 mi
```

boundaries and names shown and the designations
…d on this map do not imply official endorsement or
…eptance by the United Nations.

…tted line represents approximately the Line of
…trol in Jammu and Kashmir agreed upon by India
…Pakistan. The final status of Jammu and Kashmir
…not yet been agreed upon by the parties.

…inal boundary between the Republic of Sudan and
…Republic of South Sudan has not yet been
…rmined.

…A dispute exists between the Governments of Argentina
…the United Kingdom of Great Britain and Northern
…nd concerning sovereignty over the Falkland Islands
…vinas).

Non-UN Missions, Location of Headquarters

JCC: Joint Control Commission Peacekeeping Force, Transdniestria
KFOR: Kosovo Force, Pristina - NATO
MFO: Multinational Force and Observers, Rome
MICOPAX: Economic Community of Central African States Mission for building peace in Central Africa, Bangui
NATO Headquarters Sarajevo, Sarajevo
NTM-I: NATO Training Mission in Iraq, Baghdad
OMIK: OSCE Mission in Kosovo, Pristina
Operation Licorne, Abidjan
Operation Unified Protector, Naples
OSCE - BiH: OSCE Mission to Bosnia and Herzegovina, Sarajevo
RAMSI: Regional Assistance Mission in the Solomon Islands, Honiara - Pacific Islands Forum
TIPH 2: Temporary International Presence in Hebron, Hebron

Director's Comment

The year 2011 could have been a disastrous one for peacekeeping. At the start of the year, Côte d'Ivoire appeared to be on the brink of renewed civil war in spite of the presence of UN and French forces. South Sudan's independence referendum also had the potential to unleash mass violence. From Haiti to Liberia to the Democratic Republic of Congo, peacekeepers were charged with overseeing elections that might result in instability. In Somalia, African Union (AU) forces were locked in combat with Islamist rebels.

The risk of one or more of these situations spiraling out of control was high. Some came very close to doing so. For the first three months of the year, the UN was on the defensive in Côte d'Ivoire, and thousands of civilians lost their lives before the Security Council ordered the peacekeepers to take more robust action. The UN force in Sudan, having facilitated a successful referendum, was rendered helpless when northern and southern forces clashed in the disputed region of Abyei. The UN had known its contingent there was vulnerable, but it was necessary to deploy an entirely new mission to restore order.

Nonetheless, the most striking fact about this edition of the *Annual Review of Global Peace Operations* is that it is not a chronicle of peacekeeping failures. Instead, peace operations demonstrated an unexpected degree of resilience throughout 2011. The UN reasserted itself in Côte d'Ivoire, and helped ensure that the Haitian, Liberian, and Congolese elections were relatively smooth, if far from flawless. In Somalia, the AU scored a series of tactical victories, and the Islamists pulled back from Mogadishu.

While these established peace operations may have been relatively successful, the year brought unexpected challenges in the Middle East. Many commentators (including the Center on International Cooperation's team) believed that it might be necessary to deploy a peace operation to conclude the war in Libya. The EU briefly offered to send troops on a humanitarian mission, but a military operation in Libya ultimately proved unnecessary, with the UN sending a political mission instead. By the end of the year, the Arab League was deploying monitors to Syria—the league's first peace operation since the 1970s.

The instability in the Middle East is not yet finished. At the time of writing, it is still more than conceivable that Syria or another country in the region may require a peacekeeping force in 2012 (Turkey has alluded to the possibility of a military mission in Syria, for example, although only as a last resort). In the meantime, the peace operations already deployed in the area have to adapt to an increasingly uncertain environment. In December 2011, the UN mission in Lebanon was the subject of a series of terrorist attacks. With tensions with Iran growing, such risks may increase considerably soon.

Yet all these events and challenges have had surprisingly little impact on policy debates about the future of peacekeeping at the UN and in other organizations in 2011. Rather than talking about the effects of operations, diplomats and officials have developed one overriding obsession: what operations cost.

The last year has seen the financial crisis finally make itself felt in the world of peace operations. From 2008 to 2010, the global economic downturn had only a marginal effect on peacekeeping. Representatives of the main financiers of international operations—the United States, Europe, and Japan—noted that there was a need for austerity. Missions saw their budgets constrained or trimmed. But there were relatively few calls for deeper cuts in international peacekeeping. This is starting to change.

In New York, 2011 saw a fierce debate over the rate of reimbursements to troop contributors and quieter but serious arguments among Western countries about the costs of the UN missions in South Sudan, Haiti, and Liberia. US, British, and French officials traded barbs privately and even in the media, betraying unusual tensions among the Western powers that traditionally dominate the Security Council. Cost issues are not solely confined to the UN. The European Union, which mandated an increasing number of missions prior to the financial crisis, has now become very negative toward new operations. Analysts are still trying to interpret how North Atlantic Treaty Organization (NATO) defense cuts will restrain future operations.

What will these developments do to peace operations? Advocates of peacekeeping tend to react badly to being challenged over the costs involved. They point to the relatively low costs of UN and the AU missions (at present less than $10 billion a year combined) and compare this to the sums devoted to stimulating the US economy in 2009 or trying to save the euro in 2011. The current level of spending on operations across all organizations is also soon likely to fall significantly, as NATO draws down in Afghanistan and the UN plans to reduce its missions in a number of cases, including Haiti and the Democratic Republic of Congo.

But there is little to be gained from avoiding or dismissing debates over the costs of peacekeeping. Instead, there is a strong case for using the current combination of strategic and financial pressures as the basis for launching a much more serious debate about how international peace operations are run.

A real debate about peacekeeping would start from two basic presumptions. First, the financial pressures are real and denying them is foolish. Second, the demand for effective peace operations is equally real, whether in Côte d'Ivoire or Syria. Trying to cut peacekeeping costs just to save money is, therefore, a mistake. Refusing to accept the need to use money more effectively is just as mistaken.

Instead, it is necessary to take a hard look at the political economy and strategic logic of peacekeeping. The ongoing debates over the reimbursement rates for countries supplying peacekeepers, for example, need to be tied to more honest evaluations of the quality and impact of the forces involved. Can the systems for funding the supply of personnel and assets to the UN (or any other organization) be better calibrated to improve their effectiveness and commitment in the field? Is it possible to distinguish more reliably between those cases where significant long-term deployments are a necessity or a luxury?

The reimbursement debate in 2011 did at least result in the creation of a Senior Advisory Group of international experts tasked with reviewing how UN contributors are compensated. If the members of this group are ambitious, they could spark a broader rethinking of how to make peacekeeping work. In 2012, there will also be a debate at the UN on revising member states' "assessed contributions," the percentages of the peacekeeping and regular budgets that each country has to pay. Whereas it will be tempting to treat this as a purely financial exercise, it could also be a platform for wider strategic discussions of peacekeeping's future and the responsibilities of states in sustaining operations. In this context, this seventh edition of the *Annual Review of Global Peace Operations* is intended, like its predecessors, to provide the hard data and analysis of peacekeeping necessary for a real debate.

—*Bruce D. Jones*
Director, Center on International Cooperation

Strategic Summary 2011

*Jake Sherman and
Megan M. Gleason*

The United Nations Security Council authorized two new peacekeeping missions during 2011—the UN Mission in South Sudan (UNMISS) and the UN Interim Security Force for Abyei (UNISFA)—the first missions since the joint UN-AU Hybrid Mission in Darfur (UNAMID) was established in 2007. The Council also authorized the use of force to protect civilians in Libya, clearing the way for a NATO air campaign that divided members of the Security Council. Following the fall of Muammar Qaddafi, the Security Council mandated the civilian UN Support Mission in Libya (UNSMIL), a political mission, to help reestablish state authority.

These authorizations exhibit the range of options at the disposal of the Security Council in supporting countries in crisis and those emerging from conflict. For the past decade, the default mode of UN peacekeeping has been deployment of large, multidimensional operations. Recent missions, driven by the global financial crisis and by realities on the ground, offer alternatives to this model. UNISFA, a

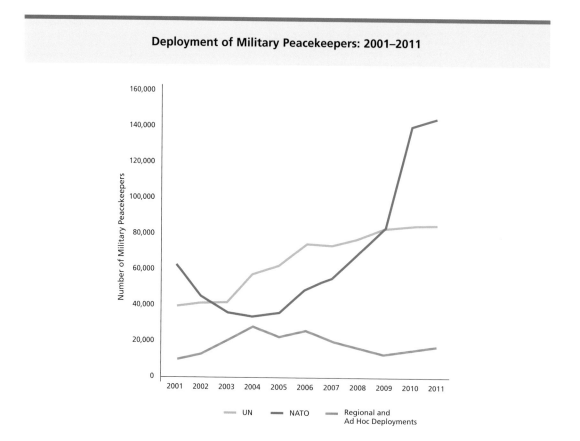

Deployment of Military Peacekeepers: 2001–2011

border-monitoring operation, was able to rapidly deploy by drawing its entire force requirement from a single, regional troop contributor. In Libya, none of the options tabled for a UN (or indeed non-UN) mission involving military troops were acceptable to the National Transitional Council. Agreement on a light civilian support mission is in line with the patterns of deployment elsewhere in the Middle East, which have favored monitoring missions and political missions.

Rapidly changing environments also tested the ability of existing missions to effectively respond to violence. Electoral crises in Côte d'Ivoire and Haiti, and at the time of writing also unfolding in the Democratic Republic of Congo, exposed limits in the capacity of UN peacekeeping operations to support political processes and reestablish legitimate state authority. Only the advanced military capabilities of France's Operation Licorne kept the UN Operation in Côte d'Ivoire (UNOCI) from irrelevance. Globally, these capabilities are predominantly—though not exclusively—possessed by Western countries largely absent from peacekeeping. Due to

the dearth of advanced military participation in peacekeeping, several of the UN's largest missions—including UNMIS, UNAMID, and the UN Organization Stabilization Mission in the Democratic Republic of Congo (MONUSCO)—have also struggled to uphold their mandates and protect civilians this past year. At the same time, NATO's experience in Afghanistan cautioned against placing too much stock in capabilities in the absence of a viable political framework. If the UN is to sustain confidence in peacekeeping as an effective means of crisis management, it requires member states to support it not just militarily, but politically as well.

Yet peacekeeping has faced increasing strain at UN headquarters and in capitals, as member states struggle with the ongoing fallout from the global financial crisis. Budgetary constraints, particularly among Western governments, have further frayed the relationship between financial contributors and troop/police contributors, and resulted in calls to quicken the pace of mission drawdown—both where missions have achieved stability and where they have not—without appropriate, practical, and

Deployment of Military Peacekeepers Excluding ISAF: 2001–2011

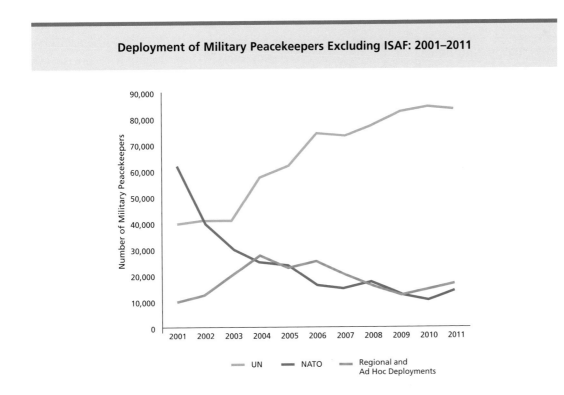

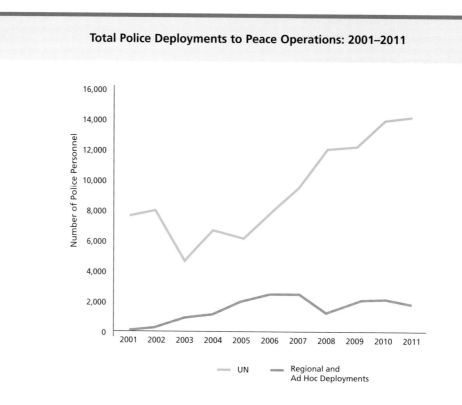

Total Police Deployments to Peace Operations: 2001–2011

cost-effective alternatives to prevent reversals and mitigate further violence.

The Year in Numbers

This year UN peacekeeping deployments experienced their first contraction since 2003. In 2011, 98,972 uniformed personnel were deployed, compared with 99,172 in 2010—a change of less than 0.5 percent.[1] However, a number of significant changes underlie this relatively stable figure. The closure of the UN Mission in Sudan (UNMIS) was roughly offset by the establishment of UNISFA and UNMISS, as well as smaller increases in a number of other missions. The post-electoral crisis prompted a troop increase in UNOCI of over 20 percent in 2011. In addition, the post-earthquake troop surge in the UN Stabilization Mission in Haiti (MINUSTAH) continued, though the mission will return to pre-earthquake levels in 2012. Peacekeepers in the UN Mission in Liberia (UNMIL) and the UN Integrated Mission in Timor-Leste (UNMIT) also

downsized, the latter in preparation for the expected withdrawal of UNMIT in 2012.

The decrease in UN peacekeeping was offset by increases in NATO and African Union deployments.[2] Thus, despite a decline in UN numbers, overall global peacekeeping continued to grow in 2011, though at a reduced pace compared with previous years; there were 263,118 peacekeepers deployed in 2011, compared with 256,170 in 2010, an increase of just 2.7 percent. NATO deployments increased this year, though troop numbers in its mission in Afghanistan remained stable. Additional contributions to the AU Mission in Somalia (AMISOM) from Burundi and Uganda strengthened the peacekeeping force by 35 percent this year, with further reinforcements pledged by Djibouti and Sierra Leone.

Pakistan, Bangladesh, and India were once again the top three troop-contributing countries to UN peacekeeping this year. However, Uruguay, Jordan, and Fiji supplied the most troops and military observers on a per capita basis. A number of countries—Ghana, Nepal, Rwanda,

Top Troop-Contributing Countries to UN Peace Operations: 2011

	Total Troops Contributed		Per Capita Troops Contributed
1	Pakistan	1	Uruguay
2	Bangladesh	2	Jordan
3	India	3	Fiji
4	Ethiopia	4	Rwanda
5	Nigeria	5	Senegal
6	Egypt	6	Nepal
7	Nepal	7	Gambia
8	Rwanda	8	Ghana
9	Ghana	9	Ireland
10	Uruguay	10	Benin

Note: Per capita calculations based on 2010 population data from the UN Population Division. Troop contributions include troops and military observers.

and Uruguay—were among the top ten troop contributors both in total and as a percentage of population.

During the past five years, military deployments to peace operations have increased by 65 percent and police deployments have grown by 56 percent. Within the UN, in the past five years military deployments have grown by nearly 13 percent, while police deployments have increased by 80 percent. Over the same period, civilian staff in UN peacekeeping missions, including international staff, national staff, and UN volunteers, increased nearly 27 percent.

Peacekeeping and the Extension of State Authority

This past year was also marked by the release of the World Bank's *World Development Report 2011* on conflict, security, and development, and the *Review of International Civilian Capacities*. The former suggests ways in which peace operations can enable countries to sustainably transition away from cycles of violence, including supporting the development of accountable, legitimate security and justice institutions. The latter provides a roadmap for UN reform and international partnerships to strengthen timely deployment of appropriate expertise to support countries emerging from crisis.

In this context, this volume of the *Annual Review* focuses on the extension and consolidation of state authority. This year's thematic essay charts the international community's experience in supporting the extension and consolidation of state authority and identifies a number of important lessons as well as ongoing challenges. As the mission reviews highlight, support to state authority has become a central function of peace operations in states recovering from protracted violence and armed conflict.

Sudan and South Sudan, which together host one-third of the UN's total global troop deployment, remain the most complex and most watched theaters in UN peace operations. The celebrations that followed South Sudan's independence from Sudan in July 2011 have been overshadowed by the failure to resolve the administration of Abyei, border demarcation, and revenue-sharing, among other contested issues. Escalating border violence in South Kordofan State and Blue Nile State and reported bombings by Sudanese armed forces in South Sudan's territory threaten a return to war between north and south, as well as a humanitarian emergency. UNISFA, unable to prevent the buildup of armed forces by both sides, has struggled to contain

The 2011 *World Development Report: Conflict, Security, and Development*

The World Bank's *2011 World Development Report* links the issues of state fragility and conflict and calls for a new approach to these challenges to break repeated cycles of violence.

In the twenty-first century, the predominant forms of conflict have changed, with fewer wars between or within states. New threats from trafficking, terrorism, and violent crime exacerbate state fragility, while local and international stresses, including high levels of youth unemployment, government corruption, and foreign security interference, create the risk of violence on multiple levels.

According to the *World Development Report*, combating these threats requires greater investment in citizen security, justice, and jobs through the creation of more resilient and legitimate institutions. However, institutional transformation requires increased confidence and commitment to the process so that potential spoilers can be turned into invested stakeholders in "inclusive-enough" coalitions. The process also occurs slowly, taking at least a generation for significant change.

The report calls for faster, more flexible international assistance targeted toward increasing the capacity of national institutions. International actors must demonstrate a long-term commitment to institution building and strengthen regional and international collaboration. The report also identifies a number of targeted steps to support sustainable peace, including basic job-creation plans, processes for addressing both national and regional threats concurrently, and quick-impact confidence-building measures.

The *World Development Report* identifies an important role for peacekeepers in helping to establish an enabling environment required for long-term security and justice reform. Peace operations are also often tasked with directly assisting in rebuilding security and justice institutions. While these efforts necessarily extend well beyond the mandate of a peacekeeping operation, peacekeepers can play a critical role in strengthening parties' confidence in and commitment to the political process, as well as in supporting, in the short term, the efforts of other actors to foster good governance and strengthen institutions.

In the report, Ramtane Lamamra, the African Union's Commissioner for Peace and Security, and Alain Le Roy, then–UN Under-Secretary-General for Peacekeeping Operations, call for creative solutions to today's peacekeeping challenges, including combining long-term security sector assistance programs with lighter monitoring missions and over-the-horizon forces to increase flexibility and enable longer engagements. The expected drawdown of a number of peacekeeping missions, including in Liberia and Timor-Leste, has renewed interest in options for rapidly deployable over-the-horizon forces as an added security guarantee during the particularly vulnerable period of mission transition.

With nearly 1.5 billion people affected by conflict globally, the *World Development Report* predicts increased risks of violence in the future due to climate change and competition over scarce natural resources. The report seeks to catalyze an improved international architecture for responding to these threats in fragile states.

the violence. The increased tensions have complicated the role of the newly established UNMISS, which is already facing the monumental task of establishing state authority and managing myriad internal conflicts among tribal groups, the Sudan People's Liberation Army (SPLA), and breakaway factions. Meanwhile, in Darfur, the political process has failed to gain traction, and UNAMID has struggled with stabilizing the region and protecting civilians.

Millions of voters queued, some for days, to vote in the Democratic Republic of Congo's general elections in November 2011. In the lead-up to the vote, significant logistical delays and sporadic incidents of violence raised concern that the election could plunge the country into renewed conflict. A shortage of helicopters lim-

ited MONUSCO's ability to protect civilians and support election preparations. National and international observers criticized the November elections for lacking credibility in the face of significant irregularities. The political opposition rejected official election results, which showed a victory for incumbent president Joseph Kabila, and the main rival candidate declared himself president. The heated rhetoric on both sides and heightened political tension run the risk of inciting large-scale violent protests and clashes, further exacerbating this political crisis.

In Haiti, MINUSTAH continues to provide critical political, security, judicial, and logistical support following the January 2010 earthquake. Following contested first-round presidential elections that triggered protests and violence,

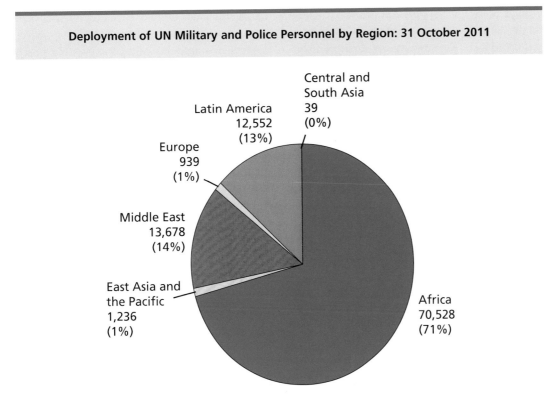

Deployment of UN Military and Police Personnel by Region: 31 October 2011

Central and South Asia
39
(0%)

Latin America
12,552
(13%)

Europe
939
(1%)

Middle East
13,678
(14%)

East Asia and the Pacific
1,236
(1%)

Africa
70,528
(71%)

Michel Martelly won a generally calm runoff election in the country's first peaceful transfer of power to the opposition. In October 2011, MINUSTAH began downsizing to pre-earthquake troop and police levels amid tense debates in the Security Council on the overall timetable for transition, and amid public outrage in Haiti over the mission's link to a deadly cholera epidemic and the alleged rape of a Haitian teenager by mission troops.

Mission drawdown is also proceeding in Timor-Leste, ahead of the national elections scheduled for 2012, and in Liberia, where in October 2011 President Ellen Johnson Sirleaf was reelected in the first nationally managed polls since the end of the civil war. While the elections were largely peaceful, clashes occurred between Liberian police and opposition supporters on the day before the runoff, requiring UNMIL peacekeepers to step in to restore order. UNMIL has faced mounting international pressure to quicken its withdrawal, despite domestic and regional security threats, including land disputes and organized crime. The regional di-

mensions of instability in the West African region were underscored during the post-election crisis when Liberian mercenaries crossed the porous border to join the conflict in Côte d'Ivoire, and refugees seeking to escape the violence crossed in the other direction.

Following months of worsening conflict between forces loyal to president-elect Alassane Ouattara and incumbent president Laurent Gbagbo, the UN Operation in Côte d'Ivoire and France's Operation Licorne intervened to ensure the integrity of the election and protect civilians. During a series of assaults on pro-Gbagbo positions, the peacekeepers destroyed heavy weapons, enabling the military victory by Ouattara supporters. The involvement of Operation Licorne, along with the deployment of attack helicopters from UNMIL to UNOCI, reversed months of humiliation suffered by UN peacekeepers, including restriction of movement, disarming of and attacks on peacekeepers, and cutting off of supplies, all of which undermined the integrity of the mission.

In Afghanistan, escalating violence and declining domestic support for military deployments among the key international partners prompted a shift in strategy from counterinsurgency to counterterrorism operations targeting militant leaders and enhancing the capacities of the Afghan government. In advance of the planned 2014 withdrawal of international forces, the International Security Assistance Force (ISAF) has been handing over security responsibilities to the Afghan army and police—despite security concerns and doubts about government capacity. The timetable for drawdown, combined with minimal progress on negotiating a settlement, has fueled uncertainty within Afghanistan about the future of the country.

Finally, in Somalia, the unexpected withdrawal of Al-Shabaab from Mogadishu has enabled the government to establish control over the capital for the first time in decades. Nonetheless, continued asymmetrical attacks by Al-Shabaab against AMISOM have exacted high casualties. The entry by Kenyan ground forces into southern Somalia—and the announcement that Ethiopia will redeploy to support AU and Kenyan operations—demonstrate the fluidity of the security situation.

Conclusion

The resulting picture underscores the contradiction facing peacekeeping. Developments on the ground—including election-related violence—demonstrate the continued need for international action, as well as the critical role for peacekeepers in stabilizing and consolidating peace in countries emerging from violent conflict. After a decade of large multidimensional missions, peacekeeping may be moving away from this template to respond more flexibly to the needs on the ground, with authorizations in 2011 reflecting the complex reality of peacekeeping needs in the future.

Yet in response to budgetary pressure, several key member states are eager to draw down existing peace operations and to limit large deployments. In fact, negotiations between troop and financial contributors this year threatened to bring UN peacekeeping to a standstill. These tensions remain. The deepening financial crisis is certain to dominate discussions on mandates and resources—including troop reimbursement rates and the scale of assessed contributions—for peacekeeping in the year ahead. Nonetheless, these negotiations also present an opportunity to galvanize support for peacekeeping as an essential tool of crisis management, and to define its future strategic direction—including strengthening partnership arrangements, mobilizing civilian expertise and military assets, and developing flexible, alternative models of deployment.

Notes

1. Uniformed personnel include military troops, military observers, and civilian police. When disaggregated, deployment of UN military personnel decreased 0.5 percent over the year, while deployment of civilian police increased slightly, from 14,025 to 14,237.

2. Year-to-year comparisons are made between September 2010 and September 2011 for non-UN-commanded missions, and between October 2010 and October 2011 for UN-commanded missions.

Peacekeeping and Support for State Sovereignty

Jake Sherman

The majority of contemporary peace operations occur in countries with weak state institutions, and where insecurity and violence continue after the signing of a peace accord. Typically, these states have had limited formal administrative, judicial, and security presence, in addition to limited capacity and resources to deliver even the most basic services beyond the capital and major urban centers. Armed conflict only broadens this gap between the center and periphery, while the continued existence of repressive or predatory regimes and unchecked elite structures can undermine the legitimacy of the state vis-à-vis citizens. In the aftermath of armed conflict, the reestablishment of legitimate, resilient national institutions is necessary for secure, sustainable peace.

In response, support to state authority[1] has become a core function of peacekeeping—and of several political missions.[2] These peace operations work in concert with multiple partners within and beyond the United Nations. Over the past two and a half decades, peace operations have gradually grown in complexity, bringing to bear a growing number of institutional actors engaged in a wide array of civilian functions—from supporting political processes and reintegrating ex-combatants, to supporting the reform of security and justice sectors—alongside military and, increasingly, police units. These multidimensional operations are staying longer and, when they do draw down, often transition to follow-on civilian missions.

In 2011 the UN Operation in Côte d'Ivoire (UNOCI), the new UN Mission in South Sudan (UNMISS), and the UN Support Mission in Libya (UNSMIL) all implemented mandates that included some form of support to the extension of state authority. UNSMIL, in addition to its good offices function, is essentially a clearinghouse for technical assistance requested by the Libyan authorities. UNMISS provides the same services to the South Sudanese government, but on a much larger scale with troops. UNOCI, with support from France's Operation Licorne, was required to use force to prevent a further escalation of violence and protect Côte d'Ivoire from being captured by the outgoing government.

UN policy documents have attempted to reflect this diversity, but there is still ambiguity regarding what restoring or supporting the extension of state authority actually means in practice, particularly for peacekeepers. There is also limited knowledge of how to prioritize and sequence engagement and assess results. The UN's Capstone Doctrine for peacekeeping identifies support to the restoration and extension of state authority as an area in which peacekeeping operations can play a "catalytic role" by "creating an enabling security environment, providing political leadership or coordinating the efforts of other international actors."[3] Support may include developing political participation, operationally supporting the "immediate activities of state institutions," small-scale capacity building, and supporting constitutional and institutional restructuring.[4] These are broad goals, encompassing complementary activities across the peacekeeping mission. At the same time, Security Council mandates, the strategy paper on early peacebuilding from the Department of Peacekeeping Operations (DPKO), its draft civil affairs handbook, and mandate implementation plans all frame support to the extension of state authority as a specific civil affairs function.

In an effort to set extension of state authority in a wider context, this chapter analyzes the use and evolution of support to state authority in five UN peacekeeping missions: the UN Mission in Sierra Leone (UNAMSIL), the first multidimensional mission authorized to support the extension of state authority;[5] the UN Organization Stabilization Mission in the Democratic Republic of Congo (MONUSCO, and its predecessor MONUC), in support of the Forces Armées du République Démocratique du Congo (FARDC); the UN Stabilization Mission in Haiti (MINUSTAH), through its joint anti-gang operations in Cité Soleil and its post-earthquake support to the Haitian government; UNOCI and Operation Licorne, in enforcement of the 2010 presidential election results in Côte d'Ivoire; and UNMISS, in support of the government of South Sudan. Also analyzed are two non-UN missions in Afghanistan and Somalia. The chapter then suggests seven lessons and three operational dilemmas for current and future missions mandated to strengthen state authority.

Extending State Authority in Practice

Since 2000, the Security Council has authorized a range of peacekeeping missions explicitly tasked with supporting the restoration and extension of state authority (see table). Yet there is no single model for this kind of work. A wide range of often context-specific activities are undertaken in support of these mandates. In certain cases, the extension of state authority has been

geographic, i.e., extending the territorial writ of the government. In other cases, it entails strengthening the capacity, effectiveness, and legitimacy of state institutions in key sectors, such as assisting the state to obtain a monopoly on the use of force. Most often, extension of state authority involves a combination of these aspects.

Thus, while there is little variation in the authorizing language for the peacekeeping missions examined here, there are variations in the forms of implementation across cases and over time. Nonetheless, the basic mode for supporting the restoration, extension, and consolidation of state authority—of creating space for the establishment of state presence and the resumption of administrative activities, gradually enhancing performance through small-scale capacity building, providing infrastructure and equipment, and strengthening local legitimacy—has built on the basic approach laid out in Sierra Leone.

Sierra Leone

In 1999, the signing of the Lomé Agreement and authorization of a UN peacekeeping mission promised an end to years of civil war in Sierra Leone. Yet within months, the country was backsliding into violence. The underresourced UNAMSIL was unable to stop the rebels' advance toward Freetown, let alone to roll back their control of the countryside. Following the

Security Council Authorizing Resolutions for Peacekeeping Missions

UNAMSIL	UNSC Res. 1313 (2000)
UNMIL	UNSC Res. 1509 (2003)
UNOCI	UNSC Res. 1528 (2004)
MINUSTAH	UNSC Res. 1542 (2004)
ONUB	UNSC Res. 1545 (2004)
MONUC	UNSC Res. 1856 (2008)[a]
MONUSCO	UNSC Res. 1925 (2010)
UNMISS	UNSC Res. 1996 (2011)

Note: a. In contrast to the mandates of other missions covered in this chapter, MONUC's did not explicitly refer to the "extension of state authority." Nonetheless, the mission's authorizing resolution did mandate provision of advice to strengthen democratic institutions and processes at the national, provincial, regional, and local levels.

intervention of British armed forces in May 2000, which halted the Revolutionary United Front, the Security Council authorized a robust new mandate for the beleaguered mission, with increased resources to match. Security Council Resolution 1313 (2000) mandated UNAMSIL "to assist, through its presence and within the framework of its mandate, the efforts of the Government of Sierra Leone to *extend state authority,* restore law and order and further stabilize the situation" (emphasis added).

The Security Council mandated UNAMSIL to assist with extending state authority as a means of enabling the national government to establish a foothold in key strategic locations and population centers. The deployment of military peacekeepers was a precondition, as it would provide a stabilizing presence and allow for the disarming of rebels, and thus create space for the return of government officials and deployment of civilian UN staff. As blue helmets progressively reestablished security and freedom of movement, the UNAMSIL civil affairs component shifted its focus to support government efforts to reinstate its presence across the country—a task complicated by the destruction of state administrative infrastructure, poor communication and transportation systems, the disruption of the civil service during the war, and rampant corruption within the existing administration.[6] Between 2000 and 2005, UNAMSIL, in cooperation with the UN Development Programme (UNDP), the World Bank, and international donors, gradually enabled the government of Sierra Leone to deploy district administrators and police in all districts, to fill positions of paramount chiefs (the system of local administration prior to its disruption by the war), and to restore elected district councils.

Democratic Republic of Congo

In January 2009, following the rapprochement between the Democratic Republic of Congo and Rwanda, Special Representative of the Secretary-General Alan Doss agreed that MONUC would support Kimia II, a ten-month FARDC military campaign against the Forces Démocratiques de la Libération du Rwanda (FDLR). The mission collaborated with FARDC brigades to stabilize eastern Congo, where peacekeepers and the Congolese army continue to face challenges from the forces of the FDLR and the Congrès National pour la Défense du Peuple (CNDP). Kimia II and the follow-on Amani Leo joint operation resulted in several tactical successes against the FDLR, but MONUC was heavily criticized for its failure to protect civilians from human rights violations committed by FARDC and FDLR troops.[7] As a corrective, Security Council Resolution 1906 conditioned future MONUC support—including joint mission planning, logistical and reconnaissance support, medical evacuation, and provision of fuel and rations—on FARDC compliance with international humanitarian, human rights, and refugee law.

Resolution 1906 also emphasized that support for the extension of state authority should be carried out under the 2009 national stabilization and reconstruction plan and the international security and stabilization support strategy. Extension of state authority is clearly stated in the goals of the latter, including opening the east to government access, stabilization, and the provision of services, with each effort meant to increase the credibility of the government in the eyes of the governed. The five priority areas of the international support strategy, and the units of MONUSCO that contribute to their implementation, are public roads (engineering contingents), policing (UN Police), penal institutions (rule of law and corrections contingents), regulation of natural resources (joint monitoring and analysis cell), and local governance (civil affairs unit in conjunction with UNDP).[8]

Haiti

MINUSTAH deployed in June 2004 with a mandate to assist the government with "extending State authority throughout Haiti."[9] Following the 2006 presidential elections, UN forces collaborated with the Haitian National Police (HNP) to minimize gang activity, restore stability, and extend governmental authority over the capital. In 2008, with the immediate threat of violence quelled, the Secretary-General identified extension of state authority as one of five priority benchmarks for MINUSTAH in preparation for a drawdown. Progress was made on all of these fronts in 2009, but was cut short by the January 2010 earthquake.

The earthquake severely weakened the capacity of the Haitian state, placing further stress on the newly established administration, police, and public service institutions. In response, MINUSTAH quickly transitioned to a multidimensional disaster-relief mission. Supporting the government to extend its authority through the provision of an enabling and stable environment for state-led reconstruction has been a key component in post-earthquake operations. MINUSTAH has provided technical, advisory, and logistical support to state institutions at national and local levels. The UN Country Team is responsible for providing direct technical assistance to the government in priority areas such as social service delivery, rule of law, state policy, and disaster management. A partial drawdown of MINUSTAH's military troops is scheduled for completion by June 2012, and will require an increased focus on the extension and consolidation of state authority. Subsequent reconfigurations to MINUSTAH's mandate will be informed by improvements in the capacity of state institutions to effectively fulfill the aforementioned functions on their own.

Brazilian peacekeepers of the UN Stabilization Mission in Haiti (MINUSTAH) stand guard in Cité Soleil, 14 July 2011. Operation Phoenix, as the security operation is called, is designed to help the Haitian authorities provide security and stability for the residents of Port-au-Prince.

UN Photo/Victoria Hazou

Côte d'Ivoire

UNOCI was deployed in 2004 to support the implementation of a cease-fire between northern rebels and government forces in the south. Its authorizing mandate, Security Council Resolution 1528, tasked the mission to "facilitate . . . reestablishment by the Government of National Reconciliation of the authority of the State throughout Côte d'Ivoire." Reunification efforts faltered in 2009 and elections were repeatedly delayed throughout 2010. When elections were finally held on 31 October, Prime Minister Alassane Ouattara defeated incumbent Laurent Gbagbo in a runoff election. Gbagbo's government pronounced the results invalid and reversed the runoff decision. In his mandated role as independent certifier for the presidential

and legislative elections in Côte d'Ivoire, Special Representative of the Secretary-General (SRSG) Choi Young-jin, dismissed the government's announcements and declared Ouattara president-elect.

Following the ensuing standoff and protracted debate in the Security Council on whether to act, UNOCI's mandate took on a different immediacy: ensuring the integrity of the electoral process. Resolution 1975 (2011) urged all "Ivorian State institutions . . . to yield to the authority vested by the Ivorian people in President Alassane Dramane Ouattara" and adopted targeted sanctions against those who obstruct the electoral process. In April, after months of armed resistance, Ouattara supporters, backed by UN and French peacekeepers, defeated Gbagbo. Ouattara was officially sworn in a month later. UNOCI's mandate has since refocused on postconflict protection and security, supporting legislative elections in December 2011—for which the SRSG again acted as the independent certifier—and the "redeployment of state administration and extension of state authority throughout the country" by

---

Box 1.1 The Review of International Civilian Capacities

Civilian personnel play an increasingly central role in international peace operations, whose growing multidimensional mandates include a broad array of peacebuilding tasks. Today, civilian personnel, including international staff, national staff, and UN volunteers, constitute approximately 17 percent of all UN staff deployed in peacekeeping operations around the world. Yet vacancy rates across these missions average 27 percent, reflecting the many obstacles the UN still faces in identifying and deploying civilian experts. These high vacancy rates present operational and strategic challenges for missions on the ground and may ultimately affect mandate implementation and peace consolidation.

Recognizing this gap in civilian capacities, in March 2010 the UN Secretary-General appointed a senior advisory group, chaired by Jean-Marie Guéhenno, former head of the UN's Department of Peacekeeping Operations, to conduct an analysis of how the international community can broaden and deepen the pool of civilian experts to support postconflict peacebuilding. Its report, *Civilian*

Capacity in the Aftermath of Conflict (also known as the Guéhenno Report), was published in February 2011. The Guéhenno Report identifies four key principles for improving international civilian capacities: stronger national ownership, enhanced global partnerships, greater efficiency in identifying and deploying expertise, and increased nimbleness in delivering these capacities on the ground. Following the release of the report, the Secretary-General formed a steering group led by Susana Malcorra, Under-Secretary-General for Field Support, to implement its recommendations.

Important progress has been made, and as an initial step toward creating a civilian partnership cell to link the UN and other international civilian capacities, Under-Secretary-General Malcorra has recommended the creation of an online Web portal to strengthen information-sharing on supply and demand. However, challenges remain and further work is needed to improve the deployment of civilian capacities. In August 2011 the Secretary-General released a report on the UN's civilian capacities that identified a

series of priority activities for the UN over the next year, including the development of guidelines for deploying national capacities, increased efforts to strengthen partnerships, and using the principle of comparative advantage in implementing mandates.

Before its closure in July 2011, the UN Mission in Sudan (UNMIS) had one of the largest civilian staff components of any UN peacekeeping mission. Yet UNMIS encountered many obstacles in hiring national staff, who represented less than 1 percent of civilian staff in the mission.[1] The new UN Mission in South Sudan (UNMISS) has been identified as a testing ground for implementation of the Guéhenno Report's recommendations, and has received requests from the government of South Sudan to enhance its civilian capacity-building activities.

Momentum must be maintained for increasing the pool of civilian experts, improving their deployment, and reducing the civilian capacity gap. Failure to do so may ultimately come at the expense of the ability of missions to fully support peace consolidation.

Note: 1. Sharon Wiharta and Stephanie Blair, "Civilian Roles in Peace Operations," in *SIPRI Yearbook 2010: Armaments, Disarmaments, and International Security* (Solna, Sweden: Oxford University Press, 2010), p. 104.

---

strengthening public administration at the national and local levels.

South Sudan

Support for the establishment of state authority is a central function of the recently mandated UN Mission in South Sudan. In contrast to the Balkans and East Timor, where the Security Council established UN transitional administrations to oversee the creation of new states, in South Sudan the UN mission is mandated to help the state to establish institutions of government simultaneous with governing. In response to the tremendous capacity and infrastructure

needs of the country, the mission is co-locating reconstruction, reintegration, and peacebuilding (RRP) officers in South Sudan's ten state capitals and, gradually, in county support bases to provide on-the-job mentoring to local government personnel. The RRP officers constitute a new category of civilian staff under the authority of the resident coordinator/humanitarian coordinator/deputy SRSG position. They provide a modality for the peacekeeping mission to support development activities, in cooperation with the UN Country Team and other partners, under the assessed budget, including implementation of stabilization and reintegration programs and support for local delivery of services at the local level through quick-impact projects. In addition to the RRP officers, some 180 civilian affairs officers focused on assessing gaps in government capacity, as well as conflict management and community engagement, are also being deployed.[10]

* * *

Two non-UN cases where peace operations are mandated to support the extension of state authority deserve brief mention: Afghanistan, where activities related to the extension of state authority are largely undertaken by NATO's counterinsurgency effort, and Somalia, where the African Union peacekeeping force is attempting to support the Transitional Federal Government (TFG) despite the absence of a civilian component. Contrary to UN peace operations, both are examples of where the international community is conducting military operations against armed groups in the absence, rather than in support, of a political settlement.

Afghanistan

Establishing and strengthening the authority of the Afghan state in rural areas has been a central goal of the international presence since 2001. Although initially focused on ending the de facto rule of the countryside by warlords, emphasis shifted, as the insurgency gathered strength, to ensuring administrative presence and providing security and basic services as part of the counterinsurgency effort. Afghanistan demonstrates the fluid relationship between presence and authority, where overlapping spheres of state and Taliban authority coexist at the local level, resulting in parallel systems of governance—if not de facto Taliban control. The surge in coalition military and civilian resources has reportedly loosened the grip of Taliban and other insurgent forces in southern territories, but insurgent activity has grown in other parts of the country where the Taliban is installing shadow governors that levy taxes, adjudicate disputes, and appoint local military commanders.[11] International efforts have taken on renewed importance over the past year as the

International Security Assistance Force (ISAF) begins to transfer responsibility for security to the Afghan state ahead of its drawdown in December 2014.

Somalia

The Security Council authorized the AU Mission in Somalia in 2007 to protect the Transitional Federal Government, support the reestablishment of Somali security forces, and facilitate humanitarian assistance. AMISOM maintained control of key government infrastructure in Mogadishu in the face of an increasingly hostile environment. Yet despite recent military gains, the mission lacks the civilian capabilities necessary to effectively support the TFG—which, with the assistance of AMISOM, only regained control of the capital in late 2011—in the area of governance. The Somali prime minister recently highlighted the urgent need for additional troops to assist the Somali state in extending its authority and presence in the areas vacated by Al-Shabaab. Funding for AMISOM remains a challenge too, as the UN is unable to fund Somali civil servants and police or to reimburse AU troop-contributing countries. Meanwhile, large swaths of Somali territory in the south are controlled by Al-Shabaab and other militias. Conversely, the two effectively autonomous "statelets," Somaliland and Puntland, have brought order to much of the north—a politically sensitive issue for the territorial integrity of the Somali state that the Security Council and the AU have so far sidestepped.

* * *

These cases highlight seven lessons and three operational challenges for the extension and restoration of state authority by peacekeepers.

Lessons

1. Extension of State Authority Often Depends on Peacekeepers' Tactical Use of Force

In all the cases, (re)establishing the territorial control of the state via the progressive deployment of military peacekeepers was a necessary first step, one that enabled the initial presence of civilian UN and often state personnel. Although consent to deployment is a fundamental principle of peacekeeping, in most of these cases peacekeepers were required to use tactical force in specific instances against armed groups opposed to the state. Often, this has been carried out jointly with state security forces—for example, MINUSTAH-HNP operations to wrest control of Haitian slums from criminal gangs, and MONUC/MONUSCO-FARDC operations in eastern Congo.

Such operations have been most successful when they are able to draw on advanced and often specialized military capabilities, for example, mobile Brazilian units experienced in anti-gang operations in MINUSTAH and rapid reaction capacities of British troops in Sierra Leone. Absent these specialized forces, UN troops have often proven incapable of rolling back or halting attacks by armed opposition groups—particularly when it is national militaries that are the spoilers, as in Côte d'Ivoire in early 2011. There, the presence of French peacekeepers in Operation Licorne proved an essential complement to the UN. However, while forces with advanced capabilities are at times necessary, they are not sufficient. Indeed, as the NATO presence in Afghanistan has demonstrated, robust military capabilities alone may be unable to hold territory and enable the reassertion of state authority.

2. Extension of State Authority Often Depends on Development of National Security Forces

Although security and justice sector reform is included as a distinct task in Security Council mandates and is supported by specialized units in peacekeeping missions, it is an important corollary to extension of state authority. At a minimum, training and deploying national police and military forces enables peacekeepers to hand over security responsibilities. Demobilization and disarmament of militias, and often their integration into national forces, constitute a common and necessary precursor. The ability of national police and military forces to take

responsibility for holding territory, providing order, and managing security is an important test of whether the state can manage on its own, and thus a key benchmark for withdrawal of a mission. For UNAMSIL in Sierra Leone, increased police presence—particularly in the eastern region, where illegal diamond mining, vigilante youth, and ex-combatants posed the greatest threat to stability—permitted the mission to begin drawing down its presence.

Nonetheless, where the state continues to face armed opposition, as in Somalia and Afghanistan, or where peacekeepers are preparing to withdraw, police training can overemphasize security at the expense of community-oriented policing and the role it can play in violence reduction and enhancing citizen security. This can negatively affect public trust in the police—particularly where there is a history of predation or abuse, as in Haiti—reinforce past negative experiences, and negatively affect efforts to strengthen state legitimacy. Likewise, in Afghanistan, ISAF transition plans are predicated on a capable Afghan National Police and Afghan National Army, prompting repeated efforts to enlarge the ranks of both. For the former, the quantity of police has arguably come at the expense of professionalism.[12]

3. Establishing State Presence Is Not the Same as Legitimate State Authority

State administrative structures have in many cases proven remarkably resilient to conflict. In Afghanistan, for example, local-level structures and officials did not "collapse" during the three decades of civil war, contrary to expectations. Rather, the political system ceased functioning, which resulted in the halting—if not reversing—of state consolidation, disruption of basic service provision, and a negative impact on state legitimacy. Such preexisting local-level structures and systems provide a framework for reconstitution of state fiscal and administrative systems, particularly where they are well understood and followed. Attempts at reform that run counter to these practices have at times resulted in confusion and parallel structures.[13]

At the same time, efforts to extend state authority are frequently focused on developing infrastructure and capacity, including establishing municipal presences, courthouses and police stations, providing office equipment, ensuring salary payments, and providing technical training like budgeting and financial management, as well as provision of logistic and communication support. Such measures facilitate state presence and, in theory, improve performance. But they do not automatically result in increased state *authority*—in the ability of the state to secure compliance with political and administrative decisions—let alone *legitimate* authority. This requires a focus beyond institution building to encompass how the state interacts with its citizens. In practice, implementation of the international security and stabilization support strategy in Congo, for instance, has focused on the "visible manifestation of state presence," like roads, infrastructure, and equipment, rather than inclusive decision-making, accountability, transparency, and effectiveness. Deployment of police, civil officials, and magistrates has suffered from insecurity and, for the latter two, serious delays in training.[14]

In conflict and postconflict environments, public trust in state institutions and processes may be extremely weak. The extension of the state can raise public expectations about delivery of basic services that the state is unable to meet, increasing the risk of dissatisfaction and mistrust.[15] Early postconflict engagement should prioritize those areas that underpin statehood and reinforce trust between the state and society, including basic security, justice, and conflict mediation. The particular form that this should take should be context-specific, but according to the World Bank's 2011 *World Development Report,* early confidence-building measures—including timely appointment of credible national or local officials, establishing or strengthening existing alternative dispute resolution mechanisms and focusing on violence reduction, increasing financial and political transparency, removing discriminatory laws, policies and practices, or removing abusive security forces[16]—can increase public trust in the state, providing time for longer-term reforms.

On the other hand, discriminatory laws, policies, and practices, as well as predatory and abusive behavior by government officials, are frequently drivers of conflict. This poses a challenge for efforts to reestablish legitimate state authority, where early "restoration" of the state may mean either bringing back or recognizing authorities or laws with contested legitimacy. In 2005 the transitional government in Congo, for example, appointed four former warlords from Ituri as generals in the FARDC, despite serious allegations of their having committed war crimes.[17] Enabling and facilitating inclusive consultative processes—for example, on the drafting and adoption of a new constitution or immediate priorities for reform—is a principal function of peace operations in supporting the extension and consolidation of a legitimate state. Yet organizing such processes takes time. In the interim, states may have to rely on imperfect legal and administrative systems characterized by conflicting legal frameworks, rivalries between institutions, and officials who may see their positions as entitlements.

Moreover, in many conflict-affected states, like Sierra Leone and Liberia, state authority has been historically weak; customary or traditional governance systems have been the prevalent form of administration and redress outside of the capital. This raises the question of what type of state is being established, and of what is "acceptable" both internally and externally as state authority. In Liberia, UNMIL is supporting the Ministry of Internal Affairs, for example, to develop a series of procedures and training for tribal governors in due process and human rights. Where local state institutions have never had a strong presence or much legitimacy, as in Congo, the UN should engage with local leaders, both official and traditional, through support to community policing, violence reduction, and alternative dispute resolution. This can be accompanied over time by gradual support to the establishment of formal state institutions that complement rather than supplant existing conflict resolution mechanisms.[18]

In such cases, decisions must be locally owned, rather than externally imposed. According to the fragile and conflict-affected countries in the g7+, international aid is "often inapplicable, unsustainable and incompatible with our in-country national agendas . . . [and] not conducive to addressing the immediate or long-term needs of our countries and regions. . . . [E]xternal mandates and ideas can no longer be imposed on our countries or regions and our peoples."[19] At the same time, many donors may find it difficult to justify support for laws and practices that are contrary to the international human rights norms, especially regarding the role of women in society.

4. Supporting States Is Distinct from Supporting Governments

During transitional periods, and after the first postconflict national election, it may be difficult for a peacekeeping mission to separate support for the state, which includes a broad range of actors and reform constituencies, from support for the newly elected government. Maintaining an arm's length from the government is essential for two reasons. First, peacekeepers at times may be in the position of working with local officials or government institutions that are viewed as suspect by local populations, and must maintain space to condemn abuses. In Congo, for example, UN assistance to the FARDC was complicated by human rights abuses that the UN could not ignore. The degree of distance between the mission and the state matters, however. If the relationship is too distant, then the mission will have limited influence and "risks condoning a system of governance based on coercion"; if the relationship is too close, then the mission risks its impartiality when faced with corruption or human rights violations.[20]

Second, for longer-term peacebuilding, state institutions need to provide access to a broad range of viewpoints and interests, including these in civil society such as opposition parties and independent media. A peace operation can facilitate this political space, particularly where these interests may run counter to the interests of governing officials and their supporters, by providing good offices, facilitating free and fair parliamentary elections, monitoring human rights, and supporting national human rights organizations, as well as through establishment of UN radio broadcasting.

A related point is the risk that incumbents will use the institutions of state, like elections commissions, state-run media, and police, to advance their candidacy or that of their political party during nationally led elections. In Afghanistan, for example, widespread electoral fraud tainted the 2009 reelection of President Hamid Karzai, undermining public perceptions of his legitimacy and that of the Afghanistan government more broadly, while nonetheless maintaining him as the key partner for international engagement. At the time of writing, questions about the independence of the national electoral commission and accusations of electoral fraud also overshadowed presidential elections in the Democratic Republic of Congo, threatening violence.

5. Extending State Authority Can Undermine Perceptions of Peacekeepers' Impartiality

Despite the fact that mandates supporting the extension of state authority are, by definition, intended to strengthen state sovereignty, there is a risk that some local actors will view certain modalities of UN assistance to government as an infringement on state sovereignty. Embedding civil affairs and technical advisers in government offices, in particular, is a common means of supporting these institutions with developing administrative systems, planning, budgeting, and program execution. Yet these roles can be perceived as an intrusion, especially if UN staff try to impose their own priorities, which underscores the need to respect principles of national ownership and buy-in. When MINUSTAH embedded international and national officers into Haiti's Department of Local Government in 2007, many of their Haitian counterparts responded with suspicion and resentment that inhibited any progress. In response, the mission shifted its approach, demonstrating a willingness to support government-identified priorities and thereby building confidence and enabling UN staff to progressively integrate with their Haitian counterparts.[21] There is a risk, however, that by yielding on points of principle in an effort to maintain good relations with the government, a mission can undermine its leverage.

Peacekeepers need to balance ownership by the government with that of broader society.

A potentially more serious threat to the legitimacy of peacekeepers is that, by explicitly supporting the state, they will jeopardize their impartiality vis-à-vis armed opposition groups. In Somalia, AU personnel and premises have been increasingly targeted by extremist groups that are opposed not only to the TFG and the perceived Western agenda of defeating Al-Shabaab, but also to the current political dispensation. This has had direct consequences for the ability of UN staff, including humanitarian and development workers, to safely access communities, and in Afghanistan informed the decision by the UN Office for the Coordination of Humanitarian Affairs to set up an office outside that of the UN Assistance Mission in Afghanistan (UNAMA).

6. Peacekeepers Need to Adjust Their Posture Over Time

Over the life of a peacekeeping mission, emphasis shifts from enabling or supporting the "extension" of state authority to supporting its "consolidation." Local-level officials gradually reestablish their presence as their capacity increases and as they become more assertive. In Sierra Leone, for example, the UNAMSIL mandate was modified in 2002 after local administrators had been reestablished in all districts. The mission shifted its focus to training and building the capacity of local officials, including provision of basic facilities and communication and office equipment.

Peacekeepers, civilian and uniformed, cannot extend state authority alone. In contemporary, multidimensional peacekeeping missions, the UN is less a surrogate for the state than an incubator. In the early months and years, it is most often the peacekeeping mission that is present in district and provincial capitals, conducting civic education, promoting dialogue between local government and constituencies, undertaking preliminary assessments, and providing logistical and administrative support. With time, the role of peacekeepers diminishes as the UN Country Team, World Bank, and other international partners initiate large-scale training, infrastructure, and development programs.

Initially, the UN peacekeeping mission may be the only actor, domestic or international, that is able to conduct basic state functions like providing security and limited basic services. Provided that other, more sustainable approaches based on local capacities do not exist, the peacekeeping mission may have a comparative advantage in such direct support. As state capacity increases, however, the peacekeeping mission should "become more involved in facilitating nationally-owned processes, while providing the guidance and tools needed to define policies and plan activities instead of simply addressing emergencies."[22] Once local government institutions operate with a degree of autonomy, more discreet and targeted assistance may be required.

In fact, as national governments become more confident and capable, the relevance and often leverage of a peacekeeping mission obsolesces over time.[23] This is especially true once countries have successfully run their own national elections. Newly elected governments often want to demonstrate resolve in moving the country forward and can request a "normalization" of international involvement through the withdrawal of troops and a shift to development assistance. At the same time, there are circumstances under which state authority remains weak, and where a peacekeeping mission is arguably still warranted. In Haiti, for instance, presidential candidate Michel Martelly campaigned on a pledge to have MINUSTAH withdraw, declaring it an "occupying force." Upon winning the elections, however, he called for a phased drawdown.[24] Still, in other circumstances, national elections have brought to power governments that are narrowly based rather than broadly legitimate, and which are resistant to the scrutiny and accountability that a peacekeeping presence brings to bear—as is arguably the case in Congo.

7. Peacekeepers Need to Be Realistic

Perhaps the most important lesson for efforts to extend and consolidate state authority is to be modest and realistic in the scope of effort and expectations of how much progress will be achieved in establishing, strengthening, and transforming governance institutions during the limited duration of a peacekeeping mission. As the 2011 *World Development Report* notes, "wishful thinking on timing pervades development assistance when it comes to governance and institution building. . . . No country today is likely to be able to make it in three to five years, the typical timeline of national leadership and the international community."[25] Indeed, the report cites the example of Haiti prior to the 2010 earthquake, when the government and international community had identified a number of wide-ranging institutional reforms—from economic restructuring and revenue reform to judicial appointments and rapid expansion of the police—within an eighteen-month time frame, an unrealistic time frame even in ideal circumstances.[26] Corruption and patronage, elite and interinstitutional competition, unforeseen external shocks, and transnational phenomena such as organized crime and terrorism can all impact effective implementation of support as well as timelines. And while peacekeeping missions have leverage that they can wield to press for legal and institutional changes, government officials have limited incentives to ensure that laws and policies are fairly applied if they run counter to other vested interests.

The effective consolidation of legitimate state authority is a basic marker of whether and when peace operations can be safely and sustainably withdrawn.[27] Yet it is easy to set the bar too high. In Haiti, the UN's benchmark for extension of state authority throughout the country is "the establishment of legitimate, transparent, accountable democratic State institutions, down to the local level, with the capacity to collect and disburse funds for the benefit of the population, including the establishment of a viable system of border management."[28] It is unlikely that Haiti will achieve these goals within the time frame of MINUSTAH, given international and national timelines.

Operational Challenges

1. Coherent Support Requires Stronger Internal and External Integration

Although civil affairs officers are typically the first civilian UN peacekeeping staff to deploy to the substate level, they rarely have specialized technical expertise in public administration and democratic governance. Instead, they support local government through assessing government capacity, facilitating consultative processes, mobilizing and coordinating resources, publicizing government policies and services, serving as intermediaries between local and central administrators, including through logistics support, and between local populations and local government, as well as supporting dispute resolution. Targeted technical expertise, by contrast, is typically the domain of UNDP, the World Bank, other specialized agencies and programs, and bilateral donors—institutions that rarely have a presence at the local level, at least during the early years of a mission.[29] However, both functions are critical for early initiatives to extend the state's authority. There are growing instances of formalized partnership between peacekeeping missions and technical programs, as between UNDP and the UN Mission in Sudan prior to the establishment of UNMISS.

Nonetheless, integration both within the UN and with external actors like the World Bank remains weaker than is necessary to coherently support governments and national constituencies for reform over the long term—both in the early phases of a mission and during transition. This is due, in part, to differing reporting lines and financial accountability among the key international stakeholders. While a peacekeeping mission is directly authorized by and accountable to the Security Council, there are weakening degrees of accountability to the Council and its mandates among the UN agencies, funds, and programs, the World Bank, and bilateral donors. In contrast to peacekeepers, development actors also view the national government as their primary partner, a relationship that remains long after the departure of a peacekeeping mission. Consequently, tasks usually fall to ad hoc and fractious groupings of bilateral and multilateral development actors. Much deeper, and earlier, partnership with the full range of actors involved in postconflict peacebuilding and broader reform efforts, including UNDP, DPKO's Office of Rule of Law and Security Institutions, the UN's Peacebuilding Support Office, and the World Bank, as well as major donors, remains a priority.[30]

2. Rapidly Deployable and Appropriate Civilian Expertise Is in Short Supply

The UN—like the broader international community—has struggled with rapid recruitment and deployment of experts needed to support and transfer skills to national and local government.[31] As the recent *Review of International Civilian Capacities* identifies, "Specialists in the design and management of programs to strengthen governance institutions, reform public administration, justice and security sectors, and management of public finance . . . are today a critical factor for stabilizing postconflict countries and expanding state authority."[32] Many of these functions fall outside the competency of civilian peacekeeping personnel, let alone the duration of peacekeeping missions. Where capacities do exist, international deployment mechanisms struggle to get the right experts on the ground at the right time.

Both the *World Development Report* and the *Review of International Civilian Capacities* highlight the relevance of tapping expertise from the global South. As the World Bank observes, "Low and middle-income countries that have gone through their own recent experiences of transition have much to offer to their counterparts."[33] The Intergovernmental Authority on Development, for instance, is deploying 200 coaches and mentors from Ethiopia, Kenya, and Uganda to support the South Sudanese civil service.[34] Such skills are especially needed at the local level in municipalities, districts, and provincial capitals, which tend to receive less attention than national-level institutions, yet are

essential to the extension and consolidation of state authority.

3. Financial Resources Are Inflexible and Programming Capacity Is Inadequate

In addition to shortages of technical expertise, UN peacekeeping missions generally lack program funding—for example, for capacity building—beyond quick-impact projects. Designed to help build public confidence in a mission's mandate and in the peace process, these projects take a variety of forms, including short-term employment generation and infrastructure development.[35] Nonetheless, quick-impact projects are small-scale; larger projects depend on the involvement of humanitarian and development agencies. This limits the scope of early confidence-building measures that a peacekeeping mission can undertake in support of its political activities, even when it has a competitive advantage in terms of presence, timeliness, or specialization (e.g., disarmament, demobilization, and reintegration of former combatants).

In response, the UN's senior advisory group on civilian capacity recommended that heads of mission, during the early phase of their mandate, be given programmatic funds from assessed contributions that can be used at their discretion to support early confidence-building measures. Examples of programmatic activities under existing rules and procedures already exist (such as MINUSTAH's support for community violence reduction), and can be endorsed if the activity is clearly mandated and the mission has the comparative advantage to carry it out.[36] However, in the current financial climate, there is little support among major financial contributors to the UN for expanding the scope of such funds due to concerns about increased budget requests.

Donor restrictions on the use of official development assistance also pose a challenge, particularly in the area of security assistance. In the Democratic Republic of Congo, for example, such restrictions have hindered voluntary funding to pay police salaries, despite the risk of predation and corruption associated with underpaid police forces. Conversely, the establishment of the multidonor Law and Order Trust Fund for Afghanistan (LOTFA) by UNDP and UNAMA in 2002 provided an innovative modality to support payment, equipping, and training of the Afghan National Police.

Conclusion

Over the past decade, the international system has increasingly sought to empower states to fulfill their sovereign responsibilities. The United Nations, other international organizations, and bilateral development partners are called upon with greater frequency to assist weak states establish their authority, carry out core functions, and provide basic services.[37] Indeed, the establishment of a legitimate, functioning state has become a primary goal of international engagement.

In Haiti, Sierra Leone, Liberia, and Timor-Leste, UN support to the restoration and extension of state authority has been a qualified success—a work in progress, but one that is being progressively realized. In other cases—Afghanistan, the Democratic Republic of Congo, and Somalia—the absence of a viable political settlement, associated armed violence, rampant corruption, and the spillover of transnational threats like organized crime, trafficking, and terrorism have undermined ambitious statebuilding efforts by peacekeepers, the wider international community, and national stakeholders.

Demand by states emerging from crisis and conflict for assistance in extending and consolidating their authority is unlikely to diminish, as demonstrated by requests from South Sudan and Libya in 2011 for UN missions. At the same time, greater pragmatism and less hubris about what can realistically be achieved by external actors is required. As peacekeeping enters a new phase of resource constraints, the willingness of countries to make significant, long-term political and financial investments is likely to diminish.

Notes

This chapter benefited from comments by the UN Department of Peacekeeping Operations Best Practices Section and, at the Center on International Cooperation, from comments by Megan Gleason, Richard Gowan, Camino Kavanagh, and Alischa Kugel, as well as from research by Matthew Carrieri. Special thanks are also due to the African Centre for the Constructive Resolution of Disputes, the Norwegian Institute of International Affairs, and the Norwegian Peacebuilding Center for providing an opportunity to present and discuss initial ideas contained in this chapter at a workshop in Oslo, Norway, in October 2011.

1. In addition to "extension of state authority," the terms "establishment," "reestablishment," "restoration," and "consolidation" have also been used by the Security Council. While "establishment of state authority" is specifically used in the case of South Sudan—befitting a new state—and use of "restoration" has been limited to Côte d'Ivoire, "extension," "reestablishment," and "consolidation" have been used more widely.

2. The inclusion of "extension of state authority" in the mandate of UNSMIL suggests creative, context-specific modalities for strengthening states emerging from armed conflict, particularly in environments where there is already a high degree of national capacity and ownership, or where there is national wariness about a large foreign presence, as is true for the UN Assistance Mission in Afghanistan (UNAMA) as well as for UNSMIL.

3. United Nations, *United Nations Peacekeeping Operations: Principles and Guidelines* [Capstone Doctrine] (New York, DPKO: 2008), pp. 26–27.

4. Ibid.

5. Resolution 425 (1978) authorized the UN Interim Force in Lebanon (UNIFIL) to assist the government in "*ensuring the return of its effective authority* in the area" (emphasis added), but through military means—that is, creating political space by removing obstacles to its authority, but without further reconstitution of the state through multidimensional means.

6. United Nations, DPKO, "Lessons Learned from UN Peacekeeping Experiences in Sierra Leone," September 2003, p. 17.

7. Human Rights Watch estimated some 1,400 civilian casualties from January to September 2009 in addition to over 7,500 cases of sexual violence and widespread destruction of infrastructure. Human Rights Watch, "You Will Be Punished: Attacks on Civilians in Eastern Congo," December 2009.

8. *International Security and Stabilization Support Strategy for the Democratic Republic of the Congo,* quarterly report, January–March 2011, http://www.unpbf.org/wp-content/uploads/ISSSS-Report.pdf.

9. UN Security Council Resolution 1542 (2004).

10. Personal communication with DPKO staff member, 8 November 2011, on file with the author.

11. International Crisis Group, *The Insurgency in Afghanistan's Heartland,* Asia Report no. 207 (July 2011), p. 8.

12. *International Security and Stabilization Support Strategy.*

13. Anne Evans, Nick Manning, Yasin Osmani, Anne Tully, and Andrew Wilder, "A Guide to Government in Afghanistan," World Bank and Afghanistan Research and Evaluation Unit, 2004, p. xvii.

14. *International Security and Stabilization Support Strategy.*

15. See World Bank, *World Development Report 2011: Conflict, Security, and Development* (Washington, D.C., 2011).

16. Ibid., p. 16.

17. Human Rights Watch, "D.R. Congo Should Not Appoint War Criminals," 13 January 2005, http://www.hrw.org/news/2005/01/13/dr-congo-army-should-not-appoint-war-criminals.

18. Camino Kavanagh and Bruce Jones, "Shaky Foundations: An Assessment of the UN's Rule of Law Support Agenda," Center on International Cooperation, 2011, http://www.cic.nyu.edu/staff/docs/kavanagh/kavanagh_rol.pdf.

19. Statement of the g7+ Heads of State, Level Plenary Meeting of the General Assembly, MDG Summit, New York City, 20 September 2011.

20. Jean-Marie Guéhenno, foreword to Center on International Cooperation, *Annual Review of Global Peace Operations 2011* (Boulder: Lynne Rienner, 2011).

21. United Nations, DPKO, draft *Civil Affairs Handbook,* p. 181, on file with author.

22. Ibid., pp. 179–180.

23. Ian Johnstone, "Peacekeeping's Transitional Moment," in Center on International Cooperation, *Annual Review of Global Peace Operations 2011.*

24. Jacqueline Charles and Steward Stogel, "Haiti's President to Make U.N. Debut," *Miami Herald,* 22 September 2011.

25. World Bank, *World Development Report 2011,* p. 108.

26. Ibid.

27. Capstone Doctrine, p. 89.

28. UN Doc. S/2008/585 (2008), Annex I.

29. United Nations, DPKO, "Early Peacebuilding Strategy," on file with author; United Nations, DPKO, draft *Civil Affairs Handbook,* p. 165.

30. Kavanagh and Jones, "Shaky Foundations: An Assessment of the UN's Rule of Law Support Agenda."

31. United Nations, Senior Advisor Group, "Civilian Capacity in the Aftermath of Conflict," March 2011.

32. Bruce Jones, Richard Gowan, and Jake Sherman, "Building on Brahimi: Peacekeeping in an Era of Strategic Uncertainty," Center on International Cooperation, 2009, p. 38.

33. World Bank, *World Development Report 2011,* p. 36.

34. K. Tarp and F. Rosén, "Building Civil Servant Capacity in South Sudan: Coaching and Mentoring for Governance Capacity in the World's Newest State," DIIS, 2011.

35. Capstone Doctrine, p. 26.

36. UN Doc. A/66/311-S/2011/527 (2011), para. 67.

37. Jean-Marie Guéhenno, foreword to Center on International Cooperation, *Annual Review of Global Peace Operations 2011* (Boulder: Lynne Rienner, 2011).

2 Mission Reviews

Afghanistan

Over the past year, the extension of state authority developed a new urgency in Afghanistan. Following the NATO summit in Lisbon in November 2010, the International Security Assistance Force (ISAF) began handing over governance and security responsibilities to the Afghan government in anticipation of the withdrawal of international forces by December 2014. Along with attempts to reconcile with the Taliban, this "transition" of greater responsibility for national security to Afghan authorities has become the pivotal component of NATO's plans to draw its decade-long deployment in Afghanistan to a close.

The transition comes at a particularly volatile time in Afghanistan. According to UN estimates, an average of 2,108 "security incidents" occurred per month in the first eight months of 2011, an increase of 39 percent over the same period in 2010.[1] The majority of the civilian deaths during this period, which increased by over 5 percent compared to the previous year, were attributed to insurgent forces. The Taliban also deepened its presence in areas beyond its traditional heartland in the east and south, including in districts surrounding Kabul. The expanding insurgency resulted in the death of approximately 573 ISAF soldiers between December 2010 and November 2011, making this one of the deadliest periods in recent years.[2]

The escalating violence, combined with growing war fatigue, prompted stark operational shifts in ISAF. Following changes in senior US military leadership, the coalition started to move away from its counterinsurgency doctrine and toward a more conventional counterterrorism operation focused on targeting key insurgent and terrorist leaders. By focusing on enhancing the capacity of the Afghan government, ISAF leadership seeks to maintain security in the country while expediting the withdrawal of international forces.

Despite the deteriorating security conditions, and lingering doubts about the capacity of the Afghan government, the transition has received considerable political support. President Hamid Karzai applauded the drawdown of ISAF forces, calling it an essential step in Afghanistan's development as a sovereign nation-state.[3] Similarly, amid diminishing public support for ISAF's mandate, voters in the United States and many parts of Europe looked favorably on the withdrawal of their troops from Afghanistan.

Nonetheless, this transition has only deepened long-standing concerns among Afghans about the future of their country. The announcement of the formal end of ISAF operations has

Map No. 4465.1 UNITED NATIONS
September 2011

Department of Field Support
Cartographic Section

stoked persistent fears that the international community will abandon Afghanistan and allow it to return to the protracted warfare and human suffering that pervaded the past three decades. These fears have been exacerbated by increasing skepticism about the viability of reconciliation efforts, particularly since the Taliban's assassination of former president Burhanuddin Rabbani, who led the Afghan government's High Peace Council.

Background

In response to the 9/11 terrorist attacks, a US-led coalition operating under the auspices of Operation Enduring Freedom (OEF) launched a military campaign in Afghanistan in October 2001. Coalition forces and their Afghan allies overthrew the Taliban government and tried to kill or capture the leaders of the Al-Qaida terrorist network. Most of the Taliban and Al-Qaida leadership escaped across the border to Pakistan. Many rank-and-file members of the Taliban returned to their villages in Afghanistan.

After the fall of the Taliban regime, a group of prominent Afghans and world leaders met in Bonn, Germany, in early December 2001 under UN leadership to form a successor government. The resulting plan, known as the Bonn Agreement, outlined a series of benchmarks for the development of a new Afghan state. To provide security in Kabul and the surrounding areas, the Security Council authorized ISAF under Security Council Resolution 1386 (2001), and extended its mandate again for a full year in October 2011. In March 2002, under Resolution 1401, the Security Council authorized the UN Assistance Mission in Afghanistan (UNAMA) to support the establishment of a permanent government as outlined in the Bonn Agreement.

In 2003, NATO assumed command of ISAF, which had previously rotated among participating troop contributors on an ad hoc basis. With more than 40 contributing countries, ISAF gradually expanded beyond Kabul, taking command of existing provincial reconstruction teams in the northern and western regions. The same year,

International Security Assistance Force (ISAF)

- Authorization Date: 20 December 2001 (UNSC Res. 1386)
- Start Date: December 2001
- Force Commander: General John R. Allen (United States)
- Budget: $292 million (1 January 2011– 31 December 2011)
- Troop Contributing Nations: 48
- Strength as of 30 September 2011: Troops: 130,670

EU Police Mission in Afghanistan (EUPOL Afghanistan)

- Authorization Date: 30 May 2007 (EU Council Joint Action 2007/369/CFSP)
- Start Date: June 2007
- Force Commander: Brigadier General Jukka Savolainen (Finland)
- Budget: $68.4 million (1 October 2010– 30 September 2011)
- Contributing Nations: 27
- Strength as of 30 September 2011: Civilian Police: 187 / Civilian Staff: 134

following the integration of nearly 12,000 US troops under NATO command, ISAF replaced OEF as the main combat force on the ground. ISAF steadily expanded into more volatile parts of the south, succeeding US forces in Helmand, Uruzgan, and Kandahar provinces and establishing a presence across the entire country by 2006.

The Afghan presidential and parliamentary elections, held in 2004 and 2005 respectively, completed the political objectives established in the Bonn Agreement. In response to the expressed need for further international cooperation, the Afghan government and its international partners signed the Afghanistan Compact in January 2006, committing to high-level benchmarks in the areas of security, governance, reconstruction, and counternarcotics. The Joint Coordination and Monitoring Board (JCMB), co-chaired by UNAMA and the Afghan government, was established to oversee implementation of the compact.

In November 2010, NATO members convened in Lisbon to establish the broad contours of the drawdown of ISAF. Several contributing countries, most notably Canada and the Netherlands, had already begun planning to withdraw their combat forces, raising questions about the fragility of the alliance. The Lisbon agreement called for a process of "transition" to full Afghan security responsibility and leadership to begin in July 2011. However, a timeline for the handover to Afghan authorities was not identified in the summit declaration, which specified that the transition would be "conditions-based, not calendar-driven." NATO officials reiterated that the plan did not amount to a withdrawal of ISAF forces and that NATO would remain committed to Afghanistan, but no details were offered about the nature of that commitment beyond 2014.

Key Developments

Inconclusive Surge
Following the Lisbon conference, the United States marked the first anniversary of its much anticipated "military surge." An additional 33,000 US soldiers and 10,000 allied forces were deployed, bringing the total number of ISAF troops to over 130,000 in November 2010. The US government celebrated the move as a decisive step in reducing the influence of the Taliban in strategic parts of Afghanistan. "The surge in coalition military and civilian resources," White House officials detailed in a December 2010 report, "along with an expanded special operations forces targeting campaign and expanded local security measures at the village level, has reduced overall Taliban influence and arrested the momentum they had achieved in recent years in key parts of the country."[4] These gains, US officials argued, were most decisive in the south, where the Afghan government had historically struggled to extend its writ amid continued Taliban presence and antigovernment sentiment.

Growing insurgent activity in other parts of the country, particularly in areas beyond the Taliban's traditional strongholds in the south and east, tempered the perceived security gains following the surge in the south. In many provinces surrounding Kabul, for instance, Taliban shadow governors operate alongside the official government, administering taxes, adjudicating disputes, and appointing local military commanders through a mixture of intimidation and corruption.[5] This proximity posed a considerable liability to the Karzai government and its international backers. Besides threatening security in the capital, as seen in several high-profile attacks in 2011, the Taliban's encroachment on Kabul underscored the Afghan government's limited political authority.

The Search for a Political Settlement
The planned strategic and political transition, combined with the inconclusive military surge, led to a decisive shift in the US-led mission in Afghanistan. After years of public reluctance to discuss the possibility of negotiations, Secretary of State Hillary Clinton announced in February 2011 that the US government had started a "new phase of our diplomatic efforts" regarding Afghanistan.[6] Alongside ongoing military activities, the United States would publicly support an Afghan-led political process to reach a negotiated settlement with the Taliban. Perhaps more important, Secretary Clinton suggested that, instead of necessary preconditions to negotiations, the Taliban's renouncement of Al-Qaida, suspension of violent activities, and acceptance of the Afghan constitution could be treated as "necessary outcomes." The policy speech marked a decisive new priority for the US-led mission in Afghanistan.

Secretary Clinton's speech had mixed effects on the ongoing negotiation process. Anticipation about a possible end to the fighting, and the willingness of the United States to deliver sufficient concessions for the Taliban to agree to a political settlement, elicited considerable support from many Afghans and commentators in ISAF-contributing countries. However, the announcement also sparked speculation that, despite assurances to the contrary, any political settlement with the Taliban would necessarily come at the expense of key social and political gains, such as women's rights, access to education, and representation of ethnic minorities in government.

Numerous rumors about the timing, scope, and participants in the negotiation process surfaced throughout 2011. Some of these revelations undermined the confidence established between the US and Afghan governments, as well as with their Taliban counterparts. More importantly, the assassination of former president Rabbani cast considerable doubt on the viability of any negotiation process with the Taliban. In response to the attacks and growing public criticism of the strategy in Afghanistan, the Karzai administration announced that it would not negotiate with the Taliban but with the government of Pakistan, which it believes to have orchestrated much of the recent insurgent activity.

The coherence of the Afghan government was further tested amid fallout from the 2010 parliamentary elections. After an investigation into widespread allegations of corruption, the Independent Election Commission (IEC) finalized the results in late 2010 after removing nearly a quarter of the ballots. However, President Karzai subsequently established a controversial special court to investigate the election results, which called for sixty-two candidates to be seated in the lower house. The ensuing constitutional crisis was resolved in August 2011, when President Karzai issued a decree annulling the special court and granting the electoral commission final authority on the issue. Four days after the special court was dissolved, the election commission announced that only nine parliamentarians would be ousted amid allegations of fraud.

Change in Strategy and ISAF Drawdown

Other decisive shifts in ISAF's operations in Afghanistan followed from the security transition and reconciliation process. In April 2011, President Barack Obama announced that General David Petraeus had been nominated as the new

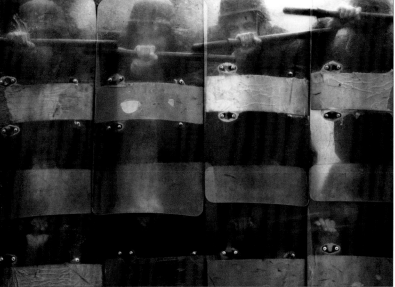

Afghan National Police (ANP) cadets stand in formation during a crowd control exercise at the ANP training facility in Kabul, Afghanistan, 5 February 2011.

director of the US Central Intelligence Agency. Petraeus had succeeded General Stanley McCrystal as the top US and NATO commander in Afghanistan less than a year earlier. The new commander, Marine Corps General John R. Allen, assumed control of ISAF forces in midJuly, promising to work closely with Afghan forces in assuming greater responsibility over national security affairs.

The change in command reflected a wider, unofficial strategic shift in ISAF's mission in Afghanistan. After several years of waging a counterinsurgency against the Taliban, the departure of Petraeus, who was one of the chief architects of the strategy in Iraq and Afghanistan, marked a return to a more traditional counterterrorism campaign in many parts of the country. Instead of trying to extend the writ of the Afghan state, largely by attempting to protect civilians, hold "secured" areas, and build up the Afghan National Security Forces (ANSF), the counterterrorism strategy calls for a more targeted, less resource-intensive campaign against key insurgent leaders. The shift seemingly addressed several of the growing concerns among the United States and other contributing countries,

Box 2.1 India-Pakistan

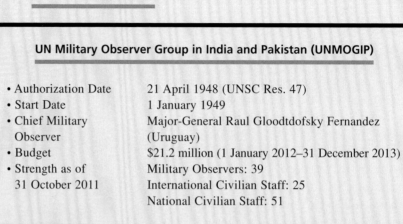

UN Military Observer Group in India and Pakistan (UNMOGIP)

- Authorization Date   21 April 1948 (UNSC Res. 47)
- Start Date   1 January 1949
- Chief Military   Major-General Raul Gloodtdofsky Fernandez
  Observer   (Uruguay)
- Budget $21.2 million (1 January 2012–31 December 2013)
- Strength as of   Military Observers: 39
  31 October 2011   International Civilian Staff: 25
     National Civilian Staff: 51

While the past year has seen several positive developments in the decades-long dispute between India and Pakistan over Kashmir, new and traditional sources of tension continue to plague the contested region. The UN Military Observer Group in India and Pakistan (UNMOGIP), the second oldest UN peacekeeping mission, continues to operate within its limited mandate while it awkwardly finds itself a focus of separatist activity in Indian-controlled Kashmir.

Since 1949, UNMOGIP has been monitoring the cease-fire line established by the Karachi Agreement, which separates the Pakistani- and Indian-controlled areas of Kashmir, a disputed territory over which three armed conflicts have been waged since the end of British rule in 1947. The 1972 Simla Agreement established the current line of control (LOC), which differs only slightly from the original 1949 cease-fire line. Since then, UNMOGIP has monitored the LOC and is mandated to engage in patrols, inspections, and investigations of alleged violations of the line. The mission may also perform other field tasks in the area when permitted by both countries. In 2010, Major-General Raul Gloodtdofsky Fernandez of Uruguay was appointed the new head of UNMOGIP.

Since the establishment of the current LOC, India has held that UNMOGIP has no operational role to play in Jammu-Kashmir. It restricts the activities of UN observers on the Indian side of the LOC and provides the mission limited support, though it has allowed UNMOGIP to operate out of its summer office in Indian-controlled Srinagar. Pakistan believes that the mandate still applies and has continued to file complaints with the mission regarding perceived violations of the LOC.

Frequent separatist protests have continued in India-controlled Kashmir, and UNMOGIP headquarters has become a symbol for protesters seeking UN intervention in the dispute, with frequent protest marches and demonstrations taking place in front of the mission's office. Tensions between Indian authorities and rebels remain high, with frequent instances of violence leading to the deaths of both civilians and Indian troops and police. In 2010, India arrested and detained over 300 separatists and imposed a broad curfew in the area.[1] The UN Special Rapporteur for Human Rights visited the country in January 2011 and expressed concern about India's treatment of separatists, citing the "arbitrary application of security laws" in Jammu-Kashmir and the country's hindrance of the work of human rights defenders.[2]

While there have been no recent hostilities between Indian and Pakistani forces, a number of Indian soldiers and separatist rebels have lost their lives in clashes near the LOC over the past year. India says it regularly intercepts Islamist rebels sneaking into Indian-held territory, but Pakistan denies allegations that it assists insurgents in their passage across the de facto border. There is long-standing speculation in India that some segments of the Pakistani government have been actively encouraging the rebellion against Indian authorities.

While Indian forces killed over a hundred Kashmiris in a two-month span in 2010, the summer of 2011 was much less violent, with tourists returning and protests diminishing. India's revised training for security forces, improved governance, greater communication with Kashmiri civilians, and renewed dialogue with Pakistan are seen as contributing to these positive developments.

Despite new tensions raised by bomb attacks in Mumbai in early July 2011, the Indian and Pakistani foreign ministers met later that month and agreed to a set of small but significant policy changes regarding Kashmir that ease LOC crossings as well as the permit process for tourists and religious pilgrims. Shortly thereafter, gunfights between Indian soldiers and Kashmiri rebels near the LOC added to the long list of fatalities in this conflict. Recent bilateral developments may give renewed hope that a solution can be reached, but without serious progress toward substantive negotiations, it appears that little will change in a dispute that has persisted for over sixty years.

Notes: 1. Amnesty International, "A 'Lawless Law,'" May 2011, http://www.amnesty.org/en/library/info/ASA20/010/2011/en.
2. "New Delhi: UN Special Rapporteur on HRDs Margaret Sekaggya Expresses Serious Concerns at End of Mission to India," *Frontline*, 24 January 2011, http://www.frontlinedefenders.org/node/14311.

including growing casualties, escalating costs, and the political need to redeploy soldiers.

The move away from counterinsurgency, along with the killing of Osama bin Laden in May 2011, has accelerated the drawdown of troops from Afghanistan. In June 2011, President Obama announced that, with the United States having largely achieved its limited goals in Afghanistan, the administration had ordered a phased withdrawal of the 33,000 troops deployed as part of the military surge. An initial 10,000 troops would return by the end of 2011, and the remainder would follow by September 2012. The scale of the drawdown surprised many officials, including several senior US military leaders, prompting widespread questions about the potential detrimental consequences for the overall military mission in Afghanistan.

The announcement led other ISAF contributors to accelerate their own drawdown plans. Twelve countries, accounting for nearly 85 percent of ISAF forces, announced that their troops would be redeployed in 2011 or 2012. Canada completed the withdrawal of combat forces in July 2011, with the remaining several hundred police and military trainers scheduled to leave by the end of 2011. The United Kingdom plans for approximately 500 or more troops to withdraw by the end of 2011. President Nicolas Sarkozy followed suit in announcing that French troops would be withdrawn "in a proportional manner and in a timeframe similar to the pullback of the American reinforcements."[7]

Security Handover

The accelerated drawdown of international forces gave greater urgency to the ongoing transition toward greater Afghan leadership over national security. Withdrawal plans were predicated on expectations that, with the assistance of ISAF and other international backers, the ANSF would be capable of assuming responsibility for national security affairs by the end of 2014. This imperative prompted a concerted effort to enlarge the army and police ranks. The Afghan National Army (ANA) enlarged to 164,000 active troops in mid-2011, an increase of approximately 25,000 soldiers since December 2010.[8] During the same period, the Afghan

National Police (ANP) enlarged to approximately 126,000 officers, from a force size of 116,300 six months earlier.

The first formal security transitions were completed in July 2011. Several relatively stable areas, including the provinces of Bamyan and Panjshir, as well as the cities of Herat, Mazar-i-Sharif, and Lashkar Gah, and the areas surrounding Kabul, were among the first transferred to Afghan security authorities. Although ISAF forces remain in these areas, their official capacity is to serve in a supportive or consultative role rather than an operational one. A subsequent round of security handovers is expected in 2012 for other provinces in northern and central Afghanistan, including several areas with greater insurgent activity and political instability.

Despite the apparent success of the initial handover, the rush to enlarge the ANSF and devolve greater leadership to Afghan officials underscores unresolved challenges. Persistent attrition, for instance, hampers plans for the ANA, as approximately one in four recruits drops out within months of entering the military. Furthermore, high illiteracy rates and drug consumption have long frustrated attempts to train ANSF recruits. In addition, in October 2011 the UN released a report detailing the systematic use of torture against detainees by the Afghan police and intelligence service. These long-standing liabilities have deepened concerns among international observers about the capacity of the ANSF, particularly following several high-profile insurgent attacks and political violence, including the assault on UNAMA offices in Mazar-i-Sharif, the British council in Kabul, and the US embassy.

Targeted Assassinations and Growing Civilian Casualties

The Taliban insurgency continued to undermine the transition by exploiting the personalities and patronage that structure the Afghan government. Several key powerbrokers, many with deep ties to the Karzai administration, have been killed in recent months in a campaign of increasingly sophisticated assassinations. Perhaps the most notable example was President Karzai's half-brother, Ahmed Wali Karzai, who was killed in a suicide attack in July 2011. As chairman of the Kandahar Provincial Council, he was one of the administration's key interlocutors in the south and an important part of US intelligence activities. The assassination of former president Burhanuddin Rabbani undermined already lagging public confidence in the reconciliation process. The death of other close Karzai allies, including Jan Mohammed Khan, Matiullah Khan, and General Daud Daud, further compounded the frailties of the Afghan government.

Assassination has long been one of the Taliban's principal tactics. Insurgent commanders have targeted opposition leaders, particularly defiant tribal leaders and public officials, to stoke greater fear and compliance. The recent wave of assassinations has been even more destabilizing, not only because of their brutality but also because of the growing complexity of and casualties caused by suicide attacks.[9] The Taliban's ability to reach the highest levels of the Afghan government has cast doubt on the ability of the ANSF to protect key leaders and heightened fears about future attacks.

This assassination campaign has compounded long-standing frustrations among Afghan and international officials regarding Pakistan's role in the ongoing transition in Afghanistan. Despite claims to support the Karzai government and the transition process, the Pakistani army and intelligence services have been indicted for supporting and directing Taliban activities in Afghanistan, including several high-profile attacks in Kabul. These frustrations reached new highs following the Rabbani assassination. As Admiral Michael Mullen, then-chairman of the US Joint Chiefs of Staff, testified before the Senate Armed Services Committee: "In supporting these groups, the government of Pakistan, particularly the Pakistani Army, continues to jeopardize Pakistan's opportunity to be a respected and prosperous nation with genuine regional and international influence."[10] The increasingly fractured relationship between the United States and Pakistan poses considerable risks to the transition process in Afghanistan and to regional stability more generally. Shortly following the Rabbani assassination,

Afghanistan signed a strategic partnership with India that included support for the ANSF, which may exacerbate tensions with Pakistan.

The violence in Afghanistan continues to be disproportionately felt by Afghan civilians. After recording the deadliest year since the fall of the Taliban, with at least 2,421 Afghan civilians killed in 2010, the first half of 2011 witnessed a 15 percent increase in deaths over the same period.[11] Insurgent groups were responsible for approximately 76 percent of civilian deaths, as compared to 21 percent attributable to ISAF and 3 percent to Afghan government troops.[12]

Casualties have been a particular source of animosity between the Karzai government and ISAF. On several occasions President Karzai has cited ISAF bombings and night raids as especially egregious examples suggesting that ISAF should relinquish greater authority to Afghan security officials. However, these charges have further frustrated ISAF leadership, as air strikes accounted for only 3 percent of civilian deaths in 2010.[13] The dynamic has compounded longstanding tensions between the Afghan government and its international backers.

Conclusion

Growing international desires to conclude combat operations in Afghanistan have imparted a new urgency in extending the authority of the Afghan state over national affairs. The emphasis on transition, however, has done little to resolve lingering questions about the capacity of the Afghan government to assume such leadership, particularly in the absence of sustained support from the international community. These doubts have deepened anticipation in Afghanistan for a strategic partnership declaration with the still reluctant United States, which would create a long-term binding commitment to the country. In addition, reconciliation attempts in 2011 and the assassination of Burhanuddin Rabbani have further complicated the fractured relationship between Afghanistan, Pakistan, and the United States and cast increasing doubt on the potential for a negotiated settlement to end the violence.

Notes

1. United Nations, *Report of the Secretary-General: The Situation in Afghanistan and Its Implications for International Peace and Security,* UN Doc. A/66/369-S/2011/590, 21 September 2011.

2. ISAF does not release casualty statistics for partner countries' military forces. These figures are based on data compiled by iCasualties.org. See http://icasualties.org/OEF/ByMonth.aspx.

3. Alissa J. Rubin and Taimoor Shah, "Karzai Welcomes Withdrawal, but Many Afghans Are Wary," *New York Times,* 23 June 2011, p. 11.

4. White House, "Overview of the Afghanistan and Pakistan Annual Review," Washington, D.C., 16 December 2010, http://www.whitehouse.gov/the-press-office/2010/12/16/overview-afghanistan-and-pakistan-annual-review.

5. International Crisis Group, "The Insurgency in Afghanistan's Heartland," Asia Report No. 207, 27 June 2011, p. 8.

6. Hillary Rodham Clinton, "Remarks at the Launch of the Asia Society's Series of Richard C. Holbrooke Memorial Addresses," New York, 18 February 2011, http://www.state.gov/secretary/rm/2011/02/156815.htm.

7. C. J. Radin, "ISAF Nations Follow US Lead, Announce Early Troop Drawdowns," *The Long War Journal,* 8 July 2011.

8. Ian S. Livingston and Michael O'Hanlon, *Afghanistan Index: Tracking Variables of Reconstruction & Security in Post-9/11 Afghanistan* (Washington, D.C.: Brookings Institution, 2011), p. 6.

9. UNAMA, "Afghanistan Midyear Report on Protection of Civilians in Armed Conflict, 2011," Kabul, July 2011, p. 17.

10. Michael Mullen, "Statement of Admiral Michael Mullen, U.S. Navy," Senate Armed Services Committee on Afghanistan and Iraq, 22 September 2011, http://armed-services.senate.gov/statemnt/2011/09-%20September/Mullen%2009-22-11.pdf.

11. Afghanistan Rights Monitor, "ARM Annual Report: Civilian Casualties of War, January–December 2010," Kabul, 2010, http://www.arm.org.af/index.php?page=en_Our+reports.

12. Ibid.

13. Susan G. Chesser, "Afghanistan Casualties: Military Forces and Civilians," Washington, D.C.: Congressional Research Service, 3 August 2011, http://www.fas.org/sgp/crs/natsec/R41084.pdf.

Côte d'Ivoire

The widespread violence that ensued after Côte d'Ivoire's second round of presidential elections in November 2010 constituted the deadliest incident of electoral violence in Africa since 1990.[1] Over 3,000 people were killed and up to 1 million displaced. While the elections were meant to advance the peace process, the post-electoral violence instead pushed the country to the brink of a new civil war. After months of clashes, a military offensive by forces loyal to the president-elect, Alassane Ouattara, and backed by UN and French peacekeepers, defeated the incumbent president, Laurent Gbagbo, in April 2011. With Ouattara installed in office, the country has refocused on national reunification and advancing the peace process, including holding parliamentary elections in December 2011. The UN Operation in Côte d'Ivoire (UNOCI) played an important role in assisting the new government with these tasks and in establishing a conducive environment for peaceful elections.

Background

Following a failed coup attempt by the country's armed forces in September 2002, civil war broke out in Côte d'Ivoire, splitting the country between the rebel-held north and the government-controlled south.

In April 2004 the UN Security Council established UNOCI to assist in the implementation of the 2003 Linas-Marcoussis Accords, which sought to end the war. Since then, the mission has supported several other follow-on peace deals, including the most recent, the 2007 Ouagadougou Agreement, which called for elections and reunification of the country. In carrying out its mandate, UNOCI receives military support from Operation Licorne, deployed by France shortly after the outbreak of the war.

Though delayed several times following the Ouagadougou Agreement, presidential elections were announced in September 2010, once serious disputes over voting lists had been resolved. Given the heightened tension during the lead-up to the elections, which were to be held on 31 October, the Security Council, through Resolution 1942, authorized an increase of UNOCI's military and police presence by 500 peacekeepers, bringing the total to 9,150. UNOCI also received two

Map No. 4465.7   UNITED NATIONS
September 2011

Department of Field Support
Cartographic Section

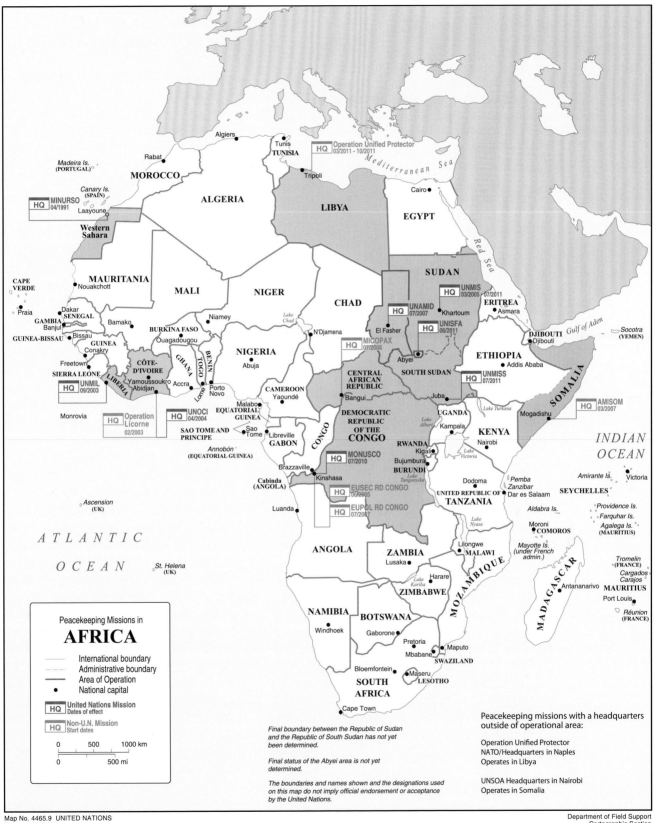

Peacekeeping Missions in
AFRICA

— International boundary
--- Administrative boundary
— Area of Operation
• National capital

HQ United Nations Mission
Dates of effect

HQ Non-U.N. Mission
Start dates

0   500   1000 km
0   500 mi

Final boundary between the Republic of Sudan
and the Republic of South Sudan has not yet
been determined.

Final status of the Abyei area is not yet
determined.

The boundaries and names shown and the designations used
on this map do not imply official endorsement or acceptance
by the United Nations.

Peacekeeping missions with a headquarters
outside of operational area:

Operation Unified Protector
NATO/Headquarters in Naples
Operates in Libya

UNSOA Headquarters in Nairobi
Operates in Somalia

UN Operation in Côte d'Ivoire (UNOCI)

- Authorization Date   27 February 2004 (UNSC Res. 1528)
- Start Date   4 April 2004
- SRSG   Albert Gerard Koenders (Netherlands)
- Force Commander   Major-General Gnakoudè Béréna (Togo)
- Police Commissioner   Major-General Jean Marie Bourry (France)
- Budget $486.7 million (1 July 2011–30 June 2012)
- Strength as of 31 October 2011   Troops: 9,356
  Military Observers: 199
  Police: 1,336
  International Civilian Staff: 397
  National Civilian Staff: 743
  UN Volunteers: 272

For detailed mission information see p. 312

Operation Licorne

- Authorization Date   24 January 2006 (UNSC Res. 1652)
- Start Date   February 2004
- Force Commander   Colonel Daniel Jaunin (France)
- Strength as of 30 September 2011   Troops: 700

military utility helicopters from the UN Mission in Liberia (UNMIL), on a temporary deployment.

On 31 October, the first round of elections failed to bring about an absolute majority victory for either incumbent president Laurent Gbagbo or his challenger and long-time political rival, Alassane Ouattara, which led to a runoff vote on 28 November. On 2 December, the Independent Election Commission (IEC) announced Ouattara as the winner of the second round. A day later, however, the president of the Constitutional Council voided the IEC's announcement and proclaimed Gbagbo victorious.

The then–Special Representative of the Secretary-General (SRSG) and head of UNOCI, Choi Young-jin, in his mandated role as independent election certifier for the presidential and legislative elections,[2] dismissed the results of the Constitutional Council and certified the outcome of the elections as announced by the IEC, again declaring Ouattara president-elect. The UN Secretary-General fully supported the SRSG's certification, which also received broad recognition by the international community. The Economic Community of West African States (ECOWAS) and the African Union (AU) called on Gbagbo to step down, and suspended Côte d'Ivoire from their organizations until Ouattara could assume power. The European Union and the United States adopted targeted sanctions against Gbagbo and his administration, while the World Bank froze $800 million in aid and $3 billion in debt relief.[3]

Aside from these punitive measures, efforts were under way to find a political solution to the ensuing crisis, particularly by the AU and ECOWAS, which held several high-level meetings on the situation and sent diplomatic delegations to mediate between the parties. The UN Secretary-General also engaged in diplomatic efforts and dispatched Said Djinnit, his Special Representative for West Africa, to Côte d'Ivoire to address the regional dimensions of the conflict.

Meanwhile, the security situation had deteriorated rapidly since the 2 December announcements, with pro-Gbagbo forces increasingly targeting perceived Ouattara supporters in Abidjan and elsewhere. UNOCI peacekeepers, stationed to protect Ouattara and his government at the Golf Hotel in Abidjan, also suffered attacks. Gbagbo's forces escalated their attempts to suffocate the UN peacekeeping operation—by denying customs clearance for supplies at port, cutting off fuel supplies, and blocking UNOCI supply vehicles and patrols.

On 20 December, concerned about the outbreak of violence against civilians and peacekeepers, the Security Council renewed UNOCI's mandate until 30 June 2011 (Resolution 1962), despite calls from Gbagbo for UN and French troops to leave the country. The Council also authorized a deployment extension, until 31 March, of the additional troops provided under Resolution 1942, as well as a temporary redeployment of troops and an aviation unit from UNMIL to UNOCI.

On 23 December, UNOCI confirmed the presence of heavily armed Liberian mercenaries in Côte d'Ivoire who had been hired by Gbagbo's regime, bringing into focus the regional dimensions of the conflict. The crisis also intensified the country's existing intercommunal and interethnic tensions. Responding to reports that the homes of Gbagbo opponents had been marked to identify the owners' ethnicity and that elements loyal to Gbagbo had incited hatred and violence against Gbagbo opponents, the UN Special Advisers on Genocide and the Responsibility to Protect issued a joint statement condemning these actions. By the end of the year, violent clashes around the country had claimed an estimated 200 lives.[4]

Key Developments

In January and February 2011, the Security Council adopted Resolutions 1967 and 1968, authorizing the deployment of an additional 2,000 troops; extending deployment of the additional military and police personnel provided under Resolution 1942; authorizing the temporary transfer of three armed helicopters with crews from UNMIL to UNOCI; and extending the deployment of the UNMIL troops and aviation unit, comprised of two military helicopters and three armed helicopters with crews under UNOCI command, for another three months, until May 2011.

On 28 March, after an extended period of unabated clashes during which civilians were increasingly targeted, President Ouattara launched a countrywide military offensive. The offensive was supported by the Forces Républicaines de Côte d'Ivoire (FRCI), under which Ouattara unified by decree the rebel group Forces Nouvelles (FN) and the state group Forces de Défense et de Sécurité (FDS). Some elements of the FDS, however, remained loyal to Gbagbo and continued fighting on his behalf.

On 30 March the FRCI encircled Abidjan, prompting pro-Gbagbo forces to increase counterattacks and escalate assaults on civilians, including with heavy weaponry. Pro-Gbagbo forces also launched attacks against UNOCI's headquarters and patrols, wounding eleven peacekeepers. One international staff member of UNOCI and one staff member of the World Health Organization (WHO) were killed during the fighting in Abidjan.[5]

In response to the continued fighting and the absence of a political solution to the crisis, ECOWAS reiterated its calls for the use of "legitimate force," first made in December,[6] if Gbagbo refused to step down, and urged the Security Council to strengthen UNOCI's mandate in order to enable the mission "to use all necessary means to protect life."[7]

Subsequently, on 30 March, in the face of the hostile operating environment and the widespread use of violence against civilians and peacekeepers, the Security Council granted UNOCI a more robust and deterrent posture, through Resolution 1975, by authorizing it to prevent the use of heavy weapons against the civilian population. The resolution also imposed sanctions on Gbagbo and his associates.

Secretary-General Ban Ki-moon arrives at Yamoussoukro Airport to attend the inauguration ceremony for Alassane Ouattara, president of Côte d'Ivoire, 21 May 2011. He was met at the airport by Prime Minister Guillaume Soro.

Box 2.2 Peace Operations and Electoral Violence

Elections play a vital role in postconflict countries and are a critical component of peace agreements, enabling the populations of war-torn societies to build democratic political processes and consolidate peace. In 2011, over eighty countries—thirty in Africa alone—held at least one election.

While the majority of elections are conducted without incidence of violence, countries that have experienced electoral violence in the past have a high risk of recurrence. At particular risk are countries—especially young democracies—with underlying systemic grievances, such as disputes concerning land rights, employment, or ethnic marginalization.

Peace operations play an important role in assisting countries in the various stages of the electoral process, from pre-election planning, to the conduct of the elections themselves, to support during the post-election period. Peace operations, along with their partners on the ground, assist in establishing independent election management bodies and forming electoral laws and guidelines; assist in establishing dispute resolution mechanisms; encourage inclusive and transparent election processes; and support the dissemination of information about the electoral process. Peace operations also assist in delivering electoral material, while military and police personnel provide crucial security functions. Mission leadership meanwhile use their good offices to mediate between the various

parties to create an environment conducive to peaceful elections.

Where electoral violence does occur, blue helmets often serve as the first responders to quell such outbreaks. When Haiti experienced violent protests in December 2010, following the announcement of preliminary results of the presidential elections that put popular candidate Michel Martelly in third place, troops from the UN Stabilization Mission in Haiti (MINUSTAH) moved to establish public order and security and to guard government buildings. Following the events of the first round of elections, MINUSTAH, along with national and international partners, identified measures to improve security for the second round, which included the replacement of electoral personnel involved in fraudulent or violent behavior. The second round of elections, in March 2011, led to the first peaceful transfer of power to the opposition in the country's history.

In Côte d'Ivoire, electoral violence broke out in December 2010 after incumbent president Laurent Gbagbo refused to step down from power and recognize president-elect Alassane Ouattara as the winner of the elections. The UN Operation in Côte d'Ivoire (UNOCI) along with France's Operation Licorne, played a decisive role in protecting civilians in the ensuing violence and in guarding the president-elect and his cabinet. UN and French peacekeepers also provided crucial backing to pro-Ouattara

forces in defeating Gbagbo and in installing the president-elect to office. UNOCI also assisted the government in preparing for the December 2011 parliamentary elections by providing security and technical assistance and fostering dialogue and reconciliation.

In the Democratic Republic of Congo, pre-electoral violence erupted in September 2011, when supporters of President Joseph Kabila's People's Party for Reconstruction and Democracy (PPRD) attacked the headquarters of the opposition Union for Democracy and Social Progress in an apparent retaliation for an arson attack on the PPRD's headquarters. The UN Organization Stabilization Mission in the Democratic Republic of Congo (MONUSCO) strongly condemned the violent incidents ahead of the November 2011 presidential and parliamentary elections and worked with the various parties to encourage dialogue. In anticipation of the election, MONUSCO also began training more than 700 police officers to provide increased security in the country's South Kivu province.

Peace operations play an important role in assisting countries throughout the electoral cycle, not least because, as first responders, they are critical in mitigating violence, protecting civilians, and reestablishing order. However, resource constraints—such as inadequate troop levels and aerial assets, particularly military helicopters—can hamper the ability of missions to perform this vital role.

In early April, UNOCI and Operation Licorne, the latter bolstered by a reinforcement of 300 troops,[8] began military operations in Abidjan to prevent the use of heavy weapons against civilians. UN peacekeepers and French troops also helped to extricate approximately 400 foreign nationals, UN staff, and diplomatic personnel who were trapped in the city, including a dramatic aerial rescue of the Japanese

ambassador by French troops. During the ensuing fighting, UNOCI forces were once again targeted both at headquarters and during patrols.

On 9 April pro-Gbagbo forces unsuccessfully attacked the Golf Hotel with mortars and heavy machine guns. In response, UNOCI and Operation Licorne troops conducted further military operations, including aerial assaults, with a focus on targeting heavy weapons in and around the presidential residence and military camps.

Two days later, Gbagbo's standoff finally came to an end when, in conjunction with sustained assaults by UN and Operation Licorne troops, FRCI forces broke through the presidential residency's defenses and apprehended the former president, his wife, and members of his family, staff, and "cabinet." Gbagbo was transferred to the north of the country, while members of the former president's extended family and retinue were either released, transferred to prisons, or placed under house arrest. Following the former president's capture, many former pro-Gbagbo commanders pledged to recognize Ouattara, while some were arrested by the FRCI and others went into hiding. Many fighters and mercenaries fled to Liberia. Acts of violence against civilians committed by these groups as well as clashes with the FRCI reportedly continued in the western part of the country.

On 21 May, in a ceremony that was attended by the UN Secretary-General and twenty heads of state, Alassane Ouattara was officially inaugurated president of Côte d'Ivoire. While the inauguration officially ended the electoral crisis, the installment of the president-elect came at a high human cost: since the outbreak of the crisis five months earlier, an estimated 3,000 people had lost their lives and between 700,000 and 1 million had been displaced.[9]

In June 2011 the Security Council adopted Resolution 1992, extending the temporary deployment of three armed helicopters from UNMIL to UNOCI until 30 September, after which they returned to Liberia to support the country's October elections. A month later, Resolution 2000 extended UNOCI's mandate at its current force level until 31 July 2012 and authorized the deployment of 205 additional police advisers. The Council also set forth terms of the mission's mandated tasks, including protection of civilians; security sector reform; addressing security threats; monitoring the arms embargo; weapons collection;

disarmament, demobilization, and reintegration (DDR); support for free, fair, and transparent legislative elections; extension of state authority throughout the country; and humanitarian assistance.

Security

The security situation in Côte d'Ivoire remained precarious throughout the second half of 2011, with the UN warning of a high risk of renewed armed conflict.[10] Continuing outbursts of violence indicated that although there had been a return to constitutional order, the crisis was not yet over. Fighting in Abidjan largely subsided, but unrest, including sporadic gunfire and looting, continued in the Abobo and Yopougon districts throughout July. In an effort to restore law and order, UNOCI and the FRCI launched joint patrols in Abidjan in mid-April, and UNOCI assisted in the collection and registration of 500 weapons and 65,000 rounds of ammunition.[11]

The security situation in the west was particularly volatile. In September, several Ivorian villages on the Liberian border suffered violent attacks allegedly carried out by Liberian mercenaries. In response, UNOCI dispatched ground forces and attack helicopters to the site, increased cooperation with UNMIL on border patrols, and began to bolster its military presence in the west. UNOCI also established eight new military camps, including four in the area along the border with Liberia. By September, two of the eight camps had been set up, while the remaining six were nearing completion. The camps are further reinforced by civilian staff working on human rights and the rule of law. The FRCI has also strengthened its presence in the west.

The post-electoral crisis led to a proliferation of armed groups around the country, which together with the large number of weapons present among the civilian population posed a challenge for DDR. In July the government reported that 11,000 former combatants had been reintegrated into the national army,[12] though disarmament among the civilian population was progressing slowly. UNOCI's DDR section supported the government in its efforts and carried out voluntary small arms collection in Abidjan's Yopougon district and throughout the country.

In September the government announced its intention to change the official name of its armed forces, the FRCI, to Forces Armées Nationales de Côte d'Ivoire (FANCI). Some see the name change as an effort to overhaul the image of the armed forces after Human Rights Watch in April and June reported that FRCI forces were increasingly targeting suspected Gbagbo supporters, particularly in the west. UNOCI's human rights section also reported an increase in attacks and violence by FRCI forces in the southwestern part of the country, which had contributed to considerable mistrust and even fear of the FRCI among the population. Beyond the change in name, further planned reforms of the army include the demobilization of 10,000 soldiers by the end of the year, troop training, and the restructuring of existing posts.[13]

UNOCI forces also came under scrutiny in August when allegations surfaced that peacekeepers had exchanged food for sex with young local girls in 2009. Following a year-long investigation into the allegations, sixteen peacekeepers from Benin were repatriated on disciplinary grounds and were barred from participating in future peacekeeping operations.[14]

Longer-term security provision and the maintenance of law and order will eventually be taken over by the Ivorian police and gendarmerie. However, the force has largely disintegrated. And although by July 85 percent reported back to resume duty, very few were actually working.[15] Even before the crisis, impunity, lack of accountability, politicization, corruption, absenteeism, and lack of training and equipment characterized the police force, pointing to a strong need for reform. The government in particular criticized the lack of weapons for the police, reportedly amounting to only fifteen handguns, and asked the UN to expedite distribution of recovered weapons to the authorities.[16] As part of the restoration of security and rule of law institutions, UNOCI assisted in rehabilitating and equipping a number of municipal offices, police stations, and gendarmeries damaged during the crisis. The mission also conducted training and sensitization sessions to prepare police personnel for the legislative elections. In November, in an effort to further strengthen the police force capacity, France, after a seven-year hiatus, resumed security cooperation with Côte d'Ivoire with the delivery of computer equipment and thirty police vehicles.

Justice and Reconciliation

In June 2011 the government of Côte d'Ivoire announced the establishment of a national commission to investigate human rights violations committed during the post-electoral violence. While the government pledged to prosecute all violators, members of a UN investigation team warned of "one-sided victory justice," as none of Ouattara's affiliates have been detained or come under investigation, by either the military or the civilian prosecutor.[17] In August, reinforcing the perception of impunity for his supporters, Ouattara appointed rebel commanders, some of whom the UN and Human Rights Watch have accused of human rights violations, to key military posts.

On 18 August, Côte d'Ivoire's state prosecutor officially charged former president Gbagbo and his wife with "economic crimes, armed robbery, looting and embezzlement." Following the indictment, both were moved from house arrest to prison. State prosecutors also indicted members of Gbagbo's party and soldiers of his regime on charges ranging from murder to attacking state security to buying illegal arms.

On 28 September, as part of a national reconciliation effort, the government launched a Truth, Reconciliation and Dialogue Commission, first proposed in May and modeled after South Africa's post-apartheid commission. The eleven-member commission, headed by former prime minister Charles Konan Banny, comprises religious leaders, regional representatives, and world-famous football star Didier

Drogba as a representative of the diaspora. UNOCI and the UN Country Team provided assistance to the commission to ensure that it would function according to international principles and standards. UNOCI also supported reconciliation efforts at the community level, to prevent and resolve further conflict.

On 29 November, the International Criminal Court (ICC) issued an arrest warrant for Gbagbo on charges of crimes against humanity, including murder, rape, persecution, and inhuman acts. Gbagbo was handed over to international custody and moved to The Hague the following day. The charges follow a request by Ouattara in May for the ICC to investigate the most serious crimes committed during the crisis. The ICC prosecutor has also opened investigations on members of the Gbagbo government, in addition to individuals in the current government. The court may also widen its investigation to include crimes committed between 2002 and 2010 and thus potentially including allegations of abuse by the FN, which during that period was under the command of the current prime minister, Guillaume Soro.

Elections

Shortly after Ouattara's inauguration, national stakeholders reiterated the importance of holding legislative elections as soon as possible to ensure full restoration of constitutional order and national reconciliation. In late June 2011, an electoral assessment mission to Côte d'Ivoire, led by the UN Department of Peacekeeping Operations, concluded that elections could be held by the end of the year if the security situation improved. At the end of September, the government announced plans to hold parliamentary elections on 11 December 2011.

A week prior to the announcement, Gbagbo's party, the Front Populaire Ivoirien (FPI), pulled out of the Independent Election Commission, criticizing a "recent modification of the electoral commission's composition in favor of the coalition of parties behind President Ouattara."[18] Ouattara, who in June had announced the formation of a new government without FPI representation, subsequently opened negotiations with opposition parties, including the FPI, in an effort to keep them from boycotting the December elections. However, in November the FPI announced its decision to boycott the election, and the parliamentary vote list closed without the party's representation.

UNOCI supported the government in the lead-up to the elections, including providing logistical and technical assistance as well as bolstering security. UNOCI stationed 7,000 peacekeepers throughout the country—a presence further augmented by the transfer of five helicopters from UNMIL to UNOCI from 3 to 31 December. The mission also worked to create a favorable environment for the elections by promoting an inclusive political process.

Considering the events that followed the 2010 elections, some members of the international community voiced concern about continuing the election certification role of the SRSG, arguing that it may have helped to fuel the crisis rather than to resolve it. However, Albert Gerard Koenders, who replaced Choi Young-jin as UNOCI's SRSG in September 2011, retained the role for parliamentary elections to ensure that the process was carried out in accordance with internationally recognized standards.

Notwithstanding several violent incidents in the lead-up to the vote, international election monitors and the UN described the conduct of the parliamentary elections as calm and peaceful. Preliminary results show that with 80 percent of the vote, President Ouattara's ruling coalition won a parliamentary majority. However, the vote took place amid a low voter turnout of around 36 percent. While this reflects in part fear among the population for renewed violence at the polls, some may interpret the low turnout as the result of the FPI's calls for a boycott.

Conclusion

UNOCI and Operation Licorne played a decisive role in ending the 2011 electoral crisis in

Côte d'Ivoire by providing military backing to the FRCI, which enabled the latter to arrest Gbagbo and facilitate the immediate transfer of power to Ouattara. Indeed, the presence of Operation Licorne, particularly its attack helicopter assets, provided an essential force complement to that of the UN during the April operations.

Although constitutional order has been restored, Côte d'Ivoire continues to face major challenges, including stabilizing the security situation, reconciliation and justice, further bolstering economic recovery, and addressing the humanitarian situation: in November, more than 138,000 refugees remained in Liberia and an estimated 25,000 remained in other countries in the region,[19] while an estimated 17,000 internally displaced persons are still living in camps.[20] The magnitude of these challenges and the fragility of national political and security institutions as demonstrated this year suggest that the presence of peacekeepers is likely to remain necessary for the foreseeable future.

Notes

1. USIP, *Prevention Newsletter,* September 2011, p. 4.

2. For more on the SRSG's certification role, see the United Nations, *Twenty-seventh Progress Report of the Secretary-General on the United Nations Operation in Côte d'Ivoire,* UN Doc. S/2011/211, 30 March 2011, para. 74.

3. United Nations, *Twenty-seventh Progress Report,* para. 24.

4. Dan Smith et al., "Ivory Coast Violence Forces Thousands to Flee," *The Guardian,* 26 December 2010.

5. United Nations, *Twenty-eighth Report of the Secretary-General on the United Nations Operation in Côte d'Ivoire,* UN Doc. S/2011/387, 24 June 2011, para. 4.

6. "Ecowas Bloc Threatens Ivory Coast's Gbagbo with Force," *BBC News,* 25 December 2010, http://www.bbc.co.uk/news/world-africa-12077298.

7. Letter from the Permanent Representative of Nigeria to the President of the UN Security Council, 24 March 2011, http://www.securitycouncilreport.org/atf/cf/%7B65BFCF9B-6D27-4E9C-8CD3-CF6E4FF96FF9%7D/Cote%20d'Ivoire%20s%202011%20182.pdf.

8. "French Troops Take Control of Airport in I. Coast Main City," *Agence France-Presse,* 3 April 2011, http://www.dawn.com/2011/04/03/french-troops-take-control-of-airport-in-i-coast-main-city.html.

9. United Nations, *Twenty-eighth Report,* S/2011/387, para. 40; UNHCR, "Escalating Violence Fuels Dramatic Rise in Displacement in Côte d'Ivoire," 25 March 2011, http://www.unhcr.org/4d8c950a9.html.

10. United Nations, *Twenty-eighth Report,* S/2011/387, para. 22.

11. Ibid., para. 13.

12. United Nations, "Restoring Order Key to National Reconciliation, Economic Recovery, All Other Tasks in Côte d'Ivoire, Special Representative Tells Security Council," press release, 18 July 2011, http://www.un.org/News/Press/docs/2011/sc10329.doc.htm.

13. "Côte d'Ivoire: Rebranding the Army," *IRIN News,* 5 October 2011, http://www.irinnews.org/report.aspx?reportid=93886.

14. "UN Peacekeepers Traded Food for Sex, Cable Says," *Associated Press,* 2 September 2011, http://articles.boston.com/2011-09-02/news/30106728_1_children-uk-peacekeepers-sexual-exploitation-and-abuse.

15. United Nations, *Twenty-eighth Report,* S/2011/387, para. IV, B, 2.

16. United Nations, "Restoring Order Key to National Reconciliation."

17. Fredrik Dahl, "U.N. Rights Chief Concerned About New Ivory Coast Army," *Reuters,* 15 June 2011, http://www.reuters.com/article/2011/06/15/us-ivorycoast-un-idUSTRE75E4FO20110615.

18. Eric Agnero, "Ouattara Opens Talks with Gbagbo Supporters," *CNN News,* 29 September 2011, http://articles.cnn.com/2011-09-29/africa/world_africa_ivory-coast-politics_1_president-alassane-ouattara-gbagbo-loyalists-gbagbo-supporters?_s=PM:AFRICA.

19. UNHCR, "New Ivorian Refugee Camp Opened in Eastern Liberia," 2 September 2011, http://www.unhcr.org/4e60afb09.html.

20. OCHA, "Côte d'Ivoire Situation Report Nr. 15," 8 September 2011.

2.3

Democratic Republic of Congo

As 2011 came to a close, the Democratic Republic of Congo (DRC) faced serious threats to its stability. Presidential and legislative elections, held on 28 November, were rejected by the political opposition and criticized by many observers for lacking credibility. Etienne Tshisekedi, veteran politician and main rival of President Joseph Kabila in the elections, declared himself "elected president" after official reports of Kabila's victory, with 49 percent of the vote versus 32 percent for Tshisekedi.

Election-related tensions in urban centers, far from the conflict in the east, have stretched the strained resources of the UN Organization Stabilization Mission in the Democratic Republic of Congo (MONUSCO) even thinner. And while regional relations in the east continued to improve, relations between the DRC and its western neighbors, the Republic of Congo and Angola, wavered. Meanwhile, MONUSCO continued to struggle with its mandate to reform the security sector, extend state authority, combat armed groups, and protect civilians in the east.

Background

The DRC's conflict can be seen as three interrelated wars, the first two of which were fought with heavy influence by neighboring states seeking to oust Congo's contentious leaders in 1996 and 1999 respectively. While the first war successfully removed then-president Mobutu Sese Seko, the second war failed to remove Mobutu's successor, Laurent Kabila, and the resulting stalemate led to the signing of a cease-fire accord, the Lusaka Agreement, in July 1999 by the various parties

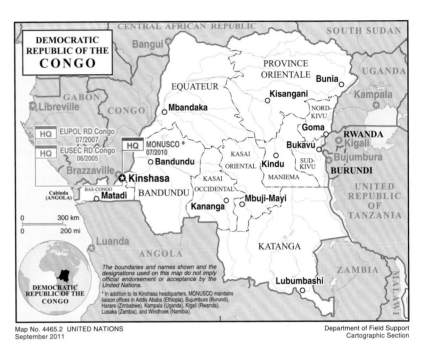

Map No. 4465.2 UNITED NATIONS
September 2011

Department of Field Support
Cartographic Section

UN Organization Stabilization Mission in the Democratic Republic of Congo (MONUSCO)

- Authorization Date   28 May 2010 (UNSC Res. 1925)
- Start Date   1 July 2010
- SRSG   Roger Meece (United States)
- Force Commander   Lieutenant-General Chander Prakash (India)
- Police Commissioner   Abdallah Wafy (Niger)
- Budget $1,419.9 million (1 July 2011–30 June 2012)
- Strength as of 31 October 2011   Troops: 16,823

  Military Observers: 731

  Police: 1,362

  International Civilian Staff: 976

  National Civilian Staff: 2,865

  UN Volunteers: 595

For detailed mission information see p. 216

and state actors. Following the agreement, the UN authorized the UN Organization Mission in the Democratic Republic of Congo (MONUC) to monitor the cease-fire and disengagement of forces. The withdrawal of foreign troops after the signing of the Lusaka Agreement left a power vacuum in the rebel-held territories, leading to a third war behind UN-monitored cease-fire lines in northeastern Congo. Following a national dialogue and series of regional agreements, a government of national unity was formed in 2003, paving the way for the 2006 UN-sponsored elections that brought Joseph Kabila to the presidency.

Following intense negotiations with the government of the DRC in early 2010 regarding the future of MONUC, the UN Security Council adopted Resolution 1925 on 28 May 2010, transforming MONUC into MONUSCO. The most recent extension of the mission's authorization, Resolution 1991, left MONUSCO's core priorities essentially unchanged. Protection of civilians under imminent threat of physical violence remains the top priority. Beyond direct action by MONUSCO to protect civilians, this includes helping the national army bring ongoing military operations against the Forces Démocratiques de Libération du Rwanda (FDLR), the Lord's Resistance Army (LRA), and other armed groups to completion, as well as supporting disarmament, demobilization, repatriation, resettlement, and reintegration (DDRRR) programs. The mission's second priority is stabilization and peace consolidation, including reform of the security sector, consolidation of state authority as per the government's Stabilization and Reconstruction Plan (STAREC) and the International Security and Stabilization Support Strategy (ISSSS), combating mineral exploitation, and providing technical and logistical support, as requested by the government, for presidential and parliamentary elections. Resolution 1991 elaborates on MONUSCO's electoral responsibilities, mandating the mission to support the Commission Électorale Nationale Indépendente (CENI) in facilitating dialogue among Congolese stakeholders, as well as monitoring, reporting, and following up on human rights violations in the context of elections.

While its mandate remained essentially unchanged in 2011, MONUSCO's available resources have been sharply curtailed, particularly its utility, attack, and observation helicopters. This has had a serious impact on the capacity of the mission, leading the Secretary-General to report that MONUSCO is "no longer able to implement critical parts of its priority mandated tasks, including in relation to the protection of civilians, providing support to the elections and putting an end to the presence of armed groups, particularly in the Kivus."[1]

The mission's stabilization work is focused around implementation of three initiatives: STAREC, the ISSSS, and the UN's peace consolidation program, developed jointly by MONUSCO and the UN Country Team. However, continued insecurity has delayed their implementation. Nearly ninety facilities were constructed in 2011 in accordance with the ISSSS, but many of the facilities have not been staffed. Magistrates are in short supply, and police detachments are under-strength. The UN's peace consolidation program is being supported by new joint MONUSCO-UN Country Team offices throughout the western provinces, in preparation for a progressive transition of leadership from MONSUCO to the UN Country Team in these areas.

Alongside MONUSCO, the EU Advisory and Assistance Mission for Security Reform in the Democratic Republic of Congo (EUSEC RD Congo) and the EU Police Mission in the Democratic Republic of Congo (EUPOL RD Congo) have provided support to the DRC's security and police institutions. EUSEC has continued to provide advice and assistance to the Congolese authorities in charge of security. Its operations have primarily focused on training Forces Armées de la République Démocratique du Congo (FARDC) units in human rights law and standards, military justice, and prevention of sexual violence, while also addressing arms stockpiling and other logistical challenges and supporting the work of the

EU Special Representative for the African Great Lakes Region.

EUPOL RD Congo, meanwhile, supports the reform and coordination of the police and justice system with a focus on capacity building. In 2011 the mission focused on training judicial police officers and assisting the police in obtaining equipment ahead of elections. Both EUSEC and EUPOL continue to make technical progress in their mandates, although pressure from some EU member states for the closure of these missions persists.

Key Developments

Developments in the East
Despite its stabilization focus, MONUSCO continues to face prevalent insecurity and armed group activity in the east. The leadership of the FDLR in the DRC remained largely intact in 2011, and the group continues to target civilians in the Kivus and northern Katanga province. While a steady stream of FDLR defectors entered DDRRR programs throughout early 2011, these defections were balanced by new recruiting. Other armed groups, including Congrès National pour la Défense du Peuple (CNDP) deserters and Mayi-Mayi militias, have consolidated their positions throughout the east, and have established loose alliances with each other and the FDLR, partially in order to secure mining interests. Human rights violations in the east continued to occur at very high levels throughout 2011, including several documented cases of mass rapes and a number of civilian deaths. The UN Joint Human Rights office in MONUSCO documented 300 human rights abuses attributed to armed groups and 320 human rights violations committed by elements of the armed forces between June and July 2011 alone.

The LRA continued to pose a significant threat to civilians in Haut Uélé and Bas Uélé. MONUSCO has provided logistical and information sharing support for operations by the FARDC and the Ugandan People's Defense Force (UPDF) against the LRA in these regions, but attacks continued throughout early

The first electoral kits are unloaded from a MONUSCO cargo aircraft at Ndjili Airport, 16 September 2011.

EU Advisory and Assistance Mission for Security Reform in the Democratic Republic of Congo (EUSEC RD Congo)

- Authorization Date   2 May 2005 (EU Council Joint Action 2005/355/CFSP)
- Start Date   June 2005
- Head of Mission   General António Martins (Portugal)
- Budget $17.6 million (1 October 2010–30 September 2011)
- Strength as of   Civilian Staff: 51
  30 September 2011

EU Police Mission in the Democratic Republic of Congo (EUPOL RD Congo)

- Authorization Date   12 June 2007 (EU Council Joint Action 2007/405/CFSP)
- Start Date   July 2007
- Head of Mission   Commissioner Jean Paul Rikir (Belgium)
- Budget $8.9 million (1 October 2010–30 September 2011)
- Strength as of   Civilian Police: 21
  30 September 2011   Civilian Staff: 19

2011, decreasing in July and August due to a possible regrouping of the armed group in the Central African Republic. In October

---

Box 2.3 Mission for the Consolidation of Peace in the Central African Republic (MICOPAX)

Since July 2008, the Mission for the Consolidation of Peace in the Central African Republic (MICOPAX) has provided support to peace and stability efforts in the Central African Republic (CAR). Under the authority of the Economic Community of Central African States (CEEAC), MICOPAX is mandated to support peace, security, and respect for human rights, including through assistance in the promotion of democratic governance, national reconciliation, security sector reform, and disarmament, demobilization, and reintegration (DDR) of former combatants. It also collaborates with the UN Integrated Peacebuilding Office in the Central African Republic (BINUCA).

MICOPAX was established to support the consolidation of peace following decades of instability, rebellions, and mutinies in the Central African Republic. The CAR's current leader, General François Bozizé, came to power in a coup in February 2003. Conflict continued until the government and nearly all main rebel groups signed a comprehensive peace agreement (CPA) in June 2008. However, the government quickly demonstrated a lack of political will for following through on the CPA and the subsequent inclusive dialogue, resulting in political and security challenges that continue to undermine the consolidation of peace in the CAR.

The 2011 presidential and parliamentary elections were held in January, with a second round of parliamentary voting in March. MICOPAX provided support to the elections, including transport of voting materials to regional polling stations. Despite the largely calm

Mission for the Consolidation of Peace in the Central African Republic (MICOPAX)

• Authorization Date	2 October 2002
• Start Date	December 2002
• Head of Mission	Ambassador Albert Akendengue (Gabon)
• Force Commander	Brigade-General Prosper Nabiolwa (Democratic Republic of Congo)
• Budget	$27.2 million (1 October 2010–30 September 2011)
• Strength as of 30 September 2011	Troops: 497 Civilian Police: 139

atmosphere that characterized both rounds of voting, the elections demonstrated the continued fragility of the CAR's political process. There was strong turnout for the January poll, and Bozizé garnered a majority and was inaugurated on 15 March. However, opposition candidates quickly denounced the election as fraudulent and several opposition candidates petitioned the Constitutional Court for a cancellation of the vote, a request that the Court denied as unfounded. After the second round of parliamentary elections, Bozizé's political party, the Kwa Na Kwa, also won a legislative majority, amid lower voter turnout and a boycott by the opposition.

In 2011 MICOPAX continued to support the reform and restructuring of the CAR's security forces and assist the government in DDR activities for former combatants. However, DDR processes in northern CAR have been repeatedly delayed due to political, security, and logistical challenges. MICOPAX plays a key role in the northwest as a guarantor of security while rebel groups disarm,

and has recently begun to expand its presence to the northeast. In April, MICOPAX, with financial support from the European Union, opened a military barracks in Ndélé in the northeastern prefecture to house several hundred soldiers through 2013.[1] The rebel group Convention of Patriots for Justice and Peace (CPJP), the last holdout, signed a cease-fire agreement with the government in June and agreed to begin the DDR process, a positive step forward.

Despite gains in 2011, the CAR remains an environment of heightened political and security concerns. Renewed hostilities between the CPJP and a rival rebel group in the central town of Bira in September over control of diamond mines demonstrates how tenuous the situation remains. The withdrawal in December 2010 of the UN's peacekeeping operation places additional pressure on MICOPAX and BINUCA to support the peace process. Continued fragility and an increasingly entrenched political elite are major obstacles to the consolidation of peace.

Note: 1. Humanitarian and Development Partnership Team, Central African Republic, *Info Bulletin* no. 167, 12–26 April 2011, http://hdptcar.net/blog/wp-content/uploads/2011/05/hdpt-car-info-bulletin-eng-167.pdf.

2011 the United States announced the deployment of 100 "combat-equipped" soldiers to LRA-affected areas, primarily to provide training to Uganda's armed forces and other national armies that are combating the LRA. MONUSCO and regional partners are paying close attention to the developing African Union regional cooperation initiative on the LRA, endorsed at its summit meeting on 1 July. An AU interim Special Envoy was appointed in late November and is expected to work closely with the governments of LRA-affected countries. Meanwhile, the Ugandan Allied Democratic Front (ADF) has increased its presence in Beni and Lubero territories.

FARDC exactions against civilians, particularly from recently integrated and poorly trained units, continue to be a very serious concern. Meanwhile, MONUSCO's progress in improving military justice and accountability has faced difficulties. MONUSCO and the UN's Office of the High Commissioner for Human Rights (OHCHR) published a report on 22 July documenting human rights violations committed on 31 December 2010 and 1 January 2011, allegedly by elements of the FARDC, but the Congolese authorities have not yet acted on the report's recommendations.

In January 2011 the FARDC began to restructure its presence in the Kivus, with the ultimate goal of establishing several regiments of 1,200 elements each. However, the withdrawal of army units has led to an increase in activity by the FDLR, Mayi-Mayi Yakutumba, and Burundian Forces Nationals de Libération (FNL) in the Kivus. While MONUSCO has carried out operations attempting to fill this security vacuum, the extended restructuring process has hindered progress in integrating former armed group elements, including the CNDP and other groups, into the national army and police. Throughout the restructuring process, elements of these groups have deserted the FARDC in significant numbers. Those remaining have often refused orders to redeploy outside their areas of operation. President Kabila issued a decree on 31 December 2010 regarding the redistribution of the ranks of former members of armed groups, but many CNDP elements continued to reject their FARDC-issued identification cards, citing confusion regarding their ranks. CNDP and other former armed group elements have also maintained parallel administration structures in the Kivus.

Throughout 2011, MONUSCO has explored various methods to improve its capacity to protect civilians with its limited resources. These efforts have mostly taken the form of improving communication and relations with local populations. The mission has established community alert networks, distributing mobile phones and some high-frequency radios to isolated communities, while also deploying community liaison assistants to communities in their areas of operation and dispatching joint protection teams aimed at increasing civil and military knowledge and analysis of protection issues. The mission has also developed a senior management group on protection. While these initiatives have been generally well assessed by the mission and many humanitarian partners, and address a crucial information gap, the loss of helicopters has curtailed not only the mission's rapid response capacity, but also its ability to maintain many of its temporary operating bases in the more remote areas of the Kivus and Orientale province.

Regional Relations

Despite ongoing violence in eastern DRC, relations in the Great Lakes region have been improving. In January 2011 the ministers of defense of Burundi, Rwanda, and the DRC adopted a draft protocol on mutual defense and security, which includes provisions for border control and interception of armed group combatants fleeing across national borders. The Ugandan and DRC defense ministers also met several times in 2011 to discuss joint military operations between the Congolese and Ugandan armies in Orientale province against the LRA and the ADF.

Improvements in relations to the east, however, were not matched in the west. Relations between the DRC and Angola deteriorated in early 2011. Beginning as a dispute over maritime boundaries in the Bas-Congo and Cabinda regions, Angola expelled over 100,000 Congolese nationals between September 2010 and August 2011. Returnees have reported serious human rights violations associated with the expulsions, including detention, forced labor, sexual violence, and beatings. Repeated high-level bilateral discussions and visits from MONUSCO, the UN Special Representative on Sexual Violence in Conflict, and the Office of the UN High Commissioner for Refugees (UNHCR) have made little progress in addressing the problem. However, relations between the two countries showed signs of improvement in late 2011, and Angola provided six helicopters to help distribute materials for the elections.

The DRC recalled its ambassador to the Republic of Congo on 25 March over disputes related to the extradition of General Faustin Munene as well as the leader of the Enyele insurgency of 2010, Mangbama Lebesse Udjani.

Elections

The lead-up to national presidential and parliamentary elections in 2011 was marked by the adoption of constitutional amendments on 15 January that replaced the former two-round presidential election with a single-round poll. The amendments aimed to strengthen the odds of President Joseph Kabila's reelection, exploiting a fractured opposition. They also created the possibility of a presidential victory with a small portion of the popular vote, with resulting concerns regarding the victor's legitimacy.

The beginning of 2011 also saw serious delays in electoral preparations. The voter registration process, for example, was initially planned to take ninety days. However, the process, launched on 9 March in most provinces, was not completed until 17 July, when the revised registration list was announced with a preliminary total of 32 million voters. Subsequently, opposition parties, including the Union pour la Démocratie et le Progrès Social (UDPS), the Union pour la Nation Congolaise (UNC), and the Mouvement de Libération du Congo (MLC), demanded an audit of the voter registration list as a precondition for their adherence to the code of conduct, which the CENI granted on 2 September. Opposition parties signed the electoral code of conduct at the second meeting of the Forum of Political Parties, on 8 September, with the notable exception of the UDPS and its allies.

Electoral materials began to arrive in the DRC on 15 September after significant delays. MONUSCO was faced with the significant challenge of distributing the ballots to 15 "hubs" and 210 "sub-hubs" around the country, where they were distributed by road to more than 63,000 polling stations. The mission also carried out training of six national police rapid response teams, with France training two and the DRC training two. However, MONUSCO reported a lack of funds from donor countries to equip the police units with nonlethal weapons.

More troubling than the numerous logistical hurdles, the period leading up to national elections was marked by an increasing number of what MONUSCO described as "politically-motivated human rights violations."[2] The mission documented over 145 reported incidents targeting political opposition members and supporters, journalists, and human rights defenders from January to October 2011, not including eighty additional allegations of human rights violations. Both the UNC and the UDPS reported cases of restrictions in conducting political activities, including arrests of and violence against supporters by the national security forces.

The days immediately preceding elections were marked by violence in urban centers. Human Rights Watch documented at least eighteen civilians killed and over a hundred injured in electoral violence between 26 and 28 November, mostly from Republican Guard elements firing into crowds of opposition supporters. The Ministry of Interior suspended short message service (SMS) communications on 3 December, allegedly due to the use of SMS to threaten domestic and international election observers.

Despite intense pressure on the CENI to briefly postpone elections to address logistical bottlenecks, the DRC held presidential and legislative elections on 28 November 2011 as scheduled, though voting was extended by two days in some polling stations. The day of elections was marred by a host of irregularities and incidents of violence. Opposition supporters clashed with security forces in Kasai and Katanga provinces. Rumors of pre-completed ballots, ballot stuffing, and vote tampering led to attacks on election officials and polling stations across the country. International observers reported confusion among electoral officials regarding voter lists and voting eligibility, and documented a number of irregularities with the handling of electoral materials, highlighting cases of electoral materials being unsealed outside of tabulation centers.

In the days following the elections, the tabulation process raised further concerns due to serious logistical problems resulting in missing ballot boxes and untabulated votes, and due to the lack of transparency in the tabulation process. The CENI released preliminary vote tallies indicating a strong lead for Kabila, but failed to disaggregate the numbers by polling station, making the numbers impossible to verify against the records provided to electoral observers and political party witnesses at each station. Tensions rose in Kinshasa and other urban centers, resulting in clashes between police forces and opposition supporters. The UDPS announced that it would reject any results showing Kabila as the winner, while a coalition of other opposition groups issued a joint call for the elections to be annulled, citing massive irregularities and fraud.

On 9 December, after three days of delays, the CENI published the full preliminary results, declaring Kabila the winner with 49 percent of votes, with Tshisekedi in second with 32 percent and Vital Kamerhe in third with 7.7 percent. The results were immediately rejected by the UDPS as fraudulent, and Tshisekedi declared himself the "elected president," citing UDPS tallies from polling stations that put his share of the vote at 52 percent.

In the days following publication of the results, national and international election observers reported significant irregularities in the published electoral results. Tabulation centers in Kabila strongholds reported suspiciously high turnout and support for Kabila, while centers in Tshisekedi bastions misplaced

boxes from thousands of polling stations. The Malemba-Nkulu tabulation center in Katanga, for example, declared all of the 266,886 votes cast in its area for Kabila, with over 99 percent turnout, compared to a national turnout average of 58.8 percent, and every polling station accounted for. In contrast, the Kinshasa tabulation center lost ballots from nearly 2,000 polling stations, resulting in 350,000 uncounted votes in a UDPS stronghold. Results from another thousand polling stations outside of Kinshasa were also lost, including a number from the major city of Lubumbashi.

The Carter Center observer mission issued a report on 10 December stating that the election results "lack credibility" and "compromise the integrity of the presidential election,"[3] and the DRC Catholic Church, the largest observer mission, announced on 12 December that the results "are not founded on truth or justice."[4] The rising tide of criticism from domestic and international observers led MONUSCO to issue a statement on 12 December calling on the CENI to "undertake a timely and rigorous review of the issues identified by observer missions."[5] On 13 December, EU election observers joined the growing group of critics, noting that the election count was chaotic and lacked transparency and credibility.

While MONUSCO was not mandated to verify or observe the electoral process, Special Representative of the Secretary-General (SRSG) Roger Meece used his good offices in the run-up to elections and the tense post-election period to urge both Kabila and Tshisekedi to refrain from resorting to violence. Although neither mass protests nor violence occurred immediately following the elections, Congolese police began door-to-door searches in opposition neighborhoods, reportedly dragging young men out of their houses and taking them away in waiting vehicles.

Kabila, rejecting criticism from observers and backed by the South African Development Community (SADC), held his inauguration on 20 December. During his speech, Kabila pledged to bolster national unity and abide by human rights. However, Tshisekedi still insisted he was president-elect and planned a rival inauguration for 23 December. The police banned Tshisekedi's swearing-in, placed tanks throughout the city, used tear gas and stun grenades to disperse rock-throwing crowds, arrested opposition supporters, and prevented Tshisekedi from leaving his house, ultimately crushing the event as planned in a Kinshasa stadium. Undeterred, Tshisekedi, along with supporters and officials of the UDSP, swore himself in as president at his house, further straining the tense postelection situation. Having proceeded with the banned act without heed to threats of arrest, it is unclear how Kabila will react to Tshisekedi's challenge, leaving the prospects for stability in the DRC uncertain.

At the time of writing, much of the capital and other major cities were gripped with confusion, with unconfirmed reports of military looting in outlying areas, widespread gunfire, and unidentified groups of armed men active in the streets.

Conclusion

The electoral process in 2011 has resulted in a shrinking of political space and left the situation in the DRC extremely tense. Troubling incidents in the lead-up to elections culminated in killings by the Republican Guard, door-to-door searches and arrests in opposition neighborhoods by Congolese police, and significant irregularities in the elections themselves. As a result, the UN mission, traditionally focused on the east, was operating in a fully fledged political crisis.

Congolese opposition and civil society groups are demanding a review of the serious flaws in the electoral process by a credible independent party. President Kabila has admitted that some "mistakes" were made, but rejects claims of widespread election rigging.[6] While Tshisekedi has so far refrained from calling on his supporters to contest the elections in the streets, the rhetoric being used by both sides is very heated. Escalation into violent protests and clashes with the authorities are a very real possibility that MONUSCO is not equipped to address. Furthermore, other Congolese actors may see the current unrest as an opportunity to further their own political agendas, both inside and outside the DRC.

The way forward is uncertain, as events in the weeks following elections will doubtless change the political landscape. The situation will likely be further destabilized with the announcement of the legislative election results in early 2012, which may prove similarly contentious. Moreover, provincial and local elections are scheduled to be held in 2012. As 2011 came to a close, MONUSCO faced both the significant challenges of its operations in the east, as well as the new challenge of a political crisis that could well engulf the rest of the country.

Notes

1. United Nations, *Report of the Secretary-General on the United Nations Organization Stabilization Mission in the Democratic Republic of the Congo,* UN Doc. S/2011/656, 24 October 2011, p. 14.

2. Ibid., p. 3.

3. Carter Center, "DRC Presidential Election Results Lack Credibility," 10 December 2011, http://www.cartercenter.org/news/pr/drc-121011.html.

4. Rukmini Callimachi and Saleh Mwanamilongo, "Growing Criticism of Congo Vote," *Associated Press,* 12 December 2011.

5. MONUSCO, "MONUSCO Calls on INEC to Address Electoral Observer Missions' Concerns," press release, 12 December 2011, http://monusco.unmissions.org/Default.aspx?tabid=932&ctl=Details&mid=5262&ItemID=15947.

6. Emmanuel Peuchot, "DR Congo's Kabila Admits Vote Flaws but Defends Re-Election," *Agence France-Presse,* 12 December 2011.

Haiti

Haiti entered 2011 still recovering from the massive earthquake that struck in January 2010, killing 230,000 and leaving 1.5 million homeless. The country has also struggled to respond to a growing cholera epidemic that began in late 2010—the outbreak of which was linked to UN peacekeepers serving with the UN Stabilization Mission in Haiti (MINUSTAH). Thousands have died due to the outbreak while hundreds of thousands more have been infected, presenting serious public health challenges. The epidemic unleashed a wave of anti-UN riots during an already volatile period of political transition.

While the unstable political environment continued in the lead-up to the second round of presidential elections in March 2011, the election and inauguration of President Michel Martelly represented the first peaceful transfer of power to the opposition in Haiti's history. However, the president and parliament quickly entered a fractious and divisive period that stalled the formation of a government, political reforms, and recovery efforts.

MINUSTAH continued to provide critical political, security, and justice support to Haiti, and in October 2011 the UN Security Council approved a drawdown of MINUSTAH's post-earthquake police and troop surge. The drawdown came in conjunction with growing public pressure on the mission related to its role in the outbreak of cholera and the alleged rape of a Haitian teenager by mission troops. These events coincided with a change in leadership for MINUSTAH, with Mariano Fernández of Chile taking over as Special Representative of the Secretary-General (SRSG) from Edmond Mulet, who returned to his duties in New York as Assistant Secretary-General for Peacekeeping Operations.[1]

Despite considerable progress in reconstruction, the overall environment in Haiti remains fragile and vulnerable to shocks, whether economic, political, or from a natural disaster.

Background

The 1991 military coup that ousted President Jean Bertrand Aristide set in motion cycles of political, economic, and security unrest in Haiti that continue to challenge stabilization. In 2000 the returned Aristide claimed victory in an election that saw a voter turnout of approximately 10 percent. The opposition and members of the international community

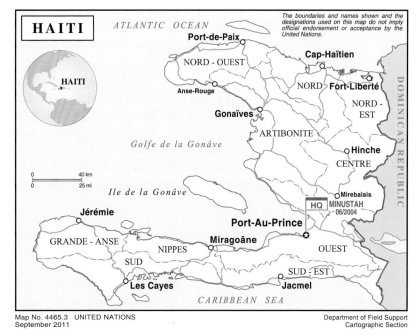

Map No. 4465.3   UNITED NATIONS
September 2011

Department of Field Support
Cartographic Section

UN Stabilization Mission in Haiti (MINUSTAH)

- Authorization Date   30 April 2004 (UNSC Res. 1542)
- Start Date   1 June 2004
- SRSG   Mariano Fernández (Chile)
- Force Commander   Major-General Luiz Eduardo Ramos Pereira (Brazil)
- Police Commissioner   Marc Tardif (Canada)
- Budget $793.5 million (1 July 2011–30 June 2012)
- Strength as of   Troops: 8,915
  31 October 2011   Police: 3,637
         International Civilian Staff: 568
         National Civilian Staff: 1,355
         UN Volunteers: 238

For detailed mission information see p. 207

---

contested the results. By 2003 a then–recently united opposition movement called for Aristide's resignation, and in 2004 armed conflict broke out in the city of Gonaïves, spreading rapidly to other cities. Aristide resigned and fled, and soon insurgents held the majority of northern Haiti, threatening to take control of Port-au-Prince.

In response, the UN Security Council authorized the deployment of a US-led multinational interim force (MIF) in February 2004 to support police, provision of humanitarian assistance, rule of law, and protection of human rights. In June 2004 the UN's peacekeeping mission, MINUSTAH, succeeded the MIF with a mandate to support the transitional government in maintaining stability; assist in the reform of the Haitian National Police (HNP); disarm, demobilize, and reintegrate armed groups; support the rule of law; assist in the preparation and conduct of elections; and monitor and report on human rights.

MINUSTAH faced a daunting environment in its first years of operation, struggling to contain increasing gang violence and insecurity. During this period, the mission also supported national elections and René Préval's successful bid for the presidency. As gang violence continued to grow, President Préval requested that MINUSTAH work with the

HNP to counter this threat. By mid-2007, joint operations between the HNP and MINUSTAH had managed to substantially reduce gang violence, allowing the mission and Haitian authorities to focus on building national justice and security capacities. These gains also encouraged stakeholders to consider scaling back MINUSTAH's future role, and in 2008 the UN Secretary-General presented a consolidation plan for MINUSTAH's eventual drawdown.

The January 2010 earthquake dealt a devastating blow to Haiti and the UN presence. In addition to the thousands of Haitians killed or displaced, 102 UN personnel lost their lives—the largest number of UN casualties ever in a single event. The earthquake required a rapid response from MINUSTAH, which quickly adapted to provide security, logistical, and political support to the Haitian state. To bolster the capacity of the mission, the Security Council authorized an additional 2,000 military troops and 1,500 police, and later an additional 680 police officers, bringing MINUSTAH's authorized strength to over 13,000 troops and police. Haitian authorities, UN officials, and international partners all worked tirelessly to "build back better."[2]

Recovery efforts were dealt a further blow in October 2010, when cholera began spreading along the Arbonite River. As there had been no cases of cholera in Haiti in nearly a century, anger was quickly directed at UN peacekeepers, resulting in violent protests. Widespread allegations that cholera was introduced by UN peacekeepers prompted the Secretary-General to task an independent panel of experts to determine the cause of the epidemic. In May 2011 the panel released its final report on the causes of the outbreak, citing contamination of a tributary of the Arbonite River, likely as a result of poor sanitation conditions at the nearby MINUSTAH camp.[3] The report also confirmed that the Haitian cholera strain was very similar to South Asian strains of the disease, further substantiating the widely held belief that the disease had been introduced by Nepalese troops serving in MINUSTAH. While the report did not place direct blame for the cholera outbreak on UN peacekeepers, several external reports have identified the strain as originating in Nepal.[4] By October 2011 the epidemic had infected 470,000 and killed 6,600.[5]

Key Developments

Political Developments

It was in this chaotic and tense environment that Haiti held its preliminary round of presidential and legislative elections, on 28 November 2010. However, the elections were marred by fraud, with fourteen of the eighteen presidential candidates calling for a cancellation. Protesters soon took to the street and demonstrations turned violent when preliminary results were announced: Jude Célestin, the ruling-party candidate, and former first lady Mirlande Manigat would face a runoff vote, excluding Michel Martelly, the third-place candidate and popular Haitian musician. During the most insecure period in late 2010, MINUSTAH troops guarded government buildings in addition to securing the mission's base.

The protests and violence that followed the announcement of the preliminary results of the first round of presidential elections prompted President Préval to request an Organization of American States (OAS) electoral observation team under joint authority of the OAS and the Caribbean Community (CARICOM) to assist in verifying the results. This team released a report in early January 2011 advising that certain vote tally sheets should be excluded from the official count. Doing so would put Martelly in second place, giving him a lead of only 3,000 votes over Célestin. In February the Haitian Provisional Electoral Council approved the OAS report's findings and announced that the runoff election between Martelly and Manigat would take place on 20 March.

Between the first and second rounds of elections, Jean-Claude "Baby Doc" Duvalier returned unexpectedly to Haiti after twenty-five years living in exile in France. After taking over from his father, François "Papa Doc" Duvalier, Baby Doc ruled Haiti from 1971 to

Brazilian UN peacekeepers of the UN Stabilization Mission in Haiti (MINUSTAH) stand guard at the entrance of a voting center as Haitians queue to cast their ballots, 20 March 2011.

1986, in an environment of corruption and terror. Arriving at the Port-au-Prince airport on 16 January 2011, Duvalier said that he had come to help his country, but Haitian authorities quickly opened investigations into alleged embezzlement and human rights crimes. On 18 March, just two days prior to the elections, exiled former leader Jean-Bertrand Aristide also returned to Haiti.

Despite the potentially destabilizing presence of these polarizing political figures, the runoff elections took place in a "generally calm and peaceful atmosphere,"[6] with limited irregularities and violence. MINUSTAH provided logistical and security support to the Haitian authorities. The results were announced in April, showing that Martelly had won with 68 percent of the vote, and he was sworn in to office on 14 May. However, he quickly faced strong resistance from parliament, which rejected his first two nominees for prime minister and thus delayed the establishment of a new government and slowed reconstruction and political and justice reform.

In October, parliament approved Martelly's third nominee for prime minister, Garry Conille, a physician with a long career at the UN, including serving as chief of staff for the

Box 2.4 UN Peacekeeping Troop Reimbursement

One of the most contentious peacekeeping debates in 2011 revolved around the reimbursement rates paid to member states for the deployment of troops to UN peacekeeping operations, clearly demonstrating the divide between troop and financial contributors and testing the member state partnership on peacekeeping. This partnership has underpinned the growth in peacekeeping operations over the past fifteen years, with key actors demonstrating their willingness to provide the political and material support required for sustaining larger and more complex peacekeeping operations. However, political and economic tensions, notably the global financial crisis, have tested the limits of these agreements, demonstrated clearly in the intense negotiations in the past year over reimbursement rates.

Troop reimbursement is governed by the UN's Contingent Owned Equipment system, which determines member state compensation for providing resources to peacekeeping missions. Troop reimbursement rates are determined by member states and applied equally across troop-contributing countries. Rates are determined for the deployment of troops, major equipment, and self-sustainment (the services that countries provide for their deployed troops).

These rates were last reviewed in 1992 and last increased in 2002, prompting calls from troop-contributing countries for their revision. Without an increase, and taking into account the costs of inflation, troop-contributing countries argue that they face a substantial financial burden in providing troops to UN peace operations, particularly in light of their expanding mandates. Troop contributors also call attention to the considerable difference between the costs of deploying UN peacekeepers compared with those of the International Security Assistance Force (ISAF) in Afghanistan, noting that the annual cost of deploying ISAF troops is more than the cost of the past twenty years of UN peacekeeping operations combined.[1] Financial contributors, however, cite the continuing challenges of the global financial crisis when calling for improved efficiency and effectiveness.

In 2011 this debate became a major point of contention for peacekeeping negotiations within the UN. After months of consultations that were labeled "very difficult and at times unorthodox" by the chairman of the UN's administrative and budget committee, the committee approved a onetime supplemental payment of $85 million to troop-contributing countries.[2] The General Assembly adopted the peacekeeping budget, including the ad hoc payment, the same day.

In addition, the General Assembly tasked the Secretary-General with establishing a senior advisory group to consider issues related to reimbursement rates. The group is comprised of five individuals with relevant experience, five representatives of troop-contributing countries, five representatives of major finance-contributing countries, and a representative from each of the five regional groups.

Without meaningful progress on the issue of troop reimbursement, the UN runs the risk of continued and protracted "unorthodox" debates around these issues, further exacerbating the divide between troop and financial contributors.

Notes: 1. Permanent Mission of India to the United Nations, "Peacekeeping: Taking Stock and Preparing for the Future—A Concept Note," 8 August 2011.

2. UN General Assembly, "Following Days of 'Very Difficult and Sometimes Unorthodox' Negotiations, Fifth Committee Approves Budgets for 13 United Nations Peacekeeping Operations," Department of Public Information, UN Doc. GA/AB/3994, 1 July 2011.

UN's Special Envoy to Haiti, former US president Bill Clinton. While Conille's confirmation represents a significant step forward, the new government will be tasked with responding to a number of political controversies, including corruption allegations against the Provisional Electoral Council in the elections and discrepancies over constitutional amendments promulgated under former president Préval.

The political environment could be further undermined by the October arrest and overnight detention of Arnel Bélizaire, a member of parliament whose name appeared on a list of post-earthquake prison escapees. Bélizaire has been a vocal critic of Martelly since taking office, and his arrest could reignite tensions between the president and parliament.

Security

While the security situation in Haiti remained largely calm throughout 2011, there were increases in incidents of civil unrest and major crimes, including murder, rape, and kidnapping. There were more than 400 protests and demonstrations in the first half of 2011, many violent. While the majority were related to the elections, a significant number were motivated by poor living conditions, unemployment, and the cholera epidemic.[7] MINUSTAH police were called in at least fifteen times in the first half of 2011 to respond to violent demonstrations. Crime reporting also increased in 2011, likely reflecting a higher level of public confidence with law enforcement.[8]

Gang violence remains a security risk, however. There are concerns that convicts who escaped after the earthquake may contribute to increased gang activities and that some gangs have established links to both political parties and drug traffickers.[9] Haiti's second largest department, the West Department, has been the most heavily affected by gang violence, particularly the department's camps for internally displaced persons (IDPs). The issue is especially pressing in Port-au-Prince. In July, 2,100 MINUSTAH troops and police launched a joint program with the HNP to quell crime and violence in three vulnerable neighborhoods—Bel Air, Cité Soleil, and Martissant. Operation Phoenix resulted in the arrest of several gang members, including escaped convicts. MINUSTAH's force commander stated that the operation was intended to "reinforce trust and confidence between the residents, HNP and MINUSTAH."[10] A similar operation, Operation Hope, was conducted in October in Bel Air and Martissant and resulted in the arrest of seven criminals, including a number of prison escapees.

Controversy erupted in September when a video surfaced that allegedly showed Uruguayan peacekeeping troops raping a Haitian teenager. The video quickly circulated on Haitian mobile phones and prompted protests outside of MINUSTAH's base. President Martelly condemned the incident and Uruguayan president José Mujica issued a letter of apology to Martelly. The UN conducted a preliminary investigation, but authority for prosecution rests with the government of Uruguay, which has initiated an investigation and stated that if the allegations are true, the perpetrators will receive the "harshest sanctions."[11]

Rule of Law and Justice

In October 2010, then-SRSG Edmond Mulet called for the creation of a rule of law compact between Haitian authorities, nongovernmental organizations (NGOs), the private sector, and international partners based on a common understanding of needs and mutually agreed criteria to support the rule of law in Haiti. As an initial step, MINUSTAH provided assistance to the government of Haiti in preparing a national rule of law strategy. However, the political stalemate between the president and parliament delayed progress on the compact in 2011, though Martelly has identified rule of law as one of the pillars of his government.

Reform of the HNP continues, with the graduation of 877 cadets this year. The police force now comprises 10,000 officers, with an expansion to 14,000 envisioned. However, even with these additions the HNP will still fall well short of the 20,000 officers that experts advise are necessary. The vetting process, stalled in the wake of the earthquake, has also been restarted, with over 900 officers vetted in 2011.

Though HNP reform and capacity are improving, the pace is slow, and significant ground remains to be covered before the force is prepared to take on full security responsibilities. Institutional and operational reforms are still needed to expand the capacity and reach of the police, which is heavily concentrated in Port-au-Prince. The HNP is hampered by logistical constraints as well as gaps in critical skills, including border management and crowd control. In addition, in December the Office of the UN High Commissioner for Human Rights and MINUSTAH released reports detailing cases of excessive use of force by the HNP, including cases where officers conducted extrajudicial executions. The UN urged the goverment to investigate the deaths, but the incidents raise concerns about the capacity and restraint of the police force. There are also some concerns that the vetting process has not been entirely successful in removing "rogue" officers.[12] Work has begun on a new five-year HNP reform plan to succeed the first plan, which is set to end in 2011. However, the political impasse through much of the year has affected Haitian ownership of and engagement with the new plan. Responding to skill gaps in the HNP, MINUSTAH has provided specialized training and support to a donor-funded project to build a police academy, slated for completion in early 2013.

Haiti's prisons remain overcrowded, vulnerable to food shortages, and below international standards. To bolster corrections capacity, MINUSTAH conducts training for prison guards, and MINUSTAH police officers are present in all Haitian prisons, providing assistance on critical issues and challenges. A 2011 training program resulted in the graduation of 300 new guards. MINUSTAH has also worked to improve cell space, which increased 28 percent between March and September. In addition, the mission has worked with Haitian officials to end cases of illegal detention, with the release of 469 individuals in 2011.

In September, parliament submitted to the president a list of eighteen candidates for six vacancies on the Supreme Court. President Martelly initially returned the list to the Senate, but subsequently named the chief justice and one additional judge from the list. However, delays in appointments have stalled the formation of the Supreme Council of the Judiciary, a key oversight body for the Haitian judiciary. The justice system continues to struggle, seen notably through the lack of progress in legal proceedings against Baby Doc Duvalier. Since the former dictator was charged in January 2011, the case has stalled, with only one judge assigned to investigate his crimes.[13]

MINUSTAH provides support to Haiti's justice system, assisting with caseload and record system management, and in the establishment of legal-aid offices and peace tribunals, low-level courts, and other infrastructure.

Post-Earthquake Recovery

Haiti continues to rebuild after the earthquake, though the list of pending activities is daunting. Immediately following the earthquake,

MINUSTAH shifted emphasis to provision of emergency relief and recovery support. The post-earthquake planning process led to the development of an integrated strategic framework (ISF), finalized in late 2010 and endorsed by the government in February 2011. The ISF, which also serves as the country's interim UN Development Assistance Framework, has identified five priority areas: institutional rebuilding, territorial rebuilding, social rebuilding, economic rebuilding, and an enabling environment.

The earthquake killed nearly one-third of Haitian civil servants and destroyed over 180 government buildings, including the national palace, the Supreme Court, the parliament, and nearly all ministries.[14] MINUSTAH has provided technical and advisory support to state institutions at the national and local levels, and logistical support for reestablishing destroyed government offices. The mission has established temporary office sites for government ministries, identified sites for co-located HNP-UN police units, and constructed a temporary parliament office block, the latter of which was completed in April 2011. The mission continues to provide support to public infrastructure and basic services. In addition, MINUSTAH and the government of Haiti signed a memorandum of understanding in February on logistical assistance to support Haitian rule of law institutions and implementation of the resettlement strategy for Haitians displaced after the earthquake. MINUSTAH military engineering units engage in a broad range of earthquake recovery projects, including removal of damaged buildings and rubble, repair of roads, and river drainage.

MINUSTAH troops have also provided community policing throughout IDP camps, maintaining a continuous presence in seven of about a thousand sites. There are still 500,000 IDPs and, despite a steady decrease in the number of Haitians living in camps, the pace of resettlement has recently slowed, at least partially due to the delay in developing longer-term housing alternatives. Forced relocation and eviction are a concern, as by September nearly 70,000 individuals had been forced to leave IDP camps by municipal authorities and private landowners.[15] MINUSTAH and humanitarian partners are working closely with the Haitian government on the long-term relocation of those still residing in camps.

The Interim Haiti Reconstruction Commission (IHRC), co-chaired by the Haitian government and the UN's Special Envoy for Haiti, former US president Clinton, was designed to support the government's coordination of international support for post-earthquake recovery. In April 2011 an aid management platform, jointly overseen by the IHRC and the Ministry of Planning, was launched to track donor funds. Donor assistance remains a concern. Only 38 percent of funds pledged by international donors had been released by July of this year.[16] In August the commission launched a major project to relocate IDPs in six camps to long-term housing in sixteen neighborhoods in Port-au-Prince, complementing other major relocation projects conducted by the Haitian government, the UN, and the World Bank. However, much of the commission's work is now on hold since its mandate expired on 21 October. Earlier in 2011, President Martelly requested a one-year extension for the commission, but parliament did not pass the legislation needed to extend its mandate.

The cholera outbreak has complicated post-earthquake recovery. Although humanitarian actors quickly mobilized to limit the spread of the disease and provide care to those infected, several large NGOs are in the process of drawing down their cholera support because of reduced donor funding,[17] which could have negative consequences for cholera response.

Drawdown of Post-Earthquake Surge

In light of the important progress made since the earthquake, in October 2011 the Security Council extended MINUSTAH's mandate for one year and decided to reduce its strength by 1,600 troops and 1,150 police, to be completed by June 2012. The drawdown will reduce the number of infantry troops on the ground, while maintaining military engineering capacity to continue support for reconstruction in Haiti. As the mission draws down, it will dedicate increasing focus to the Haitian political process and the consolidation of state authority. The Council noted that future reconfigurations of MINUSTAH would be informed by the security situation in Haiti and the capacity of national institutions.

This partial drawdown came amid growing Haitian frustration with MINUSTAH. Throughout 2011 public pressure mounted for a withdrawal of the mission, fueled by the cholera outbreak and the alleged sexual assault. It also came after the Haitian Senate adopted a resolution requesting that MINUSTAH withdraw over the next three years. Top MINUSTAH troop-contributing countries also committed to reducing the size of the mission's force.

Though President Martelly has repeatedly called for the mission to reorient its focus toward development, in September he said that Haiti still needed MINUSTAH's support in the face of continued instability.[18] Martelly has stated his desire to rebuild the Haitian army, which was disbanded in 1995, in part to take over security responsibilities from MINUSTAH. His plan to do so, which showed an estimated cost of $95 million, was leaked in September. However, it is unclear whether parliament or donors would support this proposal.

Conclusion

While MINUSTAH continued to provide important support and assistance to Haiti throughout 2011, pressure mounted for a withdrawal of the peacekeeping mission. In the wake of the alleged rape of a Haitian teenager, public demonstrations called for an end to what protesters called an "occupying" force. As MINUSTAH begins a partial drawdown to pre-earthquake levels, the mission, Haitian authorities, and international partners must consider the future role of international support in Haiti. In doing so, the capacity of

Haitian institutions, especially the HNP, for taking on full authority in the country should be the guide for the pace and structure of MINUSTAH's eventual departure. Political actors will also need to demonstrate considerable political will to overcome the divides that stalled recovery, reform, and peace consolidation efforts in 2011.

Notes

1. Mulet was appointed SRSG in the aftermath of the earthquake, and previously served with the mission in 2006–2007.

2. Reuters AlertNet, "Preview: Haiti, Donors Face Huge Task to 'Build Back Better,'" 28 March 2010, http://reliefweb.int/node/349732.

3. The report stressed that many factors contributed to the outbreak, including regular use of the Arbonite River for bathing, the salinity level of the river's water, the lack of immunity among the Haitian population, poor water and sanitation conditions, and the inability of medical facilities to prevent the further spread of the disease.

4. See, for example, Richard Piarroux, "Mission Report on the Cholera Epidemic in Haiti," December 2010; and Rene Hendriksen et al., "Population Genetics of *Vibrio cholerae* from Nepal in 2010: Evidence on the Origin of the Haitian Outbreak," *mBio*, July–August 2011.

5. UN News Centre, "Nearly 470,000 Cholera Cases Reported in Haiti over the Past Year," 21 October 2011, http://www.un.org/apps/news/story.asp?NewsID=40149&Cr=haiti&Cr1=.

6. United Nations, *Report of the Secretary-General on the United Nations Stabilization Mission in Haiti,* UN Doc. S/2011/183, 24 March 2011.

7. International Crisis Group, "Keeping Haiti Safe: Police Reform," 8 September 2011, http://www.crisisgroup.org/en/regions/latin-america-caribbean/haiti/b026-keeping-haiti-safe-police-reform.aspx.

8. Ibid.

9. Ibid.; and United Nations, *Report of the Secretary-General,* S/2011/183.

10. MINUSTAH, "Launching of Operation 'Phoenix' to Secure Port-au-Prince Key Neighborhoods," press release, 14 July 2011, http://minustah.org/?p=31133.

11. "Uruguay Apologises for Alleged Rape by Its Soldiers," *BBC News,* 7 September 2011, http://www.bbc.co.uk/news/world-latin-america-14817191.

12. International Crisis Group, "Keeping Haiti Safe."

13. Tom Phillips, "Will 'Baby Doc' Duvalier Ever Face Justice in Haiti?" *The Guardian,* 22 September 2011.

14. United Nations, *Report of the Secretary-General on the United Nations Stabilization Mission in Haiti,* UN Doc. S/2010/200, 22 February 2010.

15. UN News Centre, "Haiti: UN Concerned at Forcible Evictions of Quake Survivors from Camps," 13 September 2011, http://www.un.org/apps/news/story.asp?NewsID=39526&Cr=&Cr1=.

16. United Nations, *Report of the Secretary-General on the United Nations Stabilization Mission in Haiti,* UN Doc. S/2011/540, 25 August 2011.

17. United Nations, *Report of the Secretary-General,* S/2011/183.

18. Randal C. Archibold, "Haiti Leader Is Opposed to Reduction of U.N. Force," *New York Times,* 22 September 2011, http://www.nytimes.com/2011/09/23/world/martelly-opposes-reducing-un-force-in-haiti.html.

2.5

Liberia

The October 2011 general elections in Liberia were the first to be wholly conducted by national institutions since the end of civil war in 2003. Although the first round of voting was generally smooth, tensions escalated before the runoff, with the opposition calling for a boycott and a clash between protesters and police. As a result, turnout in the second round of elections was significantly lower, miring Ellen Johnson Sirleaf's successful reelection.

The UN Mission in Liberia (UNMIL) continues to provide critical support toward strengthening Liberian institutions, with further discussions expected in 2012 on UNMIL's future role and eventual drawdown.

Regional and domestic security threats, however, including transnational crime, refugee flows, unemployment, and land disputes, continue to present challenges to nascent national capacities. In particular, electoral violence in neighboring Côte d'Ivoire, the resulting influx of refugees to Liberia, and the threat posed by heavily armed Liberian mercenaries returning from Côte d'Ivoire, as well as the influx of Ivorian combatants, required rapid responses from the government of Liberia and UNMIL in 2011. In September the UN Security Council—cautious of prematurely withdrawing UNMIL before national institutions are able to manage these threats—extended the mission's mandate for an additional year against growing international pressure to quicken UNMIL's drawdown.

Background

Leading the National Patriotic Front of Liberia (NPFL) from bases in Côte d'Ivoire, Charles

Map No. 4465.4   UNITED NATIONS
September 2011

Department of Field Support
Cartographic Section

UN Mission in Liberia (UNMIL)

- Authorization and Start Date: 19 September 2003 (UNSC Res. 1509)
- SRSG: Ellen Margrethe Løj (Denmark)
- Force Commander: Major-General Muhammad Khalid (Pakistan)
- Police Commissioner: Gautam Sawang (India)
- Budget: $525.6 million (1 July 2011–30 June 2012)
- Strength as of 31 October 2011: Troops: 7,774
  Military Observers: 138
  Police: 1,315
  International Civilian Staff: 477
  National Civilian Staff: 991
  UN Volunteers: 240

For detailed mission information see p. 277

Taylor invaded Liberia in 1989, igniting an eight-year civil war that caused over 150,000 deaths and displaced nearly 1 million people. The Economic Community of West African States (ECOWAS) brokered peace negotiations in 1993, which led the UN Security Council to establish the UN Observer Mission in Liberia (UNOMIL) to assist the ECOWAS Military Observer Group in implementing the terms of the peace agreement. After elections in 1997 brought Taylor to power, UNOMIL withdrew and was replaced with the UN Peacebuilding Support Office in Liberia. However, the peace under Taylor's new government did not last and renewed fighting broke out in 1999, fueled by exclusionary political, economic, and security policies.

Liberia's entire fourteen-year internecine conflict caused over 250,000 deaths, displaced nearly one-third of the population, and decimated state institutions and civil society. The 2003 Comprehensive Peace Agreement (CPA) signed between Charles Taylor and the rebel groups—Liberians United for Reconciliation and Democracy (LURD) and the Movement for Democracy in Liberia (MODEL)—finally ended the conflict. The CPA provided for the establishment of a national transitional government to administer the country until the democratically elected government took office in January 2006, following elections in 2005. In addition, the CPA called for the deployment of a UN peacekeeping force, in response to which, in October 2003 under Resolution 1509, the Security Council deployed UNMIL under Chapter VII of the UN Charter to maintain peace and support implementation of the peace agreement. UNMIL was authorized at an initial level of 15,000 troops, including 3,500 rehatted ECOWAS troops, and 1,115 police personnel. The mission's multidimensional mandate authorized it to assist in the provision of security; support the reestablishment of national authority; implement disarmament, demobilization, and reintegration (DDR); protect UN personnel and civilians from violence and human rights abuses; support security sector reform; and support national elections.

The 2005 presidential elections, organized with considerable assistance from UNMIL and other international partners, saw the peaceful handover from the national transitional government to a democratic government led by Africa's first female president, Ellen Johnson Sirleaf. Since then, UNMIL has assisted the Liberian government in the development of national institutions. In light of increased stability, in 2007 the UN Secretary-General recommended a three-stage drawdown of UNMIL's military component. A series of partial troop reductions began in 2006, though formal drawdown took place in three stages from October 2007 to May 2010, bringing the mission to its current strength of 7,774 military troops and 1,315 police. In September 2011 the Security Council renewed UNMIL's mandate at its current strength for an additional year, with the expectation that, in 2012, a technical assessment mission will present further recommendations for the next reconfiguration of the mission.

To facilitate long-term peacebuilding and stability, Liberia requested to be placed on the agenda of the UN's Peacebuilding Commission in 2010, complementing ongoing assistance from the UN's Peacebuilding Fund. In late 2010 the government of Liberia and the Peacebuilding Commission signed a statement of mutual commitments that outlined three peacebuilding priorities: strengthening the rule of law, security sector reform, and national reconciliation. Subsequently, in May 2011 a Liberia peacebuilding program was adopted for a total value of $72 million.

Key Developments

Political Developments

The organization of the 2011 constitutional referendum and presidential and parliamentary elections was a historic milestone for Liberia. While UNMIL provided logistical support, the onus for conducting the elections fell on Liberian institutions, with the national electoral commission responsible for organizing the elections, and the Liberian National Police (LNP) largely responsible for maintaining law and order. The Liberian-run voter registration campaign in early 2011 succeeded in registering nearly 1.8 million Liberians—approximately 85 percent of eligible voters—paving the way for the referendum and national elections.[1]

The constitutional referendum in August 2011 proposed a number of important election-related constitutional amendments that, if passed, would have significantly impacted the October national elections. However, turnout was low amid criticism that the Liberian public lacked information about the proposals and amid calls from the opposition for a boycott due to allegations that the changes unfairly favored the ruling party. Only one of the four proposals tabled—the elimination of runoff elections in local and legislative polls—garnered the two-thirds majority required for a constitutional amendment. Proposals to shorten the residency requirement clause, to delay elections until November, and to increase the mandatory retirement age for Supreme Court justices were all rejected.

The failure of the proposal to shorten the residency clause from ten years to five temporarily plunged the presidential election into turmoil, as many of the sixteen candidates, including frontrunner Ellen Johnson Sirleaf and leading opposition candidate Winston Tubman, failed to meet the ten-year requirement. However, one week before the election the Supreme Court determined that the civil war overrode the clause for this election and cleared all candidates to run.

The presidential election took place on 11 October in a mostly peaceful atmosphere, with larger turnout than was initially expected. To support the election, UNMIL coordinated international assistance, increased air patrols, and stationed ground troops at strategic locations around the country. ECOWAS, the African Union, and the Carter Center provided international observation missions, and more

Liberia's incumbent president and joint Nobel Peace Prize laureate Ellen Johnson Sirleaf meets with residents after casting her ballot in her hometown of Fefeh on 8 November 2011, the day after at least four opposition supporters were killed amid a boycott protest by the challenger in this disputed presidential runoff. Early voting was slow amid the tense atmosphere in the capital following the previous day's violence, in marked contrast to long lines that greeted the opening of polls during the previous month's first round.

AFP Photo/Getty Images/Issouf Sanogo

than 4,000 national observers were accredited to observe the process. Johnson Sirleaf, with 43.9 percent of the vote, fell shy of the absolute majority required to win in the first round, necessitating a November runoff with Tubman. While election day was largely calm, isolated incidents of arson in the immediate aftermath raised concern but did not spark widespread violence. In the weeks between the first and second rounds of voting, opposition parties, citing allegations of fraud by the national electoral commission, threatened to pull out of the elections unless their demands—including the resignation of the electoral commission's chairman, James Fromayan—were met. At the end of October, Fromayan resigned, citing his interest in a peaceful runoff, and his deputy for administration and civic education, Elizabeth J. Nelson, became acting chair.

However, the reconfiguration of the commission did not mollify Tubman, who withdrew from the 8 November runoff citing fraud, though some observers have suggested

---

Box 2.5 Helicopters in Peacekeeping Operations

Helicopters play a key role in implementing peacekeeping mandates and reinforcing the UN's presence on the ground. However, the UN struggles with a severe shortage of these critical assets. As of September 2011, there were only 148 helicopters deployed across UN peacekeeping missions, leaving a shortfall of over 30 percent.

Helicopters have been used in peacekeeping missions primarily in a utility capacity, for logistical tasks such as transporting troops, search and rescue, following rebel movements, and conducting evacuations of wounded personnel, particularly in areas with limited road access or vast geographies. However, more recently and especially in 2011, helicopters have been deployed in an attack capacity, in order to support a much more assertive deterrent posture.

This was seen most recently in Côte d'Ivoire, where helicopters under UN command were a decisive component in the defeat of Laurent Gbagbo and his forces. UNOCI's helicopters, reinforced with rotary-wing asset transfers from the neighboring mission in Liberia (UNMIL), as well as from France's Operation Licorne, proved critical in the standoff. They extended the UN's presence and eventually fired on forces loyal to

incumbent leader Gbagbo, an act both of self-defense and to protect civilians.

In the Democratic Republic of Congo (DRC), utility and attack helicopters have been critical for the UN's mission, MONUSCO. In accordance with its mandate to protect civilians, the mission has used its rotary-wing assets to assert its presence in the eastern regions and to deter rebel attacks. However, in 2011 India withdrew its remaining utility and attack helicopters from the mission to address domestic security needs, leaving MONUSCO with only fourteen rotary-wing assets (a shortfall of fifteen) and no attack helicopters. According to the Secretary-General, the shortage impacted the deployment of troops, joint operations with Congolese forces, and the mission's ability to support the November elections.

In Darfur, the UN and AU's joint mission, UNAMID, currently has only five helicopters out of the required twenty-four. This crippling shortfall has limited the mission's ability to protect civilians from attacks, or help facilitate the necessary distribution of humanitarian aid.

The process of finding replacement helicopters to strengthen the UN's missions in the DRC and Darfur has been difficult. So far, only a few African nations have pledged assistance.[1] Generally, the

pool of helicopter-contributing countries is limited. Of the 193 member states of the United Nations, just 13 provide all the military utility and attack helicopters currently deployed. Many countries simply lack the needed rotary assets to cover their own domestic needs, let alone the needs of UN peacekeeping. Meanwhile, those countries with a sufficient inventory are tied down in theaters of operation elsewhere.

There is hope that as NATO operations in Afghanistan draw down, Western helicopter units may be transferred to UN peacekeeping missions. Given the reluctance of many Western states regarding the handover of command and control, reforms to the use and management of UN helicopters—both in the field and at headquarters—are needed to address their concerns and to ensure that helicopters are used to maximum effect. The UN may also need to increase incentives for potential helicopter contributors, and improve its system of reimbursement for deployed assets.

Until a solution can be found, the shortfall in helicopter assets will continue to significantly impede the ability of UN peace operations, particularly in geographically diverse and less secure settings, to implement their mandates.

Note: 1. As of 30 June, UNAMID reports that an Ethiopian multirole logistics unit, a Rwandan medium rotary-wing utility aviation unit, and Nigerian reconnaissance and reserve companies are expected to deploy later in the year, while an incoming Senegalese battalion is expected to reach full strength by October 2011. MONUSCO has secured commitments from one country only, South Africa, in the form of one utility helicopter.

that he withdrew because he was unlikely to surpass Johnson Sirleaf in the vote. In the lead-up to the second round, clashes occurred between the LNP and opposition supporters, resulting in at least two deaths.[2] The runoff took place in a tense atmosphere, with many voters staying home because of security concerns or in support of Tubman's boycott. Turnout was under 40 percent of registered

voters, approximately half that of the initial vote,[3] but international observers have stated that the election was largely free, fair, and transparent.[4] Johnson Sirleaf won 90 percent of the vote and has vowed to prioritize reconciliation during her second term, calling upon fellow Nobel laureate Leymah Gbowee to lead the newly created Peace and Reconciliation Initiative.

While Liberia focused mainly on electoral preparations during the past year, the government has also strengthened its capacity through extension of administrative services at the district level and more regular payment of government salaries. Both the Law Reform Commission, which is tasked with reviewing Liberia's legal framework, and the Land Commission, designed to formulate a much-needed land policy, became operational, filling a crucial governance gap. The government also announced its first corruption conviction, though the Anti-Corruption Commission still lacks independent prosecutorial powers.[5] Outside of Monrovia, service delivery is inconsistent and largely dependent on considerable assistance from UNMIL.

Although the economy has incrementally improved, rampant unemployment among youth and former combatants remains a potential threat. Increased interest by multinational corporations in energy and mining could open up Liberia to much-needed investment and help fill the budgetary gaps that beset many of Liberia's national institutions. However, any potential economic growth will require stability, government transparency, and credible security guarantees. Looking forward, the Governance Commission and the Ministry of Planning and Economic Affairs introduced "Liberia Rising 2030," a national visioning paper that aims to provide a roadmap for long-term consolidation of good governance, decentralization, and the fostering of economic growth.

Security Situation

Regional instability, particularly from crises in Guinea and Côte d'Ivoire, significantly tested Liberian security forces in 2011. Over 200,000 refugees fleeing electoral violence in Guinea and Côte d'Ivoire arrived in Liberia during the year, while heavily armed Liberian mercenaries recruited by pro-Gbagbo forces in Côte d'Ivoire used the region's porous borders to move between the two countries.

To increase border surveillance and to help stabilize the situation in Côte d'Ivoire, UNMIL shared mission assets, including troops and military utility and attack helicopters, with the UN Operation in Côte d'Ivoire (UNOCI) under an intermission agreement. While the helicopters and troops were returned to UNMIL, the two operations continue the intermission agreement on an as-needed basis and coordinate their strategies and operations in the border area to "prevent armed groups from exploiting the seam of political boundaries."[6]

Accordingly, UNMIL, UNOCI, and the LNP have increased their border patrols to monitor activities and the return of the estimated 2,000 Liberian mercenaries. These patrols, which have been instrumental in shoring up previously inaccessible areas of the border, have also seized multiple large weapons and ammunitions caches on Liberian territory, an important step in combating regional weapons trafficking.

To further strengthen the regional response to these challenges, in July 2011 President Ellen Johnson Sirleaf hosted the Ivorian prime minister for bilateral discussions on common security concerns, including the thousands of Ivorian refugees now residing in Liberia. Later that month, the Mano River Union held a security summit in Monrovia and established a technical committee to better coordinate border security.

Transnational mercenaries are not the only regional security concern for Liberia. Drug trafficking continues to destabilize the country as cocaine, heroin, and marijuana are transported across borders in the region. In particular, trafficking of domestically produced marijuana for the global market has raised concerns that the drug was replacing other agricultural activities in some areas. Human trafficking is also an increasing problem. In May the government of Liberia joined three other pilot countries as part of the UN-ECOWAS West Africa Coast Initiative (WACI), which seeks to institutionalize ECOWAS's regional action plan to combat transnational crime. Several months later, the LNP's Transnational Crime Unit was established to complement the WACI's regional framework.

Internal security remains stable, albeit with occasional violent flare-ups and persistent criminal activity. Ethnic and communal tensions continue. Recurring land and labor disputes led to violent incidents in Maryland and Grand Kru counties, requiring LNP operations with UNMIL support.[7] On one such occasion, the LNP's Emergency Response Unit remained in the area to independently manage domestic threats and maintain peace. General criminal activity, especially rape, gun violence, and armed robbery, remain endemic in Liberian society.[8]

Security Sector Reform
Long-term peace and security in Liberia will be predicated on capable and accountable security institutions, underscoring the importance of continued security sector reform by the government of Liberia and UNMIL. These efforts were boosted in 2011 by the enactment of a national security reform and intelligence bill that provides a roadmap for improving Liberia's security architecture. However, as in years past, uneven progress puts the viability of a smooth transition from UNMIL to a Liberian-run security sector into question.

The Liberian government began 2011 by assuming full responsibility for the Armed Forces of Liberia (AFL) from the United States.[9] The United States has provided support to the Liberian military since 2003, and in the past eight years has worked to develop the AFL through vetting processes, training exercises, and mentoring programs. While initial projections indicated the AFL would attain full operational capability in 2012, delays in obtaining new assets and in endorsing the national defense strategy will postpone this transition until 2014. Insufficient budget allocations have compounded infrastructural and logistical problems, including equipment deficits, hindering the AFL's ability to operate independently. In preparing for an eventual transfer of responsibilities, UNMIL continued its mentoring role in 2011 by training the AFL in civil-military cooperation, rule of law, unexploded ordnance identification, and radio operations, and conducting joint operations, including the transportation of suspected former combatants returning from Côte d'Ivoire. UNMIL also prepared the AFL for potential future peacekeeping duties in other countries.

While the LNP managed to maintain stability in the lead-up to the first round of elections, the clashes that erupted between the police and opposition supporters the day before the runoff raised concerns about the command and control of the force. According to a preliminary statement by the Carter Center, evidence suggests that the LNP used excessive force and that UNMIL played a critical role in restraining the police and reestablishing order.[10]

More broadly, much work remains until the force is able to operate independently. For example, while the LNP exceeded its pre-election goal of training 600 officers for the Police Support Unit—a specialized unit intended to respond to instances of civil unrest—members of the unit are still not fully operational due to lack of equipment and logistical support, while issues relating to accountability and command and control present an even larger challenge than the capacity question. In addition, the LNP must also contend with poor community relations due to a historical pattern of abuse, despite some progress. Lax oversight and poor vetting processes further weaken the LNP, although the number of internal police investigations into allegations of crime and corruption by police officers grew in 2011 in an effort to rid the institution of spoilers. UNMIL provided critical infrastructural support to the LNP in 2011, including rehabilitation of stations, barracks, and regional headquarters to support LNP capacity to provide security, especially outside of Monrovia.

The Bureau of Immigration and Naturalization (BIN), a government security agency, played an important role during the year in response to regional instability, particularly through its increased activity on Liberia's border with Côte d'Ivoire. However, responses by both the BIN and the LNP to security incidents emphasized their chronic reliance on UNMIL for mobility and information-gathering.[11] Recognizing these gaps, the UN-supported Justice and Security Trust Fund provided vehicles, training, and communication equipment to support both institutions ahead of the October elections.[12]

Justice and Rule of Law

National reconciliation has been hampered by limited implementation of the Truth and Reconciliation Commission's 2009 final report. In January 2011 the Supreme Court held that implementation of the report's recommendation of political debarment would be unconstitutional, further adding to setbacks. Many former war criminals indicted in the report continue to avoid prosecution for their crimes, including former rebel leader and presidential candidate Prince Johnson, identified by the report as a notorious perpetrator of war crimes during the civil conflict. Finishing third in the October elections, Johnson supported President Johnson Sirleaf in the runoff, publicly rallying beside the president days before the second round of voting. Delays in initiating the Palava Hut program, a forum in which former combatants seek public forgiveness, also hampered national reconciliation. Further rifts could occur if Charles Taylor, currently facing war crimes charges in the Special Court for Sierra Leone for his role in the Sierra Leone civil war, is acquitted and returns to Liberia.

With UNMIL's drawdown looming, Liberia's justice sector is still weak and access to justice for the average Liberian remains limited. A severe backlog of unprosecuted cases and outdated laws that limit courts' jurisdiction have led to delays and reduced the public's confidence in the justice system. The courts also suffer from a severe shortage of qualified personnel as well as infrastructure and equipment constraints, exacerbating structural and logistical pressures.

As a result, the majority of Liberians use customary justice mechanisms, such as community courts headed by tribal governors, as recourse for grievances. The Liberian Ministry of Justice and Law Reform Commission have led efforts in harmonizing the customary and formal justice systems. In addition, the Liberian Ministry of Internal Affairs and UNMIL's legal and judicial support division are supporting the establishment of standardized procedures for community courts and training governors in due process and human rights.

The deficiencies in the justice sector have also led to high rates of pretrial detention, a problem that Liberia's overcrowded corrections facilities, which struggle just to maintain basic human living conditions, have been unable to address. Furthermore, rule of law sector staff regularly complain of not receiving their salaries, and strikes have been threatened or taken place in a number of institutions. These limitations in infrastructure and personnel, and their impact on staff morale, mean that prisons are often unable to provide sufficient security. In 2011, more than ten escape incidents occurred at facilities in cities including Monrovia and Buchanan, requiring responses from the LNP's Police Support Unit with UNMIL assistance.[13]

To address these shortcomings, UNMIL provided technical assistance for a two-day retreat in February to strengthen coordination between the Ministry of Justice and the judiciary. Also considered at the meeting were key reforms needed to improve the criminal justice system. An additional meeting facilitated by UNMIL brought together units of the LNP with prosecutors from the Ministry of Justice to foster greater cooperation and efficiency. A government-run Pretrial Detention Task Force additionally seeks to address the underlying causes of legal delays in the justice system. UNMIL also built courthouses in Kolahun, Foya, and Voinjama districts in 2011, and construction started on the five Peacebuilding Fund–supported regional security and justice hubs, including one in Gbarnga that is set to be completed in early 2012. These hubs will expand the rule of law outside of

Monrovia through co-location of security and justice authorities, pooling of resources, and increased cooperation among agencies. The hubs are one element of a joint justice and security program, currently under development by the government, UNMIL, and the UN Country Team in Liberia. It is envisaged that the hubs will assist the government of Liberia to prepare for UNMIL's eventual transition. The Peacebuilding Fund also supported education programs intended to build respect for rule of law and formal training for legal staff.

For long-term peace consolidation, state institutions in the criminal and justice system will need to improve their credibility and expand their reach into regional and local sectors to promote rule of law and good governance.

a broadly free and fair environment, the boycott of the opposition and the performance of the police the day before the runoff underscore the continued need for reconciliation. Renewed discussions are expected in 2012 on the future role of UNMIL, amid continued pressure from the international community for the mission to draw down. Mission transition is a particularly vulnerable period, presenting new risks for sparking latent tensions and undermining fragile stability, particularly in the context of ongoing regional instability. The delay in transition planning during the election period means that significant work remains, especially in the security and justice sectors. Gains here will be imperative for ensuring Liberia's institutional capacity to respond to domestic and international security threats transparently and effectively.

Conclusion

The 2011 elections were a critical milestone for Liberia, and while they were conducted in

Notes

1. International Crisis Group, "Liberia: How Sustainable Is the Recovery?" *Africa Report* no. 177, 19 August 2011, http://www.crisisgroup.org/~/media/Files/africa/westafrica/liberia/177%20Liberia%20%20How%20Sustainable%20is%20the%20Recovery.pdf.

2. Alphonso Toweh and Richard Valdmanis, "Liberia's Sirleaf Eyes Reconciliation After Landslide," *Reuters,* http://www.reuters.com/article/2011/11/11/us-liberia-election-idUSTRE7AA3GE20111111.

3. "Liberia Election: Sirleaf Promises Reconciliation," *BBC News,* 11 November 2011, http://www.bbc.co.uk/news/world-africa-15684787.

4. Emily Schmall, "Liberia's President Wins Boycotted Runoff Vote," *New York Times,* 10 November 2011, http://www.nytimes.com/2011/11/11/world/africa/liberias-president-ellen-johnson-sirleaf-wins-election.html?ref=global-home.

5. United Nations, *Twenty-third Progress Report of the Secretary-General on the United Nations Mission in Liberia,* UN Doc. S/2011/497, 1 August 2011.

6. UN Security Council Resolution 2008 (2011), S/RES/2008.

7. United Nations, *Twenty-third Progress Report,* S/2011/497.

8. United Nations, *Twenty-second Progress Report of the Secretary-General on the United Nations Mission in Liberia,* UN Doc. S/2011/72, 14 February 2011.

9. International Crisis Group, "Liberia: How Sustainable Is the Recovery?" This followed the AFL's 2010 resumption of responsibility for managing its development and maintenance, but other areas, including weapons control, remained under the responsibility of the United States.

10. Carter Center, "Carter Center Preliminary Statement on the Liberia 2011 Presidential Run-Off Election," 10 November 2011, available at http://www.cartercenter.org/resources/pdfs/news/peace_publications/election_reports/liberia-prelim-111011.pdf.

11. United Nations, *Twenty-second Progress Report,* S/2011/72, 14 February 2011.

12. United Nations Liberia, "UN Hands Over Vehicles and Equipment to Liberia's Bureau of Immigration and Naturalization," press release, 5 October 2011.

13. United Nations, *Twenty-third Progress Report,* S/2011/497.

2.6

Sudan and South Sudan

Sudan and South Sudan, which together host nearly one-third of the UN's total global troop deployment, experienced profound and dramatic changes in 2011 and remain among the most challenging theaters for UN peace operations. In 2011 an increasingly complex and diverse architecture for UN operations emerged, involving three separate peacekeeping missions and numerous political processes.

The secession of Sudan's southern region as the Republic of South Sudan is a historical and structural political transformation with significant implications for UN peace operations. The January 2011 referendum proceeded peacefully, with substantial operational support from the UN Mission in Sudan (UNMIS), with southerners voting overwhelmingly for independence. South Sudan's procession to independence on 9 July 2011 was marked by notable political compromise and restraint by both Juba and Khartoum and concerted third-party engagement from the African Union, the UN, and key members of the international community. South Sudan's independence prompted the closure of UNMIS and the authorization of a new peace operation, the UN Mission in South Sudan (UNMISS).

While the implementation period for the 2005 Comprehensive Peace Agreement (CPA) came to a close in July 2011, key provisions from the CPA have yet to be implemented, most importantly those concerning the relationship and borders between north and south. Negotiations failed to reach agreement on the referendum for the status of the Abyei area, border demarcation, oil revenue sharing, and citizenship issues. Abyei in particular remained a hotly contested flashpoint, witnessing renewed hostilities and ongoing disagreement

over eligibility to participate in its referendum. In response to the violence and in the context of an agreement by the parties on temporary arrangements for the security and administration of Abyei, the Security Council authorized deployment of the UN Interim Security Force for Abyei (UNISFA) in June 2011.

There has also been a deterioration of conditions in areas of the north covered by the CPA—the Southern Kordofan State and the Blue Nile State—with the eruption of severe hostilities between the Sudan Armed Forces (SAF) and northern units of the Sudan People's Liberation Army that may portend a return to protracted civil conflict. Coinciding with the conclusion of the UNMIS mandate, this outbreak of violence presented serious -

UN Mission in Sudan (UNMIS)

- Authorization and Start Date — 24 March 2005 (UNSC Res. 1590)
- SRSG — Haile Menkerios (South Africa)
- Force Commander — Major-General Moses Bisong Obi (Nigeria)
- Acting Police Commissioner — Klaus Dieter-Tietz (Germany)
- Budget — $137.5 million (1 July 2011–30 June 2012)
- Strength as of 31 October 2011 — Troops: 8,572
  Police: 409
  International Civilian Staff: 90
  National Civilian Staff: 507
  UN Volunteers: 12

Note: In accordance with S/RES/1996 of 8 July 2011, the appropriate functions of UNMIS were transferred to UNMISS effective 9 July 2011. The 2011–2012 budget reflects proposed costs for the liquidation of UNMIS. Figures for troops and police as of 31 July 2011.

For detailed mission information see p. 287

UN Mission in South Sudan (UNMISS)

- Authorization Date — 8 July 2011 (UNSC Res. 1996)
- Start Date — 9 July 2011
- SRSG — Hilde Johnson (Norway)
- Force Commander — Major-General Moses Bisong Obi (Nigeria)
- Budget — $738.3 million (1 July 2011–30 June 2012)
- Strength as of 31 October 2011 — Troops: 4,920
  Military Observers: 182
  Police: 382
  International Civilian Staff: 697
  National Civilian Staff: 1,117
  UN Volunteers: 212

For detailed mission information see p. 287

humanitarian and political challenges, while also compounding the problems faced in resolving north-south issues. The November bombing of a refugee camp in South Sudan, reportedly by SAF, led to further deterioration in the relationship between the neighboring states. Direct clashes in December between

Sudan and South Sudan led to large-scale displacement and further raised concern about the possibility of a return to conflict.

With much attention drawn to north-south developments, the eight-year-old conflict in Darfur continued without significant progress. In some areas, intensification of hostilities between rebels and the government of Sudan caused civilian displacement and deterioration of security and humanitarian conditions. The UN-AU Hybrid Mission in Darfur (UNAMID) has struggled with its mandate to improve the security situation and protect civilians. AU- and UN-led negotiations on Darfur, though they did result in the brokering of an accord between the government of Sudan and one rebel coalition, continued to face opposition from other rebel groups and erratic engagement from the government and the international community.

Progress on outstanding post-independence issues and resolution of the ongoing tensions in South Kordofan and Blue Nile states will require intensive international engagement, from the UN, the AU, and other key stakeholders. In addition, maintaining the internal cohesion of the two states will be a central challenge for UN peace operations in 2012, as state authority is weak and violently contested in a number of areas.

Background

The 2005 CPA ended the decades-long conflict between the government of Sudan and the Sudan People's Liberation Army/Movement (SPLA/SPLM). On 24 March 2005, Security Council Resolution 1590 mandated UNMIS as a fully fledged peacekeeping mission focused on supporting implementation of the CPA. Its responsibilities included monitoring and verification of troop redeployments, investigating CPA violations and providing good offices for the resolution of disputes arising from CPA implementation, and supporting elections and referendums. UNMIS's mandate also included coordination of humanitarian assistance, promotion of human rights, and protection of civilians.

The CPA interim period ended on 9 July 2011, which also brought an end to the UNMIS mandate. At its conclusion, UNMIS had deployed personnel across the whole of southern Sudan and in the CPA areas of Abyei, Blue Nile State, and Southern Kordofan State through a system involving sectoral headquarters and numerous remote sites. Despite the persistence of important unresolved CPA issues and the onset of violent conflict, the government of Sudan indicated that it would not consent to an extension of the UNMIS mandate beyond 9 July 2011.

UNAMID was mandated in July 2007 to help provide security for humanitarian assistance and protect any civilian populations under imminent threat of physical violence. The mission was also called on to monitor compliance with cease-fire agreements, investigate human rights abuses, and assist with implementation of the 2006 Darfur Agreement and any subsequent peace accords. After a notably delayed deployment, UNAMID neared full strength through 2010.

Citizens celebrate in the streets as the Republic of South Sudan proclaims its independence, 9 July 2011.

Key Developments

*Referendum and Conclusion
of the Interim CPA Period*

On 9 January 2011, six years to the day after the CPA came into effect, southerners went to the polls for the referendum on independence. The official results, announced on 7 February, showed that over 98 percent of voters had opted for separation. The UN Secretary-General's panel on the referendum, established in a monitoring capacity, found that the referendum reflected the free will of the people of South Sudan and that the process was free, fair, and credible. National and international observers, including the Carter Center and the European Union Observer Mission,[1] publicly concurred with these findings. The results were immediately accepted by the National Congress Party (NCP) and were later endorsed by the national legislature.

Given the inherent risks in the referendum process and delayed preparations, the outcome was a significant achievement. Considerable technical and operational support was undertaken by the UN Integrated Referendum and Electoral Division (UNIRED), which brought together elections staff from UNMIS and the UN Development Programme (UNDP) into one team. UNIRED worked in partnership with the Southern Sudan Referendum Commission to overcome the daunting logistical challenges of conducting the vote across South Sudan—with its vast and inaccessible terrain, extremely limited infrastructure, and sparsely distributed population. The mission provided transportation and procurement of all referendum-related materials,[2] assisted in the design of operational plans for conducting voter registration and polling, and provided referendum-related security training for the police forces of both South Sudan and Sudan.

The conclusion of the CPA interim period marked a transformation in the framework for UN and international engagement in regard to the peaceful resolution of issues between the north and the south. Secession created a new state, with previously internal issues now existing between two sovereign nations.

The AU has hosted the post-CPA negotiations, with the AU High-Level Implementation

Box 2.6 Safety and Security

Staff of peacekeeping missions regularly operate in highly volatile and insecure environments, risking injury, harassment, abduction, civil unrest, terrorism, and conflict. While these risks are present in all peacekeeping contexts, they are particularly acute in the least-secure environments, including Afghanistan, Somalia, and Sudan. In Afghanistan, the ten-year international operation suffered its deadliest month ever in August 2011, with 66 peacekeeping fatalities; between January and September, over 300 troops were killed.[1] As of October, UN peacekeeping as a whole suffered 91 fatalities in 2011, with significant losses in Côte d'Ivoire and Sudan.

Recognizing these risks, the UN has made a number of improvements in its approach to ensuring the safety and security of personnel. In 2005 it established the Department of Safety and Security, which is mandated to lead and oversee the UN's security management system in reducing the risks that UN personnel face in the field. The UN bases its security approach on a "how to stay" principle aimed at finding ways to keep personnel safe and secure during their engagements.

In January 2011 the UN introduced a new security system, based on objective threat assessment, to assist missions in identifying the most acute threats and possible options for mitigation. The UN has also extended security training to nationally recruited staff and introduced a new security policy manual. It has also established an executive group on security to advise and support the Under-Secretary-General for Safety and Security.

Despite these advancements, it is ultimately the host governments that bear the primary responsibility for the security of UN personnel. To date, only 89 of the UN's 193 member states have signed the Convention on the Safety of United Nations and Associated Personnel, which requires states "to take all appropriate measures to ensure the safety and security" of these personnel. The challenge of addressing this significant gap in the provision of safety and security for peacekeepers was brought into sharp focus in 2011 in Sudan, where in August three peacekeepers serving with the UN Interim Security Force for Abyei (UNISFA) died after the government of Sudan threatened to shoot down a helicopter dispatched for their evacuation after their patrol was hit by a landmine.[2] While the Sudanese government denies any interference, the incident fits a pattern of previous action on its part to limit peacekeeping activity, and violates the status of forces agreement between the UN and the government of Sudan. The incident also underscores the significant risks for UN personnel operating in these insecure and volatile environments.

Notes: 1. "August Was 'Deadliest Month' for US in Afghan War," *BBC News,* 30 August 2011, http://www.bbc.co.uk/news/world-us-canada-14720918.

2. UN News Centre, "Sudan Delayed Evacuation Flight for Wounded Peacekeepers," 4 August 2011, http://www.un.org/apps/news/story.asp?NewsID=39235&Cr=Abyei&Cr1.

Panel managing talks between the CPA parties. This process has received significant support from the government of Ethiopia, UNMIS leadership, and key AU member states. UNMIS Special Representative to the Secretary-General (SRSG) Haile Menkerios was appointed as the Secretary-General's Special Envoy on Sudan and South Sudan in July 2011 to continue political engagement after the conclusion of the UNMIS mandate.

The Abyei dispute (addressed in detail later) is just one of many pending post-independence issues on the agenda for negotiations between Sudan and South Sudan. There are also other contested areas along the north-south border that must be negotiated before border demarcation can take place, and pending issues on financial arrangements, including the sharing of oil revenues (the majority of revenues come from oil fields in the south) and access to oil pipelines and refineries (located in the north). On 18 September 2011, Sudan and South Sudan did reach agreement on the opening of ten border-crossing points during the first meeting of the Joint Political and Security Mechanism, which is designed to strengthen cooperation between the two countries.

The issue of citizenship also remains to be settled. Khartoum has taken the line that all those eligible to vote in the southern referendum automatically became citizens of South Sudan at the succession of the south. This has created uncertainty among the 1–2 million individuals from the south living in the north. It is estimated that since August

2010 approximately 150,000 southerners have left the north for the south. Many are now dependent on aid, due to the limited infrastructure and economic opportunities at their places of arrival in the south.

Relations between the two states deteriorated in November when Sudanese armed forces reportedly bombed two locations in South Sudan, including a refugee camp in Yida, which hosts more than 20,000 individuals fleeing fighting in the north. Sudan has denied the charges, but the incident raised tensions between Sudan and South Sudan, with each accusing the other of supporting insurgent groups in its territory. The UN and the AU urged restraint from both parties. However, following the bombings, direct fighting between Sudan and South Sudan erupted in the disputed Jau border region, leading South Sudan's foreign minister to warn that the two states were on the brink of war.

Equally crucial to peace and stability will be the internal cohesion and dynamics within the two new states. Sudan is host to the lingering eight-year-old insurgency in Darfur and the recently erupted conflicts with the northern contingents of the SPLA in Southern Kordofan State and Blue Nile State. Similarly, South Sudan experiences regular and extremely violent intercommunal and factional conflicts, which has led the UN to report that the main political driver of conflict in post-CPA South Sudan will be internal tensions.[3]

Continued Conflict in the North: Southern Kordofan and Blue Nile States

For the first half of 2011, UNMIS maintained its support for implementation of the CPA in Southern Kordofan State and Blue Nile State, with particular focus on the organization of the Popular Consultations, the Southern Kordofan State elections, and the security arrangements for SPLA troops from the two states. The mission provided continued support to the redeployment of SPLA forces from above the north-south border into the south. At the March meeting of the Cease-Fire Political Commission, the mission agreed to concentrate its monitoring and verification efforts on

determining the actual SPLA presence in Southern Kordofan State and Blue Nile State. The future of northern contingents of the SPLA was also taken up in the AU-managed post-CPA negotiations on security arrangements.

UNMIS supported and monitored preparations for the Popular Consultations, a CPA-mandated mechanism designed to provide citizens of the two states with the opportunity to express their views on the implementation of the CPA and deliver recommendations that would rectify any shortcomings in the constitutional, political, administrative, and economic arrangements of the agreement. In Blue Nile State, the mission provided logistical and material assistance and a series of preparatory workshops in support of public hearings that took place in January and February in 108 centers across the state, during which 69,429 people expressed their opinions on implementation of the agreement. In Southern Kordofan, preparations for the Popular Consultations were delayed in order to hold the state elections.

After a one-year delay, the Southern Kordofan elections were held in May 2011. UNMIS provided technical and logistical support and voter education training and materials. The elections pitted previous partners in the state power-sharing government, Ahmed Haroun from the NCP and Abdul Aziz al-Hilu from the SPLM, against each other in an environment of heightened tensions. Voting took place without incident between 2 and 4 May 2011. UNMIS SRSG Menkerios met with both candidates and urged the eventual winner to form an inclusive government to avoid a winner-take-all situation that could exacerbate tensions.

However, prior to the national electoral commission's announcement that Haroun had won by a narrow margin, the SPLM declared that it was withdrawing and would not recognize the outcome. Post-election pronouncements that the government of Sudan intended to forcibly disarm SPLA soldiers in Blue Nile and Southern Kordofan further increased tensions. Amid mutual accusations, fighting between the two forces broke out in Southern Kordofan's capital, Kadugli, in June and quickly spread across the state. Widespread fighting, including the use of aerial bombardment, led to large-scale displacement and serious abuses against the civilian population. Khartoum alleges that the SPLM continues to support SPLM-North, further contributing to north-south tensions.

With the NCP and the SPLM's northern faction failing to reach an agreement to halt fighting in Southern Kordofan, hostilities spread to Blue Nile in September. Fighting between government and SPLA forces broke out in the state capital and again quickly spread across the state. At the same time, UNMIS was in the position of commencing liquidation and withdrawal as these conflicts broke out around it. The end of the mission's mandate and the absence of a negotiated cease-fire or settlement meant that the UN and other stakeholders had limited opportunities to engage in peacemaking activities. The withdrawal also cast serious doubt over the future of the remaining CPA provisions in these areas, with some observers warning of a return to wide-scale civil war.

Establishment of UNMISS

Security Council Resolution 1996 established UNMISS on 9 July 2011 for an initial period of one year at an authorized strength of 7,000 troops and 900 police. UNMISS inherited the infrastructure, assets, and personnel from UNMIS, enabling the mission to deploy quickly. Broadly, UNMISS is charged with consolidating peace and security and helping to establish the conditions necessary for development in the Republic of South Sudan. The logic of the mission's mandate is peace consolidation through state consolidation. As such, UNMISS is tasked with providing good offices, advice, and support on political transition; capacity building of key government institutions, including security sector reform; popular and inclusive participation in political processes; and the prevention, mitigation, and resolution of local conflicts.

Like its predecessor, UNMISS is authorized to use force under Chapter VII of the UN Charter to protect civilians under imminent threat of violence and to deter violence through proactive deployments and patrols, particularly when the government is not providing such security.

While UNMIS was largely guided in its priorities by the provisions and timeline of the CPA, the new mission is centered on supporting the new government and the institutional consolidation of the new state. The mission's activities are focused on enhancing national capacities to meet political, security, and protection challenges in a way that helps the government extend its authority and create the space for statebuilding and socioeconomic development. UNMISS has no executive governing authority or direct responsibilities for establishing the institutions of the state. Rather, the mission is tasked with supporting and advising the government of South Sudan and providing technical advice on various processes.

One significant change from UNMIS to UNMISS is the structure and approach to mission deployments. No longer designed to monitor the redeployment of CPA forces, UNMISS pursues a more flexible approach, deploying military contingents and civilian experts based on the needs of local security and guided by detailed conflict tracking and early warning mechanisms. To do so, the mission is restructuring its deployment toward the state level and critical *payams* (counties). For instance, in late August 2011, after inter-communal fighting in the state of Jonglei resulted in the deaths of approximately 600 people, UNMISS deployed troops to sensitive locations and conducted roaming patrols and surveillance flights to deter further violence. Civilian experts were also deployed to politically engage local leaders and communities and provide good offices for reconciliation efforts.

Although the main emphasis of the mission is political, coordination and partnership with the UN Country Team, nongovernmental organizations, and donors will be vital given the breadth of needs evident in South Sudan, particularly since South Sudan may have only a short window to establish itself as a successful state.

Political and Security Developments in South Sudan

The security challenges facing South Sudan are daunting. There are frequent and severe conflicts among heavily armed tribal groups and between the SPLA and breakaway factions. In the first half of 2011, insecurity resulted in more than 116,000 internally displaced persons in the southern region. Rivalry and mistrust between communities is high. As the year came to a close, violence again erupted between feuding ethnic groups in Jonglei State, with UNMISS warning that thousands of armed men were moving toward Pibor. The movements prompted UNMISS to deploy a battalion of troops to deter violence and protect civilians, though rapid deployment was hampered by a lack of helicopters to transport troops.

Largely reliant on international aid for service provision during the war, rural areas outside of state capitals are out of reach of the authority and institutions of the government. Having achieved independence, South Sudan now faces the challenge of building a state and a sense of citizenship among its people and communities. An important step was taken in August when President Salva Kiir announced the appointment of the first governmental cabinet of South Sudan, a geographically representative group comprising twenty-nine ministers, of whom 30 percent are female.

The strongest and most visible of South Sudan's institutions, the SPLA, plays the central role in providing security. Seen in some areas of the south as a partisan force, it is very often deeply integrated into local political power structures. It has on occasion obstructed or hindered humanitarian access and has committed transgressions against the civilian population during security operations. It is also extremely bloated from the integration of large numbers of opposition militias during the CPA period. One of the immediate—and most politically sensitive—priorities facing the mission is supporting the government in transforming the SPLA from a rebel group into a national army. This transition includes

UN Interim Security Force for Abyei (UNISFA)	
• Authorization and Start Date	27 June 2011 (UNSC Res. 1990)
• Force Commander	Lieutenant-General Tadesse Werede Tesfay (Ethiopia)
• Budget	$180.7 million (1 July 2011–30 June 2012)
• Strength as of 31 October 2011	Troops: 2,812 Military Observers: 80 Police: 2 International Civilian Staff: 20

For detailed mission information see p. 262

"right-sizing" the force through the demobilization of an estimated 150,000 SPLA members, including 70,000 soldiers and 80,000 police, prison officers, and other security actors, as well as through professionalization.

The capacities of the South Sudan Police Service (SSPS) are improving, but they remain inadequate to secure public safety and police international borders. UNMISS will intensify efforts initiated by UNMIS to develop the security and justice sector and coordinate donor support. Mission police contingents and civilian expert advisers will be co-located with the SSPS at the state and *payam* level.

Abyei

The contested resource-rich region of Abyei remains the most combustible unresolved issue of the CPA and, to date, the most intractable. The CPA stipulated that the residents of Abyei would vote in their own referendum, to be held at the same time as the larger southern referendum, to determine whether to secede with the south or remain in the north. Abyei's political weight is disproportionate to its geographical size and economic value. It looms large in the calculations of the two parties to the CPA, as both have important and relatively powerful constituencies connected to the area, constituencies whom neither side wants to disappoint.

After the two parties failed to agree on the modalities for the Abyei referendum, the area witnessed a buildup of regular and irregular forces, and a deterioration of security, through the first months of 2011. This culminated in an outbreak of intense fighting between the SAF and the SPLA in May 2011, which displaced an estimated 100,000 Abyei residents southward and resulted in SAF forces taking over the town of Abyei and surrounding area. The UNMIS contingent in Abyei faced criticism for inaction; perceiving themselves to be outmanned and outgunned, the peacekeepers were unwilling to intercede forcefully between the fighting parties.[4]

In response to the situation in Abyei, the AU facilitated high-level meetings in Addis Ababa between the CPA parties, which were attended by President Omar al-Bashir and then–first vice president Salva Kiir. On 20 June the government of Sudan and the SPLM signed an agreement on interim security and administrative arrangements for Abyei. The agreement called for the establishment of a civilian administration for the Abyei area, though the parties have yet to agree on a chairperson. The agreement also called for the deployment of a new armored brigade from the Ethiopian Defense Force and an Ethiopian force commander. Based on the agreement, Security Council Resolution 1990 established UNISFA.

The agreement also called for both the SAF and the SPLA to withdraw troops from the Abyei area. Accordingly, monitoring and verifying the withdrawal is one of the primary tasks for the new mission. To date, however, full withdrawal has not taken place. In September, the government of Sudan and the SPLM agreed to withdraw their troops from the border by the end of the month, though Khartoum subsequently denied the agreement, maintaining that it would not redeploy troops until the 20 June agreement was implemented, including the establishment of the Abyei administration. South Sudan maintains that it will fully withdraw at the same time as Sudan.

UNISFA is further mandated to participate in relevant Abyei area bodies established under the agreement.[5] Acting under Chapter VII, UNISFA is also authorized to ensure the security and freedom of movement of UN and humanitarian personnel and of members of the joint observer teams, protect civilians, and protect Abyei from incursions. As in previous instances of fighting between the CPA parties, the fighting in Abyei was precipitated by the unregulated proximity and interaction between the two hostile forces. Thus, UNISFA's ability to uphold its mandate to protect the Abyei area from unauthorized incursions will be an important factor in deescalating tensions between the two countries.

In a further agreement between the Sudanese government and the SPLM on border security, signed in June, the parties have agreed to establish a ten-kilometer demilitarized border zone, pending resolution of disputed areas and final border demarcation. This agreement also requested UNISFA to provide support for a joint border-monitoring verification mechanism, and in December the UN Security Council expanded UNISFA's mandate to include support for border verification through investigations, monitoring, arbitrations, patrols, and security. The enhanced mandate expands the mission's area of operations and tasks UNISFA to work with Sudan and South Sudan to further develop bilateral border management initiatives.

As of November, 2,872 of an authorized 4,250 UNISFA troops had arrived in the Abyei area. Despite logistical difficulties caused by the rainy season and denials of flight clearance, the mission's deployment has been one of the fastest on record.

While UNISFA may prove effective at maintaining security and stability in the interim, the parties have still not reached a final settlement on the future of Abyei and negotiations are ongoing.

Darfur

In Darfur, despite the efforts of UNAMID and the AU- and UN-led mediation, progress toward improved security and a comprehensive resolution to the conflict proved elusive in 2011. A resurgence of fighting between rebel groups and government forces in some areas displaced an estimated 70,000 people in early 2011. Throughout the year, UNAMID military and civilian staff, as well as humanitarian aid workers, have been the target of attacks, ambushes, kidnappings, car-jackings, and violent robberies. With much attention and engagement drawn to north-south developments, and given the discord among UN and AU member states over the best way to proceed in Darfur, various efforts and initiatives failed to gain traction.

The AU- and UN-led negotiations for Darfur in Doha succeeded in the brokering of an accord between the government and the Liberation and Justice Movement in July 2011, but opposition from other rebel groups continued. Efforts are ongoing to bring other groups into the so-called Doha Agreement, but the continued fractiousness of the rebel groups and erratic engagement from the government of Sudan render the prospects for a comprehensive and credible agreement extremely challenging.

Efforts to shape the negotiations were pursued by the AU-UN mediation team and supported on the ground in Darfur by UNAMID. The mission implemented a series of consultations with a large number of stakeholders and facilitated civil society participation in Doha at a number of conferences aimed at forging consensus on key issues of the conflict.

UNAMID has also been engaging the government of Sudan politically so that certain unilateral measures can be taken in an effort to improve the situation on the ground. Such improvements, including lifting the state of emergency, are intended to create an enabling environment for an AU-conceived approach to localizing the peace process. This process is intended to empower the people of Darfur while limiting the role of rebel groups, who are often viewed as obstructionist. However, these attempts have not yielded any improvements to date, and the discord among AU and

UN member states over the effectiveness and feasibility of such a strategy remains ongoing.

The Doha negotiations were dealt a further blow in September with the return of top rebel leader Khalil Ibrahim from Libya after the fall of the Qaddafi regime. Ibrahim led the Justice and Equality Movement (JEM), the region's most heavily armed rebel group. In November, the JEM joined the Sudan Liberation Army and the SPLM-North in Southern Kordofan State and Blue Nile State in a political and military alliance, the Sudanese Revolutionary Front, uniting the groups to overthrow the government of Sudan. However, just weeks after JEM joined the alliance, Ibrahim was killed in an airstrike, which may prove to be a major setback for rebel movements in the region.

In December, the International Criminal Court prosecutor announced that he would seek an arrest warrant for Sudan's current defense minister, Abdelrahim Mohamed Hussein, for his part in atrocities committed in Darfur in 2003 and 2004. The impact on the government of Sudan and the conflict in Darfur are unclear,

---

UN-AU Hybrid Mission in Darfur (UNAMID)

• Authorization Date	31 July 2007 (UNSC Res. 1769)
• Start Date	Implement mandated tasks no later than 31 December 2007
• Joint AU/UN Special Representative	Ibrahim Gambari (Nigeria)
• Force Commander	Lieutenant-General Patrick Nyamvumba (Rwanda)
• Police Commissioner	James Oppong-Boanuh (Ghana)
• Budget	$1,689.3 million (1 July 2011–30 June 2012)
• Strength as of 31 October 2011	Troops: 17,723 Military Observers: 239 Police: 4,920 International Civilian Staff: 1,124 National Civilian Staff: 2,904 UN Volunteers: 481

For detailed mission information see p. 225

but this could prove to further destabilize the already precarious environment.

Conclusion

Enormous change took place in Sudan in 2011, and the consequences for regional stability and the implications for peace operations are not yet fully clear. Ongoing political processes and negotiations are certain to impact and make further demands upon UN operations. Another important factor for the future will be regional dynamics. Although for months Sudan appeared insulated from the popular protests sweeping the Middle East and North Africa, hardening economic conditions stimulated street protests in Khartoum in September. The fall of the Qaddafi regime in Libya, though it removed an interventionist and often-destabilizing factor from Sudanese politics, could also exacerbate an already fragile situation.

Sudan and South Sudan will remain extremely challenging environments for peacekeeping operations in 2012, with multiple missions pursuing numerous priorities. While allowing for flexibility and responsiveness in achieving peace and stability, this approach also heightens the risk of strategic and operational incoherence.

Notes

1. Carter Center, "Carter Center Finds Sudanese Referendum Peaceful and Credible," 17 January 2011, http://www.cartercenter.org/news/pr/sudan-011711.html; European Union, *Final Report: Southern Sudan Referendum,* Election Observation Mission, 9–15 January 2011, http://www.eueom.eu/files/press releases/english/final-report-eueom-referendum-south-sudan-2011_en.pdf.

2. Referendum-related materials included 7.5 million ballot papers, 8,500 ballot booths, 4,300 voter registration kits, and 600 registration training kits.

3. United Nations, *Special Report of the Secretary-General on the Sudan,* UN Doc. S/2011/314, 17 May 2011.

4. "Exclusive: UN Probes Absences Amid Sudan Clashes," *Reuters,* http://www.reuters.com/article/2011/06/04/us-sudan-abyei-un-idUSTRE7531WF20110604.

5. The agreement calls for a joint oversight committee and a joint military observer committee to be stationed in Abyei, comprising an equal number of members and observers from the two parties. The agreement also calls for a power-sharing administration and a police force for the Abyei area; details for the latter are to be determined by the joint oversight committee.

3 Mission Notes

Bosnia and Herzegovina

Bosnia and Herzegovina (BiH) experienced political deadlock in 2011, but the European Union judged that the security situation was stable enough to allow a reduction in its peacekeeping presence. This consists of the EU Police Mission in Bosnia and Herzegovina (EUPM), launched in 2003 to replace a UN police force, and the EU Force in Bosnia and Herzegovina (EUFOR Althea), a military mission authorized in 2004 to replace the NATO forces that had patrolled Bosnia since the mid-1990s.

Background

The past two years have seen significant political uncertainty and tension in BiH. After the October 2010 national elections, Bosniak, Croat, and Serb politicians failed to form a national government for over a year. The main Croat and Bosniak parties also failed to form a government within the Muslim-Croat Federation, one of the two constituent parts of the country, while leaders of their counterpart, the Republika Srpska, have continued to agitate for secession. Against this uncertain background, the EU continues to conduct two peace operations in BiH.

Since 2010 the EUPM's key tasks have been focused on combating organized crime and corruption in BiH, with an emphasis on state-level law enforcement agencies. To this end, the mission works to strengthen law enforcement capacity to promote criminal investigative capabilities, enhance police-prosecution cooperation, strengthen police-penitentiary cooperation, and promote accountability. The EUPM also provides operational advice to the EU Special Representative.

EUFOR Althea is an EU-led military operation that contributes to safety and security in BiH, works to ensure compliance with the Dayton Accords, and supports capacity building and training for the armed forces of BiH. The mission has a police presence throughout the country and a limited deterrent military force, with the potential for rapid reinforcements from EU member states. The mission includes liaison and observation teams that gather information on the general security situation throughout BiH and monitor joint military affairs in BiH, particularly in the movement of weapons and military equipment and the disposal of surplus weapons and ammunition. EUFOR Althea also supports the EUPM's efforts to combat organized crime, while also assisting the International Criminal Tribunal for the Former Yugoslavia in searching for war crimes suspects.

EU Military Operation in Bosnia and Herzegovina (EUFOR Althea)

- Authorization Date   21 July 2004 (EU Council Joint Action 2004/570/CFSP); 22 November 2004 (UNSC Res. 1575)
- Start Date   December 2004
- Operation Commander   General Sir Richard Shirreff (United Kingdom)
- Force Commander   Major-General Bernhard Bair (Austria)
- Budget $29.9 million (1 October 2010–30 September 2011)
- Strength as of 30 September 2011   Troops: 1,291

Both of these missions have shrunk considerably in recent years. EUFOR Althea comprised 7,500 personnel when it began, but reduced to only 1,300 troops by the middle of 2011. The EUPM, meanwhile, dwindled from a peak of 540 international staff after its launch to under 200 in the second half of 2011.

Key Developments

In May 2011, the High Representative for Bosnia and Herzegovina, Valentin Inzko, warned the Security Council that Bosnia faced "the most serious and direct challenges" to the Dayton peace agreement since it was signed in 1995. In June 2011, political parties at least managed to form a parliamentary assembly, and it was only in late December that political parties reached an agreement to form a government, ending a fourteen-month deadlock. The Republika Srpska continued to distance itself from the Bosnian state in the second half of the year. These political tensions, though significant, did not spill over into violence.

The EU has placed increasing emphasis on its civilian presence in Bosnia. Until 2011, the High Representative in Sarajevo doubled as the EU Special Representative. In September, however, a separate EU Special Representative was appointed to work in parallel with Valentin Inzko. The logic for this split is to give Inzko more time to focus on the state of the Dayton Accords while the EU prioritizes integrating Bosnia into the European system—although it is unlikely to join the Union for many years.

The EUPM's future was cast in considerable doubt after a meeting in Brussels in July at which EU ambassadors reportedly agreed to close the mission in June 2012. This decision was not formally confirmed, however, and the mission's head in Sarajevo indicated in interviews that it might not be final. Within the EU, Britain appeared skeptical about closing the operation. Nonetheless, by the last quarter of 2011, preparations for assisting the Bosnian police forces in taking over duties from the EUPM were under way.

EU Police Mission in Bosnia and Herzegovina (EUPM)

- Authorization Date — 11 March 2002 (EU Council Joint Action 2002/210/CFSP)
- Start Date — January 2003
- Head of Mission — Brigadier-General Stefan Feller (Germany)
- Budget — $24.5 million (1 October 2010–30 September 2011)
- Strength as of 30 September 2011 — Civilian Police: 83 Civilian Staff: 34

OSCE Mission to Bosnia and Herzegovina

- Authorization Date — 8 December 1995 (Fifth Meeting of the OSCE Ministerial Council)
- Start Date — December 1995
- Head of Mission — Ambassador Fletcher M. Burton (United States)
- Budget — $20.8 million (1 October 2010–30 September 2011)
- Strength as of 30 September 2011 — Civilian Staff: 73

NATO Headquarters Sarajevo

- Authorization Date — 28 June 2004 (Communiqué of NATO Istanbul Summit); 22 November 2004 (UNSC Res. 1575)
- Start Date — December 2004
- Head of Mission — Brigadier-General Gary E. Huffman

While EUFOR Althea has not been scheduled for closure, EU officials reportedly agreed in October to halve its strength to between 600 and 700 personnel, with a continued emphasis on capacity building coupled with the ongoing provision of "situational awareness and a credible reserve."[1] As with the EUPM, the UK expressed skepticism regarding this proposal.

EUFOR/Sergeant Marcus Rumpold

The Multinational Battalion participates in a training exercise during a visit of EUFOR Althea's force commander, 11 August 2011.

Conclusion

The year in review saw progress toward normalization of Bosnia's security framework in operational terms, albeit in an environment of political deadlock for much of the year. The EUPM and EUFOR Althea play a vital role in BiH as they continue to face the challenge of successfully transferring responsibilities to the government and promoting reform while significant political tensions persist. In November, the UN Security Council extended authorization of EUFOR Althea for one year, stressing that responsibility for further peace consolidation lies with BiH political authorities.

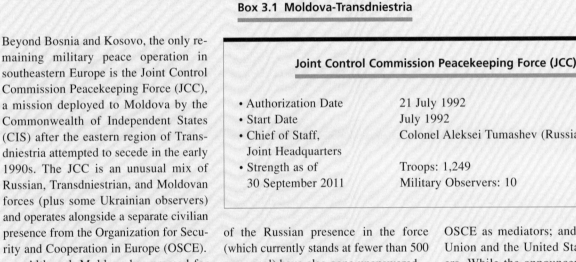

Box 3.1 Moldova-Transdniestria

Joint Control Commission Peacekeeping Force (JCC)

• Authorization Date	21 July 1992
• Start Date	July 1992
• Chief of Staff, Joint Headquarters	Colonel Aleksei Tumashev (Russia)
• Strength as of 30 September 2011	Troops: 1,249 Military Observers: 10

Beyond Bosnia and Kosovo, the only remaining military peace operation in southeastern Europe is the Joint Control Commission Peacekeeping Force (JCC), a mission deployed to Moldova by the Commonwealth of Independent States (CIS) after the eastern region of Transdniestria attempted to secede in the early 1990s. The JCC is an unusual mix of Russian, Transdniestrian, and Moldovan forces (plus some Ukrainian observers) and operates alongside a separate civilian presence from the Organization for Security and Cooperation in Europe (OSCE).

Although Moldova has pressed for the peacekeeping operation to be wound down, with some progress occurring in talks between the Moldovan and Transdniestrian authorities in 2011, the JCC continues to operate. Conversely, calls by Transdniestria for a significant expansion of the Russian presence in the force (which currently stands at fewer than 500 personnel) have also gone unanswered.

In September it was announced that official negotiations, which were suspended in 2006, would resume in the so-called 5+2 format, which brings together Moldova and Transdniestria as parties to the conflict; Russia, Ukraine, and the OSCE as mediators; and the European Union and the United States as observers. While the announcement was welcomed as a promising first step, the unchanged positions of both Moldova and Transdniestria indicate that much work remains before a permanent settlement to this conflict can be reached.

Note

1. Council of the European Union, "Council Conclusions on Bosnia and Herzegovina," presentation at the 3117th meeting of the Foreign Affairs Council, Luxembourg, 10 October 2011.

Cyprus

Despite increased UN engagement in Cyprus in 2011, few gains were made in the country's decades-long conflict. Since attaining statehood in 1960, Cyprus has endured violence and partition resulting from tensions between ethnic Turks in the island's north and Greeks in the south. As frequent talks in recent years have shown little progress in resolving the dispute, the UN Peacekeeping Force in Cyprus (UNFICYP) continues to monitor the de facto border and provide essential services to Cypriot civilians. International pressure on both sides to come to an agreement has been building, but until such an accord is reached, UNFICYP will continue to play a vital role.

Background

The island of Cyprus is divided between a predominantly ethnic Greek south and a minority of Turks concentrated in the north. Upon independence in 1960, the country attempted through its constitution to balance the interests of both the Greek and Turkish Cypriot communities. Political crises erupted early on, however, resulting in the outbreak of violence in 1963. When further division occurred in 1974, the UN brokered a de facto cease-fire, which established the status quo of a divided Cyprus.

UNFICYP was established in 1964 with a mandate to prevent the recurrence of fighting and contribute to the maintenance and restoration of law and order and a return to "normal conditions." Following renewed hostilities in 1974, its mandate was expanded, with monitoring of the de facto cease-fire becoming a top priority. After 1974, cease-fire lines and a buffer zone were established between the areas controlled by the opposing Cyprus National Guard and Turkish Cypriot forces. This de facto border stretches across the island and varies in width from less than twenty meters to seven kilometers, covering about 3 percent of the island and some of Cyprus's most valuable agricultural land. The zone also cuts through Nicosia, capital of both north and south, dividing it in two. UNFICYP utilizes a system of observation posts and air, vehicle, and foot patrols to monitor maintenance of the military status quo in the buffer zone. The mission's civilian police maintain close cooperation with the Greek and Turkish Cypriot police on intercommunal matters, contribute to law and order in the buffer zone, and assist in investigations and humanitarian activities.

UNFICYP maintains the crossing points on the buffer zone and is examining new potential crossing locations. From 21 November 2010 through 7 May 2011, there were more

---

UN Peacekeeping Force in Cyprus (UNFICYP)

• Authorization and Start Date	4 March 1964 (UNSC Res.186)
• SRSG	Lisa Buttenheim (United States)
• Force Commander	Major-General Chao Liu (China)
• Budget	$58.2 million (1 July 2011–30 June 2012)
• Strength as of 31 October 2011	Troops: 856
	Police: 66
	International Civilian Staff: 38
	National Civilian Staff: 112

For detailed mission information see p. 243

than 778,000 official crossings through the seven points along the buffer zone, in addition to several million euros' worth of trade. Though the main thoroughfare in Nicosia had been closed for forty-four years, hundreds of crossings now occur there every day.

The mission addresses day-to-day issues for Cypriots who live and work in the buffer zone, supporting education and medical services, maintaining roads across the zone, facilitating the supply of electricity and water across the de facto border, and delivering mail and Red Cross messages between north and south. UNFICYP provides permits for civilian activities in the buffer zone, including housing construction, farming, and other commercial ventures. The mission conducts outreach activities in villages near the buffer zone to explain these procedures and process applications.

UNFICYP also undertakes activities benefiting Greek Cypriots and Maronites living in the northern part of the island and Turkish Cypriots living in the south. The mission assists in addressing legal and humanitarian concerns regarding such individuals, including attending court hearings and facilitating family visits. UNFICYP also delivers humanitarian assistance, including in cooperation with the UN High Commissioner for Refugees (UNHCR), and liaises with authorities in the south to provide welfare services, including medical care and education.

One of UNFICYP's most important activities has been assisting in the clearance of landmines from Cyprus. The mission has supported the UN Mine Action Centre in Cyprus (UNMACC), which was established by the UN Development Programme (UNDP) with funding from the European Union in 2003. Teams working with UNMACC have cleared over 27,000 mines from the island that were laid during the outbreak of violence in the 1960s. In February 2011, however, mine removal operations came to an end, as both sides continued to withhold access to remaining mined areas in the buffer zone and no agreement was reached on extending de-mining operations outside the zone. UNMACC estimates

that 15,000 landmines may still remain in Cyprus, and 2 million square meters of land could still contain mines and unexploded ordnance. The Security Council has urged the parties to agree to further de-mining, but there has been no progress in this effort.

In the June 2011 resolution that extended the mission's mandate for six months, the Security Council called on both sides to intensify the momentum of negotiations and increase the participation of civil society in the process, as well as to facilitate removal of the remaining mines. Lisa Buttenheim of the United States is the Special Representative of the Secretary-General (SRSG) for UNFICYP. The mission's force commander, appointed in January 2011, is Major-General Chao Liu of China.

Key Developments

While there were some tense exchanges in 2011 between UNFICYP and Turkish Cypriot military forces, these incidents were generally quickly resolved and the situation in the buffer zone largely remained calm, with no significant cease-fire violations. No major exercises were carried out by either military, with only occasional low-level activities provoking a reaction from the other side. These mostly occurred around Nicosia, where forces are in close proximity to each other. Both opposing forces continued to report alleged violations to UNFICYP, but the number has decreased since 2010. Some previously reported military positions established by both sides in violation of the status quo remain in place. There have also been restrictions imposed on UN staff members of Greek Cypriot origin seeking to undertake their duties in the north. The mission supports measures such as unmanning or closing observation posts where opposing troops are in close proximity, but there has been no progress in advancing proposals for military confidence-building measures.

The current series of reunification talks began in 2008 under UN sponsorship and with UNFICYP support. Dimitris Christofias, the president of the Republic of Cyprus, and his

Box 3.2 Women, Peace, and Security

In February 2011, following the tenth anniversary of Security Council Resolution 1325 and the subsequent resolutions that constitute the UN's Women, Peace, and Security (WPS) framework, the Department of Peacekeeping Operations (DPKO) and the Department of Field Support (DFS) released a ten-year impact study on the implementation of Resolution 1325.[1]

The impact study assessed the effects of DPKO's work on several WPS components, including participation in peace negotiations, political participation, sexual- and gender-based violence, and judicial reform. The findings reveal mixed success in advancing the WPS agenda. While disparities persist, peacekeeping support for women's political participation resulted in tangible and significant impacts over the past decade. Lessons learned were tested this year by national elections held in Haiti, Liberia, and the Democratic Republic of Congo.

DPKO and DFS, with the assistance of a gender advisory team and mission-specific gender advisers, have successfully promoted women's engagement in political processes both as voters and as candidates. UN-led voter education campaigns, gender-sensitive voter information, improved election security, and women-only voting booths have yielded greater female turnout during elections and increased involvement of women in the formation of government and the strengthening of democratic institutions.

Peacekeeping operations like the UN Stabilization Mission in Haiti (MINUSTAH) also support the mobilization of female electoral candidates through enhanced security (such as specialized communication lines), production of campaign posters, and the airing of candidates' profiles on mission radio stations in the lead-up to elections.

Through active lobbying for gender equality in government, peacekeeping missions helped enact legislative quotas in countries including Sudan and Timor-Leste, and in the latter women now occupy more than a quarter of the legislative seats. The rise in women's governmental participation is smaller without quotas, but can still lead to more representative state institutions, as seen in Liberia, Darfur, and Afghanistan over the past decade. Problems remain, however, as women who transcend cultural barriers to governmental participation face the additional challenge of developing their leadership skills while concurrently fulfilling their duties in office. DPKO and the UN Entity for Gender Equality and the Empowerment of Women (also known as UN Women) work to build upon their capacity through multiday training and coaching programs aimed at improving awareness of gender-sensitive policies and providing technical support.

There are more women involved in government than ever before, although they are far from achieving gender equality. By increasing the participation of women as voters, candidates, and government officials, UN peace operations have created more inclusive and therefore more sustainable postconflict governments and civil societies. Looking to build upon the successes in women's political participation and to continue moving toward gender parity, DPKO and DFS are now working with the Department of Political Affairs to revise joint field guidelines on women's roles in postconflict electoral processes, with a slated release in early 2012. Elections scheduled for spring 2012 in Timor-Leste may be the first beneficiaries of the improved guidelines.

Gaps in implementing other aspects of the WPS framework still remain, including women's roles in peace processes, women's security sector involvement, and prevention and prosecution of sexual- and gender-based violence. In addition, while gender-mainstreaming efforts are now core components of UN peacekeeping mandates, the 2011 impact report recommends that additional resources, improved commitment by senior leadership, and clearer guidelines for crosscutting issues are needed to improve mission-level execution. More consistency between missions and thematic areas will also be necessary to build sustainable peace and propel Resolution 1325 and the WPS framework into the next decade of peacekeeping.

Note: 1. The report is available at http://www.un.org/en/peacekeeping/documents/10year_impact_study_1325.pdf.

northern counterpart at the time met with the SRSG and agreed on a path toward a comprehensive settlement, committing to the concept of a federal government with a single international identity and two constituent states of equal status. The meetings continued after a leadership change in the north, with Dervis Eroglu becoming de facto president of Northern Cyprus. The leaders of the two sides have met over a hundred times since 2008, and the UN Secretary-General has been closely involved in the discussions, meeting with them several times in 2011. The sides have found broad convergences regarding EU representation, international treaties, federal-level decisionmaking, and economic issues, but specific details have been lacking despite frequent meetings. A number of important issues regarding governance and power-sharing remain significant obstacles.

In July the two leaders met with the Secretary-General and accepted his offer for an enhanced UN mediation role in reunification talks, with the Secretary-General urging the two parties to reach convergence on core issues by October. Later that month the two sides began a series of nineteen intensive UN-supported meetings. In August the Secretary-General reported that talks were taking longer than had been hoped, with an agreement not likely for some time.[1] The leaders met with the Secretary-General again in late October and were invited to an additional meeting in January 2012, with the eventual goal of a multilateral conference on the Cyprus issue.

Negotiations have been increasingly undermined by developments in 2011. In July an explosion occurred at a military facility in the Republic of Cyprus, knocking out a major power plant and weakening the economy. The republic has seen its credit rating downgraded by three major rating agencies and is facing fears that it will become the next country to seek an EU bailout. Controversial austerity proposals have increased political uncertainty, leading to the collapse of the governing coalition and presenting a further challenge to resolving the north-south situation.

Cypriot affairs have been further worsened by recent strains between the Republic of Cyprus and Turkey. In September, despite warnings from Turkey, the Greek Cypriot government began exploratory drilling for oil and gas off the coast of Cyprus. Turkey called this an act of provocation, and stated that Turkish military assets would monitor developments in the area. Turkey has also expressed the intention to start its own seismic exploration program in the area near Northern Cyprus through an agreement with the north's de facto government. Turkey does not accept Greek Cypriot claims to the area, and believes that any development projects should be shelved until the dispute over the political status of the island is resolved.

Conclusion

The European Commission has indicated that it would like to see a settlement to the political status of the island before Cyprus assumes the EU presidency in the second half of 2012, but this currently seems unlikely. If negotiations fail to produce a resolution to this decades-old dispute, UNFICYP will continue to play an essential role in monitoring the situation and improving the lives of Cypriots affected by the partition.

Note

1. United Nations, *Assessment Report of the Secretary-General on the Status of the Negotiations in Cyprus*, UN Doc. S/2011/498, 8 August 2011.

3.3

Georgia

Since attaining independence from the Soviet Union in 1991, Georgia has grappled with persistent separatist movements in the regions of Abkhazia and South Ossetia. These disputed territories have been a long-standing source of contention between Georgia and Russia, which shares a border with the two regions, and led to a five-day war in 2008. In 2011 the situation remained tense and uncertain.

The EU Monitoring Mission in Georgia (EUMM) deployed shortly after the 2008 war. The mission plays a vital role as the only remaining peacekeeping presence in the country, but its inability to regularly access the disputed territories themselves has prevented it from fulfilling its mandate.

Background

After the dissolution of the Soviet Union, South Ossetia and Abkhazia sought independence from Georgia. Armed conflicts between Georgian authorities and separatists prompted the deployment of peacekeeping and observer missions by the UN, the Commonwealth of Independent States (CIS), and the Organization for Security and Cooperation in Europe (OSCE). The situation was stable through the early 2000s, but the basic issues underlying the conflict remained unresolved. A new Georgian administration in 2004, led by President Mikhail Saakashvili, made "territorial integrity" a priority and sent troops to Georgia's de facto border with South Ossetia. A military confrontation that year ended with a cease-fire, but the situation remained tense. Russia took steps to strengthen its ties to Abkhazia and South Ossetia in 2008, forming direct relationships with their de facto authorities, and the breakaway regions called for international recognition.

The situation climaxed in August 2008 as a series of military incidents led to a five-day war between Georgia and Russia. The war caused hundreds of casualties, displaced over 100,000 people, and devastated South Ossetia's capital. The EU negotiated a cease-fire and peace agreement, but Russia recognized the sovereignty of Abkhazia and South Ossetia and signed bilateral agreements providing them border protection and establishing military bases in the two territories. Due to loss of support from the disputants and stalemates at the UN and OSCE, all multilateral peace missions except for the newly created EUMM ceased operations within a year of the conflict.

The EUMM began operations in October 2008 and currently comprises more than 200 monitors from twenty-six EU member states. Its initial primary task, monitoring the withdrawal of Russian forces from Tbilisi-controlled Georgia, was largely completed in the first months of the mission's deployment.

EU Monitoring Mission in Georgia (EUMM)

- Authorization Date   15 September 2008 (EU Council Joint Action 2008/736/CFSP)
- Start Date   October 2008
- Head of Mission   Andrzej Tyszkiewicz (Poland)
- Budget $37.1 million (1 October 2010–30 September 2011)
- Strength as of 30 September 2011   Civilian Police: 89   Civilian Staff: 218

Since then, it has focused on monitoring the stabilization process, compliance with the 2008 peace agreement, normalization of civil governance, restoration of the rule of law, return of displaced persons, and the promotion of confidence-building measures. The mission facilitates conflict resolution between the parties and generally works to improve the security situation through its presence in relevant areas. EUMM conducts day and night patrols in areas adjacent to Abkhazia and South Ossetia, but has not been permitted regular access within the borders of the disputed territories. EUMM works to make the areas adjacent to the administrative boundary lines (ABLs), which serve as the de facto borders, safe for local residents, and seeks to facilitate civilian crossings in both directions without obstruction. In addition to its headquarters in Tbilisi, the EUMM has three field offices in Georgia located near the ABLs. In July, Andrzej Tyskie-wicz was appointed head of EUMM.

The mission maintains a high level of contact with Georgian authorities, including through liaison officers in government ministries, and it benefits from agreements restricting Georgian police and military movements near the ABLs. While EUMM is mandated to cover the whole territory of Georgia within the country's internationally recognized borders, Abkhazian and South Ossetian authorities have denied it regular access to the disputed territories. EUMM contact with Abkhazian and South Ossetian officials is also very limited. Despite these shortcomings, the mission still plays an important early warning function. The EUMM is able to gather information on new developments, which is then passed on to the relevant local, national, and international bodies. The mission asserts that access to Abkhazian and South Ossetian territory would increase transparency, bring clarity to events that have already taken place, and decrease the risk of destabilizing incidents.

EUMM maintains working contact with Russian security forces. The continued presence of 7,000 to 9,000 Russian military personnel and Russian military equipment in both South Ossetia and Abkhazia, along with the construction of permanent military bases, is seen by EUMM as a violation of the 2008 agreement that brought an end to the conflict, but Russia holds that its recognition of the territories nullified that commitment.

Key Developments

The UN and OSCE have been facilitating a series of discussions in Geneva bringing together Georgian, Russian, Abkhazian, and South Ossetian representatives. The fifteenth round of these talks occurred in March 2011, but the parties have been unable to agree on the larger issues the negotiations are intended to address. In June, Georgia threatened to pull out of the talks, but this has yet to happen.

The Incident Prevention and Response Mechanism (IPRM), founded in 2009, provides a framework for regular meetings of representatives of the EUMM, the OSCE, the UN, Georgia, Russia, and the de facto governments of Abkhazia and South Ossetia. This serves as a forum for discussing and resolving specific incidents and issues, with the aim of developing greater confidence and cooperation between the parties. The IPRM is facilitated by the EUMM and OSCE and includes a "hotline" telephone system, which has helped to de-escalate tensions quickly through development of common understandings of specific incidents. IPRM is the primary vehicle through which to exchange information on ABL incidents and related issues. Recurring issues during meetings in 2011 involved troop movements, military asset deployments, missing persons, detention cases, and a number of ABL-related matters, including border-crossing procedures and access to resources around the ABLs. Through the IPRM, the EUMM has also been able to participate in some investigations in the disputed territories.

Events in 2011 illustrate the high level of mistrust and suspicion existing between Georgia and Russia. In February, Georgian police crossed the ABL to arrest a suspect in a series of bombings that occurred in Georgia in 2010 and 2011. Georgia has asserted Russian involvement in these attacks and released a document in June purporting to show evidence supporting that accusation. In August, Russia accused Georgia of preparing a peaceful incursion of displaced individuals into South Ossetian territory on the third anniversary of Abkhazia and South Ossetia's proclaimed independence; however, no such march occurred.

Incidents in the breakaway territories are difficult to evaluate, as the facts are often disputed between the two sides and the EUMM cannot cross the ABL to verify any details. In April, a shootout in Abkhazia resulted in the deaths of a Russian border guard and two Georgians. Russia says the Georgians were working for the Interior Ministry, but Georgia asserts that they were criminals. In May, two Georgian civilians were wounded while straying across the ABL with South Ossetia. Georgia claims they were shot by Russian soldiers, while South Ossetian officials assert that they were in fact South Ossetian border guards.

Also in May, the EUMM sought to engage with both sides as Georgian authorities increased their presence near South Ossetia as part of recently enhanced security measures. The mission maintained contact with Georgian authorities and expressed concerns about the implications for freedom of movement of the local populations. EUMM was in touch with Russian border guards and South Ossetian authorities to share information on developments. The mission increased its visible presence in these areas and urged restraint from all sides.

The EU and NATO have supported Georgia's position regarding the breakaway republics. Both organizations have stated that they do not recognize the results of the August 2011 Abkhazian presidential election and have issued statements referring to Abkhazia as a "Georgian region." Georgia has been working with the EU on creating status-neutral travel documents that would allow residents of the disputed territories to travel abroad. Currently, Georgia does not recognize the Russian passports issued to some of those inhabiting the disputed areas.

In June, the UN General Assembly adopted a resolution recognizing the right of return of internally displaced persons (IDPs) and refugees from Abkhazia, South Ossetia, and Tbilisi-controlled Georgia. The resolution condemns forced demographic changes in the area and calls for unimpeded access for humanitarian activities for all IDPs, refugees, and other persons residing in conflict-affected areas throughout Georgia.

Conclusion

As 2011 came to a close, it did not appear that South Ossetia or Abkhazia would give up their aspirations of independence or that Georgia and Russia were moving any closer to an agreement resolving their bilateral disagreements. Georgian leadership asserts that it is ready for direct talks with Russia without preconditions, but Moscow has said it will not talk to current Georgian president Saakashvili and will wait for a change of power in Georgia to open direct bilateral talks. The legacy of 2008 lives on, as over 20,000 ethnic Georgians displaced during the war are still prevented from returning to their homes.

With the EUMM unable to access the contested territory, it remains unable to properly fulfill its mandate and monitor activity within the disputed areas. While it serves a vital role as the only peacekeeping presence in Georgia and has helped to lessen violence and increase communication between the key actors, the threat of a return to armed conflict is still very real.

3.4

Kosovo

The overall situation in Kosovo remained stable in the first half of 2011. This period was marked by progress in the dialogue between Serbia and Kosovo, sponsored by the European Union, particularly in the areas of civil registries, diplomas, and freedom of movement. In July, however, ethnic tensions erupted in the north following a failed attempt by Kosovo institutions to take control of two northern boundary-crossing points. The incident, which was only resolved in December by an agreement between Kosovo and Serbia, highlights the risk of continued instability in the region. If the situation in northern Kosovo, which is currently outside the control of Kosovo's institutional domain, remains unsettled, the potential for ethnic flare-ups and regional volatility will remain.

Background

In 1998, Serbian president Slobodan Milosevic's attempts to bring Kosovo under direct Serbian rule ignited conflict between the Kosovo Liberation Army and Serbian armed forces. NATO responded with an intense four-month bombing campaign and the deployment of Kosovo Force (KFOR) to supervise the withdrawal of Serbian troops from Kosovo as laid out in Security Council Resolution 1244. This resolution also authorized the establishment of an interim civilian administration, the UN Interim Administration Mission in Kosovo (UNMIK). The OSCE Mission in Kosovo (OMIK) was established soon thereafter, tasked with addressing democracy, human rights, and rule of law issues.

With status negotiations reaching an impasse after nine years of international administration, Kosovo declared independence unilaterally in February 2008. Serbia's refusal to recognize the newly independent Kosovo created a complex political scenario for international actors. This was particularly true in the north, where Kosovo Serbs rejected Pristina's

---

UN Interim Administration Mission in Kosovo (UNMIK)

• Authorization and Start Date	10 June 1999 (UNSC Res. 1244) (note: paragraph 19 of the resolution states that international civil and security presences are established for an initial period of twelve months, to continue thereafter unless the Security Council decides otherwise)
• SRSG	Farid Zarif (Afghanistan)
• Budget	$44.9 million (1 July 2011–30 June 2012)
• Strength as of 31 October 2011	Military Observers: 9
	Police: 8
	International Civilian Staff: 150
	National Civilian Staff: 215
	UN Volunteers: 26

For detailed mission information see p. 269

EU Rule of Law Mission in Kosovo (EULEX)

• Authorization Date	4 February 2008 (EU Council Joint Action 2008/124/CFSP)
• Start Date	February 2008
• Head of Mission	Xavier Bout de Marnhac (France)
• Budget	$230 million (1 October 2010–30 September 2011)
• Strength as of 30 September 2011	Civilian Police: 1,044
	Civilian Staff: 541

authority, and in turn created a significant constituency who remain largely under Serbian control.

Soon after, UNMIK concluded its administrative role, transferring operational responsibility for law and order to the EU Rule of Law Mission in Kosovo (EULEX). EULEX was deployed under the legal framework of Resolution 1244 to support the rule of law, including police, justice, and customs. Serbia agreed to the reconfiguration of UNMIK and the deployment of EULEX in the so-called Six-Point Plan, which allowed EULEX to deploy to the north. Under the plan, EULEX, UNMIK, and OMIK are all to continue operating under Resolution 1244 and to remain "status neutral" regarding Kosovo. However, the plan failed to address the numerous obstacles and challenges these organizations have faced on the ground, particularly in the north, where EULEX has struggled to fully implement its mandate.

Key Developments

Political and Security Situation
In September 2010 the EU and Serbia jointly drafted a UN resolution calling for an EU-mediated dialogue on technical issues to promote cooperation between Serbia and Kosovo, achieve progress on the path to EU accession, and, more generally, to improve the lives of the populace. An initial agreement was reached in early July 2011 on civil registries, school and university diplomas, and freedom of movement. Disagreements over customs stamps, however, resulted in the postponement of further negotiations.

Tensions quickly escalated in light of the customs stamp issue, and Pristina organized a unilateral boycott of Serbian goods on 22 July. The boycott was then followed three days later by a failed attempt on the part of Kosovo institutions to take control of two northern boundary-crossing points previously under the control of Serb members of the Kosovo Police and EULEX officers. These

developments were criticized by international actors and caused a strong outcry from Kosovo Serbs, who quickly organized roadblocks and engaged in open fire with Kosovo's special police forces, resulting in the death of one Albanian police officer. On 26 July, KFOR troops took control of the two disputed border posts under an agreement with Pristina, but these forces encountered armed resistance and roadblocks manned by local Serbs. The crisis was ultimately averted by a KFOR-brokered deal negotiated with Pristina and Belgrade on 5 August. Under the terms of the agreement, both boundary-crossing points were designated as restricted military areas.

On 2 September, Serbia recognized status-neutral stamps from Kosovo within the EU-sponsored dialogue, paving the way for the lifting of mutual trade embargoes and an easing of tensions. However, the agreement failed to address the disputed border posts, and efforts to deploy EULEX customs officers to the contested border gates, jointly with Kosovo police and customs officers in an observer capacity, were met with local resistance and new roadblocks. Teams of customs officers were deployed by helicopters amid protests by the Serbian government and Kosovo Serbs. Kosovo Serbs reinforced existing roadblocks and built additional ones to protest the presence of Kosovo officials at the border gates. Tensions continued and clashes erupted on 27 September, when protesters attempted to remove barbed wire laid by KFOR at one of the gates. The clash left nearly thirty Kosovo Serbs and nine KFOR soldiers injured. The Serbian government boycotted the EU-sponsored dialogue, scheduled for 28 September, and talks were not resumed until late November.

In October, KFOR attempted to disassemble the roadblocks, using tear gas to disperse protesters. Ethnic Serbs resisted NATO forces, arguing that they would be willing to allow KFOR troops access as long as they did not transport Kosovo authorities to the north. An agreement was reached in late October to partially remove the barricades to allow KFOR troops through. However, tensions remained high and violence erupted again between Albanians and Serbians in early November, resulting in one death and two injuries. Fighting broke out again in late November when KFOR attempted to remove a roadblock, leaving twenty-five KFOR troops and dozens of Kosovo Serbs injured. An agreement between Kosovo and Serbia was finally reached in December to establish joint border patrols. Shortly after, Serbs began removing the roadblocks to allow freedom of movement.

In addition to the intercommunal divides exacerbated by the standoff in the north, Kosovo's institutions face numerous political challenges, including fragile democratic structures and widespread corruption. Snap elections in December 2010, for example, were marred by charges of fraud, and the new government has been unable to garner a strong mandate. In April 2011, parliament appointed Atifete Jahjaga, then–deputy police chief, as president in an emergency session. The appointment of

Jahjaga, who lacks previous political experience, was reportedly mediated by the United States.

The newly formed government suffered a public relations disaster in December 2010, when allegations of organ trafficking came to light in a Council of Europe report naming Prime Minister Hashim Thaci as the head of an organized crime syndicate. These accusations are likely to remain a destabilizing factor while a special prosecutor attached to EULEX continues to expand the investigation. It was in this environment of political fragility that EULEX issued a house arrest order on 22 September 2011 for Fatmir Limaj, the deputy head of the ruling party, on war crimes charges. This episode represents yet another challenge to the government's credibility.

Peace Operations

Now in its thirteenth year of operations, UNMIK has shifted to a largely diplomatic focus. Its activities include mediating between the communities in northern Kosovo, engaging with local, regional, and international stakeholders, and facilitating the participation of Kosovo institutions in multilateral forums. The mission's activities also include the promotion of stability and human rights in Kosovo.

With respect to the border crisis, UNMIK has been largely concerned with facilitating communication between the relevant parties, advocating peace, and discouraging independent action.[1] On 25 September 2011, then–acting chief of UNMIK Farid Zarif requested free movement for KFOR and EULEX in the north and encouraged all parties to resolve the crisis through dialogue. In October, Zarif was appointed Special Representative of the Secretary-General (SRSG) and head of UNMIK.

EULEX has continued to focus on its responsibilities in the areas of police, justice, and customs reforms, with recent successes in the fight against organized crime, corruption, and the pursuit of war criminals.[2] On 5 October, EULEX conducted a search-and-arrest

---

NATO Kosovo Force (KFOR)

- Authorization Date   10 June 1999
- Start Date   June 1999
- Head of Mission   Major-General Erhard Drews (Germany)
- Strength as of   Troops: 6,240
  30 September 2011

OSCE Mission in Kosovo (OMIK)

- Authorization Date   1 July 1999
- Start Date   July 1999
- Head of Mission   Ambassador Werner Almhofer (Austria)
- Budget $31.5 million
  (1 October 2010–30 September 2011)
- Strength as of   Civilian Police: 12
  30 September 2011   Civilian Staff: 177

Box 3.4 HIV/AIDS and UN Peacekeeping

It has been eleven years since the UN Security Council passed the landmark Resolution 1308 (2000), recognizing the impact of HIV/AIDS on international peace and security. The resolution stressed that HIV/AIDS, if left unchecked, can pose great risks to global security and stability, and in the most severe instances can contribute to state breakdown. It also noted that violence and instability play a significant role in exacerbating the pandemic and spreading the disease. Resolution 1308 mandated the Secretary-General and the UN's Department of Peacekeeping Operations (DPKO) to take relevant steps to raise awareness and provide training to peacekeeping personnel on HIV prevention.

Since the adoption of Resolution 1308, over 186 reports of the Secretary-General to the Security Council have cited HIV/AIDS-related concerns. DPKO has sought to train its peacekeepers to raise awareness of the disease and has made it a priority to curb the transmission of HIV among peacekeepers and host communities. To do so, DPKO established pre-deployment training, induction training on arrival, and continuing education for peacekeepers. It has also integrated HIV prevention and awareness into its peacekeeping missions, with HIV/AIDS units in larger missions and focal points in smaller peacekeeping and political missions.

In 2011 DPKO and the Joint UN Programme on HIV/AIDS (UNAIDS) released a report reviewing progress in implementing Resolution 1308. *On the Front Line* assesses progress since 2005, the last time a review of this type was conducted.[1] During this period, HIV induction training increased from 11 to 55 percent, an especially significant increase given an overall increase in the number of peacekeeping troops. Voluntary confidential counseling and testing (VCCT) services also increased significantly, with the number of personnel requesting these services increasing from 1,830 in 2005 to over 14,000 by the end of 2010. Moreover, the number of sites at which VCCT is available increased from two to thirteen over the same period. DPKO has also prioritized the training of HIV peer educators, with 1,500 trained in 2010. In addition, many current troop-contributing countries provide mandatory HIV testing policies for their uniformed personnel before or after deployment.

However, the report also notes that major challenges remain in effectively implementing Resolution 1308, including low funding for HIV/AIDS programs and the need for a greater focus on prevention. Continued stigma around the disease may also discourage individuals from educating themselves and being tested. The report also acknowledges that the increase in induction training has been inconsistent across missions.

In June 2011 the Security Council met to discuss HIV/AIDS for only the second time, and unanimously adopted Resolution 1983. The resolution welcomed efforts by DPKO and other actors to strengthen HIV awareness and prevention and noted the important role of peace operations in providing a holistic response. Shortly thereafter, the UN General Assembly adopted a political declaration on HIV/AIDS that stressed the critical role of mission leadership in prevention, treatment, and care.

DPKO's efforts to integrate HIV prevention and awareness into peacekeeping operations have helped to mitigate the risks posed by the spread of the virus. However, the prevalence of HIV and AIDS worldwide still remains a concern to global stability and security, particularly in vulnerable postconflict environments.

Note: 1. The report is available at http://www.unaids.org/en/media/unaids/contentassets/documents/document/2011/20110519_OnTheFrontLine.pdf.

---

operation relating to fraud within the Kosovo police, which resulted in the arrest of six individuals, including Kosovo police officers. EULEX has also played an active role in monitoring, mentoring, and advising local customs officials, police officers, judges, prosecutors, and investigators.

Since his appointment in October 2010, EULEX head Xavier Bout de Marnhac has focused on expanding the mission's footprint in northern Kosovo by increasing contacts with local authorities and revamping efforts to combat criminal institutions in the area with support from KFOR. This strategy produced a major EULEX special forces operation, launched in February 2011, that resulted in the arrest of several individuals associated with smuggling and other criminal activities.[3] EULEX has also continued to support the reenactment of the multiethnic courthouse in Mitrovica, but has pushed to resolve the issue within the framework of the EU-sponsored dialogue.[4] Kosovo continues to criticize EULEX for its failure to fully implement its mandate in the north.

EULEX's response to the flare-ups in northern Kosovo involved coordinating activities with KFOR to maintain security, reinforcing its presence with special forces in the two disputed boundary areas, and increasing EULEX police patrols in the north. EULEX also supported the restoration of full customs controls throughout the territory. EULEX prosecutors also launched a criminal investigation into the July death of the Albanian police officer mentioned earlier and other criminal incidents. These investigations triggered a EULEX police action on 30 August in which several suspects were indicted.

On 5 August, only a few days after the start of the border crisis, an e-mail communication by the EULEX deputy head was made public, indicating a plan to begin downsizing EULEX by October. However, no formal statements have been made at this juncture and the specifics remain uncertain.

KFOR has been steadily reducing its footprint. By mid-2011, the force had been curtailed to just over 6,000 soldiers, versus a high of 10,000 in 2010. KFOR has also initiated plans to devolve responsibilities to local authorities. In March 2011 it withdrew from the border between Kosovo and Macedonia, transferring its control to the Kosovo police. More recently, KFOR turned over control of the border with Montenegro in September. However, the administrative line with Serbia will remain under KFOR control. Plans to further downsize KFOR to 2,000 troops were announced in May 2011; however, the border crisis has delayed preparations.[5]

KFOR adopted a prominent leadership role during the crisis, including extensive mediation and consultation activities in an effort to maintain security and ensure freedom of movement. Further reinforcements from Germany and Austria totaling 700 troops arrived in early August to replace soldiers on the ground. After the customs stamp agreement was signed in September, NATO peacekeepers remained stationed at the two disputed border gates to prevent potential violence. Outgoing KFOR commander Erhard Buehler warned that the situation in northern Kosovo remains KFOR's most significant operational challenge on the ground.

OMIK has remained engaged in supporting institutional development and democracy building, promoting human and community rights, and providing substantial assistance in the improvement of security and public safety, especially in combating organized crime and supporting community policing. The mission has also taken on a reinforced monitoring role in the context of UNMIK's downsizing.

Conclusion

The resumption of the EU-sponsored dialogue in November is a positive development for Serbia-Kosovo relations; however, further international engagement may be needed to address the underlying conflict in the north. Despite the EU's postponement of a decision on its candidacy until 2012, Serbia's EU bid remains a powerful incentive, especially following the arrest of war crimes suspect Ratko Mladic and in the context of the 2012 elections. This also comes at a time when the EU is beginning a significant institutional overhaul of its presence in the Balkans, where the EU Special Representative is no longer "double hatted" with the International Civilian Office. This process has been delayed, however, largely as a result of EU divisions concerning the status of Kosovo and the stalemate in the north.

Belgrade has expressed a willingness to discuss northern Kosovo as part of the EU-sponsored dialogue, but Pristina has expressed opposition and favors an approach that unilaterally extends its presence in the north. Should the status quo remain, the potential for ethnic tensions and instability will likely disrupt plans for the continued downsizing of KFOR as part of a larger international withdrawal.

Notes

1. UN News Centre, "UN Urges Kosovo and Serbia to Show Restraint and Avoid Unilateral Actions," 15 September 2011, http://www.un.org/apps/news/story.asp?NewsID=39572&Cr=kosovo&Cr1=.

2. EULEX Kosovo, "EULEX Carries Out Arrest Near Zubin Potok Related to Organised Crime," 17 May 2011, http://www.eulex-kosovo.eu/en/pressreleases/0125.php.

3. "EULEX Arrests Three in Northern Kosovo," *Balkan Insight,* 15 February 2011, http://www.balkaninsight.com/en/article/eulex-arrests-three-in-northern-kosovo. See also EULEX, "EULEX Carries Out Arrest Near Zubin Potok Related to Organised Crime," press release 17 May 2011, http://www.eulex-kosovo.eu/en/pressreleases/0139.php.

4. See UNMIK press summary of 14 April 2011 at http://www.unmikonline.org/Pages/MediaMonitoring.aspx.

5. See J. Benitez, "NATO Puts Off Planned Troop Reduction in Kosovo Because of Upsurge in Violence," *Associated Press,* 30 August 2011.

3.5

Middle East

The political and security situation in the Middle East changed radically during 2011. The "Arab Spring" began in December 2010, with street protests in Tunisia that led to the overthrow of the Ben Ali regime. By the end of January, Egyptian protesters had ousted President Hosni Mubarak. Demonstrations broke out in other Arab countries during the spring and summer, including Jordan, Algeria, Yemen, Bahrain, Iraq, Morocco, Libya, and Syria. These demonstrations achieved further political changes, including dismissal of the Jordanian government and agreement by President Ali Abdullah Saleh of Yemen to step down from office. Violence escalated in some areas, notably in Libya and Syria, with the crisis in the latter prompting the deployment of the first Arab League peace operation since the 1970s.

The wave of change continues, so the extent to which it will transform the political landscape of the Middle East is not yet clear. Some important developments relating to the Arab-Israeli conflict are already evident, however. With the overthrow of Mubarak and the

revolt against Bashar al-Assad, Israel's relationships with its two largest neighbors are less predictable than they have been for decades. Instability and anti-Israeli sentiment are also evident in Jordan. To Israel's north, the situation in Lebanon remains tense, and in November an exchange of rocket fire between Israel and Lebanon, the first since 2009, underscored the fluid security environment. The Palestinian issue has shifted significantly: the leadership of the Palestine Liberation Organization (PLO) decided to pursue its case for statehood at the UN; meanwhile, on the ground, Palestinians began to employ new modes of political action. Israel is concerned by regional developments, but has offered no alternative proposal for progress toward regional peace and continues to approve construction of settlements in East Jerusalem and the West Bank.

Peace operations in the Middle East are being pushed to respond to rapidly changing circumstances and to interact with a broadening range of regional actors. The UN Interim Force in Lebanon (UNIFIL) and the UN Disengagement Observer Force (UNDOF) have faced new challenges, notably the mobilization of Palestinian refugees who marched toward Israel in May and June 2011 and were fired upon by Israeli soldiers. The internal security situation has deteriorated in both Syria and Lebanon, and UNIFIL troops were attacked three times inside Lebanon during the year.

Background

UNIFIL is the largest UN peace operation in the region. First established in 1978 by Security Council Resolutions 425 and 426, UNIFIL was tasked with confirming the withdrawal of Israeli forces and helping the government of

---

UN Interim Force in Lebanon (UNIFIL)

• Authorization and Start Date	19 March 1978 (UNSC Res. 425/426)
• Force Commander	Major-General Alberto Asarta Cuevas (Spain)
• Budget	$545.5 million (1 July 2011–30 June 2012)
• Strength as of 31 October 2011	Troops: 12,488 International Civilian Staff: 353 National Civilian Staff: 666

For detailed mission information see p. 252

For detailed mission information see p. 252

Map No. 4465.10   UNITED NATIONS
September 2011

Department of Field Support
Cartographic Section

Lebanon to reestablish control over the south. In May 2000, UNIFIL assisted in the withdrawal of Israeli forces behind a Blue Line identified by the UN.

The Lebanese government was unable to deploy forces in the south, and in 2004 the Security Council again demanded extension of Lebanese governmental authority. It also called for withdrawal of Syrian troops, accomplished in 2005, and the disbanding and disarmament of all Lebanese and non-Lebanese militias.

A Cambodian peacekeeper with the UN Interim Force in Lebanon (UNIFIL) leaves the site where a de-mining procedure was conducted, close to the village of Maroon al-Rass and the Blue Line demarcating the Israeli-Lebanese border, 23 May 2011.

War erupted in Lebanon in July 2006 when Hezbollah attacked an Israeli patrol and abducted two soldiers. Israel bombed Lebanon and invaded Lebanese territory; Hezbollah fired rockets into Israel. Over a thousand Lebanese and 161 Israelis were killed, and thousands were displaced.

The war ended with the adoption of Security Council Resolution 1701. This resolution established a new mandate for UNIFIL, adding to its original responsibilities the tasks of monitoring the cessation of hostilities, ensuring that no foreign forces would be present in Lebanon without government consent, assisting the Lebanese Armed Forces (LAF) in preserving an area free of unauthorized armed personnel between the Blue Line and the Litani River, and fully implementing the Taif Accords. Resolution 1701 allowed for the expansion of UNIFIL up to 15,000 troops and the inclusion of a maritime task force.

Key Developments

Lebanon's stability was threatened in early January 2011 by a political crisis relating to the Special Tribunal for Lebanon (STL).

Divisions among members of Saad Hariri's government of national unity relating to this issue had become increasingly pronounced during 2010, and on 12 January 2011 the government collapsed when eleven ministers from the March 8 coalition resigned. The infuriated March 14 leadership described this as a "coup."

The collapse of the Hariri government was followed by a five-month governmental vacuum, during which the prime minister–designate, Najib Mikati, struggled to form a new cabinet. The political atmosphere worsened. The March 14 coalition held a large political rally at which all speakers denounced the existence of arms outside the control of the state. Meanwhile, the March 8 leadership was vocal in its denunciation of the STL, which Hezbollah leader Hassan Nasrallah condemned as an "Israeli project." The Lebanese press speculated feverishly about when the STL would issue indictments, and what would happen when this occurred. Dialogue between the main political camps broke down.

Lebanese internal security deteriorated during this period. Seven Estonian cyclists were kidnapped in the Bekaa on 23 March and held captive for 113 days. Illegal construction accelerated, leading to violent clashes between offenders and state authorities. The uprising in Syria contributed to tensions. At the political level, the Syrian government accused March 14 members of parliament of supporting the Syrian opposition, and on the ground, Syrian nationals began to cross into north Lebanon. Lebanese leaders' responses to the crisis in Bahrain contributed to sectarian tensions.

UNIFIL's area of operations south of the Litani River remained largely calm for most of the year. However, in late November a rocket was fired from southern Lebanon, prompting the Israeli army to return fire. UNIFIL called for restraint from both parties and deployed additional troops in the area to discourage further incidents. The event was followed by further rocket fire in December, raising concern about the escalating security breaches in southern Lebanon.

Box 3.5 Libya

After forty-two years in power, Colonel Muammar Qaddafi's regime crumbled in August 2011, as Libyan rebel forces took control of Tripoli and sent the dictator and his remaining supporters into hiding. The UN General Assembly subsequently ceded Libya's seat to the National Transitional Council (NTC) in September, recognizing the body as the country's legitimate representative. Qaddafi was killed on 20 October during the Battle of Sirte, a month-long offensive waged by NTC forces against his final stronghold. Three days later, NTC chairman Mustafa Abdel Jalil pronounced the end of the uprising and declared Libya "liberated."

Antigovernment protests erupted in Benghazi in February 2011 and quickly spread to neighboring regions in the east. Decades of political repression, socioeconomic disparity, and entrenched patronage fueled opposition to the regime. Qaddafi's regime responded by harshly cracking down on protesters, triggering further dissidence across the country and the defection of a number of top officials. The international community widely condemned Qaddafi's use of force and on 26 February the Security Council unanimously passed Resolution 1970, demanding an immediate end to the violence, levying sanctions against the regime, and calling for the International Criminal Court to investigate the regime for war crimes. The following day, the opposition in Benghazi formed the NTC in an effort to coordinate resistance efforts.

On 17 March, the Security Council passed Resolution 1973, calling for member states to protect civilians by all means necessary, authorizing the use of force, and imposing a no-fly zone over Libya. NATO eventually assumed responsibility for conducting air strikes through Operation Unified Protector, with the United States, the United Kingdom, and France playing particularly central roles. The NATO campaign was initially opposed by a number of states. The African Union, led by South Africa, was especially critical, calling instead

NATO Operation Unified Protector

- Authorization Date — 17 March 2011 (UNSC Res. 1973)
- Start Date — 23 March 2011
- End Date — 31 October 2011
- Head of Mission — Vice Admiral Rinaldo Veri (Italy)
- Budget — $7 million (23 March 2011–30 September 2011)
- Strength as of 30 September 2011 — Troops: 8,000 Civilian Staff: 80

for a political solution to the conflict. Moreover, NATO faced internal divisions over the scale and intensity of operations, with only eight of its twenty-eight member states participating. By mid-April, however, NATO had ramped up its attacks, striking Qaddafi's compound in Tripoli among other high-profile targets. The mission's activities have highlighted the thin boundary between protection of civilians and peace enforcement in international peace operations.

In April the European Union announced the creation of EUFOR Libya, a military operation designed to support humanitarian relief in the country. The mission's mandate stated that deployment was predicated on a request for assistance from the UN's Office for the Coordination of Humanitarian Affairs (OCHA). However, because the assistance was never requested, the mission never deployed.

NTC forces made rapid gains throughout June and July, due in part to NATO military assistance and arms shipments from France. At the same time, the divide between supporters and critics of the NATO operation widened as the international community increasingly called for a political solution to the conflict, with a possible role for Qaddafi in negotiations. Such a settlement seemed unlikely, however, as NTC forces swiftly entered Tripoli on 22 August and captured the capital shortly thereafter. Following the

rebels' ultimate victory at the Battle of Sirte, the UN Security Council adopted Resolution 2016, ending authorization for Operation Unified Protector as of 31 October.

During the conflict, UN diplomatic and mediation efforts were carried out by Special Envoy Abdel-Elah al-Khatib, appointed by the Secretary-General to broker a political solution. In April, Ian Martin was appointed Special Adviser to the Secretary-General on postconflict planning in Libya and, with support from the UN system (in addition to the World Bank and the International Organization for Migration), developed a preassessment plan for UN engagement in the postconflict period. While the initial analysis included contingencies for both military and police, the NTC has since made clear that it would not be receptive to foreign military personnel on Libyan soil, though it is open to police assistance.[1] The NTC has also requested the UN's aid in planning for elections.

On 16 September, the Security Council unanimously adopted Resolution 2009, establishing the UN Support Mission in Libya (UNSMIL) for an initial period of three months and subsequently extended it for an additional three months. This political mission will assist the NTC in a number of efforts, including restoring the rule of law, drafting a new constitution, preparing for elections, and extending state authority.

Note: 1. "UN Shelves Libya Military Observer Plan," *CBC News,* 31 August, 2011, http://www.cbc.ca/news/world/story/2011/08/31/libya-united-nations-military.html.

Throughout 2011, UNIFIL enjoyed freedom of movement with the exception of some small-scale incidents in which local people blocked UNIFIL patrols. UNIFIL reports that the attitude of the local population toward the peace operation has remained largely positive.

UNIFIL was attacked three times outside its area of operations, however. On 27 May, an explosion caused by a remotely controlled roadside bomb hit a UNIFIL logistics convoy north of Saida. The attack injured six Italian peacekeepers, two of them seriously. A further attack on UNIFIL troops occurred on 26 July, when another roadside bomb exploded near Saida, injuring six French soldiers. A third roadside bomb injured five French peacekeepers in December. These direct attacks on UNIFIL troops were the first since January 2008. Responsibility for these attacks has not yet been established.

Attacks against the peacekeepers have contributed to concerns that major European countries will withdraw their troops from UNIFIL. Italy has already scaled down its presence, and President Nicolas Sarkozy of France wrote to Lebanese counterparts in August calling on Lebanon to "confront the dangers" facing the force, and warning that France "may reconsider its participation in UNIFIL" if it is attacked again. After the December attack, the French ambassador to Lebanon said that France would decide whether to reduce its troop contribution to UNIFIL after the completion of a UN strategy review of the mission, expected in early 2012. Italian foreign minister Franco Frattini also hinted in April that UNIFIL's mandate might need to be revised as a consequence of regional changes,[1] though this seems unlikely to occur.

UNIFIL and UNDOF were also affected by Palestinian demonstrations staged to mark the Nakba (the "catastrophe" of Palestinian displacement in 1948) and Naksa (the "setback" of Israel's victory in June 1967). Palestinians have traditionally commemorated these events, but their destabilizing effect was greater in 2011 than in previous years because Lebanese and Syrian authorities permitted demonstrators to access areas adjacent to the Blue Line and separation area.

In Lebanon, 8,000–10,000 people, mainly Palestinian refugees, held a ceremony at the southern village of Maroun ar-Ras on 15 May. After the event, about a thousand demonstrators marched toward the Blue Line. Some unearthed mines, threw stones and petrol bombs, and sought to scale the technical fence. The Israeli Defense Forces (IDF) responded with live fire. Seven demonstrators were killed and 111 were injured, making this the "most deadly incident in the Blue Line area" since the adoption of Resolution 1701.[2] The LAF then sought to disperse the demonstration. UNIFIL was present but not directly involved, as it had received a request from the LAF "to avoid close contact with the demonstrators so as not to potentially aggravate the situation."[3] UNIFIL's subsequent investigation found that both the demonstrators and the IDF had violated Resolution 1701. In Syria, parallel demonstrations took place. About 4,000 demonstrators gathered in the "family shouting place," opposite Majdal Shams, and about 300 passed through a minefield and crossed the cease-fire line and IDF technical fence. Four were killed by IDF fire and approximately forty others were wounded.

Further Palestinian demonstrations were planned for Naksa Day on 5 June. In preparation for this event, the UNDOF force commander met Israeli and Syrian authorities. UNIFIL convened a special tripartite meeting and held separate coordination meetings with both the LAF and the IDF. UN political and peacekeeping operations established special communication networks. In Lebanon, the planned Naksa demonstration was called off because the LAF decided to deny demonstrators access to the area south of the Litani. Demonstrations did occur, however, on 5 June in Syria. This time, up to twenty-three people were killed and many more were wounded. UNDOF monitored developments and the force commander engaged with IDF and Syrian authorities on the ground in an effort to de-escalate tensions.

Political and Regional Dynamics

Lebanon remains highly vulnerable to crisis provoked by events elsewhere in the region, although its domestic political atmosphere has calmed slightly since Najib Mikati unveiled his cabinet in mid-June 2011. The cabinet is dominated by the March 8 coalition, and although Hezbollah has been assigned only two ministerial portfolios, the party clearly plays a major role in policy formation. Polarization between the main political camps has not decreased, though the Mikati government has been able to make progress in several practical areas, notably in relation to the electricity crisis. However, the government only narrowly averted a crisis in November when Mikati announced that Lebanon would pay its share of the costs for the STL out of the budget for the prime minister's office. In the absence of action by Lebanese authorities to act on the tribunal's indictment, the STL may move to try the four indicted members of Hezbollah in absentia.

The crisis in Syria poses a grave threat to Lebanon's security and stability. Outgoing UN Special Coordinator Michael Williams warned in September 2011 that Lebanon must "prepare for the storm" hailing from Syria. Williams highlighted several threats, including the risk that Syrian Sunnis might turn against Alawites or Christians in Syria: "That could have consequences in Lebanon." Williams also identified the economic impacts of the crisis in Syria and the possibility of increased refugee flows as potential threats to Lebanon.[4]

Lebanese political actors of all stripes are aware of the potential impact of change in Syria on the balance of political and military power inside Lebanon. March 8 parties would lose an important political ally if Assad were to be removed from power. In November the government voted against the Arab League suspension of Syria and "disassociated" itself from sanctions imposed against the regime. Hezbollah could also lose its logistics route through Syria and therefore be unable to transport military hardware from Iran. Although Hezbollah already possesses a substantial arsenal inside Lebanon, resupply in the event of conflict with Israel may become more difficult. In December Hezbollah's leader made a rare public statement in support of the Assad regime. How March 8 and particularly Hezbollah would respond to further change in Syria is far from clear.

The March 14 response to the Syria crisis was muted during the summer of 2011. The leadership of the "new opposition" was abroad, and Syrian accusations that March 14 members of parliament were supporting the anti-Assad uprising may have contributed to the coalition's nervousness. In early October, March 14 leaders voiced strong criticism of Syrian incursions into Lebanon, which Kataeb party leader Amin Gemayel described as "very dangerous" and "an attack on Lebanese sovereignty."

In December, in the face of growing armed resistance and international pressure, Syria signed an agreement to allow Arab League observers into the country to monitor the implementation of a regional peace agreement. The agreement seeks to bring an end to the crisis, which, according to UN estimates, had killed over five thousand people by December. Approximately 50 Arab League monitors entered the country on 26 December as violence continued. Activists argued that the Syrian government limited the observers' movements, and in the six days between the start of the mission and the end of 2011 more than 150 people were killed in the continued crack down. The Arab League responded by arguing that the operation had achieved important objectives including the agreement to release thousands of political prisoners and the withdrawal of military tanks from cities. However, as 2011 came to a close the Arab Parliament, an advisory body independent of the Arab League, called for the withdrawal of the observers, arguing that the mission was providing cover for the continued violence perpetrated by the Syrian government. At the time of writing, the mission's findings were expected to be released in early January.

Israeli political actors are also awaiting the outcome of the uprising in Syria with anxiety. Despite its hostile rhetoric, the Assad regime had maintained stability in the Golan for many years. This stability has already faded. If the Assad regime were to be removed from power, Israel could face more forceful challenges to its occupation of the Golan. Israeli actors are also concerned about the possible impact of change in Syria on the stability of Lebanon.

UNIFIL's relationship with the Lebanese authorities has not deteriorated since the formation of the Mikati government. The government affirmed its commitment to Resolution 1701 in its 7 July ministerial statement, and on 16 July Mikati visited UNIFIL headquarters, where he expressed support for the peace operation. UNIFIL has made progress in addressing technical issues, both bilaterally and within the tripartite forum, and notes that technical cooperation between the parties has recovered from the crisis caused by the LAF-IDF clash of August 2010.

Further substantial progress toward implementation of Resolution 1701 looks almost impossible in the current political climate, however. The resolution calls for "disarmament of all armed groups in Lebanon, so that . . . there will be no weapons or authority in Lebanon other than that of the Lebanese State." It is hard to imagine the current Lebanese government taking steps to implement this provision. While the government of Israel believes that Hezbollah is building its arsenal, it has failed to respect the Blue Line (as called for in Resolution 1701), for example, by ending air violations. In the long run, UNIFIL's credibility may be eroded if no further progress is made toward implementing outstanding provisions of 1701.

The Israeli-Palestinian impasse is another destabilizing factor, both within the occupied territory and in countries hosting Palestinian refugees. Palestinians around the region have begun to interact with each other more intensively, inspired by the Arab Spring, through use of social media and Internet-based telecommunications. This has facilitated dialogue across borders, making coordinated political mobilization easier. The events of May and June 2011 highlighted the potential impact of mass mobilization of Palestinian refugees. Further demonstrations would pose substantial new challenges, both for the IDF and for peacekeeping operations in the region.

Progress toward a permanent cease-fire and long-term solution to the Israel-Lebanon conflict would probably require interim steps, which the outgoing UN Special Coordinator argues could include "undertakings by the Israelis for example [to] diminish or suspend" overflights, accompanied by "undertakings on behalf of the Lebanese state and Hezbollah that . . . would correspond with decommissioning arms." However, no agreement is likely unless Palestinians make progress toward statehood and there is change in Damascus: "Any breakthrough . . . has to take place in a regional context which is more propitious."[5]

UNDOF

The UN Disengagement Observer Force was established in May 1974 to supervise the cease-fire and Israel-Syria disengagement agreement. UNDOF's mandate, force structure, and composition did not change during 2011. However, the force was affected by two significant developments: first, the antigovernment protests in Syria that took place in some villages in the area of limitation; and

---

UN Disengagement Observer Force (UNDOF)

- Authorization and Start Date : 31 May 1974 (UNSC Res. 350)
- Force Commander : Major-General Natalio C. Ecarma (Philippines)
- Budget : $50.5 million (1 July 2011–30 June 2012)
- Strength as of 31 October 2011 : Troops: 1,040
  International Civilian Staff: 41
  National Civilian Staff: 103

For detailed mission information see p. 235

second, the Palestinian protests that led to breaches of the cease-fire line (as described earlier).

UNDOF has faced new restrictions since April 2011, when the Syrian authorities denied the Golan observer group access to several villages, "ostensibly to ensure the safety and security of the military observers."[6] In response to new challenges, UNDOF has raised its alert status, affecting the readiness and availability of troops, and has increased patrols in the separation area. UNDOF has also established a new, permanently occupied position and taken measures to improve force protection, including fortification of UN positions. UNDOF has also begun crowd-control training to support self-defense of UNDOF soldiers and installations.

On 30 June the Security Council renewed UNDOF's mandate and called on the Secretary-General to provide an assessment and recommendations regarding the operational capacity of UNDOF to ensure that the peace operation is best configured to fulfill its mandated tasks. The assessment found that the mission was appropriately configured for its mandate and did not require changes, though it did find some areas where adjustments would strengthen UNDOF's capacity.

UNTSO

The UN Truce Supervision Organization (UNTSO) was established in 1948 to monitor observance of cease-fires negotiated between Israel and its neighbors. UNTSO provides observers and logistical and financial support to UNIFIL and UNDOF, as well as a small observer group in Egypt at the request of its government. UNTSO did not undergo any formal changes to its mandate or authorized strength during 2011, nor did it suffer casualties or injuries. Operations by the Golan observer group were affected by the demonstrations on Nakba and Naksa Days, with more personnel needed at some duty stations and observing positions, and at UNTSO headquarters. The UNTSO's situation center was also activated to monitor the situation.

UN Truce Supervision Organization (UNTSO)

- Authorization and Start Date — 29 May 1948 (UNSC Res. 50)
- Chief of Staff — Major-General Juha Kilpia (Finland)
- Budget — $69.7 million (1 January 2012–31 December 2013)
- Strength as of 31 October 2011 — Military Observers: 150; International Civilian Staff: 101; National Civilian Staff: 132

For detailed mission information see p. 322

EU Border Assistance Mission at Rafah (EUBAM Rafah)

- Authorization Date — 5 November 2005 (Agreement on Movement and Access); 12 December 2005 (EU Council Joint Action 2005/889/CFSP)
- Start Date — 30 November 2005
- Head of Mission — Colonel Alain Faugeras (France)
- Budget — $2 million (1 October 2010–30 September 2011)
- Strength as of 30 September 2011 — Civilian Police: 5; Civilian Staff: 8

EU Coordinating Office for Palestinian Police Support (EUPOL COPPS)

- Authorization Date — 14 November 2005 (EU Council Joint Action 2005/797/CFSP)
- Start Date — January 2006
- Head of Mission — Henrik Malmquist (Sweden)
- Budget — $11 million (1 October 2010–30 September 2011)
- Strength as of 30 September 2011 — Civilian Police: 17; Civilian Staff: 32

EUBAM Rafah

The EU Border Assistance Mission at Rafah (EUBAM Rafah) was established in 2005 to help implement the Israeli-Palestinian Agreement on Movement and Access by providing a third-party presence at the Rafah crossing point. When Hamas forces took control of

Temporary International Presence in Hebron (TIPH)

- Authorization Date   17 January 1997 (Protocol Concerning the Redeployment in Hebron); 21 January 1997 (Agreement on the Temporary International Presence in Hebron)
- Start Date   February 1997
- Head of Mission   Brigadier-General Einar Johnsen (Norway)
- Strength as of 30 September 2011   Civilian Police: 28   Civilian Staff: 39

Multinational Force and Observers in Sinai (MFO Sinai)

- Authorization Date   3 August 1981 (Protocol to the Treaty of Peace)
- Start Date   April 1982
- Head of Mission   Ambassador David M. Satterfield (United States)
- Force Commander   Major-General Warren J. Whiting (New Zealand)
- Budget $78.3 million (1 October 2010–30 September 2011)
- Strength as of 30 September 2011   Military Observers: 1,656   Civilian Staff: 60

NATO Training Mission in Iraq (NTM-I)

- Authorization Date   8 June 2004 (UNSC Res. 1546); 30 July 2004 (establishment of mission); 16 December 2004 (modification into full-fledged training mission)
- Start Date   August 2004
- Force Commander   Lieutenant-General Michael Ferriter (United States)
- Strength as of 30 September 2011   Troops: 170

Gaza in June 2007, EUBAM suspended its operations. The Council of the EU has continued to extend the mission's mandate.

The EU welcomed the decision by Egyptian authorities to open the Rafah crossing on 28 May 2011. However, the Egyptian decision did not directly affect the overall situation of the EUBAM. As a third-party mission, EUBAM Rafah must be invited by Israel and the Palestinian Authority in order to be reactivated, and so far neither party has made such a request. The EU is nonetheless currently assessing the implications of the opening of the Rafah crossing point on a permanent basis, and following closely the implementation of the Palestinian reconciliation agreement in this regard. The mission has a redeployment plan to increase its strength should conditions allow.

EUPOL COPPS

The EU Coordinating Office for Palestinian Police Support (EUPOL COPPS) is a European Common Security and Defense Policy mission based in the West Bank. The mission assists the Palestinian Authority in building Palestinian policing and criminal justice institutions and increasing the safety and security of the Palestinian population.

EUPOL COPPS aims to ensure that the Palestinian Civil Police have sufficient capacity to sustain an efficient, transparent, and accountable policing organization within a sound legal framework. EUPOL COPPS promotes "civilian police primacy," meaning that the civilian police should have ultimate charge over policing, and that civilian control of security forces should be guaranteed. EUPOL COPPS also assists the Palestinian Authority in building professional capacity within judicial institutions, enacting modern legislation, and facilitating reform.

TIPH

Established by Israeli-Palestinian agreement in 1994, the Temporary International Presence in Hebron (TIPH) is mandated to provide security for Hebron residents and promote stability through monitoring, reporting, and assistance. TIPH is coordinated by Norway and staffed by personnel from Denmark, Italy, Norway, Sweden, Switzerland, and Turkey. There have been no changes to TIPH's mandate since December 2010.

MFO Sinai

The Multinational Force and Observers in Sinai (MFO Sinai) was established in 1981 following withdrawal of the UN Emergency Force II and the conclusion of the Israeli-Egyptian peace treaty. The MFO supervises implementation of security provisions of this treaty. On 1 September 2005, the MFO took on responsibility for monitoring the deployment of guards along the Egyptian side of the Egypt-Gaza border.

There have been no changes to the MFO's mandate in 2011. The overthrow of the Mubarak regime in January led to disruption of supplies in Egypt, which presented the MFO with logistical challenges. The security situation in the Sinai has deteriorated significantly since January, requiring the MFO to implement movement controls and upgrade force protection at its main camps and remote sites. A terrorist attack took place across the Egypt-Israel border in August 2011, leading to temporary suspension of MFO verification missions in the area.

NTM-I

The NATO Training Mission in Iraq (NTM-I) was established in 2004 at the request of the Iraqi interim government, under the provisions of UN Security Council Resolution 1546. In December, the NATO Secretary-General announced that despite intense negotiations, it was not possible to extend NTM-I's mandate in Iraq and that the mission would close by the end of 2011. The NTM-I operated under the political control of NATO's North Atlantic Council. The mission sought to help support Iraq in developing a credible and self-sustaining security sector. During the period of its operations, the NTM-I trained over 5,200 Iraqi officers and noncommissioned officers and over 9,000 Iraqi police.

Notes

1. "The role that Syria has played and will continue to play with Hezbollah has removed one—I repeat, 'one'—of the important raisons d'être of the UNIFIL mission. In an apparent paradox, if Hezbollah feels weakened by the absence of the strength provided by Syrian 'cover,' weaponry and 'guardianship,' it could become more aggressive. It could get out of control. And if that happens, UNIFIL's mandate will need to be changed. If UNIFIL is no longer useful, let's remove it. If it does have a use, its mandate needs to be up-dated to keep pace with a crisis whose endgame is not yet clear. . . . UNIFIL has played its role of settling the crisis well since 2006. It could be an excellent deterrent in the face of a new crisis in the region. But that's not an easy decision, nor one that can be taken for granted. Certainly not on the basis of resolution 1701." Interview with Foreign Minister Franco Frattini on the Syrian crisis and UNIFIL, *Il Foglio,* Rome, 28 April 2011; translation available at the website of the Italian Ministry of Foreign Affairs, http://www.esteri.it.

2. United Nations, *Sixteenth Report of the Secretary-General on the Implementation of Security Council Resolution 1701 (2006),* UN Doc. S/2011/406, 1 July 2011, para. 3.

3. Ibid., para. 10.

4. "Interview: UN Envoy Tells Lebanon: Prepare for Storm from Syria," *Daily Star,* 12 September 2011.

5. Interview with UN Special Coordinator for Lebanon Michael Williams, "Era of One-Man Rule over in Arab World—UN Envoy," *Reuters,* 29 September 2011.

6. United Nations, *Report of the Secretary-General on the United Nations Disengagement Observer Force for the Period from 1 January to 30 June 2011,* UN Doc. S/2011/359, 13 June 2011.

Solomon Islands

Increased stability in the Solomon Islands in 2011 has paved the way for greater focus on national capacity development and institutional strengthening. It has also prompted discussion on the eventual drawdown and transition of the Regional Assistance Mission in the Solomon Islands (RAMSI). RAMSI underwent a turnover in leadership during 2011, with Special Coordinator Graeme Wilson handing over responsibility to Nicholas Coppel in April and Paul Osborne joining the mission as the new police commander for the Participating Police Force (PPF) in June.

Background

RAMSI was established in 2003 by the Pacific Islands Forum in response to a five-year conflict between the Malatians and the Guale ethnic groups in the Solomon Islands. The conflict had eroded law and order and given way to rampant corruption, intimidation, and violence. The Solomon Island government was unable to function effectively and incapable of delivering basic services. In RAMSI's earliest days, the mission focused on security and stabilization, contributing to the surrender of armed criminal gangs supported by both the Malatians and the Guale.

The 2007 election of Manasseh Sogavare ushered in a period of tense relations between the Solomon Island government and RAMSI. The Sogavare government openly questioned the intentions of the RAMSI contingent and threatened to oust the mission. A 2007 vote of no confidence and the subsequent election of Derek Sikua helped to strengthen relations and demonstrated the broader support among Solomon Islanders for RAMSI's work. Elections in 2010 brought former foreign minister Danny Philip to power with a narrow majority.

As security and stability have improved and the Solomon Islands moves further away from crisis, the mission has turned its attention to long-term capacity building and institution strengthening. The 2009 partnership framework between the Solomon Island government and RAMSI identified three pillars of the mission's work: law and justice, economic governance and growth, and machinery of government. The framework established the overall goals for RAMSI, with specific targets and timelines for achievement, intended to facilitate a smooth transfer of activities to national actors in tandem with capacity building and institutional strengthening.

Regional Assistance Mission in the Solomon Islands (RAMSI)

- Authorization Date   23 October 2000
  (Pacific Islands Forum Communiqué)
- Start Date   July 2003
- Head of Mission   Nicholas Coppel (Australia)
- Force Commander   Lieutenant-Colonel Campbell Smith (Australia)
- Budget $42.5 million
  (1 October 2010–30 September 2011)
- Strength as of   Civilian Police: 250
  30 September 2011

Key Developments

In 2011 RAMSI entered into a series of open discussions on its future role in the Solomon Islands and its eventual drawdown. The talks

Box 3.6 Regional Organizations: ASEAN and the CSTO

Regional organizations have long been identified as important actors in peacekeeping and conflict resolution. The African Union, European Union, and the Organization for Security and Cooperation in Europe (OSCE), among others, all play critical roles in regional stability. In 2011, two regional organizations, the Collective Security Treaty Organization (CSTO) and the Association of Southeast Asian Nations (ASEAN), took important though still untested steps forward in their efforts to respond to regional conflict.

In mid-2010, widespread protests erupted into large-scale violence in Kyrgyzstan, resulting in over seventy-five deaths and the resignation of the president. During the violence, Kyrgyzstan requested intervention from the CSTO; however, the organization stated that the unrest was an internal matter and limited its support to humanitarian assistance. The events pointed to weakness in the CSTO's ability to provide security guarantees within the region.

Though CSTO members had discussed creating a collective peacekeeping force for several years, these efforts gained momentum in late 2010, at least partially due to the failure to act during the violence in Kyrgyzstan. In April 2011, the CSTO formed a collective peacekeeping force with approximately 4,200 peacekeepers. This force is complemented by an existing 17,000-strong CSTO rapid reaction force. The peacekeepers have yet to deploy, but the CSTO has agreed that they may be deployed within its member states and globally under the authorization of the UN Security Council. Further amendments to the CSTO's charter are anticipated, including efforts to develop the organization as the primary peacekeeping force in Central Asia.

In Southeast Asia, tensions flared along the border between Cambodia and Thailand in 2011, reigniting a long-standing territorial dispute between the two countries over the Preah Vihear temple. In 1962 the International Court of Justice (ICJ) awarded the temple to Cambodia, but both countries claim the territory around the temple. The dispute escalated in 2008 when Cambodia applied for and successfully registered the temple as a World Heritage site under the UN Educational, Scientific, and Cultural Organization (UNESCO). Hostilities resumed in 2011, with the resulting exchange of fire killing eight people and displacing thousands.

In response, Indonesia, acting in its capacity as the 2011 chair of ASEAN, invited ASEAN foreign ministers to meet informally on the conflict. It also offered to provide observers to monitor the cease-fire. When negotiations stalled, Cambodia brought the matter back to the ICJ, which ruled that troops from both countries should withdraw to allow Indonesian observers to monitor the border. Though Thailand initially rejected the decision of the Court, both countries agreed in September to comply with its decision.

The observers have yet to deploy and when they do, they will be deployed bilaterally by Indonesia, likely with a limited mandate. Still, this represents an important advancement in ASEAN's engagement in conflicts between its member states, demonstrating an increased willingness under the Indonesian chair to take an active role in member conflicts. However, Cambodia assumed the chairmanship in 2012, all but guaranteeing a substantially different role for ASEAN in this conflict.

included community leaders and chiefs, church leaders, students, teachers, and public servants who met to reflect on RAMSI's past achievements and share views on the future of the mission. During these discussions RAMSI stressed that any transition would occur within the parameters of the partnership framework and would take place in close consultation with the Solomon Island government.

RAMSI is currently funded through 2013, but stakeholders emphasize that any drawdown or withdrawal will occur gradually and that the mission will exist in some form for a number of years to come. RAMSI-contributing countries are already adapting their support in light of increasing stability in the Solomon Islands. Australia, the main contributor to RAMSI, has reduced the size of its contingent, many of whom are currently deployed as reservists.[1] New Zealand has also emphasized the importance of a greater focus on the shift from security to development.[2]

A key precondition for a smooth transition process will be strengthened capacity of the Royal Solomon Islands Police Force (RSIPF). RAMSI has therefore given priority to training and mentoring the police, with expectations of long-term support.[3] In addition, RAMSI will increasingly focus on handing over policing tasks to the RSIPF. In this vein, it is envisioned that over the next two years RAMSI will gradually withdraw from the thirteen police posts where it maintains a presence in order to allow the RSIPF to take a leadership role. This transition began in August 2011 in Buala, Isabel province, where RAMSI PPF officers began to gradually scale down their operational presence and dedicate greater attention to mentoring. This was followed by a handover in October in Isuna, where the RSIPF, in response, pledged to increase its own policing services.

The transition is also predicated on the expanded presence of police officers throughout the Solomon Islands. To facilitate officer relocation and ensure that they have adequate housing in their new stations, in 2011 RAMSI initiated a project, funded by Australia and New Zealand, to build police houses throughout the country. RAMSI's Special Coordinator noted that the housing project plays an important role in police recruitment, heightening the image of the RSIPF as an "employer of choice."[4]

The 2010 edition of the independent annual People's Survey, released in April 2011, showed continued support for RAMSI's work in the Solomon Islands, with 84 percent of respondents supporting the mission as a whole and 76 percent supporting the military component.[5] The results also revealed continued concern about a return to conflict, with nearly half of respondents believing that law and order would break down if RAMSI were to depart immediately. In addition, 40 percent of respondents said they trusted the police, with 28 percent dissenting. These results underscore wide support for a continued role for RAMSI, particularly in the context of handover of policing responsibilities to national authorities.

Conclusion

As RAMSI moves forward with its assistance through the three pillars of the partnership framework, continued close consultation with the Solomon Island government will be critical. This is particularly important as discussions increasingly focus on transition and RAMSI's future role in the Solomon Islands.

Notes

1. Sean Dorney, "RAMSI in 'Transition' but No Word on Exit," *Australia Network News,* 12 July 2011, http://australianetworknews.com/stories/201107/3268533.htm?desktop.

2. "New Zealand Pushes for RAMSI to Shift to Development Work," *Solomon Island Times,* 16 June 2011, http://www.solomontimes.com/news.aspx?nwID=6199.

3. Stephen Smith, Australian minister of defense, interview with Dorothy Wickham and Koroi Hawkins, *One Television,* Solomon Islands, 13 July 2011, http://www.minister.defence.gov.au/2011/07/13/minister-for-defence-interview-with-dorothy-wickham-and-koroi-hawkins-one-television-solomon-islands/.

4. Thomas Perry, "More Police Houses Handed Over," RAMSI, 21 September 2011.

5. "People's Survey 2010," ANU Enterprise, April 2011.

3.7

Somalia

Somalia underwent enormous political and security change in 2011. Al-Shabaab's August announcement that it would retreat from Mogadishu brought hope that conditions in the capital city would improve. While security gains have been made, Al-Shabaab has scaled up asymmetric attacks in the city since ceding control. The militia has also threatened reprisal against Kenya, after that country's military entered Somalia in October to drive Al-Shabaab from its northern border. The efforts against Al-Shabaab were also bolstered by the November announcement that Ethiopia would send troops to Somalia for a short deployment.

A massive drought and poor harvests in 2011 resulted in a declaration of famine in June, and this acute humanitarian situation has expanded to cover nearly all of south-central Somalia. While a rapid increase in humanitarian assistance has improved conditions, progress remains fragile and the crisis has resulted in the displacement of hundreds of thousands of Somalis, both inside the country and into refugee camps in Kenya and Ethiopia.

At the same time, Somalia underwent important political developments. Somali political stakeholders agreed to extend the transitional period, which was set to end in 2011, until August 2012. While the timeline to complete the transitional period is ambitious, the agreement may be an important milestone for developing the critical long-term political structures needed in Somalia. However, the political and security gains of 2011 remain fragile. The humanitarian crisis and the continued threat from Al-Shabaab could reverse the year's progress.

Background

Somalia, the prototypical "failed state" and one of the most dangerous countries in the world, has struggled with political instability and insecurity for over two decades. In 1991, Somalia was confronted with clan-based violence after the collapse of Siad Barre's regime. A year later, drought in the region sparked a famine in Somalia that resulted in the death of over 300,000 people and the displacement of thousands more.

In 1992 the UN imposed an arms embargo, followed by the establishment of the first UN Operation in Somalia (UNOSOM I)

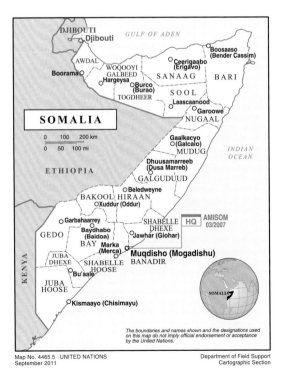

Map No. 4465.5   UNITED NATIONS
September 2011

Department of Field Support
Cartographic Section

AU Mission in Somalia (AMISOM)

• Authorization Date	21 February 2007 (UNSC Res. 1744)
• Start Date	March 2007
• Force Commander	Major-General Fred Mugisha (Uganda)
• Budget	$152 million (1 October 2010–30 September 2011)
• Strength as of 30 September 2011	Troops: 9,754 Police: 50 Civilian Staff: 13

to monitor a cease-fire in the Somali capital of Mogadishu and provide military support to the UN humanitarian relief operation. However, attacks on aid convoys and humanitarian staff continued, and aid efforts were slowed dramatically as 1.5 million people were declared to be at risk of starvation.

It was these circumstances that prompted US president George H. W. Bush to deploy the UN-authorized and US-led Unified Taskforce (UNITAF). The mission, deployed under Chapter VII of the UN Charter, comprised 37,000 soldiers authorized to use "all necessary means" to open up space for the delivery of humanitarian aid.

In 1993 the UN assumed control of the operation, under the new name UNOSOM II, with a wider statebuilding mandate. In October of that year an attempt by US forces to capture warlord Mohamed Farrah Aidid resulted in the infamous "Blackhawk down" incident and the death of eighteen US soldiers. In the aftermath, US and other Western military forces withdrew from Somalia; the effect of this incident on popular perceptions of peacekeeping, and of Somalia, continues to impact Western policymaking in the region.

The UN operation struggled following the withdrawal of Western forces and assets, and in 1995 the mission withdrew from the country and established the UN Political Office in Somalia (UNPOS) in Nairobi, to continue its monitoring and negotiation efforts.

Political Context

After approximately a dozen peacemaking attempts in Somalia, discussions led by the Inter-Governmental Authority on Development (IGAD) in 2004 resulted in the establishment of the Transitional Federal Charter and the Transitional Federal Government (TFG). Many Somalis viewed the TFG as a puppet of Ethiopia, and its legitimacy continues to be deeply challenged both inside Somalia and abroad.

After the establishment of the TFG, the president quickly requested the support of a peacekeeping mission, but the planned AU-sponsored IGAD mission was never deployed and the TFG—unable to control the capital on its own—was forced to meet in exile.

In 2006 the Islamic Courts Union (ICU), a coalition of moderate and extreme Islamist groups and exiled Somali parliamentarians, came to power in Mogadishu, initiating the first period of relative stability and security in over fifteen years. In December 2006 the Ethiopian military, concerned about the emergence of an Islamist state on its border, intervened with tacit support from the United States, ousting the ICU and reinstalling the TFG in the capital. In response, Al-Shabaab, a hard-line faction of the ICU, launched an insurgency. Large-scale fighting in 2007 and 2008 displaced over 1 million Somalis.

In 2007 the UN Security Council authorized the deployment of the AU Mission in Somalia (AMISOM). The mission was mandated to support the TFG, provide assistance to ongoing political dialogue, create secure space for the delivery of humanitarian assistance, and support the reform and reestablishment of a professional Somali security sector. Initial discussions cast AMISOM as a "bridging" mission, intended to pave the way for a UN deployment. Following serious disagreements at senior levels of the UN and among Security Council member states, it was determined that conditions on the ground were not appropriate for the deployment of blue helmets.

In the context of continued fighting in 2007, ICU members, diaspora leaders, and exiled Somalis joined together to form the Alliance for the Reliberation of Somalia (ARS). This group also included Al-Shabaab and other hard-line militant groups. Under what came to be known as the Djibouti process, ARS leaders and the TFG met in Djibouti in 2008 to hammer out an agreement that would precipitate the withdrawal of Ethiopian forces, the incorporation of ARS elements into the TFG, and the creation of an "international security presence."

The hard-line members of the ARS, including Al-Shabaab, rejected the agreement and intensified their efforts to oust the TFG and AMISOM forces, while the Djibouti process moved forward without them. In early 2009, after the withdrawal of Ethiopian forces and the selection of Sharif Sheikh Ahmed, the former head of the ICU, as president, there was a lull in the violence and some businesspeople began to return to Mogadishu to reclaim property and resume their affairs. However, Al-Shabaab resumed its insurgency with renewed vigor, and by June 2009 the TFG had declared a state of emergency. The militant group continues to control large swathes of south-central Somalia today.

Key Developments

Security Developments

In 2010 and 2011, AMISOM took a more forward-leaning approach, mounting offensive operations against Al-Shabaab throughout Mogadishu, an effort that was bolstered by the December 2010 UN Security Council authorization to increase troop levels. In August 2011, weary of continuing direct confrontations with the growing AMISOM force, Al-Shabaab declared that it was withdrawing from the capital to regroup. Since Al-Shabaab's withdrawal, the TFG and AU peacekeepers now control all of Mogadishu.

A Ugandan soldier serving with the AU Mission in Somalia (AMISOM) stands guard in a doorway inside Mogadishu Stadium, north of the Somali capital, on 7 August 2011, two days after the insurgent group Al-Shabaab withdrew the majority of its forces overnight. Transitional Federal Government (TFG) forces, backed by AMISOM troops, fought sporadic gun battles in the area as pockets of resistance erupted and "mopping-up operations" took place, according to an AMISOM commander on the ground.

UN Photo/Stuart Price

Al-Shabaab has also returned to a more asymmetric style of attacks, however. A number of suicide bombings in the capital in October 2011 have resulted in many civilian deaths, including a truck bomb that killed more than 100 people.

On 17 October, the government of Kenya launched military operations aimed at creating a large buffer area inside Somalia, between Al-Shabaab and the Kenyan border area. The Kenyan government initially stated that the operations were in response to a number of high-profile kidnappings, despite Al-Shabaab's denial of involvement in the abductions. However, the Kenyan government subsequently acknowledged that the operations had been planned further in advance and were in reaction to long-term security threats.[1]

The incursion is likely to draw Al-Shabaab forces into combat in the southwest of the country. Militants have also promised to mount attacks inside Kenya, adding a new—and wider—dimension to the Al-Shabaab threat. To date, the majority of violence has taken place in Somalia, with the notable exception of the 2010 suicide bombing in Uganda, the first bombing outside the country for which Al-Shabaab claimed responsibility. However, shortly after the Kenyan government launched the operation, Nairobi suffered several grenade attacks, carried out by a Kenyan member of Al-Shabaab.[2]

In addition, in late 2011 Ethiopia, responding to an IGAD request for support, agreed to provide assistance to the efforts of Kenya and the AU to oust Al-Shabaab. The form and scale of this support is yet to be determined, but it is expected that the deployment will be brief and that Ethiopian troops will remain outside AMISOM command. The decision followed media reports that Ethiopian troops entered Somalia in late November.

Separate from these operations, US officials confirmed in October that the US military is flying unarmed surveillance drones from a base in Ethiopia to monitor Al-Shabaab's activities in Somalia. The drones are part of a broader counterterrorism effort in the region aimed at militant groups with links to Al-Qaida.

Meanwhile, as the acute humanitarian situation continues, Al-Shabaab has hindered international efforts to provide aid to famine-affected people in two ways. First, severe insecurity throughout most of the famine-affected area, as well as an Al-Shabaab–declared ban on the World Food Programme and other aid organizations, has meant that humanitarians must negotiate access day by day, village by village, in order to operate. In November, Al-Shabaab looted the offices of a number of aid agencies and announced a ban on more humanitarian organizations in areas under its control, striking a further blow at relief efforts. Second, Al-Shabaab is considered a terrorist organization by the United States, which restricts the delivery of assistance funded by the US government or by any donors based in the United States that operate in areas controlled by the militants.

Political Developments

Continued infighting between President Sharif Sheikh Ahmed and the Transitional Federal Parliament, particularly the speaker of the parliament as well as a series of prime ministers, has stymied achievement of key transitional benchmarks, including the establishment of a Somali constitution and preparation for elections. The transitional process was slated to end in August 2011, but on 9 June the president and the speaker of the parliament, with the support of IGAD, agreed to extend the transitional period to August 2012 under the Kampala Accords.

The accords commit the TFG to a new "roadmap" for stabilization and development. In conjunction with UNPOS, the TFG has agreed to a set of priority benchmarks that must be met in the lead-up to an election in August 2012. This timeline is ambitious, especially because the benchmarks include activities that went unrealized during the first three years of the transitional period, and also because donor support for the effort has been tied to results that the TFG may struggle to achieve. Nonetheless, the first major milestone—the drafting of a new national security and stabilization plan—was completed in October and has been viewed as a successful, Somali-owned process with a greater chance of long-term success than its donor-driven predecessors.

The Kampala Accords also included a provision requiring the resignation of Prime Minister Mohamed Abdullahi Mohamed, who was widely respected as a reformer who could rise above the clan divisions that often dictate Somali politics. While his resignation was based on an agreement between the president and the speaker of the parliament to strengthen parliament's support for the accords and unify the TFG, it prompted large-scale protests in Somalia and throughout the diaspora community. There is hope, however, that the new prime minister, Abdiweli Mohamed Ali, a US-trained economist, will strengthen international support and confidence in the Somali political process.

Peace Operations

Since its deployment in 2007, AMISOM has pursued a three-phase approach to stabilizing south-central Somalia. The first phase involves stabilizing and establishing control over Mogadishu; while the force established control over the city in 2011, the recent trend of suicide attacks by Al-Shabaab suggests further challenges. In the second phase, the force is to expand southwest, toward Kismayo and Baidoa, though mission leadership has emphasized that AMISOM will need significant air and sea assets—including attack and utility helicopters—as well as strengthened logistical and engineering capacity in order to progress past the first phase. The third phase would entail consolidation and the full implementation of AMISOM's mandate.

In order for AMISOM forces to move out of Mogadishu, TFG security forces, including police and military, must be able to hold and maintain order in the capital. AMISOM, with European Union support, completed the training of 1,000 soldiers in January 2011, and a second cohort of 998 troops completed training at the end of October. The TFG and AMISOM are also currently seeking strong leaders from within the ranks of the newly trained troops, as well as from the TFG-allied militia groups operating inside Mogadishu, who can be trained as midlevel officers. Somali soldiers are now being registered in a biometric database in an effort to minimize corruption and help ensure that troops receive their salary.

Somali police have also made strides toward becoming a more professional force. AMISOM police provide operational training and capacity building for the Somali police force, roughly 500 of whom were trained in 2011. Still, there is a tremendous need for continued donor support to enhance individual troop and officer capacity, and to better equip the police for the difficult task of maintaining law and order in Mogadishu. The TFG also requires support to develop institutional processes and controls to manage its new security institutions.

AMISOM has struggled to find balance between difficult counterinsurgency in densely populated Mogadishu and the need to minimize civilian casualties. The more aggressive posture of the mission has come with increased accusations of indiscriminate killing of civilians. In 2011, with the assistance of the nonprofit organization Campaign for Innocent Victims in Conflict, AMISOM instituted a new indirect fire policy in an effort to reduce the likelihood of civilian casualties. The mission also instituted a policy of making "amends" with families and communities when its actions result in harm to people or property.

AMISOM itself has been the target of serious attacks, including an October attack on an AU military base that resulted in an undisclosed number of AMISOM troop fatalities.[3] Though the mission has sustained heavy casualties, troop-contributing countries—Uganda and Burundi—regard the operation and the containment of the threat posed by Al-Shabaab to be national priorities, and have sustained support in spite of the human and economic costs of continued involvement.

The UN Security Council first authorized the expansion of AMISOM troop levels—from 8,000 to 12,000 (still 8,000 fewer than the requested ceiling of 20,000)—in December 2010. But in October 2011 there were still just 9,700 troops deployed, though additional deployments, including from Djibouti and Sierra Leone,[4] are expected to bring the troop levels to 12,000 by early 2012.[5] The Somali prime minister has stated that these troops are urgently needed to support the extension of the state's presence to those areas vacated by Al-Shabaab.

Further, in December the Kenyan parliament approved a request from the AU to rehat Kenyan troops under AMISOM, contingent on approval from the UN Security Council to increase the mission's troop ceiling. The AU's Peace and Security Commissioner noted that including Kenya's forces in AMISOM would provide the mission with critical force enablers including helicopters and war ships,[6] which may provide the necessary support for the mission to move to its second phase.

The UN Support Office for AMISOM (UNSOA) is mandated to provide support and supplies to the overstretched mission, including logistical, engineering, medical, and transport support. UNPOS is also working to build AMISOM capacity through training in communications and public information. This support has allowed for significant improvements to AMISOM's capabilities in recent years, but the mission remains extremely under-resourced for the complex tasks it is mandated to perform. Gaps in information-gathering and analytical capacity still hamper the mission's ability to operate in this highly fluid and insecure environment.

The EU Training Mission in Somalia was established to provide assistance to the Somali security sector. Deployed in 2010, the mission's original twelve-month mandate was extended for an additional year in July 2011 to support the training of 2,000 Somali soldiers. The training takes place in Uganda and focuses on strengthening the TFG security forces. In addition to military assistance, the mission provides training on human rights, international humanitarian law, and protection of civilians.

Piracy continues to present a major threat off the Somali coast, and incidents continue to occur in spite of the international naval presence in the Gulf of Aden (see Box 3.7.1). The EU Naval Force (EU NAVFOR), also known as Operation Atalanta, is tasked primarily with deterring and preventing acts of piracy and armed robbery off the coast of Somalia, including protecting transports by the World Food Programme, AMISOM, and other vulnerable vessels. In 2010, EU NAVFOR's mandate was extended two years, until December 2012. In June 2011, Operation Atalanta escorted its 100th AMISOM vessel, ensuring the secure delivery of important humanitarian and security supplies.

Conclusion

In December 2011, Ban Ki-moon visited Mogadishu, the first trip by a UN Secretary-General to Somalia in nearly two decades, underscoring the tremendous change that took place in the country this year. The ambitious agenda set out in the roadmap for stabilization and development will require renewed efforts by Somali political stakeholders and international partners if the transitional period is to be brought to an end in 2012. Significant challenges remain: the TFG's legitimacy is still contested, and both the famine and the continued threat from Al-Shabaab could further destabilize the already tenuous security environment.

AMISOM's ability to support the TFG and stabilize Somalia will depend critically upon the availability of troop reinforcements and military assets. Without these resources, while it may be able to hold its positions in Mogadishu, AMISOM will likely face significant challenges in extending its presence beyond the capital.

Notes

1. Jeffrey Gettleman, "Kenyan Motives in Somalia Predate Recent Abductions," *New York Times,* 26 October 2011.
2. "Kenyans in First Al-Shabab Battle in Somalia," *BBC News,* 28 October 2011.
3. Josh Kron, "Militants Strike at Troops at Base in Somali Capital," *New York Times,* 29 October 1.
4. Josh Kron, "Somalia: Sierra Leone to Send Troops," *New York Times,* 3 November 2011. South Sudan has also offered to send troops.
5. Mohamed Ahmed and Richard Lough, "Suicide Bomber Hits Somali Capital, Dozens Killed in South," *Reuters,* 6 December 2011.
6. Peter Heinlein, "Regional Summit Urges Ethiopia to Send Troops to Somalia," *Voice of America,* 28 November 2011.

Box 3.7.1 Piracy off the Coast of Somalia

Piracy off the Somali coast continues to present a significant challenge to international security, prompting concerted effort from a diverse group of actors to counter the threat. Since 2008, over 1,900 individuals have been kidnapped from Somali coastal waters[1] and hundreds of millions of dollars have been paid in ransom, disrupting one of the world's key shipping routes. In 2011 alone there were twenty-six successful ship hijackings in Somalia, representing nearly 70 percent of the global total.[2] While the success rate of attacks off the Somali coast has decreased over the past several years, mainly due to the presence of naval vessels, the level of violence, sophistication, and frequency of attacks hit a record high in 2011.

International collaborative efforts through the Contact Group on Piracy off the Coast of Somalia (CGPCS) and the group Shared Awareness and Deconfliction (SHADE) to counter piracy continue. As a voluntary international forum, the CGPCS coordinates the responses of over seventy member states and several major international organizations, including on operational matters, legal issues, shipping self-awareness, and public information. In 2011 the CGPCS created a group to strengthen international efforts aimed at dismantling complex pirate financial networks—an area of increasing international attention. SHADE, a voluntary international military group, continued facilitating coordination between independently deployed navies in the Gulf of Aden and the Indian Ocean. In May, members agreed to further bolster communication mechanisms, strengthen operational cooperation, and enact regional capacity-building measures to increase the organization's efficacy.

NATO's Operation Ocean Shield and the EU's Operation Atalanta also maintained critical assistance and protection through their presence in the waterways. Operation Ocean Shield engaged in a number of counter-piracy operations, successfully freeing pirate-held ships and dismantling mother ships. The NATO operation also liaises with regional states, including Djibouti and Somalia, to promote anti-piracy efforts. Additionally, Operation Atalanta continued to provide assistance to the anti-piracy efforts of Somalia's Transitional Federal Government and the African Union's peacekeeping mission in Somalia through 2011.

During the course of the year, international attention also turned to bolstering onshore anti-piracy mechanisms, particularly in the judicial and security sectors. Although 1,046 individuals are currently being prosecuted or have faced prosecution for piracy in twenty countries,[3] more than 90 percent of captured pirates are immediately released due to judicial obstacles, including the absence of a Somali legal framework for prosecution. UN Security Council Resolutions 2015 (2011) and 1976 (2011) call for Somalia to strengthen its governance and rule of law structures to play a more substantial role in combating piracy. In the resolutions, the Council further reiterated its call for the adoption of a comprehensive set of counter-piracy laws and the construction of correctional facilities for convicted pirates. In addition, the Council also noted the need for specialized anti-piracy courts in Somalia and other states in the region. As a first step, Resolution 2015 requests the UN Secretary-General to provide further information on the technical and financial requirements needed to implement these courts.

Piracy in the Gulf of Aden and the Indian Ocean is inextricably linked to the crisis in Somalia, and many of the root causes, including political instability and poverty, persist. However, the challenge is not isolated to Somalia, and the threat of piracy in the Gulf of Guinea is an increasingly pressing international concern. Concerted international support and a multipronged approach that targets piracy offshore, supports the development of institutions and capacity onshore, and addresses root causes such as widespread poverty and high unemployment, will be critical for responding to international maritime piracy.

Notes: 1. United Nations, *Report of the Special Adviser to the Secretary-General on Legal Issues Related to Piracy off the Coast of Somalia,* S/2011/30, 25 January 2011.

2. International Maritime Bureau, Piracy Reporting Center, "Piracy News & Figures," http://www.icc-ccs.org/piracy-reporting-centre/piracy newsafigures.

3. Contact Group on Piracy off the Coast of Somalia, "WG2: Chairman's Conclusions from the 9th Meeting," fact sheet, 11–12 October 2011, http://www.thecgpcs.org/doc.do?action=doc.

Box 3.7.2 From Host Nation to Troop Contributor

As United Nations peacekeeping struggles with debates on troop reimbursement and divides between troop contributors and financial contributors, a growing number of troops and police are deploying from familiar places: countries that have previously hosted or currently host peace operations.

Former hosts to peacekeeping missions including Bosnia and Herzegovina, Cambodia, and El Salvador now provide troops and police to multilateral peace operations. Rwanda, former host to the UN Assistance Mission in Rwanda (UNAMIR), is currently ranked among the top ten UN military contributors globally, with Rwandan troops and police stationed in UN missions in Haiti, Liberia, Sudan, and South Sudan. With the support of the UN Development Programme (UNDP), Rwanda also runs one of the main peacekeeping training centers in Africa, helping to prepare current and future troop-contributing countries using lessons learned from both the UN and its own experiences.

Burundi also plays a critical role in peacekeeping in Africa. A former host to African Union and United Nations peacekeeping missions, Burundi is now one of the two main troop contributors to the

AU Mission in Somalia (AMISOM), and has deployed five battalions to the mission since 2007. Sierra Leone, previously host to a six-year UN peace operation, responded to the AU's September 2011 call for more AMISOM troops by signaling its intention to send a troop battalion to join Sierra Leonean police officers already serving with the mission.

Countries with current peacekeeping missions are also readying themselves for future contributions through training and capacity building exercises. The UN Integrated Mission in Timor-Leste (UNMIT) has trained the national army for potential deployment as military observers in peacekeeping operations. In July 2011, Timor-Leste Defense Force engineers also began training ahead of their integration with a Portuguese contingent serving the UN Interim Force in Lebanon (UNIFIL), which will mark the first international military contribution by Timor-Leste. In Liberia, security forces received training for potential peacekeeping duties in 2011 from both the UN Mission in Liberia (UNMIL) and the US African Command (AFRICOM), which assisted in a regional communications exercise.

Meanwhile, some countries have already begun participating in global operations even as missions continue within their national borders. The Democratic Republic of Congo (DRC), current host to the UN Organization Stabilization Mission in the DRC (MONUSCO), has a small number of police deployed to the UN Operation in Côte d'Ivoire (UNOCI), while Côte d'Ivoire has contributed over a hundred police to MONUSCO and UN missions in Haiti and Darfur.

Through proactive training, countries are increasingly emerging from robust peacekeeping missions with the ability and desire to contribute to global multilateral operations. Their own recent experiences of transition may also provide valuable lessons for peace operations and peace consolidation. Supporting these new and emerging troop and police contributors is especially important as many peace operations, including AMISOM, face chronic troop and police shortages. Further diversifying the group of contributing countries in peacekeeping missions also helps bolster the flexibility of these operations and strengthen their ability to deploy to crises around the world.

Timor-Leste

As 2011 came to a close, Timor-Leste began preparations for elections in 2012 in a largely calm and stable environment.

There is widespread expectation that 2012 will be the last year of the UN Integrated Mission in Timor-Leste (UNMIT). Now entering its sixth year of operations, the mission dedicated much of its focus in 2011 to the modalities for this transition.

A key milestone in this process was the resumption of policing responsibilities by the Timorese national police. While concerns about the capacity of the police remain, there has been no increase in crime rates since this handover took place in March. The handover was followed by the development of a joint transition plan between the mission and the government to guide UNMIT's transition. However, while Timor-Leste remained largely calm and stable in 2011, the timing and pace of the mission's withdrawal will depend heavily on the peaceful conduct of elections in 2012 and the security environment facing the new government.

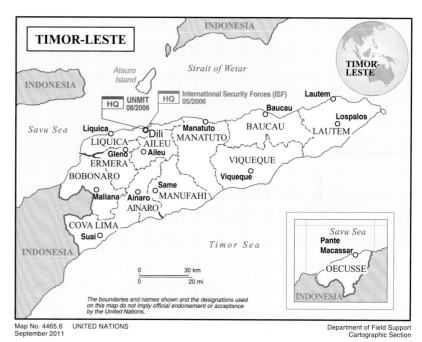

Map No. 4465.6   UNITED NATIONS
September 2011

Department of Field Support
Cartographic Section

Background

After the UN-organized 1999 referendum, in which the overwhelming majority of Timorese voted for independence from Indonesia, Indonesian troops and their Timorese proxies launched an aggressive campaign of violence that left approximately 1,400 Timorese dead and hundreds of thousands displaced. The emergency deployment of a UN-authorized Australian stabilization force paved the way for the establishment of the UN Transitional Administration in East Timor (UNTAET), which was mandated to support East Timor during its

transition to independence in 2002. A successor mission was established in 2002 and then replaced by the UN Office in Timor-Leste (UNOTIL) in 2005, a considerably smaller political mission mandated to support the development of state institutions.

Violence erupted shortly thereafter, prompted by long-standing grievances within the armed forces. In response to a call from the Timorese government for international assistance, the Australian-led International Security Forces (ISF) were deployed. The Security Council subsequently authorized UNMIT, a multidimensional peacekeeping mission with a broad mandate including support to government institutions, interim law enforcement and support to the Timorese police, assistance in conducting the 2007 elections, and

---

UN Integrated Mission in Timor-Leste (UNMIT)

- Authorization and Start Date   25 August 2006 (UNSC Res. 1704)
- SRSG   Ameerah Haq (Bangladesh)
- Police Commissioner   Luis Miguel Carrilho (Portugal)
- Budget $196.1 million (1 July 2011–30 June 2012)
- Strength as of 31 October 2011   Military Observers: 33
  Police: 1,203
  International Civilian Staff: 394
  National Civilian Staff: 883
  UN Volunteers: 206

For detailed mission information see p. 297

International Security Forces (ISF)

- Authorization Date   20 June 2006 (UNSC Res. 1690)
- Start Date   May 2006
- Force Commander   Colonel Luke Foster (Australia)
- Budget $184.6 million (1 July 2010–30 June 2011)
- Strength as of 30 September 2011   Troops: 460

To guide the transition process, a joint high-level committee on transition was established, comprising the president, the prime minister, relevant senior government officials, the army and police commanders, UNMIT's Special Representative of the Secretary-General (SRSG), as well as the senior UNMIT management team. Its first meeting was held in November 2010, at which the committee agreed to establish seven working groups on key focus areas to guide the transition: democratic governance; police and security sector; rule of law, justice, and human rights; socioeconomic development; mission support; training for national UN staff; and the impact of UNMIT's withdrawal on the Timorese economy. Thus, as UNMIT entered 2011, led by SRSG Ameerah Haq, its focus was on identifying, jointly with the government, the processes and modalities for its transition.

Key Developments

Elections and Political Developments

Elections in 2012 will follow those of 2007, which elected José Ramos-Horta as president and brought a coalition government to power led by Prime Minister Kay Rala Xanana Gusmão. As political parties and candidates began preparations for the 2012 elections, the political atmosphere was calm, with less friction seen between parties and opposing candidates compared to the heightened tension during the 2007 elections. A July 2011 meeting between political parties, national electoral management bodies, and civil society organizations stressed the importance of maintaining peace and stability during the electoral period. The government also unveiled its long-term development plan, further articulating its map for socioeconomic development in order to spur employment and investment.

UNMIT's logistical and technical support for the elections will be coordinated by the UN electoral support team and reinforced by additional UN volunteers throughout the period. The mission will also provide support to

support for human rights. In 2009, UNMIT developed a medium-term strategy that identified objectives, targets, and benchmarks across four priority areas of the mission's mandate: security and stability; rule of law, justice, and human rights; democratic governance; and socioeconomic development.

Timor-Leste has been largely calm since UNMIT's establishment, even in the face of a 2008 assassination attempt on the lives of the president and prime minister. National institutions have become increasingly capable of carrying out their respective functions, and stakeholders have largely managed to channel political disputes through democratic processes. It was in this environment that in 2010 UNMIT and the government of Timor-Leste turned to considerations of drawdown and eventual withdrawal of the mission.

Timor-Leste's technical electoral secretariat and its national electoral commission. UNMIT police will provide further security assistance throughout the electoral period. As the country moves closer to elections, the SRSG continues her good office role, meeting weekly with the Timorese leadership and monthly with a broader group of political actors, including civil society organizations and all political parties. While the political environment has thus far remained calm, some stakeholders, including business owners, remain concerned about the risk of renewed violence or conflict.[1]

The relationship between the government and UNMIT suffered a setback in May with the leak of an internal UN presentation that identified Prime Minister Gusmão as an obstacle to democratic governance. The prime minister quickly rejected the report and UNMIT rapidly issued two statements underscoring that the report did not reflect the official position of the mission and stressing the democratic nature of the prime minister's tenure.

UN Police Commissioner for Timor-Leste Luis Carrilho (left) gives a flag to Longuinhos Monteiro (right) of the Polícia Nacional de Timor-Leste (PNTL) during a ceremony in Dili, 7 March 2011, marking the UN Police's return of full control of Timor-Leste to the national force, more than four years after bloody clashes threatened to push the country into civil war.

Transition Planning

In September 2011 UNMIT and the government of Timor-Leste released a joint transition plan to provide a framework for the mission's assistance through the end of 2012. The plan, which is intended to be a living document, is guided by four assumptions: continued stability, the holding of national elections in line with international standards, the formation of a new government, and the protection of political space for the opposition. It identifies priority areas for assistance through 2012, objectives, and resource implications across each of the seven thematic focus areas, as well as an assessment of continued support beyond 2012. The plan also provides a matrix of mission activities, their expected completion dates, and handover arrangements if applicable. In addition, the plan identifies possible models for a UN presence after UNMIT withdraws. Throughout the planning process, the government and UNMIT have provided briefings to relevant stakeholders, including donors and civil society.

As part of the transition process, UNMIT is providing a comprehensive, three-phase training program for the mission's national staff members, focused on expanding their skills and preparing them for employment when the mission withdraws. Trainings are also extended to government ministries; requests so far have focused on language, computer, and administrative skills.

Police Handover

On 27 March 2011, UNMIT police formally handed over responsibilities to the Timor-Leste national police (Polícia Nacional de Timor-Leste [PNTL]), completing a process that began in May 2009. The handover occurred at the district level based on joint assessments of mutually agreed criteria between the government of Timor-Leste and UNMIT. As national authorities assumed control of each district, UNMIT police stayed on in monitoring and advising roles and stood ready to provide operational support if needed and requested. As districts were turned over, UNMIT police

Box 3.8 Mindanao, Philippines

Since 2004, the International Monitoring Team (IMT) has provided support to an intermittent and frequently stalled peace process between the government of the Philippines and the Moro Islamic Liberation Front (MILF) in Mindanao. Talks between the two groups have repeatedly fallen apart, most recently in 2008, with resulting violence killing 200 and displacing hundreds of thousands. When President Benigno Aquino III took office in June 2010, he announced that resolving the conflict in Mindanao would become a priority for his administration, giving new life to negotiations.

The 1996 peace agreement signed by the Moro National Liberation Front (MNLF) and the government of the Philippines established the Autonomous Region of Muslim Mindanao (ARMM). This agreement did not satisfy the demands of the Moro Islamic Liberation Front, which splintered from the MNLF in 1978 and continues to push for an autonomous substate with devolved control over major aspects of governance. After several failed attempts at negotiation between the government and the MILF, talks brokered by Malaysia resulted in both parties agreeing to establish the International Monitoring Team in 2004. Negotiations have since broken down, in 2006 and again in 2008, after which the IMT's mandate expired without renewal.

International Monitoring Team (IMT)

- Authorization Date: 22 June 2001 (Tripoli Peace Agreement)
- Start Date: October 2004
- Head of Mission: Major-General Mahdi Yusof (Malaysia)
- Strength as of 30 September 2011: Military Observers: 38

Hostilities continued until both parties agreed to a new round of peace negotiations in 2009, which led to the renewal of the IMT's mandate in 2010. The mandate was again renewed in February 2011 for twelve months.

The IMT comprises representatives from Malaysia, Brunei, Japan, and Libya and, as of 2011, the European Union and Norway. Indonesia is in the process of joining and Saudi Arabia is also expected to join, which would bring the team to a full strength of sixty personnel.[1]

Despite its small size, the IMT has played a critical role in monitoring the cease-fire between the government of the Philippines and the MILF and in investigating violations. In 2010 a civilian protection component was created within the IMT. Composed of nongovernmental organizations, this component is designed to ensure that both parties comply with their international obligations to protect civilians.

Peace negotiations, which were restarted in early 2011, have been delayed by the government's concern over the Malaysian facilitator, who was replaced in April. In mid-August the process halted again when the MILF announced that it would not accept the draft proposal prepared by the government because it excluded the creation of a substate with governance authority. The fragile peace process deteriorated further in October when renewed fighting between the MILF and government forces left nearly thirty dead and forced thousands to flee their homes. It also prompted the first government air strikes against the group since 2008.[2] Negotiations resumed in November and the IMT is investigating the clashes; however, the hostilities, the worst seen in recent years, have dashed popular support for a negotiated settlement with the MILF.

Notes: 1. International Crisis Group, "The Philippines: Back to the Table, Warily, in Mindanao," 24 March 2011, http://www.crisisgroup.org/en/regions/asia/south-east-asia/philippines/B119-the-philippines-back-to-the-table-warily-in-mindanao.aspx.
2. Jason Gutierrez, "First Air Strikes on Philippine Rebels Since 2008," *Agence France-Presse,* 24 October 2011.

dedicated an increasing focus to capacity building and institutional development.

Prior to the full handover, observers raised concern over the significant number of uncertified officers in the last remaining districts. This was a particularly critical issue for Dili, where many officers had been transferred to allow police resumption to proceed in other districts. In late 2010 the Secretary for State and Security decided to certify 199 PNTL officers facing criminal or disciplinary issues, of which 52 faced serious charges, though the certification would not exempt officers from criminal or disciplinary proceedings. A special investigation team, supported by two UNMIT police officers, reviewed the cases and determined that 121 of the 199 officers would face criminal or disciplinary action and that no further action would be taken against the remaining 78 officers.

At the first meeting of the high-level transition committee, the general commander of the PNTL noted key areas that would require further strengthening: legislation, training, administration, discipline, and operations. In February, the UN Police (UNPOL) and the PNTL signed a joint development plan covering the period through December 2012 and focusing on these five areas.

UNMIT police have responded to their shifting role by drawing down from 1,608 officers to 1,203 officers in October 2011, with this level expected to be maintained through the elections. In addition, recruitment has emphasized the advising and mentoring role of the police, and nineteen civilian expert posts have been added to provide key capacity building support. Eighteen of the nineteen have been deployed; however, there have been delays in identifying and deploying police officers with the required skills, highlighting a gap in the UN's police recruitment and deployment model.

The government of Timor-Leste has also requested police advisers with critical skill sets to be identified within the UNPOL contingent. As of September, UNMIT, working with government partners, had identified 257 adviser posts and filled 225 of these. Recognizing that advising is a long-term task and not well-suited to the typical six-month deployment of police officers to peacekeeping missions, the UN is requesting that police-contributing countries allow for extended deployments for these advisers. However, the receptivity of member states to this request remains to be seen.

A critical issue for the police transition will be the transfer of ongoing support from UNPOL to other international actors. The government of Timor-Leste has established several bilateral agreements for future assistance with partners including Australia, Indonesia, and Portugal.[2] With multiple actors providing multiple aspects of police assistance, the government will need to take a strong coordination role.

Security and Justice
While the security environment in Timor-Leste remained largely peaceful in 2011, a number of violent incidents involving martial arts groups were a cause for concern. The most serious incident occurred in August and resulted in the death of an off-duty police officer and the burning of fifty-eight homes.

UNMIT has continued to provide support for the Timorese defense forces (the Falintil-Forças de Defesa de Timor-Leste [F-FDTL]), including providing development advice and mentoring support. A joint security sector review project undertaken by UNMIT and the UN Development Programme (UNDP) continued to provide technical and operational trainings, and also supported the opening of Timor-Leste's National Defence Institute in late 2010. In addition, in September 2011 UNMIT and UNDP initiated a security sector development project intended to strengthen civilian oversight and management capacity of the security sector.

In 2011 the F-FDTL developed a new force structure that included recruitment of 600 additional officers. In addition, twelve F-FDTL officers began a six-month joint training program in July in preparation for deployment with a Portuguese contingent to the UN Interim Force in Lebanon (UNIFIL), Timor-Leste's first contribution to a UN peacekeeping operation. However, the overarching national security policy has still not been finalized, and was recently returned to the Secretariat of State for Security by the Council of Ministers for revision. In addition, the comprehensive review of the security sector remains in draft form and is unlikely to be finalized in the near term.

The International Security Forces continue to provide assistance and support capacity building in the Timorese security sector. The government of Timor-Leste has requested that the ISF continue to assist until after the 2012 elections, with future reconfigurations to be made in consultation with the government and the UN.

In addition to its support to the security sector, UNMIT has also continued to provide support to the justice sector, focused on strengthening the capacity of judicial institutions. In May 2011, fourteen judicial officials graduated from Timor-Leste's UNDP-supported Legal Training Center, expanding the country's nascent justice system to sixty-four officials. As more national actors are able to take on official functions within the justice sector, international actors continue to move to advisory roles, with only twenty-two international officials remaining in line functions. Under the supervision of the Office of the Prosecutor-General, UNMIT's Serious Crimes Investigation Team continues to investigate serious crimes committed in 1999.

In addition to providing support to the country's Legal Training Center, UNDP has assisted in developing its case management system, which continues to be a major challenge for Timor-Leste's justice sector. From January to August 2011, the Timorese justice system processed 2,963 criminal cases, though over 2,600 new cases were registered during the same period, leaving nearly 5,000 cases pending. Though the increase in new cases may indicate increasing public confidence in the justice system, the continued backlog of cases risks undermining this growing trust.

Conclusion

Elections in 2012 will serve as a critical test for peace consolidation in Timor-Leste and the resilience of its institutions. UNMIT's technical, political, and security assistance will be important throughout the period, after which a rapid drawdown is envisioned. As the history of UN peacekeeping in Timor-Leste demonstrates, there are risks associated with mission transitions. To avoid renewed conflict, UNMIT, the government of Timor-Leste, and its international partners will need to adopt a flexible and honest approach to UNMIT's drawdown and eventual withdrawal.

Notes

1. Stephen Coates, "Testing Times for East Timor As Polls Loom," *Agence France-Presse,* 11 September 2011.

2. International Crisis Group, "Timor-Leste: Time for the UN to Step Back," *Asia Briefing* no. 116, 15 December 2010, http://www.crisisgroup.org/~/media/Files/asia/south-east-asia/timor-leste/B116%20Timor-Leste%20-%20Time%20for%20the%20UN%20to%20Step%20Back.pdf.

3.9

Western Sahara

The decades-long dispute over the African territory of Western Sahara remained in deadlock through 2011, as meetings between the government of Morocco and the Frente Popular para la Liberación de Saguia el-Hamra y de Río de Oro (POLISARIO) yielded no progress on the fundamental points of contention. Since the departure of its Spanish colonial rulers thirty-five years ago, conflict and uncertainty have plagued the territory and defied determination of its final status.

The UN Mission for the Referendum in Western Sahara (known by its French acronym MINURSO) was formed to conduct a self-determination vote after a 1991 cease-fire agreement. September 2011 marked the twentieth anniversary of the mission's establishment, but MINURSO finds itself continuing to monitor a cease-fire line and support confidence-building measures, while the two sides appear no closer to an agreement on the future of Western Sahara. POLISARIO, the dominant political power among the area's Sahrawi people, long ago claimed an independent Sahrawi Arab Democratic Republic, while since 2004, the government of Morocco has categorically rejected the possibility of independence or the option in a referendum. The gulf between the two sides suggests that the mission will continue to act as an observer in the absence of progress on the political track.

Background

Western Sahara, a Spanish colony for nearly a century, was annexed by Morocco and Mauritania upon Spain's exit in 1976. Mauritania abandoned its claim in 1979, and Morocco has considered the entire region part of its

---

UN Mission for the Referendum in Western Sahara (MINURSO)

- Authorization Date   29 April 1991 (UNSC Res. 690)
- Start Date   6 September 1991
- SRSG   Hany Abdel-Aziz (Egypt)
- Force Commander   Major-General Abdul Hafiz (Bangladesh)
- Budget $63.2 million (1 July 2011–30 June 2012)
- Strength as of   Troops: 27
  31 October 2011   Military Observers: 201
     Police: 6
     International Civilian Staff: 102
     National Civilian Staff: 165
     UN Volunteers: 18

For detailed mission information see p. 198

---

territory ever since. POLISARIO was founded in 1973 to fight Spanish control, and refocused its attention on Morocco after Spain's departure. It operates in exile from the Algerian city of Tindouf, and has gained recognition from a number of countries in addition to African Union membership.

Approximately 500,000 people live in Western Sahara, while more than 100,000 Sahrawi refugees reside in Algerian refugee camps. Morocco has invested heavily in Laayoune, Western Sahara's largest city, which is now home to approximately 200,000 people, fewer than 40 percent of whom are Sahrawi. Socioeconomic grievances have heightened tensions between the Sahrawi population and Moroccan settlers. In addition, some Sahrawis in the Tindouf refugee camps are growing increasingly frustrated by the lack of political progress achieved by the POLISARIO leadership.

MINURSO was founded in 1991 with a mandate that includes monitoring the cease-fire, verifying Moroccan troop reductions, implementing a repatriation program, identifying and registering qualified voters, and organizing and proclaiming the results of a self-determination referendum. The referendum was originally scheduled for January 1992, but no real progress has been made toward its execution in over a decade. The mission identified voters in the 1990s, resulting in a final list published in 1999, but disagreements between the two sides on the eligibility of three groups of applicants derailed the process.

Due to the absence of staff tasked with organizing a referendum, MINURSO's staff numbers are much smaller than originally planned, with an authorized strength of 237 military and 6 police personnel, in addition to a civilian component, which includes a political affairs unit and public information office. It currently monitors the cease-fire and supports assistance programs for displaced and separated Sahrawi families. The mission tracks troop movements and military activity around the "berm," an extensive system of sand walls constructed by Morocco as a buffer strip between the territory it administers and that controlled by POLISARIO. MINURSO receives complaints from both sides, reports on violations, and acts as the means of contact between the Moroccan military and POLISARIO's armed forces, as the two parties do not communicate with each other directly. The mission also visits units on both sides to monitor their adherence to military agreements. In July 2011, Major-General Abdul Hafiz of Bangladesh was appointed head of MINURSO, replacing Major-General Zhao Jingmin of China.

Both Morocco and POLISARIO maintain restrictions on MINURSO operations, including limitations on its access to military positions and units. This has been detrimental to the mission's ability to achieve its mandated tasks, but the cease-fire has generally held.

MINURSO is the only UN peacekeeping mission established since 1978 without a human rights role in its mandate, and there are currently no UN staff in the territory to address human rights issues. In April 2011 the Security Council decided against the establishment of a full-time human rights monitoring mechanism in Western Sahara. POLISARIO and states including South Africa have called for augmenting the mission's mandate to encompass these issues, while a group of Western powers has presented a compromise initiative calling for more periodic visits by independent UN rights investigators. With long-standing allegations of human rights violations by both sides, this has been a prominent recurring issue in annual Security Council discussions on the renewal of MINURSO's mandate.

Key Developments

In 2011 MINURSO continued to actively assist the UN High Commissioner for Refugees (UNHCR) in conducting confidence-building measures. The mission provides logistical support, including aircraft transportation and police escorts, for a family visitation program that reunites refugees in Algeria with their families in Western Sahara. Since the beginning of the program in 2004, over 14,000 Sahrawis have participated, with 27,000 individuals currently registered on waiting lists. Disagreements between Morocco and POLISARIO have led to periodic interruptions in the visitations, but both sides agreed in 2011 on plans to enhance the program. To support this, MINURSO participated in a technical assessment mission to examine a potential ground route to allow more families, some separated for over thirty years, to be transported by road. The mission also provides humanitarian medical support for UNHCR-led family visits.

MINURSO also plays a critical role in the removal of landmines and other explosive remnants of war (ERW), which have been prevalent in the territory. In March 2011, the mission reported that POLISARIO had destroyed 1,506 antipersonnel mines in its stockpiles, the fourth such operation carried out by the group since 2005. MINURSO's Mine Action Coordination Centre conducts quality-control of stockpile destruction, while a UN implementing partner hires local Sahrawis to clear mines east of the berm, with the Moroccan military responsible for removing mines to the west. The program has resulted in the destruction of many thousands of mines and other explosive ordnance, but the death of a Sahrawi mine clearer in June 2011 was only the latest of over 500 mine- and ERW-related fatalities since the conflict began.

From April 2010 to March 2011, MINURSO performed 8,168 ground patrols and 710 aerial patrols. During these patrols, the mission observed and recorded 126 new violations by the Moroccan military, a considerable increase from the previous reporting period, and 12 new violations by POLISARIO. Morocco argues that some acts reported by MINURSO as violations were in fact justified by security enhancements to combat terrorism and smuggling activities, though under the military agreement with MINURSO, any such construction altering the military status quo is prohibited. Both parties would like revisions to the agreement codifying these rules, but for different reasons, and thus are unlikely to agree to each other's proposals.

MINURSO also received a number of allegations by each party concerning violations of the cease-fire agreement during the most recent reporting period. Morocco submitted twenty-one allegations and POLISARIO eight. One POLISARIO allegation, concerning unauthorized Moroccan defense infrastructure work, was confirmed, but none of the other allegations, from either side, could be confirmed. MINURSO lacks the technical capability for ground-to-air surveillance, making it difficult to confirm allegations of Moroccan overflights.

The parties have still not addressed their long-standing infringement on MINURSO operations, and restrictions by both parties increased significantly in the mission's most recent reporting period. POLISARIO committed eighty-one freedom-of-movement violations against MINURSO, which it claimed were due to its frustration with the UN's lack of progress in resolving the conflict. After the mission agreed to provide POLISARIO with information on mission flights and ground patrols, the number of violations decreased. Morocco committed four such violations, preventing the mission from visiting facilities and military units in certain areas.

Since the 1999 voter list was published, negotiations between Morocco and MINURSO have not seen any progress on the core issues of the conflict, despite the considerable efforts of the UN Secretary-General to promote dialogue. Since 2003, a series of Personal Envoys to the Secretary-General have presented proposals and organized meetings between the sides. Ambassador Christopher Ross was named to this position in 2009 and initiated the current series of informal discussions. Ross has sought to involve regional stakeholders Algeria and Mauritania in the discussions, and has reasserted Western Sahara's right to self-determination. Despite a crisis in November 2010 involving the dismantling of a Sahrawi camp by Moroccan authorities and consequent rioting in Laayoune, talks remained on schedule through 2011, with four rounds of discussion occurring during the year. However, the talks have failed to generate meaningful progress to date.

Since the November 2010 violence, the general situation in the territory has remained tense, particularly between the Sahrawi population and Moroccan authorities. Several demonstrations have occurred, with allegations of repression and detention by Moroccan forces. In February 2011, there were incidents of violence between groups of Moroccan and Sahrawi civilians in the city of Dakhla, leading to Sahrawi demonstrations. MINURSO took enhanced security measures in all its locations in response to the deteriorating regional situation and increased tension in the territory.

In January 2011, Morocco arrested twenty-seven people accused of operating an Al-Qaida–connected terrorist cell in Western Sahara. The government claimed this group was planning suicide and car bomb attacks against Moroccan and foreign security forces, as well as bank robberies. MINURSO could not corroborate these claims. In October, three aid workers were kidnapped from a Sahrawi refugee camp near Tindouf—reportedly by Al-Qaida in the Islamic Maghreb, though the organization did not claim responsibility.

Security Council discussions in April regarding the renewal of MINURSO's mandate were contentious, with intense lobbying from both sides of the dispute. Criticisms were raised that the draft resolution had not taken a stronger stance on human rights. On 27 April, MINURSO's mandate was extended by one year, with the authorizing resolution taking a slightly stronger stance on human rights and, for the first time, specifically referencing the human rights situation in the Moroccan-administered territory. The resolution also referenced the human rights situation in POLISARIO camps and supported registration of refugees in Tindouf, a position Morocco has supported.

Conclusion

While informal talks are expected to continue in 2012, a solution to the dispute over Western Sahara does not seem likely in the near future. The core issue of the right to self-determination remains at odds with Morocco's insistence that the territory cannot become independent. While MINURSO maintains the cease-fire with only isolated instances of violence, its ultimate role remains unclear. It appears that the stalemate will persist while the mission bides its time, unable to pursue its original goal of organizing a referendum.

4 Global Statistics on UN-Commanded Missions

This chapter contains data on all current missions of the UN Department of Peacekeeping Operations (DPKO) and the UN Department of Field Support (DFS). The data presented here is aggregated from the mission-by-mission material in Chapter 6. It is based on public UN documents and sources, combined with data provided by DPKO and DFS, and in some cases by the UN Department of Management and the United Nations Volunteer Programme in Bonn.

This chapter covers the period running from 1 July 2010 to the third quarter of 2011. The coverage reflects the UN's 1 July 2010–30 June 2011 budgetary year in addition to information available on later months. Data for UNMIS is included up to the date of termination, 9 July 2011, prior to the inception of its successor mission, UNMISS.

4.1 Total UN Troops: 1 July 2010–31 October 2011

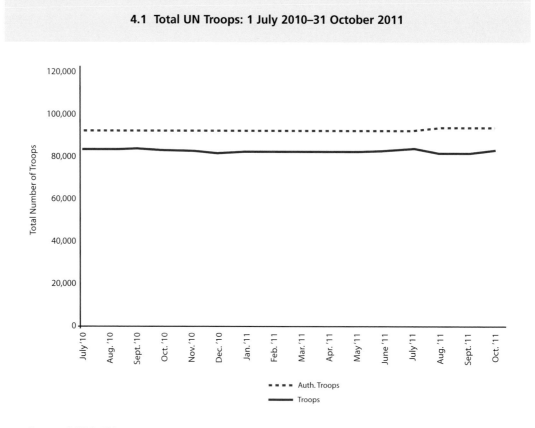

- - - - Auth. Troops
—— Troops

Source: DPKO FGS.

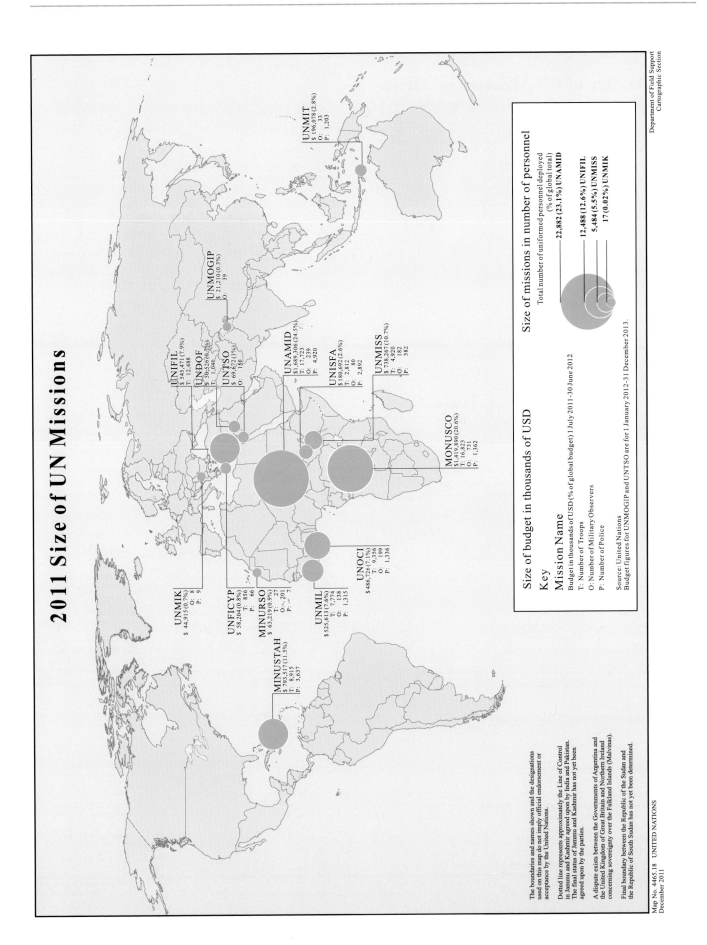

2011 Size of UN Missions

UNMIT
$ 196,078(2.8%)
O: 33
P: 1,203

UNMOGIP
$ 21,210(0.3%)
O: 39

UNIFIL
$ 545,471(7.9%)
T: 12,488

UNDOF
$ 50,526(0.7%)
T: 1,040

UNTSO
$ 69,672(1%)
O: 150

UNAMID
$1,689,306(24.5%)
T: 17,723
O: 239
P: 4,920

UNISFA
$ 180,692(2.6%)
T: 2,812
O: 80
P: 2,892

UNMISS
$ 738,267(10.7%)
T: 4,920
O: 182
P: 382

MONUSCO
$1,419,890(20.6%)
T: 16,823
P: 1,362

UNOCI
$486,726(7.1%)
T: 9,356
O: 199
P: 1,336

UNMIK
$ 44,915(0.7%)
T: 8
P: 9

UNFICYP
$ 58,204(0.8%)
T: 856
P: 66

MINURSO
$ 63,219(0.9%)
T: 27
O: 201
P: 7

UNMIL
$525,613 (7.6%)
T: 7,774
O: 138
P: 1,315

MINUSTAH
$ 793,517(11.5%)
T: 8,915
P: 3,637

Size of missions in number of personnel

Total number of uniformed personnel deployed
(% of global total)

22,882 (23.1%) UNAMID

12,488 (12.6%) UNIFIL

5,484 (5.5%) UNMISS

17 (0.02%) UNMIK

Size of budget in thousands of USD

Key

Mission Name
Budget in thousands of USD (% of global budget) 1 July 2011–30 June 2012

T: Number of Troops
O: Number of Military Observers
P: Number of Police

Source: United Nations
Budget figures for UNMOGIP and UNTSO are for 1 January 2012–31 December 2013.

The boundaries and names shown and the designations used on this map do not imply official endorsement or acceptance by the United Nations.

Dotted line represents approximately the Line of Control in Jammu and Kashmir agreed upon by India and Pakistan. The final status of Jammu and Kashmir has not yet been agreed upon by the parties.

A dispute exists between the Governments of Argentina and the United Kingdom of Great Britain and Northern Ireland concerning sovereignty over the Falkland Islands (Malvinas).

Final boundary between the Republic of the Sudan and the Republic of South Sudan has not yet been determined.

Map No. 4465.18   UNITED NATIONS
December 2011

Department of Field Support
Cartographic Section

2011 Size of UN Missions in Africa

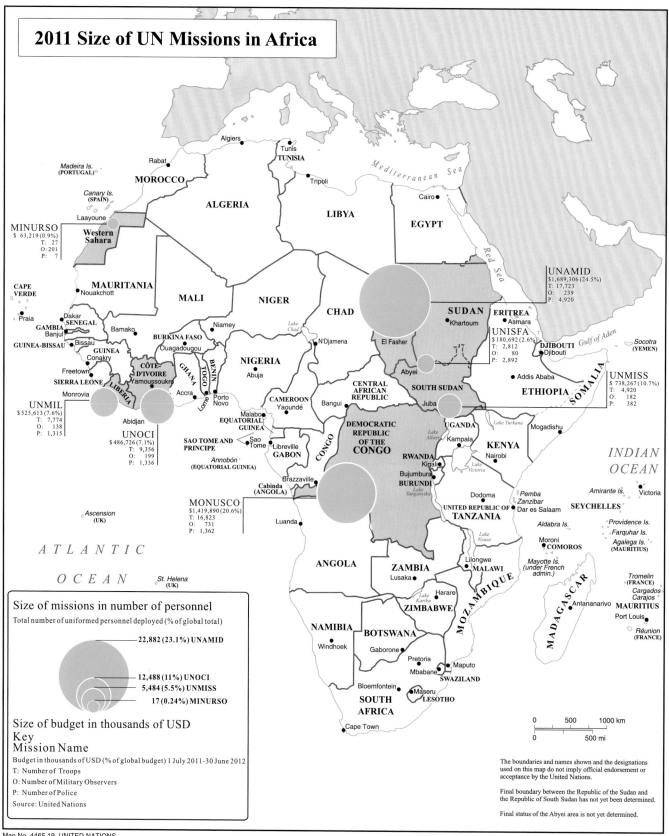

MINURSO
$ 63,219 (0.9%)
T: 27
O: 201
P: 7

UNAMID
$1,689,306 (24.5%)
T: 17,723
O: 239
P: 4,920

UNISFA
$ 180,692 (2.6%)
T: 2,812
O: 80
P: 2,892

UNMISS
$ 738,267 (10.7%)
T: 4,920
O: 182
P: 382

UNMIL
$ 525,613 (7.6%)
T: 7,774
O: 138
P: 1,315

UNOCI
$ 486,726 (7.1%)
T: 9,356
O: 199
P: 1,336

MONUSCO
$1,419,890 (20.6%)
T: 16,823
O: 731
P: 1,362

Size of missions in number of personnel

Total number of uniformed personnel deployed (% of global total)

22,882 (23.1%) UNAMID

12,488 (11%) UNOCI

5,484 (5.5%) UNMISS

17 (0.24%) MINURSO

Size of budget in thousands of USD
Key
Mission Name

Budget in thousands of USD (% of global budget) 1 July 2011-30 June 2012
T: Number of Troops
O: Number of Military Observers
P: Number of Police
Source: United Nations

The boundaries and names shown and the designations used on this map do not imply official endorsement or acceptance by the United Nations.

Final boundary between the Republic of the Sudan and the Republic of South Sudan has not yet been determined.

Final status of the Abyei area is not yet determined.

0   500   1000 km
0   500 mi

4.2 Top Twenty Troop Contributors to UN Missions: 31 October 2011

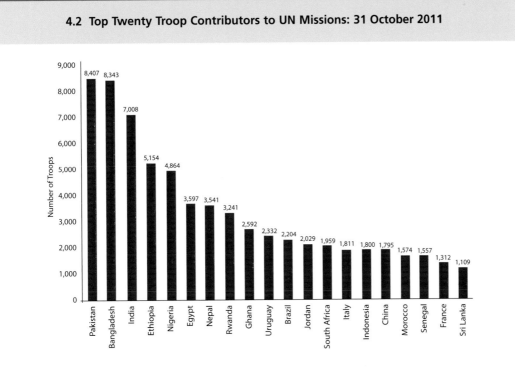

Source: DPKO FGS.

4.3 Troops Deployed by UN Mission: 31 October 2011

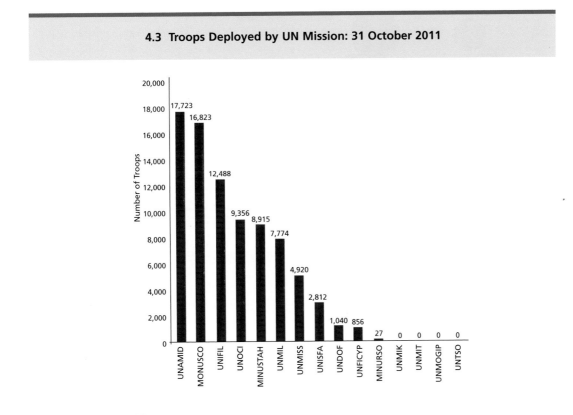

Source: DPKO FGS.

2011 Top Twenty Troop Contributors to UN Missions

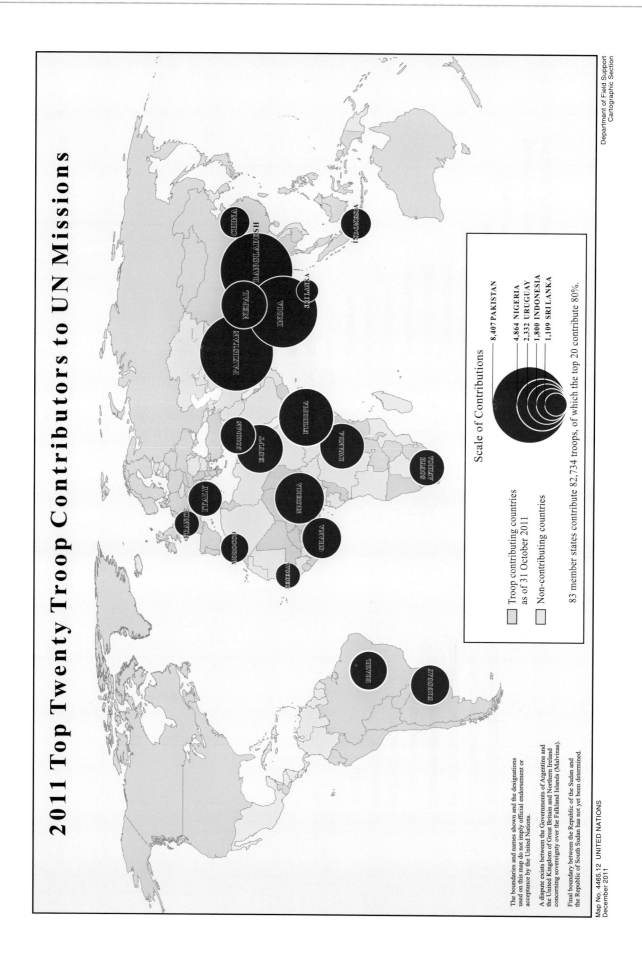

Scale of Contributions

8,407 PAKISTAN

4,864 NIGERIA
2,332 URUGUAY
1,800 INDONESIA
1,109 SRI LANKA

☐ Troop contributing countries
as of 31 October 2011

☐ Non-contributing countries

83 member states contribute 82,734 troops, of which the top 20 contribute 80%.

The boundaries and names shown and the designations used on this map do not imply official endorsement or acceptance by the United Nations.

A dispute exists between the Governments of Argentina and the United Kingdom of Great Britain and Northern Ireland concerning sovereignty over the Falkland Islands (Malvinas).

Final boundary between the Republic of the Sudan and the Republic of South Sudan has not yet been determined.

Map No. 4465.12 UNITED NATIONS
December 2011

Department of Field Support
Cartographic Section

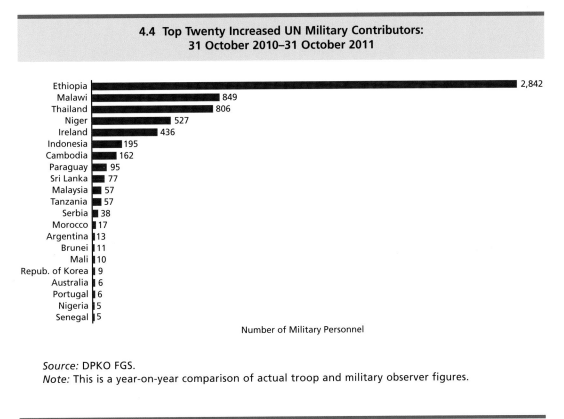

4.4 Top Twenty Increased UN Military Contributors: 31 October 2010–31 October 2011

Number of Military Personnel

Source: DPKO FGS.
Note: This is a year-on-year comparison of actual troop and military observer figures.

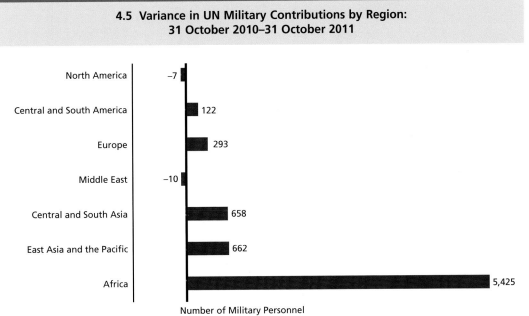

4.5 Variance in UN Military Contributions by Region: 31 October 2010–31 October 2011

Number of Military Personnel

Source: DPKO FGS.
Note: This is a year-on-year comparison of actual troop and military observer figures.

2011 Top Twenty Military Observer Contributors to UN Missions

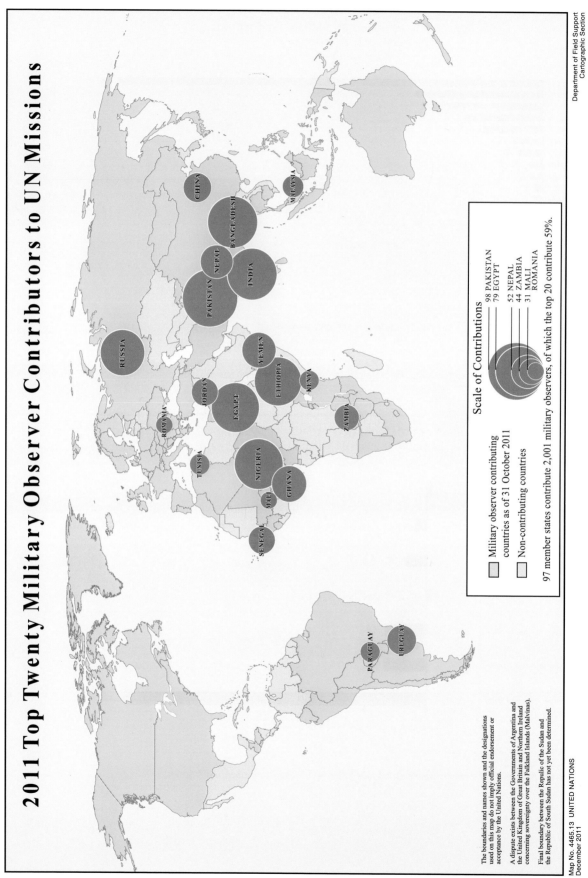

Scale of Contributions

98 PAKISTAN
79 EGYPT
52 NEPAL
44 ZAMBIA
31 MALI
   ROMANIA

97 member states contribute 2,001 military observers, of which the top 20 contribute 59%.

Military observer contributing countries as of 31 October 2011

Non-contributing countries

The boundaries and names shown and the designations used on this map do not imply official endorsement or acceptance by the United Nations.

A dispute exists between the Governments of Argentina and the United Kingdom of Great Britain and Northern Ireland concerning sovereignty over the Falkland Islands (Malvinas).

Final boundary between the Republic of the Sudan and the Republic of South Sudan has not yet been determined.

Department of Field Support
Cartographic Section

4.6 Total UN Military Observers: 1 July 2010–31 October 2011

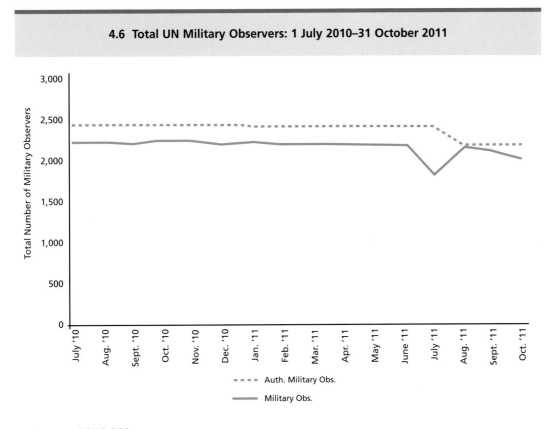

Source: DPKO FGS.

4.7 Top Twenty Military Observer Contributors to UN Missions: 31 October 2011

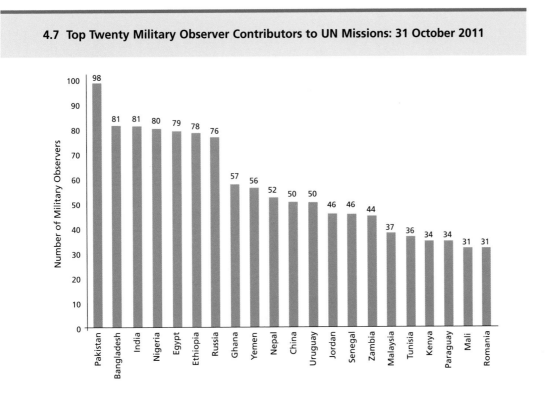

Source: DPKO FGS.

4.8 Military Observers Deployed by UN Mission: 31 October 2011

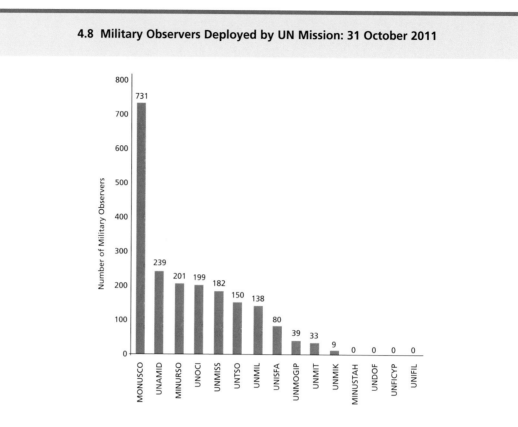

Source: DPKO FGS.

4.9 Total UN Police: 1 July 2010–31 October 2011

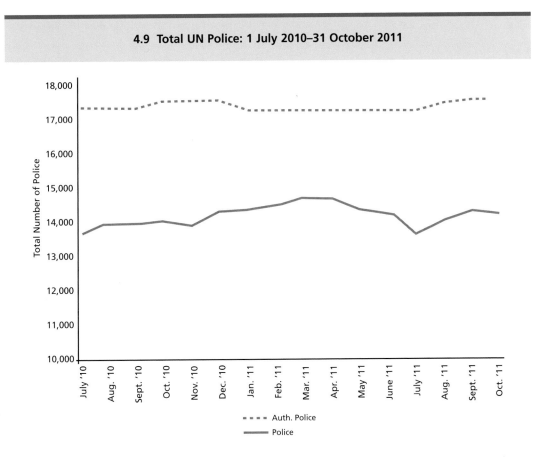

Source: DPKO PD.
Note: Formed police units included.

2011 Top Twenty Police Contributors to UN Missions

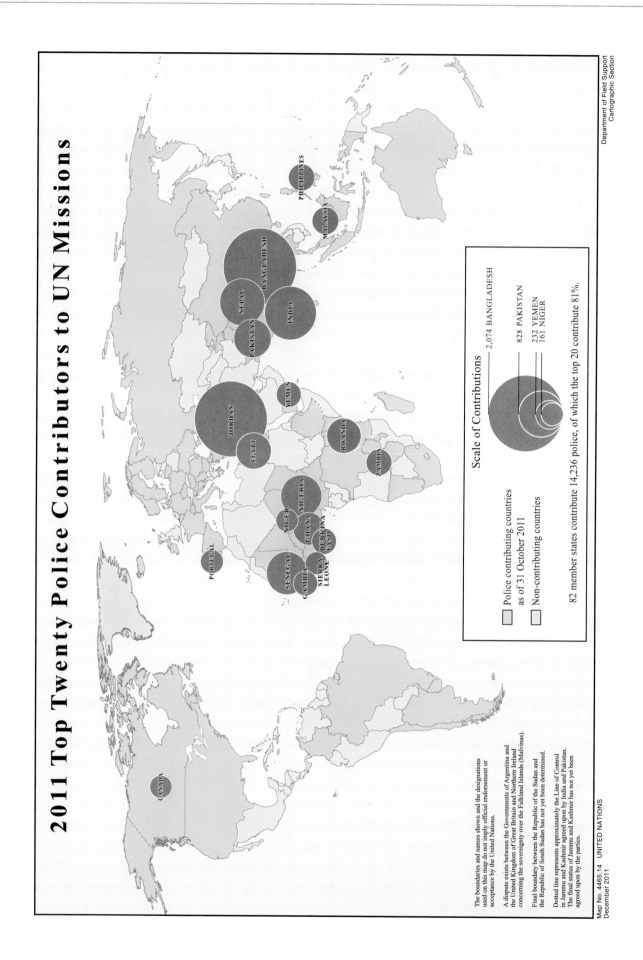

Scale of Contributions

2,074 BANGLADESH

828 PAKISTAN

232 YEMEN
161 NIGER

- Police contributing countries as of 31 October 2011
- Non-contributing countries

82 member states contribute 14,236 police, of which the top 20 contribute 81%.

The boundaries and names shown and the designations used on this map do not imply official endorsement or acceptance by the United Nations.

A dispute exists between the Governments of Argentina and the United Kingdom of Great Britain and Northern Ireland concerning the sovereignty over the Falkland Islands (Malvinas).

Final boundary between the Republic of the Sudan and the Republic of South Sudan has not yet been determined.

Dotted line represents approximately the Line of Control in Jammu and Kashmir agreed upon by India and Pakistan. The final status of Jammu and Kashmir has not yet been agreed upon by the parties.

Map No. 4465.14   UNITED NATIONS
December 2011

Department of Field Support
Cartographic Section

4.10 Top Twenty Police Contributors to UN Missions: 31 October 2011

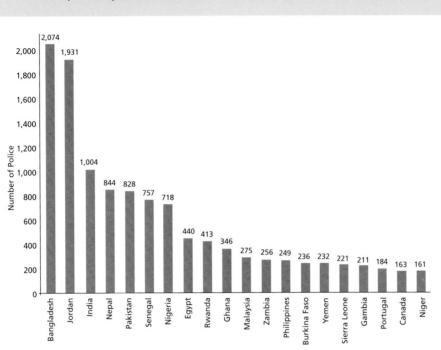

Source: DPKO PD.
Note: Formed police units included.

4.11 Police Deployed by UN Mission: 31 October 2011

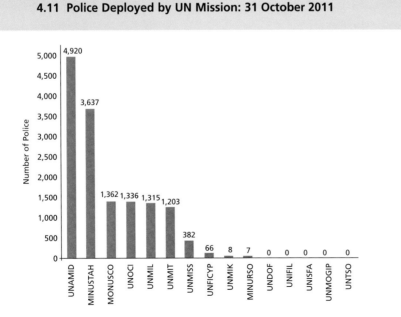

Source: DPKO PD.
Note: Formed police units included.

4.12 Top Twenty Increased UN Police Contributors: 31 October 2010–31 October 2011

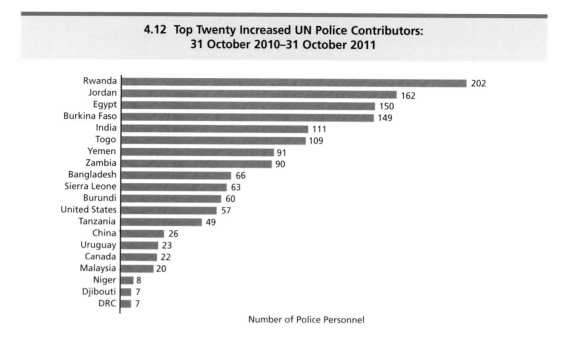

Number of Police Personnel

Source: DPKO PD.
Note: This is a year-on-year comparison of actual police figures.

4.13 Variance in UN Police Contributions by Region: 31 October 2010–31 October 2011

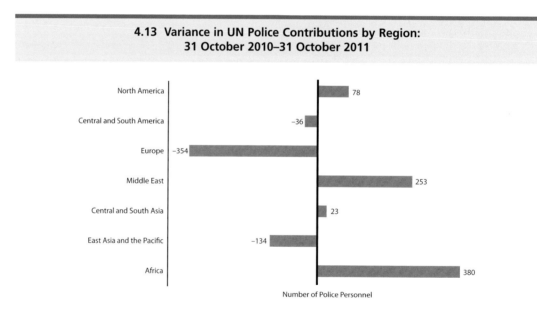

Number of Police Personnel

Source: DPKO FGS.
Note: This is a year-on-year comparison of actual police figures.

4.14 Formed Police by UN Mission: 31 October 2010–31 October 2011

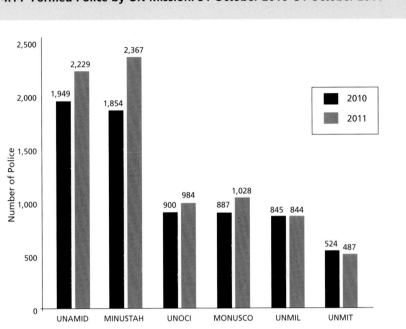

Source: DPKO PD.
Note: This is a year-on-year comparison of actual formed police unit figures.

4.15 Formed Police Contributions by UN Mission: 31 October 2011

	MINUSTAH	MONUSCO	UNAMID	UNMIL	UNMIT	UNOCI	Total
Bangladesh	479	389	558	—	104	354	1,884
Jordan	479	—	279	240	—	489	1,487
India	453	250	—	245	—	—	948
Senegal	140	250	276	—	—	—	666
Pakistan	277	—	138	—	103	141	659
Nepal	239	—	140	239	—	—	618
Nigeria	140	—	280	120	—	—	540
Egypt	—	139	140	—	—	—	279
Rwanda	160	—	—	—	—	—	160
Indonesia	—	—	140	—	—	—	140
Malaysia	—	—	—	—	140	—	140
Portugal	—	—	—	—	140	—	140
Burkina Faso	—	—	139	—	—	—	139
Togo	—	—	139	—	—	—	139
Total	**2,367**	**1,028**	**2,229**	**844**	**487**	**984**	**7,939**

Source: DPKO PD.

4.16 Origin of UN Military Personnel by Region: 31 October 2011

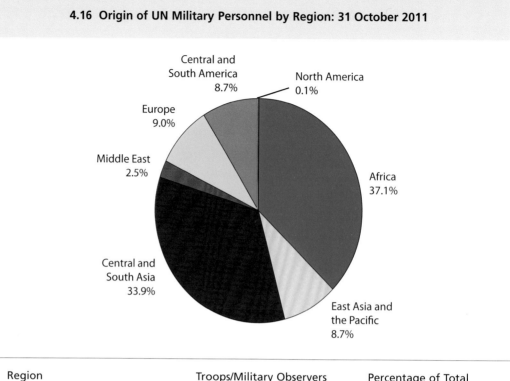

Region	Troops/Military Observers	Percentage of Total
Africa	31,448	37.1%
East Asia and the Pacific	7,331	8.7%
Central and South Asia	28,734	33.9%
Middle East	2,145	2.5%
Europe	7,623	9.0%
Central and South America	7,389	8.7%
North America	65	0.1%
Total	**84,735**	

Source: DPKO FGS.

Note: The regions used here and in the charts below are defined as follows: **Africa:** all members of the African Union and Morocco. **Central and South Asia:** all members of the South Asia Association for Regional Cooperation (including Afghanistan) and all members of the Commonwealth of Independent States to the east of the Caspian Sea, other than Russia. **East Asia and the Pacific:** all states in or bordering on the Pacific, the states of South-East Asia, and Mongolia. **Central and South America:** all members of the Organization of American States other than Canada, the United States, and Mexico. **Europe:** all states to the north of the Mediterranean, Armenia, Azerbaijan, Cyprus, Georgia, Malta, Russia, and Turkey. **Middle East:** all members of the Gulf Cooperation Council, Lebanon, Iraq, Iran, Israel, Jordan, Syria, and Yemen. **North America:** Canada, the United States, and Mexico.

4.17 Deployment of UN Military Personnel by Region: 31 October 2011

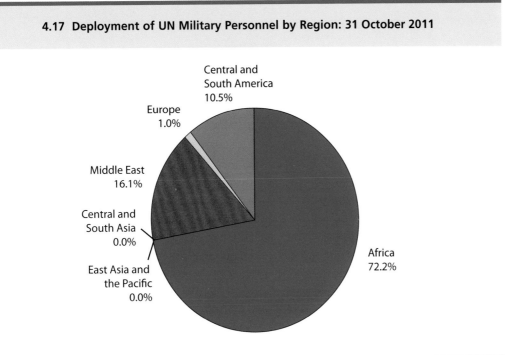

Region	Troops/Military Observers	Percentage of Total
Africa	61,205	72.2%
East Asia and the Pacific	33	0.0%
Central and South Asia	39	0.0%
Middle East	13,678	16.1%
Europe	865	1.0%
Central and South America	8,915	10.5%
North America	—	—
Total	**84,735**	

Source: DPKO FGS.

4.18 Origin of UN Police Personnel by Region: 31 October 2011

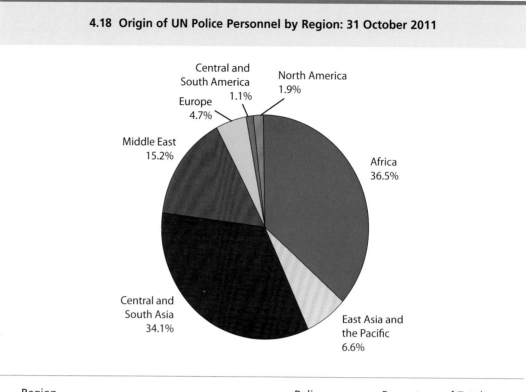

Region	Police	Percentage of Total
Africa	5,189	36.5%
East Asia and the Pacific	934	6.6%
Central and South Asia	4,850	34.1%
Middle East	2,163	15.2%
Europe	665	4.7%
Central and South America	162	1.1%
North America	272	1.9%
Total	**14,235**	

Source: DPKO PD.
Note: Formed police units included.

4.19 Deployment of UN Police Personnel by Region: 31 October 2011

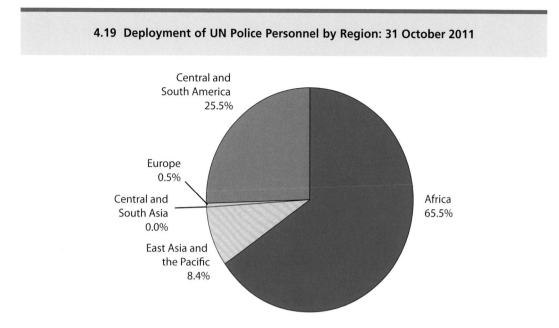

Region	Police	Percentage of Total
Africa	9,323	65.5%
East Asia and the Pacific	1,203	8.4%
Central and South Asia	—	0.0%
Middle East	—	—
Europe	74	0.5%
Central and South America	3,637	25.5%
North America	—	—
Total	**14,237**	

Source: DPKO PD.
Note: Formed police units included.

4.20 Origin of UN Military Personnel in Africa by Region: 31 October 2011

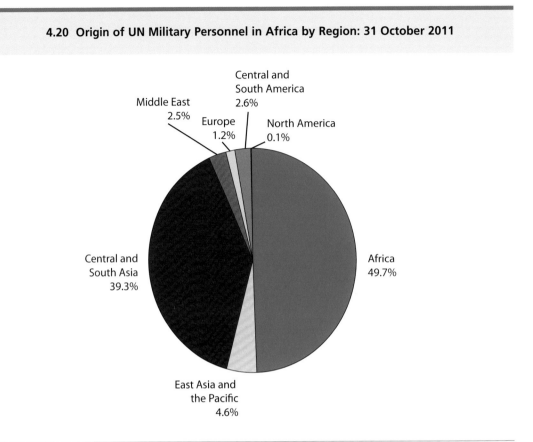

Region	Troops/Military Observers	Percentage of Total
Africa	30,414	49.7%
East Asia and the Pacific	2,830	4.6%
Central and South Asia	24,048	39.3%
Middle East	1,533	2.5%
Europe	733	1.2%
Central and South America	1,612	2.6%
North America	35	0.1%
Total	**61,205**	

Source: DPKO FGS.

4.21 Origin of UN Police Personnel in Africa by Region: 31 October 2011

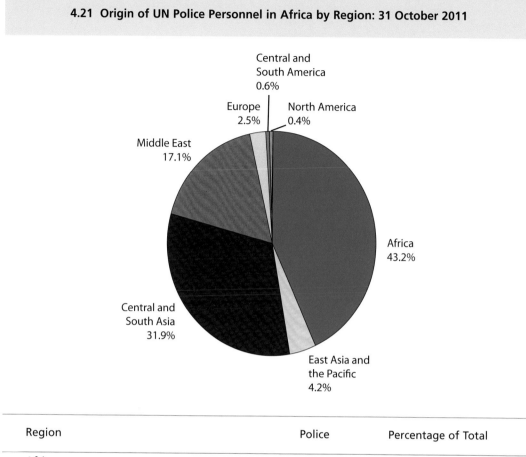

Region	Police	Percentage of Total
Africa	4,031	43.2%
East Asia and the Pacific	387	4.2%
Central and South Asia	2,977	31.9%
Middle East	1,592	17.1%
Europe	237	2.5%
Central and South America	59	0.6%
North America	38	0.4%
Total	**9,321**	

Source: DPKO PD.
Note: Formed police units included.

**4.22 Origin of UN Military Personnel in the Middle East by Region:
31 October 2011**

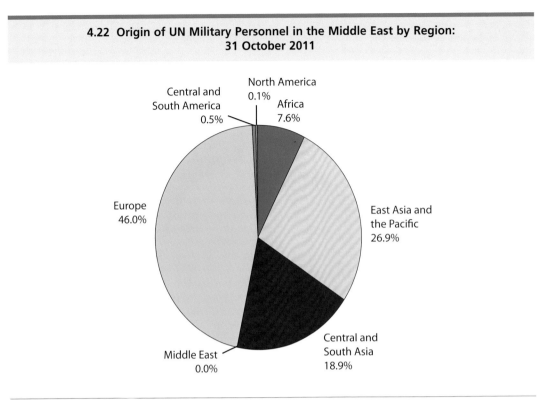

Region	Troops/Military Observers	Percentage of Total
Africa	1,033	7.6%
East Asia and the Pacific	3,678	26.9%
Central and South Asia	2,587	18.9%
Middle East	3	0.0%
Europe	6,290	46.0%
Central and South America	75	0.5%
North America	12	0.1%
Total	**13,678**	

Source: DPKO FGS.

4.23 Total UN Civilian Personnel (international, national and UNV): 1 July 2010–31 October 2011

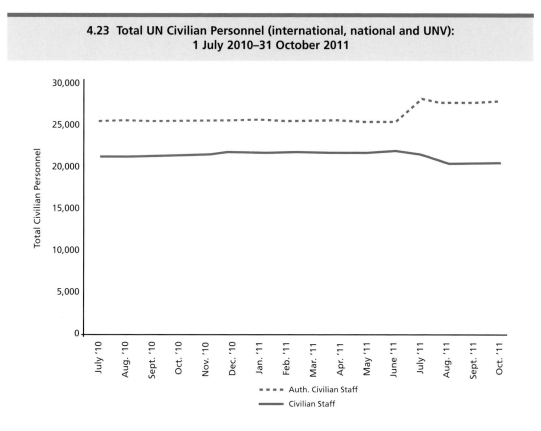

Sources: DFS FPD; UNV Programme.

Notes: Staff at UN Logistics Base in Brindisi not included. Figures do not include staff from UN specialized agencies, funds, and programs, but do include UNMIS personnel following the mission's termination in July 2011 and the subsequent drawdown of the mission.

4.24 UN Mission International Civilian and DFS and DPKO Headquarters Staff Occupational Groups: 31 October 2011

Occupation	International Civilian Staff	Percentage International Staff	DFS HQ Staff	Percentage DFS HQ Staff	DPKO HQ Staff	Percentage DPKO HQ Staff
Administration	686	12.6%	113	28.5%	123	30.4%
Aviation	189	3.5%	13	3.3%	—	—
Cartography	—	—	7	1.8%	—	—
Civil Affairs	165	3.0%	—	—	—	—
Economic Affairs	3	0.1%	—	—	—	—
Electoral Affairs	56	1.0%	—	—	—	—
Engineering	336	6.2%	8	2.0%	—	—
Financial Management	216	4.0%	47	11.9%	4	1.0%
Human Resources	276	5.1%	86	21.7%	17	4.2%
Human Rights	147	2.7%	—	—	—	—
Humanitarian Affairs	24	0.4%	—	—	—	—
Information Management	53	1.0%	8	2.0%	10	2.5%
Information Systems and Technology	512	9.4%	28	7.1%	4	1.0%
Legal Affairs	60	1.1%	5	1.3%	14	3.5%
Logistics	805	14.7%	55	13.9%	—	—
Management and Program Analysis	3	0.1%	—	—	—	—
Medical Services	78	1.4%	3	0.8%	—	—
Military	—	—	—	—	74	18.3%
Police	—	—	—	—	34	8.4%
Political Affairs	310	5.7%	4	1.0%	60	14.9%
Procurement	120	2.2%	—	—	—	—
Programme Management	159	2.9%	8	2.0%	33	8.2%
Public Information	134	2.5%	—	—	—	—
Relations and Liaison	—	—	—	—	3	0.7%
Rule of Law	166	3.0%	—	—	—	—
Security	675	12.4%	—	—	9	2.2%
Social Affairs	49	0.9%	—	—	6	1.5%
Training	—	—	—	—	13	3.2%
Transportation	241	4.4%	11	2.8%	—	—
Total	**5,463**		**396**		**404**	

Sources: DFS FPD; DPKO EO.
Notes: Staff at UN Logistics Base in Brindisi not included. DPKO HQ occupations include both professional and general service staff, but exclude professional staff on contracts of less than one year.

4.25 UN Mission International Civilian Staff Occupations: 31 October 2011

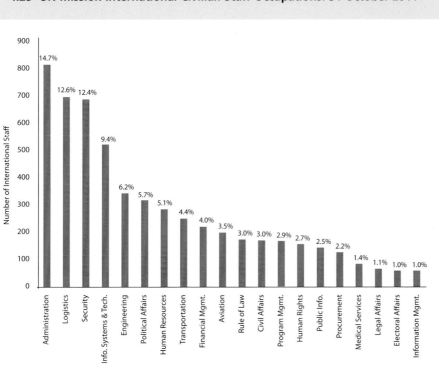

Source: DFS FPD.
Note: Staff at UN Logistics Base in Brindisi not represented.

4.26 DFS and DPKO Headquarters Staff Occupations: 31 October 2011

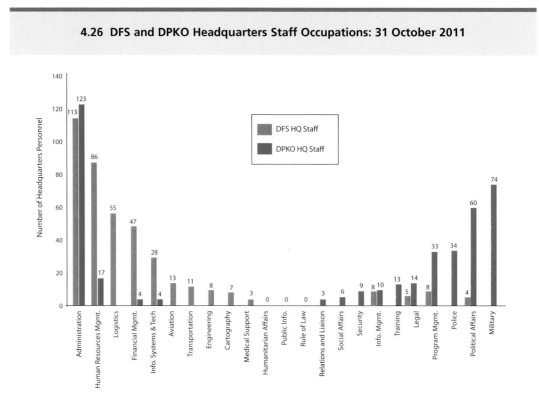

Source: DPKO EO.

Note: HQ occupations include both professional and general service staff, but exclude professional staff on contracts of less than one year.

4.27 Highest National Representation in UN Missions: 31 October 2011

UN Missions – International Professional and General Service Staff Total International Staff in Missions = 7,037				DPKO Missions – National Professional and General Service Staff Total National Staff in Missions = 12,302			
Rank	Country	Number of International Staff	Percentage of Total International Staff	Rank	Mission	Number of National Staff	Percentage of Total National Staff
1	United States	355	5.0%	1	UNAMID	2,904	23.6%
2	Kenya	331	4.7%	2	MONUSCO	2,865	23.3%
3	Philippines	270	3.8%	3	MINUSTAH	1,355	11.0%
4	India	240	3.4%	4	UNMISS	1,117	9.1%
5	Canada	212	3.0%	5	UNMIL	991	8.1%
6	Sierra Leone	203	2.9%	6	UNMIT	883	7.2%
7	United Kingdom	197	2.8%	7	UNOCI	743	6.0%
8	Ghana	194	2.8%	8	UNIFIL	666	5.4%
9	Nigeria	161	2.3%	9	UNMIK	215	1.7%
10	Ethiopia	158	2.2%	10	MINURSO	165	1.3%
11	Serbia	155	2.2%	11	UNTSO	132	1.1%
12	France	140	2.0%	12	UNFICYP	112	0.9%
13	Pakistan	127	1.8%	13	UNDOF	103	0.8%
14	Uganda	124	1.8%	14	UNMOGIP	51	0.4%
15	Cameroon	117	1.7%	15	UNISFA	0	0.0%
16	Tanzania	106	1.5%				
17	Côte d'Ivoire	99	1.4%				
18	Russia	94	1.3%				
19	Australia	93	1.3%				
20	Lebanon	93	1.3%				

Source: DFS FPD.
Note: Staff at UN Logistics Base in Brindisi not represented.

**4.28 Highest National Representation in UN DPKO Headquarters:
31 October 2011**

Total DPKO and DFS Headquarters Staff: 800
535 Professional Staff and 265 General Service Staff

Rank	Country	DFS	DPKO	DFS and DPKO	Percentage of Total DPKO HQ Staff
1	United States	95	82	177	22.1%
2	Canada	18	18	36	4.5%
3	Philippines	20	15	35	4.4%
4	United Kingdom	11	19	30	3.8%
5	France	11	17	28	3.5%
6	India	13	13	26	3.3%
7	Germany	6	17	23	2.9%
8	Italy	4	15	19	2.4%
9	Japan	4	12	16	2.0%
10	Pakistan	6	9	15	1.9%
11	Brazil	5	8	13	1.6%
12	Nigeria	5	8	13	1.6%
13	Russia	8	5	13	1.6%
14	Argentina	8	4	12	1.5%
15	Uruguay	7	5	12	1.5%
16	Australia	7	4	11	1.4%
17	Kenya	7	4	11	1.4%
18	Republic of Korea	4	6	10	1.3%
19	Myanmar	5	4	9	1.1%
20	Nepal	6	3	9	1.1%
21	Romania	5	4	9	1.1%
22	Uganda	7	2	9	1.1%

Source: DPKO EO.
Note: HQ occupations include both professional and general service staff, but exclude professional staff on contracts of less than one year.

4.29 Total Personnel in UN Missions: 31 October 2011

Mission	Troops	Military Observers	Police	International Staff	National Staff	UNVs	Total
UNAMID	17,723	239	4,920	1,124	2,904	481	27,391
MONUSCO	16,823	731	1,362	976	2,865	595	23,352
MINUSTAH	8,915	—	3,637	568	1,355	238	14,713
UNIFIL	12,488	—	—	353	666	—	13,507
UNOCI	9,356	199	1,336	397	743	272	12,303
UNMIL	7,774	138	1,315	477	991	240	10,935
UNMISS	4,920	182	382	697	1,117	212	7,510
UNISFA	2,812	80	2	20	—	—	2,914
UNMIT	—	33	1,203	394	883	206	2,719
UNDOF	1,040	—	—	41	103	—	1,184
UNFICYP	856	—	66	38	112	—	1,072
MINURSO	27	201	6	102	165	18	519
UNMIK	—	9	8	150	215	26	408
UNTSO	—	150	—	101	132	—	383
UNMOGIP	—	39	—	25	51	—	115
Total	**82,734**	**2,001**	**14,237**	**5,463**	**12,302**	**2,288**	**119,025**

Sources: DFS FPD; DPKO FGS; DPKO PD; UNV Programme.
Note: Police figures include formed police units.

4.30 UN Personnel Gender Statistics: 31 October 2011

Personnel Type	Male	Female	Percentage Male	Percentage Female
Troops	80,555	2,179	97.4%	2.6%
Military Observers	1,927	74	96.3%	3.7%
Police	12,895	1,340	90.6%	9.4%
International Civilian Staff	3,843	1,620	70.3%	29.7%
National Civilian Staff	10,158	2,144	82.6%	17.4%
DFS HQ Professional	144	89	61.8%	38.2%
DFS HQ General Service	48	115	29.4%	70.6%
DPKO HQ Professional	204	98	67.5%	32.5%
DPKO HQ General Service	30	72	29.4%	70.6%
UN Logistics Base in Brindisi	238	118	66.9%	33.1%
Total	**110,042**	**7,849**	**93.3%**	**6.7%**

Sources: DFS FPD; DPKO FGS; DPKO PD; DPKO EO.
Notes: Police figures include formed police units. HQ staff includes all general service staff and all professional staff with contracts of one year or more.

4.31 Total Monthly Fatalities in UN Missions: 1 July 2010–31 October 2011

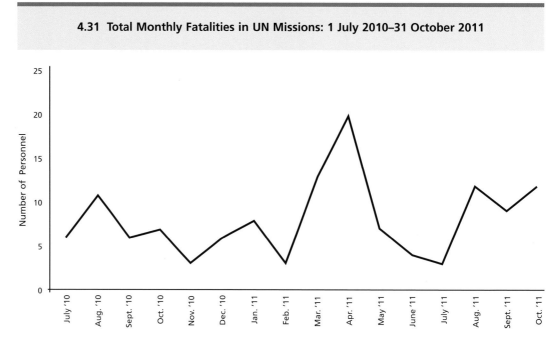

Source: DPKO Situation Center.
Note: UN Logistics Base in Brindisi not included.

4.32 Fatalities by UN Missions: 1 July 2010–31 October 2011

	Number of Fatalities	Percentage of Fatalities
UNAMID	35	26.9%
MONUSCO	32	24.6%
UNOCI	18	13.8%
UNMIL	16	12.3%
MINUSTAH	8	6.2%
UNMISS	7	5.4%
UNIFIL	5	3.8%
UNISFA	5	3.8%
UNMIT	3	2.3%
UNFICYP	1	0.8%
MINURSO	—	—
UNDOF	—	—
UNMIK	—	—
UNMOGIP	—	—
UNTSO	—	—
Total	**130**	

Source: DPKO Situation Center.

4.33 Fatalities in UN Missions by Incident Type: 1 July 2010–31 October 2011

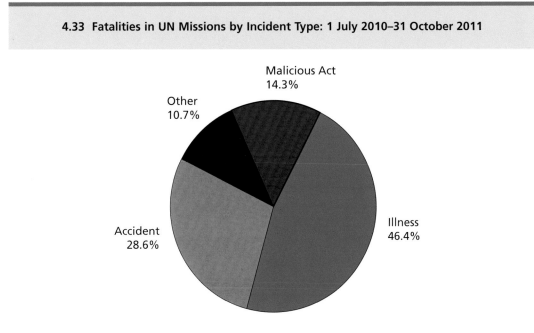

Source: DPKO Situation Center.
Notes: UN Logistics Base in Brindisi not included. Malicious acts include both what were previously referred to as hostile acts and crime. Other includes what were previously qualified as self-inflicted.

4.34 Fatalities in UN Missions by Personnel Type: 1 July 2010–31 October 2011

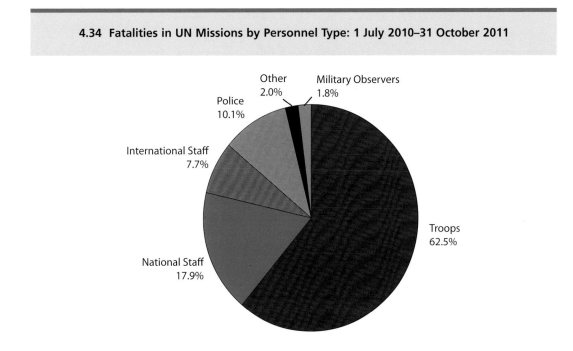

Source: DPKO Situation Center.
Notes: UN Logistics Base in Brindisi not included. Other refers to consultants, UNVs, etc.

4.35 UN Peacekeeping Budgets: 1 July 2010–30 June 2011

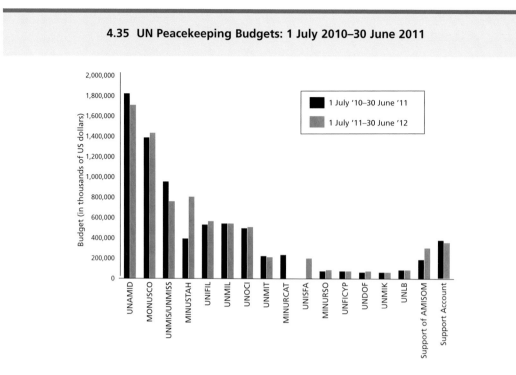

Sources: UN Documents A/66/532 and A/C.5/65/19; DFS FBFD.

Notes: Figures above include only peacekeeping operations funded out of the peacekeeping budget; see table below for missions funded from the regular UN budget. In accordance with S/RES/1996 of 8 July 2011, the appropriate functions of UNMIS were transferred to UNMISS effective 9 July 2011.

4.36 Other Peace Operations Budgets: 1 January–31 December 2012 (in thousands of US dollars)

	Appropriations
DFS	4,141.1
DPKO	5,340.5
UNMOGIP	10,605.0
UNTSO	34,836.0
Total	**54,922.6**

Sources: UN Document A/66/6(Sect.5); DFS FBFD.

Notes: DPKO and DFS budget lines are for peacekeeping operations executive direction and management costs, programme of work and programme support. The budgets for DFS, DPKO, UNMOGIP and UNTSO are based on one-half of the proposed programme budget for the biennium 2012–2013. 2012–2013 appropriations for DFS and DPKO are preliminary and subject to change.

2011 Top Twenty Providers of Assessed Contributions to UN Peacekeeping Budget

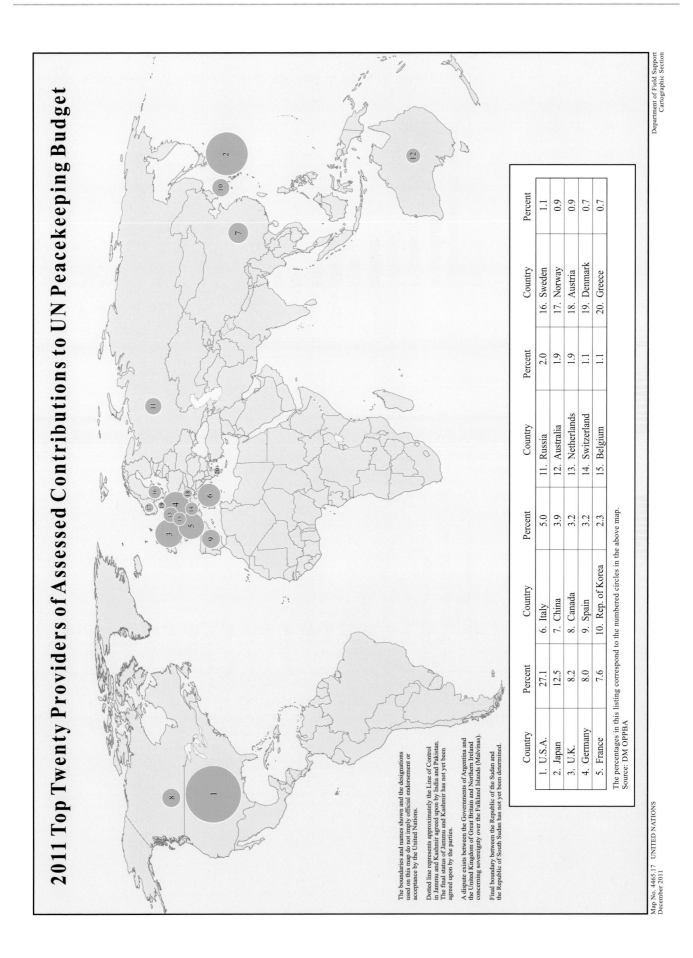

Country	Percent	Country	Percent	Country	Percent	Country	Percent
1. U.S.A.	27.1	6. Italy	5.0	11. Russia	2.0	16. Sweden	1.1
2. Japan	12.5	7. China	3.9	12. Australia	1.9	17. Norway	0.9
3. U.K.	8.2	8. Canada	3.2	13. Netherlands	1.9	18. Austria	0.9
4. Germany	8.0	9. Spain	3.2	14. Switzerland	1.1	19. Denmark	0.7
5. France	7.6	10. Rep. of Korea	2.3	15. Belgium	1.1	20. Greece	0.7

The percentages in this listing correspond to the numbered circles in the above map.
Source: DM OPPBA

The boundaries and names shown and the designations
used on this map do not imply official endorsement or
acceptance by the United Nations.

Dotted line represents approximately the Line of Control
in Jammu and Kashmir agreed upon by India and Pakistan.
The final status of Jammu and Kashmir has not yet been
agreed upon by the parties.

A dispute exists between the Governments of Argentina and
the United Kingdom of Great Britain and Northern Ireland
concerning sovereignty over the Falkland Islands (Malvinas).

Final boundary between the Republic of the Sudan and
the Republic of South Sudan has not yet been determined.

Department of Field Support
Cartographic Section

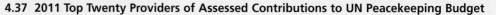

4.37 2011 Top Twenty Providers of Assessed Contributions to UN Peacekeeping Budget

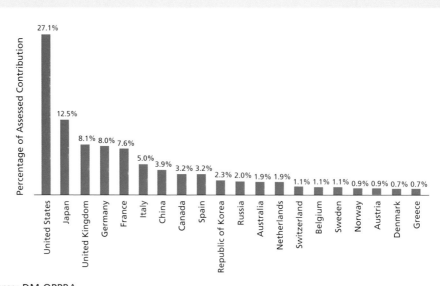

Source: DM OPPBA.

4.38 2011 Top Twenty Providers of Assessed Contributions to UN Regular Budget

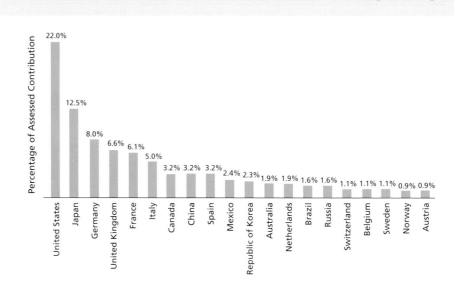

Source: DM OPPBA.

Member State	2011 Effective Assessment Rate	Outstanding Contributions as at 31 December 2010	Assessments Issued in 2011	Collections and Credits Received in 2011	Oustanding Contributions as at 30 September 2011
United States	27.4%	430,630,946	2,057,094,330	2,067,005,501	420,719,775
Japan	12.5%	674,354,947	924,570,557	951,088,770	647,836,734
United Kingdom	8.1%	105,771,447	601,210,631	533,415,548	173,566,530
Germany	8.0%	—	591,636,605	553,886,305	37,750,300
France	7.6%	54,507,239	557,421,662	529,412,156	82,516,745
Italy	5.0%	95,168,667	368,868,970	213,408,293	250,629,344
China	3.9%	1,459,068	290,318,093	170,906,448	120,870,713
Canada	3.2%	—	236,639,886	221,540,708	15,099,178
Spain	3.2%	298,040,499	234,426,230	42,285,033	490,181,696
Republic of Korea	2.3%	130,837,777	166,762,121	129,438,182	168,161,716
Russia	2.0%	45,383,376	145,841,828	141,529,730	49,695,474
Australia	1.9%	—	142,633,274	133,532,334	9,100,940
Netherlands	1.9%	—	136,877,763	128,144,063	8,733,700
Switzerland	1.1%	—	83,381,067	78,060,807	5,320,260
Belgium	1.1%	31,359,884	79,322,695	53,982,067	56,700,512
Sweden	1.1%	—	78,511,020	73,501,502	5,009,518
Norway	0.9%	—	64,269,832	42,367,103	21,902,729
Austria	0.9%	—	62,794,057	18,579,854	44,214,203
Denmark	0.7%	1,172,546	54,308,370	50,709,228	4,771,688
Greece	0.7%	93,605,688	50,987,887	28,065,768	116,527,807

Source: DM OPPBA.

Note: Credits utilized are derived from unencumbered balance of appropriations and other income for peacekeeping operations utilized at the time that assessments for the same operations were issued.

4.40 UN Mandate Renewals: 1 July 2010–31 December 2011

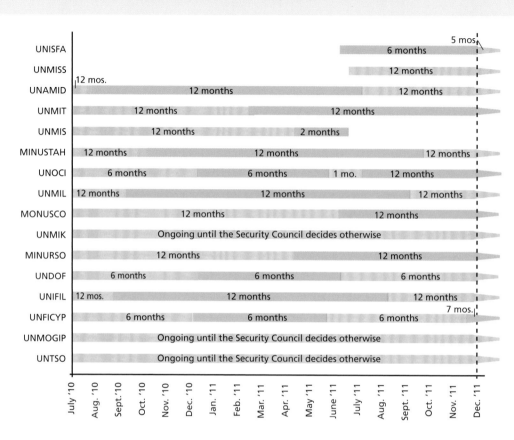

Source: UN Security Council Resolutions.

Notes: Mandate duration noted is mission authorization as per initial Security Council resolution. In some cases, mission authorization was renewed prior to the end of the previous mandate; in such cases the mandate duration may not match the timeline on the graph.

4.41 UN Operations Timeline: 1945–2011

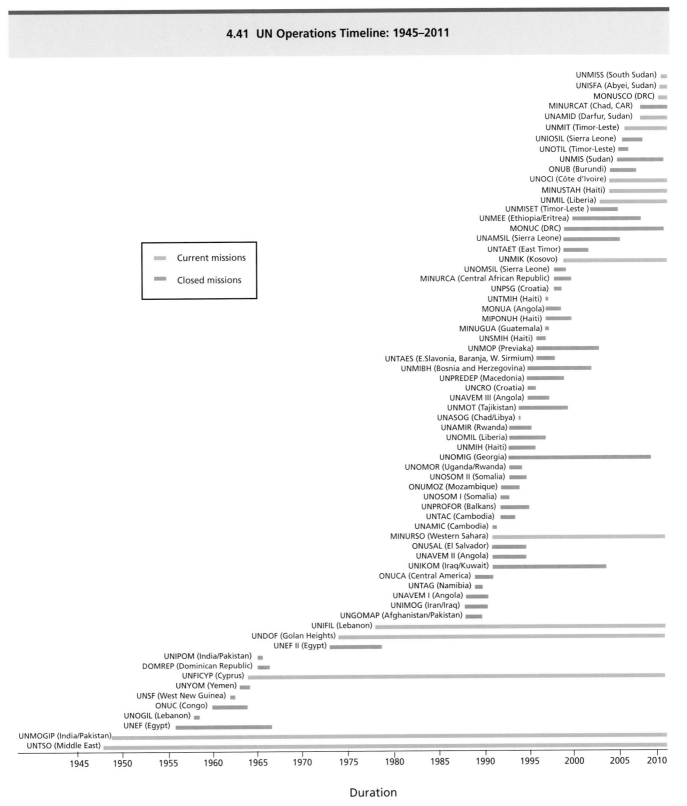

Source: UN Security Council Resolutions.

5 Global Statistics on Non-UN-Commanded Missions

This chapter presents data on peace operations conducted under the authority of regional organizations and non-standing coalitions of states; the data is compiled by the Stockholm International Peace Research Institute (SIPRI).

* * *

Listed are 27 non-UN multilateral peace operations that started, were ongoing, or terminated during 2011. Figures provided in this chapter are as of September 2011 or, in the case of operations that were terminated in 2011, the date of closure.

The chapter covers a broad range of peace operations, reflecting the growing complexity of operation mandates and the potential for operations to change over time. The chapter does not include good offices, fact-finding, or electoral assistance missions. The operations provided in this chapter are specifically compiled for the Center on International Cooperation and do not reproduce the operations included in the SIPRI Multilateral Peace Operations Database.[1]

The operations are divided into two loosely defined categories: those including military and observer functions (Table 5.10) and those focusing on policing and other civilian functions (Table 5.11). The operations are grouped in the tables by the entity conducting them and are listed chronologically within these groups. The tables provide information on the legal instruments underlying the establishment of an operation—UN Security Council resolutions or formal decisions by regional organizations, the missions' locations,

the start dates, the principal contributors, and the personnel fatalities. The start dates for the operations refer to dates of first deployments. The list of contributing countries presented in this volume does not necessarily refer to the total number of contributing countries: in the case of missions including contributions by more than ten countries the principle contributors are stated, in the case of smaller missions the full list of contributors is provided. For a complete list of countries' participation in each mission, see the SIPRI database. The actual missions' strengths represent international personnel located in theater. Due to constant rotation of mission personnel, the numbers provided are estimates. Mission fatalities are recorded as a total since the beginning of an operation and as a total for October 2010 until September 2011. Causes of death—whether by hostile act, accidental, or through illness—are recorded for fatalities in 2011. As some deaths were the result of other causes, the breakdown of the causes of death does not always add up to the total number of fatalities.

Table 5.12 lists the estimated declared costs of the operations underway in 2011. Budget figures are given for the period 1 October 2010 to 30 September 2011. The figures are given in millions of US dollars. Conversions from budgets set in other currencies are based on the International Monetary Fund's aggregated market exchange rates for October 2010 to September 2011.

The way in which various regional organizations finance peace operations is different. Unlike UN budgets, figures of operations conducted by regional organizations such as

NATO refer only to common costs. This includes mainly the running costs of the headquarters (i.e., costs for civilian personnel and costs for operation and maintenance) and investments in the infrastructure necessary to support the operation. The costs of deploying personnel are borne by individual contributing states and are not reflected in the figures given here. Most EU operations are financed in one of two ways: civilian missions are funded through the Community budget, while military operations or operations with a military component are funded by contributions by the participating member states through the Athena mechanism. In missions by other organizations—and generally the ad hoc missions—budget figures may include program implementation.

There are certain limitations to the data. The main problems of reliability are due to varying definitions of what constitutes the total cost of an operation. The coverage of official data varies significantly between operations; sometimes a budget is an estimate while in other cases it is an actual expenditure. For all these reasons, budget figures presented in Table 5.12 are best viewed as estimates, and the budgets for different operations should not be compared.

Data on multilateral peace operations are obtained from the following categories of open source: (1) official information provided by the secretariat of the authorizing organization; (2) official information provided by the mission on the ground, either in official publications or in written responses to annual SIPRI questionnaires; and (3) information from national governments contributing to the operation in question. These primary sources are supplemented with a wide selection of publicly available secondary sources consisting of specialist journals; research reports; news agencies; and international, regional, and local newspapers.

Note

1. For detailed explanations and further information on SIPRI's multilateral peace operations dataset, consult the SIPRI website (http://www.sipri.org/databases/pko/pko) or the SIPRI Yearbook.

5.1 Top Twenty Troop Contributors to Non-UN-Commanded Missions: 30 September 2011

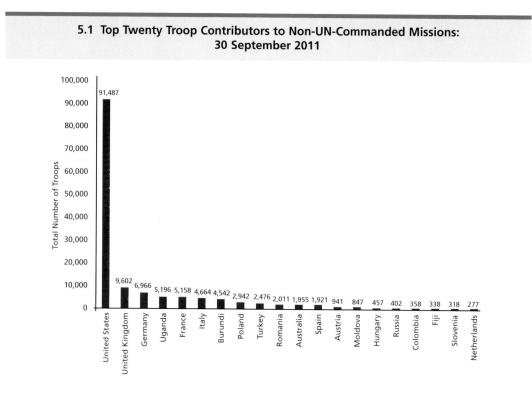

Note: These figures represent the number of personnel deployed in large-scale units and may exclude some additional personnel deployed individually or in small scale units. Figures for Moldova include troops deployed from Transdniestria in the Joint Control Commission Peacekeeping force (JCC).

5.2 Top Twenty Police Contributors to Non-UN-Commanded Missions: 30 September 2011

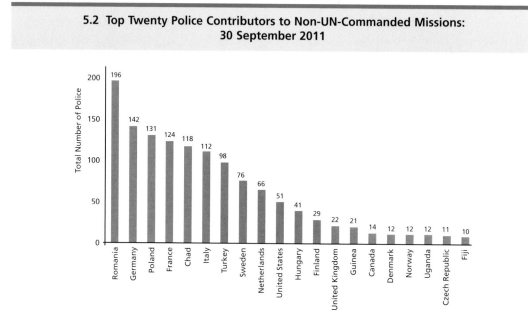

Note: As the figures for largest contributors represent personnel deployed in large scale units, there may be variations with actual field strength.

2011 Top Twenty Troop Contributors to Non-UN Missions

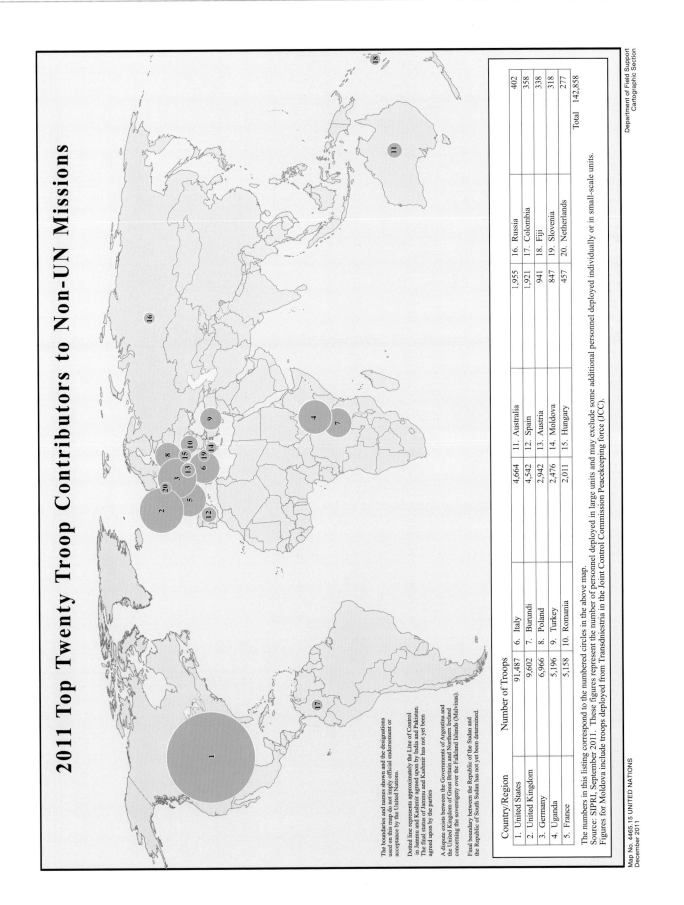

Country/Region	Number of Troops				
1. United States	91,487	6. Italy	1,955	16. Russia	402
2. United Kingdom	9,602	7. Burundi	1,921	17. Colombia	358
3. Germany	6,966	8. Poland	941	18. Fiji	338
4. Uganda	5,196	9. Turkey	847	19. Slovenia	318
5. France	5,158	10. Romania	457	20. Netherlands	277
		11. Australia	4,664		
		12. Spain	4,542		
		13. Austria	2,942		
		14. Moldova	2,476		
		15. Hungary	2,011		
				Total	142,858

The numbers in this listing correspond to the numbered circles in the above map.
Source: SIPRI, September 2011. These figures represent the number of personnel deployed in large units and may exclude some additional personnel deployed individually or in small-scale units.
Figures for Moldova include troops deployed from Transdniestria in the Joint Control Commission Peacekeeping force (JCC).

The boundaries and names shown and the designations used on this map do not imply official endorsement or acceptance by the United Nations.

Dotted line represents approximately the Line of Control in Jammu and Kashmir agreed upon by India and Pakistan. The final status of Jammu and Kashmir has not yet been agreed upon by the parties

A dispute exists between the Governments of Argentina and the United Kingdom of Great Britain and Northern Ireland concerning the sovereignty over the Falkland Islands (Malvinas).

Final boundary between the Republic of the Sudan and the Republic of South Sudan has not yet been determined.

Department of Field Support
Cartographic Section

Map No. 4465.15 UNITED NATIONS
December 2011

2011 Top Twenty Police Contributors to Non-UN Missions

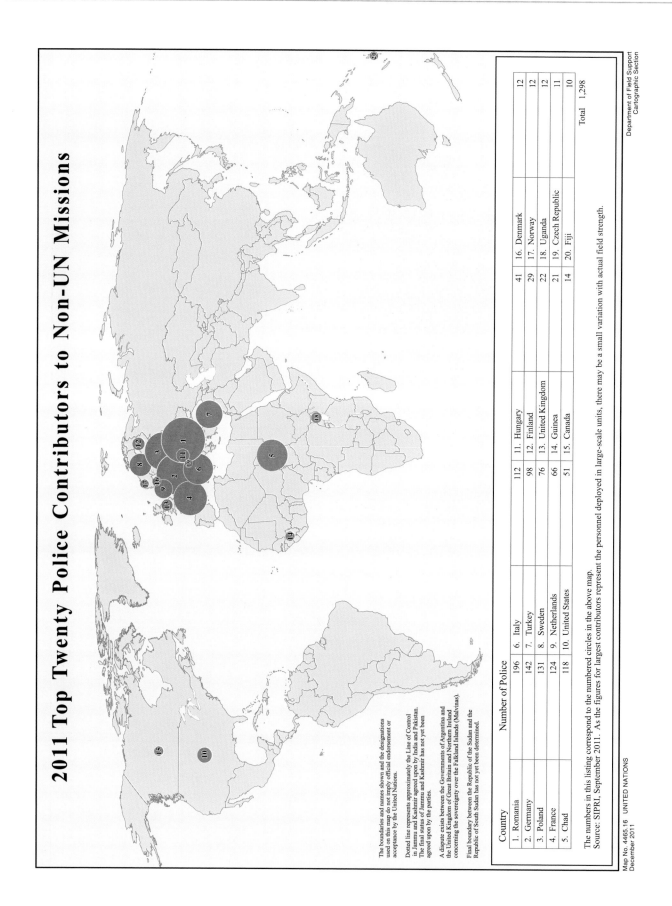

The boundaries and names shown and the designations used on this map do not imply official endorsement or acceptance by the United Nations.

Dotted line represents approximately the Line of Control in Jammu and Kashmir agreed upon by India and Pakistan. The final status of Jammu and Kashmir has not yet been agreed upon by the parties.

A dispute exists between the Governments of Argentina and the United Kingdom of Great Britain and Northern Ireland concerning the sovereignty over the Falkland Islands (Malvinas).

Final boundary between the Republic of the Sudan and the Republic of South Sudan has not yet been determined.

Country	Number of Police				
1. Romania	196	6. Italy	142	11. Hungary	112
2. Germany	142	7. Turkey	131	12. Finland	98
3. Poland	131	8. Sweden	124	13. United Kingdom	76
4. France	124	9. Netherlands	118	14. Guinea	66
5. Chad	118	10. United States	51	15. Canada	51

16. Denmark	41		
17. Norway	29		
18. Uganda	22		
19. Czech Republic	21		
20. Fiji	14		
		Total	1,298

The numbers in this listing correspond to the numbered circles in the above map.
Source: SIPRI, September 2011. As the figures for largest contributors represent the personnel deployed in large-scale units, there may be a small variation with actual field strength.

Map No. 4465.16   UNITED NATIONS
December 2011

Department of Field Support
Cartographic Section

5.3 Contributions of Military Personnel to Non-UN-Commanded Missions by Organization: 30 September 2011

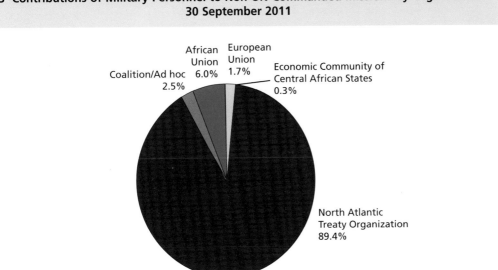

Organization	Troops/Military Observers	Percentage of Total
North Atlantic Treaty Organization	145,080	89.4%
African Union	9,754	6.0%
Coalition/Ad Hoc	4,113	2.5%
European Union	2,777	1.7%
Economic Community of Central African States	497	0.3%
TOTAL	**162,221**	

5.4 Deployment of Non-UN-Commanded Military Personnel to Regions: 30 September 2011

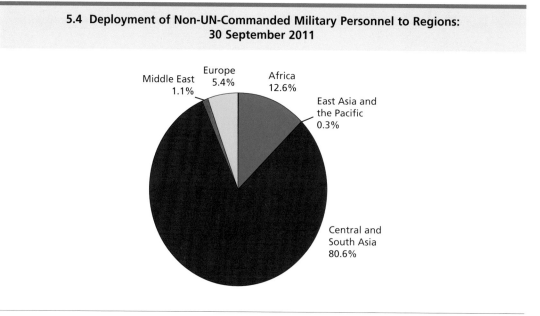

Region	Troops/Military Observers	Percentage of Total
Central and South Asia	130,670	80.6%
Africa	20,437	12.6%
Europe	8,790	5.4%
Middle East	1,826	1.1%
East Asia and the Pacific	498	0.3%
TOTAL	**162,221**	

5.5 Deployment of Non-UN-Commanded Police By Organization: 30 September 2011

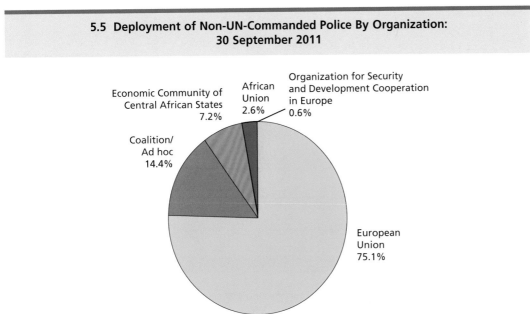

Organization	Police	Percentage of Total
European Union	1,446	75.1%
Coalition/Ad Hoc	278	14.4%
Economic Community of Central African States	139	7.2%
African Union	50	2.6%
Organization for Security and Development Co-operation in Europe	12	0.6%
TOTAL	**1,925**	

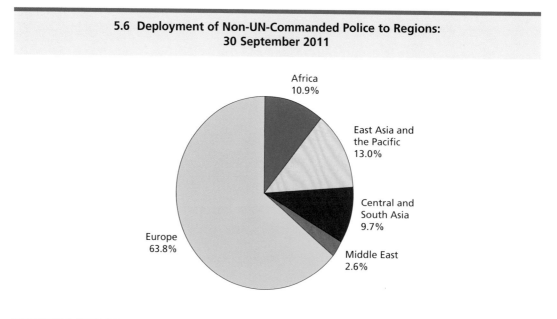

**5.6 Deployment of Non-UN-Commanded Police to Regions:
30 September 2011**

Region	Police	Percentage of Total
Europe	1,228	63.8%
East Asia and the Pacific	250	13.0%
Africa	210	10.9%
Central and South Asia	187	9.7%
Middle East	50	2.6%
TOTAL	**1,925**	

5.7 Deployment of Non-UN-Commanded Troops to Africa by Organization: 30 September 2011

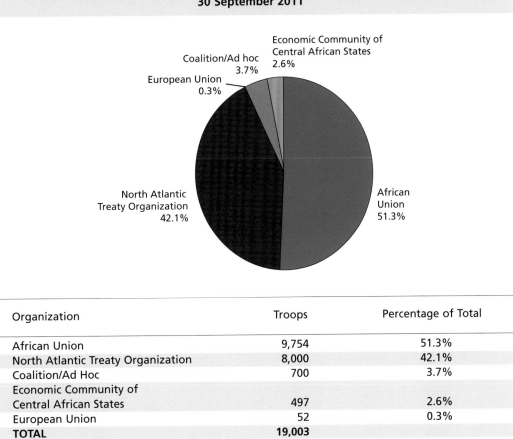

Organization	Troops	Percentage of Total
African Union	9,754	51.3%
North Atlantic Treaty Organization	8,000	42.1%
Coalition/Ad Hoc	700	3.7%
Economic Community of Central African States	497	2.6%
European Union	52	0.3%
TOTAL	**19,003**	

Note: EU NAVFOR Somalia is excluded because it does not deploy troops in Somalia.

5.8 Deployment of Non-UN-Commanded Troops in Europe by Organization: 30 September 2011

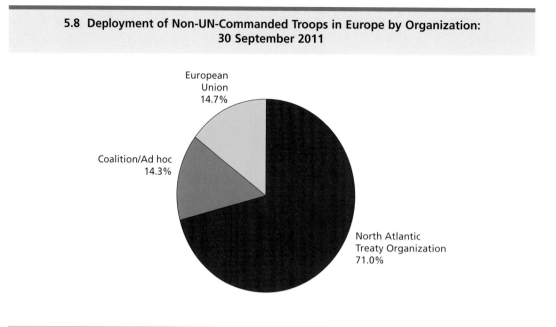

Organization	Troops	Percentage of Total
North Atlantic Treaty Organization	6,240	71.0%
European Union	1,291	14.7%
Coalition/Ad Hoc	1,259	14.3%
TOTAL	**8,790**	

5.9 Deployment of Non-UN-Commanded Police in Africa by Organization: 30 September 2011

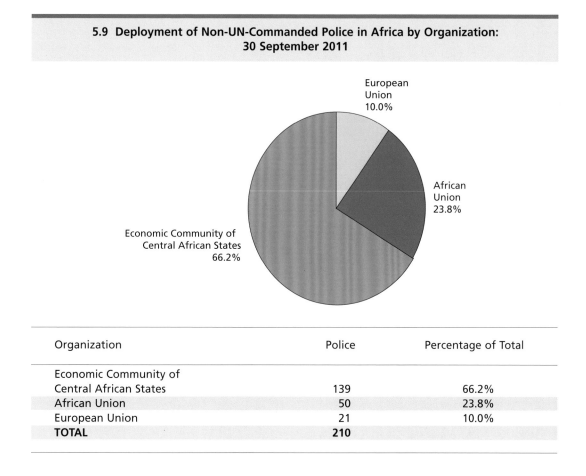

Organization	Police	Percentage of Total
Economic Community of Central African States	139	66.2%
African Union	50	23.8%
European Union	21	10.0%
TOTAL	**210**	

5.10 2011 Non-UN-Commanded Military and Observer Missions

Name	Location	Authorization Date	Start Date	Principal Troop Contributors	Principal Military Observer Contributors	Principal Civilian Police Contributors	Principal Civilian Staff Contributors	Troops, Military Observers, Civilian Police, Civilian Staff (Actual)	Total Deaths to Date/ in 2011 (due to hostilities, accidents, illness, other)
African Union Mission in Somalia (AMISOM)	Somalia[1]	PSC/PR/Comm (LXIX) (19 Jan. 2007) and SCR 1744 (21 Feb. 2007)[2]	March 2007	Burundi (4,542), Cameroon (1), Comoros (1), Djibouti (1), Ethiopia (3), Kenya (8), Senegal (1), Uganda (5,196), Zambia (1)	—	Burundi (1), Gambia (1), Ghana (8), Kenya (10), Nigeria (9), Sierra Leone (9), Uganda (12)	Burundi (1), Kenya (4), Ivory Coast (2), Libya (1), Sudan (1), Swaziland (1), Tanzania (1), Uganda (2)	Troops: 9,754 Civilian Police: 50 Civilian Staff: 13	../83[3]
Mission for the Consolidation of Peace in Central Africa (MICOPAX)	Central African Republic	Libreville Summit (2 Oct. 2002)[4]	December 2002	Cameroon (120), Chad (124), Republic of the Congo (114), Gabon (138)	—	Chad (118), Guinea (21)	—	Troops: 497 Civilian Police: 139	3/1 (–, –, 1, –)
Joint Control Commission Peacekeeping Force (JCC)	Moldova-Transdniestria	Agreement on the Principles Governing the Peaceful Settlement of the Armed Conflict in the Transdniester Region (21 July 1992)[5]	July 1992	Moldova (355), Russia (402), Transdniestria (492)	Ukraine (10)	—	—	Troops: 1,249 Military Observers: 10	../..

Mission	Legal basis	Start date	Troop contributors		Staff contributors	Size	
EU Military Operation in Bosnia and Herzegovina[6] (EUFOR Althea)	CJA 2004/570/CFSP (12 July 2004) and SCR 1575 (22 November 2004)[7]	December 2004	Austria (349), Bulgaria (109), Chile (22), Greece (24), Hungary (166), Netherlands (62), Poland (49), Romania (59), Slovakia (45), Turkey (279)	—	—	Troops: 1,291	21/–
EU Naval Force against Piracy (EU NAVFOR Somalia)	CJA 2008/851/CFSP (10 November 2008)[8]	December 2008	Estonia (10), Finland (4), France (197), Germany (513), Italy (6), Luxembourg (14), Netherlands (210), Spain (394), UK (60)	—	France (1), Germany (2), UK (5)	Troops: 1,434 Civilian Staff: 8	–/–
EU Training Mission in Somalia (EUTM)	CJA 2010/197/CFSP (31 March 2010)[9]	April 2010	Belgium (6), Finland (1), France (22), Germany (4), Hungary (1), Ireland (5), Italy (2), Malta (1), Portugal (3), Spain (4), Sweden (1), UK (2)	—	France (1), Kenya (6), Uganda (5)	Troops: 52 Civilian Staff: 12	–/–

1. The mission's headquarters are based in Nairobi, Kenya. The operation is currently deployed to secure the air and sea ports, Villa Somalia, the old university, the military academy, and other strategic sites in Mogadishu.

2. AMISOM was mandated to support the dialogue and reconciliation process in Somalia by supporting the Transitional Federal Institutions, facilitating the provision of humanitarian assistance and contributing to the overall security situation. On 29 June 2008 the operation's mandate was expanded to include assisting the implementation of the Djibouti Agreement (19 August 2008), including training of Somalia security forces to promote security in the area of Mogadishu. UN SCR 2010 (30 September 2011) extended the mission's mandate until 31 October 2012.

3. This figure covers the period October 2010 to April 2011.

4. MICOPAX was established by a decision of the CEMAL Libreville Summit (2 October 2002) to secure the border between Chad and CAR and to guarantee the safety of former CAR President Patassé. In 2003, following the 15 March coup, its mandate was expanded by a decision of the Libreville Summit (3 June 2003) to include contributing to the overall security environment, assisting in the restructuring of CAR's armed forces, and supporting the transition process. The latest decision of 12 July 2008 expanded the operation's mandate to include promoting political dialogue and human rights. The operation is mandated for 6 months, renewable up to 2013.

5. The JCC Peacekeeping Force was established pursuant to the Agreement on the Principles Governing the Peaceful Settlement of the Armed Conflict in the Transdniester region, signed in Moscow by the presidents of Moldova and Russia (21 July 1992). The JCC—a monitoring commission comprising representatives of Moldova, Russia, and Transdniestria—was established to coordinate the activities of the joint force.

6. A multinational maneuver battalion (made up of Hungarian, Polish, Spanish, and Turkish troops) is stationed in Sarajevo. An integrated police unit and liaison and observer teams are also deployed throughout Bosnia and Herzegovina. EUFOR ALTHEA can be reinforced by KFOR and by EU Operational and Strategic Reserve Forces.

7. EUFOR ALTHEA was established by CJA 2004/570/CFSP (12 July 2004) and endorsed by the UN SCR 1575 (22 November 2004) under UN Charter Chapter VII. It is mandated to maintain a secure environment for implementation of the 1995 Dayton Agreement, to assist in the strengthening of local capacity, and to support Bosnia and Herzegovina's progress toward EU integration. UN SCR 1948 (18 November 2010) extended the mandate of EUFOR ALTHEA until November 2011.

8. EU NAVFOR Somalia was established by CJA 2008/851/CFSP (10 November 2008) and endorsed by the UN SCR 1846 (2 December 2008) under UN Charter Chapter VII. It is mandated to contribute to the deterrence, prevention, and repression of acts of piracy and armed robbery off the Somali coast. Council Decision 2010/766/CFSP (7 December 2010) extended the mission's mandate until 12 December 2012.

9. EUTM was established by CJA 2010/96/CFSP (31 March 2010). It is mandated to contribute to the development of Somali security sector by strengthening Somali security forces. Council Decision 2011/483/CFSP (28 July 2011) extended the mission's mandate to 2012 after two 6-month training periods.

continues

5.10 Continued

Name	Location	Authorization Date	Start Date	Principal Troop Contributors	Principal Military Observer Contributors	Principal Civilian Police Contributors	Principal Civilian Staff Contributors	Troops, Military Observers, Civilian Police, Civilian Staff (Actual)	Total Deaths to Date/ in 2011 (due to hostilities, accidents, illness, other)
NATO Kosovo Force (KFOR)	Kosovo[10]	SCR 1244 (10 June 1999)[11]	June 1999	Austria (592), France (303), Germany (1,451), Hungary (245), Italy (583), Poland (295), Slovenia (318), Switzerland (220), Turkey (357), USA (783)	—	—	—	Troops: 6,240	127/..
International Security Assistance Mission (ISAF)	Afghanistan[12]	SCR 1386 (20 December 2001)[13]	December 2001	Australia (1,550), France (3,935), Germany (4,998), Italy (3,918), Poland (2,580), Romania (1,948), Spain (1,523), Turkey (1,840), UK (9,500), USA (90,000)	—	—	—	Troops: 130,670	2,403/633 (-, 20, 7, 45)
NATO Training Mission in Iraq (NTM-I)	Iraq	SCR 1546 (8 June 2004)[14]	August 2004	Denmark (7), Hungary (3), Italy (77), Netherlands (5), Poland (18), Romania (4), Ukraine (10), UK (39), USA (11)	—	—	—	Troops: 170	../..

Operation Unified Protector (OUP)	Libya	SCR 1970 (26 February 2011) and SCR 1973 (17 March 2011)[15]	March 2011	Belgium, Bulgaria, Canada, Denmark, France, Greece, Italy, Jordan, Netherlands, Norway, Qatar, Romania, Sweden, Spain, Turkey, UAE, UK, USA[16]	—	—	—	Troops: 8,000 Civilian Staff: 80	1/1 (–, 1, –, –)
Multinational Force and Observers (MFO)	Sinai (Egypt)	Protocol to the Treaty of Peace between Egypt and Israel (26 March 1979)[17]	April 1982	Australia (25), Canada (28), Colombia (358), Czech Republic (3), Fiji (338), Hungary (42), Italy (78), New Zealand (28), Norway (3), Uruguay (40), USA (693)	—	Australia (3), Canada (3), France (1), New Zealand (1), UK (29), USA (23)[18]	—	Military 1,656 Observers: Civilian Staff: 60	67/2 (–, 1, 1, –)

10. The Headquarters of Kosovo Force (HQ KFOR) are located in Pristina. It supports a NATO-led mission of two Multinational Battle Groups (MBG) and five Joint Regional Detachments. MBG West is located in Pec and is led by Italy, and MBG East is located in Urosevac and is led by the United States. A Multinational Specialized Unit (MSU) and a Tactical Reserve Manoeuvre Battalion (KTM) are also stationed in Pristina.

11. KFOR was established by UN SCR 1244 (10 June 1999). Its mandated tasks include deterring renewed hostilities, establishing a secure environment, supporting UNMIK, and monitoring borders. In 2008, NATO expanded the operation's task to include efforts to develop professional, democratic, and multiethnic security structures in Kosovo. A positive decision of the UN Security Council is required to terminate the operation.

12. The territory of Afghanistan is divided into six areas of responsibility: Regional Command (RC) Centre (Kabul), currently led by Turkey; RC North (Mazar-e Sharif), led by Germany; RC West (Herat), led by Italy; RC South (Kandahar), led by the United States; RC Southwest (Helmand), led by the United States; and RC East (Bagram), led by the United States.

13. ISAF was established by UN SCR 1386 (20 December 2001) under UN Charter Chapter VII as a multinational force mandated to assist the Afghan Government to maintain security, as envisaged in Annex I of the 2001 Bonn Agreement. NATO took over command and control of ISAF in August 2003. UN SCR 2011 (12 October 2011) extended the mandate to 13 October 2012.

14. NTM-I was established pursuant to UN SCR 1546 (8 June 2004) and approved by the North Atlantic Council on 17 November 2004. It is mandated to assist in the development of Iraq's security institutions through training and equipment of, in particular, middle- and senior-level personnel from the Iraqi security forces. Since 2007 the mission is mandated to focus on mentoring and to advise an Iraqi-led institutional training program.

15. Operation Unified Protector was established pursuant to UN SCR 1970 (26 February 2011) and UN SCR 1973 (17 March 2011) under UN Charter Chapter VII. Its aim was to enforce the arms embargo and the no-fly zone decided upon by the Security Council and to protect civilians and civilian-populated areas under attack or threat of attack. The mission ended on the 31 October 2011.

16. Operation Unified Protector's personnel supported air and maritime operations. Media reports indicate the following national breakdown for the principal troop contributors: Belgium (170), Bulgaria (160), Canada (560), France (800), Netherlands (205), Norway (140), Romania (205), Spain (500), the United Kingdom (1,300), and the United States (8,507).

17. MFO was established on 3 August 1981 by the Protocol to the Treaty of Peace between Egypt and Israel, signed 26 March 1979. Deployment began on 20 March 1982 following the withdrawal of Israeli forces from the Sinai but the mission did not become operational until 25 April 1982, the day that Israel returned the Sinai to Egyptian sovereignty. The mission is mandated to observe the implementation of the peace treaty and to contribute to security.

18. Civilian staff are not seconded personnel; they are contracted by the mission directly.

continues

5.10 Continued

Name	Location	Authorization Date	Start Date	Principal Troop Contributors	Principal Military Observer Contributors	Principal Civilian Police Contributors	Principal Civilian Staff Contributors	Troops, Military Observers, Civilian Police, Civilian Staff (Actual)	Total Deaths to Date/ in 2011 (due to hostilities, accidents, illness, other)
Operation Licorne	Côte d'Ivoire	SCR 1464 (4 Feb. 2003)[19]	February 2003	France (700)	—	—	—	Troops: 700	24/–
Regional Assistance Mission to Solomon Islands (RAMSI)	Solomon Islands	Biketawa Declaration (2000)[20]	July 2003	Australia, New Zealand, Papua New Guinea, Tonga	—	Australia, Cook Islands (1), Federated States of Micronesia (2), Fiji (10), Kiribati, Marshall Islands (1), Nauru, New Zealand, Niue (2), Palau (2), Papua New Guinea (8), Samoa, Tonga, Tuvalu (2), Vanuatu	Australia, Fiji, New Zealand, Papua New Guinea, Samoa, Tonga	Civilian Police: 250[21]	8/..

International Security Forces (ISF)	Timor-Leste	SCR 1690 (20 June 2006)[22]	May 2006	Australia (380), New Zealand (80)	—	—	Troops: 460	./. (-, 1[23] -,-,-)
International Monitoring Team	Philippines[24]	27 October 2009 (Agreement on the Civilian Protection Component (CPC) of the IMT) 22 June 2001 (Agreement on Peace between the GPH and the MILF)[25]	10 October 2004[26]	Brunei (15), France (1), Japan (2), Libya (3), Malaysia (20), Norway (2), UK (1)[27]	—	—	Military Observers: 38	./.

19. Operation Licorne was deployed under the authority of UN SCR 1464 (4 February 2003) and given UN Charter Chapter VII powers to support the ECOWAS mission (2003–2004) in contributing to a secure environment and, in particular, to facilitate implementation of the 2003 Linas-Marcoussis Agreement. UN SCR 1528 (27 February 2004) provides its current authorization and revised the mandate to support UNOCI. UN SCR 1795 (15 January 2008) expanded the mandate to support implementing the Ouagadougou political Agreement (4 March 2007) and the Supplementary Agreements (28 November 2007), in particular assisting in preparations for elections scheduled in October and November 2010. UN SCR 2000 (27 July 2011) extended the mandate to 31 July 2012.

20. RAMSI was established under the framework of the 2000 Biketawa Declaration, in which members of the Pacific Islands Forum agreed to mount a collective response to crises, usually at the request of the host government. It is mandated to assist the Solomon Islands government in restoring law and order and in building up the capacity of the police force.

21. Figures for RAMSI's troop component and civilian staff component are not available.

22. ISF was deployed at the request of the government of Timor-Leste to assist in stabilizing the security environment in the country and endorsed by UN SCR 1690 (20 June 2006). The operation cooperates closely with UNMIT.

23. Information on total number of fatalities and other causes of death (if any) was not available.

24. IMT operates on the island of Mindanao.

25. IMT is tasked to observe and monitor the implementation of cessation of hostilities, humanitarian, socioeconomic aspects, and the civilian protection component of the agreements signed between the GPH and MILF.

26. Following a dramatic increase in conflict and a withdrawal from the ceasefire agreement by MILF in late 2008, the IMT decided to remove its monitors until the ceasefire was renewed. IMT's mandate was renewed on 8 December 2009.

27. Observers from France, Norway, Japan, and the United Kingdom are civilian observers.

5.11 2011 Non-UN-Commanded Civilian Police and Civilian Missions

Name	Location	Authorization Date	Start Date	Principal Troop Contributors	Principal Military Observer Contributors	Principal Civilian Police Contributors	Principal Civilian Staff Contributors	Civilian Police, Civilian Staff (Actual)	Total Deaths to Date/ in 2011 (due to hostilities, accidents, illness, other)
EU Police Mission in Bosnia and Herzegovina (EUPM)	Bosnia and Herzegovina	CJA 2002/210/CFSP[1] (11 March 2002)	January 2003	—	—	Finland (6), France (5), Germany (12), Hungary (3), Ireland (3), Italy (9), Netherlands (7), Romania (8), Slovakia (3), Slovenia (3), Spain (3), Sweden (4)	Bulgaria (2), Finland (4), France (3), Germany (4), Ireland (2), Italy (7), Netherlands (1), Portugal (1), Romania (1), Slovenia (1), Switzerland (1), Turkey (2), Ukraine (1), UK (4)	Civilian Police: 83 Civilian Staff: 34	3/–
EU Advisory and Assistance Mission for DRC Security Reform (EUSEC RD Congo)	Democratic Republic of the Congo	CJA 2005/355/CFSP[2] (2 May 2005)	June 2005	—	—	—	Belgium (8), France (9), Germany (3), Hungary (2), Netherlands (3), Portugal (3), UK (4)	Civilian Staff: 51[3]	2/–

Mission	Location	Legal basis	Start		Contributing states		Contributing states	Personnel	
EU Border Assistance Mission for the Rafah Crossing Point (EU BAM Rafah)[4]	Rafah Crossing Point, (Egypt and Palestinian Territories)	CJA 2005/889/CFSP[5] (12 December 2005)	November 2005	—	France (2), Germany (2), Italy (1)	—	Finland (2), France (1), Hungary (1), Italy (1), Romania (1), Spain (1), UK (1)	Civilian Police: 5 Civilian Staff: 8	–/–
EU Police Mission for the Palestinian Territories (EUPOL COPPS)	Palestinian Territories	CJA 2005/797/CFSP[6] (14 November 2005)	January 2006	—	Belgium (2), Canada (2), Finland (1), France (2), Germany (2), Italy (1), Netherlands (1), Spain (1), Sweden (3), UK (2)	—	Denmark (3), Estonia (2), Finland (4), France (1), Germany (4), Ireland (2), Italy (2), Netherlands (2), Spain (3), Sweden (2), UK (3)	Civilian Police: 17 Civilian Staff: 32	–/–
EU Police Mission in Afghanistan (EUPOL Afghanistan)	Afghanistan	CJA 2007/369/CFSP[7] (30 May 2007)	June 2007	—	Canada (11), Czech Republic (8), Denmark (8), Finland (21), Germany (24), Ireland (6), Netherlands (22), Norway (12), Romania (6), Sweden (10), UK (15)	—	Canada (12), Finland (15), Germany (26), Hungary (4), Ireland (5), Italy (8), Netherlands (11), Norway (10), Romania (17), Sweden (16), UK (13)	Civilian Police: 187 Civilian Staff: 134	–/–

1. EUPM was established by CJA 2002/210/CFSP (11 March 2002) and tasked with the establishment of a sustainable professional and multi-ethnic police service in Bosnia and Herzegovina under Bosnian ownership through monitoring, mentoring, and inspection. At the request of the Bosnian authorities, the mandate was modified to focus on the police reform process, strengthening of police accountability, and efforts to fight organized crime. CJA 2009/906/CFSP (8 December 2009) extended the mandate to 31 December 2011.

2. EUSEC RD Congo was established by CJA 2005/355/CFSP (2 May 2005). The mission's initial mandate was to advise and assist the authorities of the DRC, specifically the Ministry of Defense, on security matters, ensuring that policies are congruent with international humanitarian law, the standards of democratic governance, and the principles of the rule of law. In 2009 the mission's mandate was broadened to include facilitating the implementation of the guidelines adopted by the Congolese authorities in the revised plan for reform of the armed forces of DR Congo. In carrying out its activities, EUSEC operates in coordination with MONUSCO and EUPOL DR Congo. CJA 2010/565/CFSP (21 September 2010) extended the mandate to 30 September 2012.

3. The majority of the deployed personnel (37) are military advisers.

4. The mission is based in Ashkelon, Israel.

5. EU BAM Rafah was established pursuant to CJA 2005/889/CFSP (12 December 2005) and on the basis of the Agreement on Movement and Access between Israel and the Palestinian Authority (15 November 2005). It is mandated to monitor, verify, and evaluate the performance of Palestinian Authority border control, security, and customs officials at the Rafah Crossing Point with regard to the 2005 Agreed Principles for the Rafah Crossing; and to support the Palestinian Authority's capacity building in the field of border control. Following riots in 2007, the Rafah Crossing Point was closed and only to be opened under exceptional circumstances. However, EU BAM Rafah retains full operational capabilities. Council Decision 2011/312/CFSP (26 May 2011) extended the mandate to 31 December 2011.

6. EUPOL COPPS was established by CJA 2005/797/CFSP (14 November 2005). It is mandated to provide a framework for and advise Palestinian criminal justice and police officials, and coordinate EU aid to the Palestinian Authority. Council Decision 2010/784/CFSP (17 December 2010) extended the mandate to 31 December 2011.

7. EUPOL Afghanistan was established by CJA 2007/369/CFSP (30 May 2007) at the invitation of the Afghan Government. The operation is tasked to contribute to the establishment of civilian policing arrangements and law enforcement under Afghan ownership. CJA 2010/279/CFSP (18 May 2010) extended the mandate to 31 May 2013.

continues

5.11 Continued

Name	Location	Authorization Date	Start Date	Principal Troop Contributors	Principal Military Observer Contributors	Principal Civilian Police Contributors	Principal Civilian Staff Contributors	Civilian Police, Civilian Staff (Actual)	Total Deaths to Date/ in 2011 (due to hostilities, accidents, illness, other)
EU Police Mission in the Democratic Republic of the Congo (EUPOL RD Congo)	Democratic Republic of the Congo	CJA 2007/405/CFSP[8] (12 June 2007)	July 2007	—	—	Belgium (6), Finland (1), France (11), Italy (2), Sweden (1)	Belgium (5), France (3), Germany (2), Italy (1), Poland (1), Portugal (4), Sweden (3)	Civilian Police: 21 Civilian Staff: 19	–/–
EU Rule of Law Mission in Kosovo (EULEX Kosovo)	Kosovo	CJA 2008/124/CFSP[9] (4 February 2008)	February 2008	—	—	France (88), Germany (87), Hungary (35), Italy (99), Netherlands (36), Poland (122), Romania (173), Sweden (51), Turkey (85), USA (51)	Bulgaria (47), Denmark (23), Finland (37), France (23), Germany (45), Italy (41), Poland (26), Romania (30), Sweden (34), UK (79)	Civilian Police: 1,044 Civilian Staff: 541	2/–
EU Monitoring Mission in Georgia (EUMM)	Georgia	CJA 2008/736/CFSP[10] (15 September 2008)	October 2008			Austria (3), Czech Republic (3), Denmark (4), Estonia (4), France (16), Germany (14), Hungary (3), Poland (9), Romania (8), Sweden (7), UK (3)	Bulgaria (18), Czech Republic (11), Finland (25), Germany (23), Italy (15), Netherlands (9), Poland (15), Romania (21), Sweden (21), UK (18)	Civilian Police: 89 Civilian Staff: 218[11]	–/–

Mission	Location	Establishing decision			Participating states	Personnel	
OSCE Mission to Moldova	Moldova	19th OSCE Committee of Senior Officials meeting[12] (4 February 1993)	April 1993	—	—	Bulgaria (1), Czech Republic (1), Estonia (2), France (2), Germany (1), Italy (1), Latvia (1), Poland (1), Russia (1), Sweden (2), UK (1), USA (4)	Civilian Staff: 18	-/-
OSCE Mission to Bosnia and Herzegovina	Bosnia and Herzegovina	5th Meeting of the OSCE Ministerial Council[13] MC(5).DEC/1 (8 December 1995)	December 1995	—	—	Germany (4), Greece (3), Ireland (5), Italy (5), Russia (4), Slovakia (3), Spain (3), UK (5)	Civilian Staff: 73	-/-
OSCE Mission in Kosovo (OMIK)	Kosovo	PC.DEC/305[14] (1 July 1999)	July 1999	—	—	Canada (1), Georgia (1), Germany (1), Romania (1), Turkey (6), UK (2)	Austria (16), Bosnia and Herzegovina (10), Canada (8), Croatia (8), Germany (8), Italy (19), Macedonia (9), Spain (8), UK (10), USA (20)	Civilian Police: 12 Civilian Staff: 177	-/-

8. EUPOL RD Congo was established by CJA 2007/405/CFSP (12 June 2007). CJA 2009/769/CFSP (19 Oct 2009) mandated the mission to assist the Congolese authorities in reforming and restructuring the Congolese Police; improving interaction between police and criminal justice system; supporting efforts against sexual violence; and promoting gender, human rights, and the children aspects of the peace process. The mission cooperates with EUSEC DR Congo and MONUSCO. Council Decision 2011/537/CFSP (12 September 2011) extended the mandate to 30 September 2012.

9. EULEX Kosovo was established by CJA 2008/124/CFSP (4 February 2008). With certain executive responsibilities, in terms of investigating and prosecuting serious and sensitive crimes, the operation is tasked to monitor, mentor, and advise Kosovo rule of law institutions. It cooperates closely with UNMIK and OMIK. CJA 2010/322/CFSP (8 June 2010) extended the mandate to 14 June 2012.

10. EUMM was established by CJA 2008/736/CFSP (15 September 2008) in accordance with the agreement on 8 September 2008, following the conflict in South Ossetia in August 2008. The operation is tasked with monitoring and analyzing progress in the stabilization process, focusing on compliance with the 6-point peace plan of 12 August 2008, and in the normalization of civil governance; monitoring infrastructure security and the political and security aspects of the return of internally displaced persons and refugees, and supporting the confidence-building measures. Council Decision 2011/536/CFSP (12 September 2011) extended the mandate to 14 September 2012.

11. Figure includes 73 observers.

12. The OSCE Mission to Moldova was established at the 19th CSO meeting (4 February 1993) and authorized by the Moldovan Government through an MOU (7 May 1993). Its tasks include assisting the conflicting parties in pursuing negotiations on lasting political settlement and gathering and providing information on the situation. PC.DEC/970 (16 December 2010) extended the mandate to 31 December 2011.

13. The OSCE Mission to Bosnia and Herzegovina was established by a decision of the fifth meeting of the OSCE Ministerial Council MC(5).DEC/1 (8 December 1995), in accordance with Annex 6 of the 1995 Dayton Agreement. The operation is mandated to assist the parties in regional stabilization measures and democratization. PC.DEC/974 (16 December 2010) extended the mandate to 31 December 2011.

14. The OSCE Mission in Kosovo was established by PC.DEC/305 (1 July 1999). Its mandate includes training police, judicial personnel, and civil administrators, and monitoring and promoting human rights. The mission is a component of UNMIK. Since PC.DEC/835 (21 December 2007) the mission's mandate is extended on a monthly basis unless one of the participating states objects.

continues

5.11 Continued

Name	Location	Authorization Date	Start Date	Principal Troop Contributors	Principal Military Observer Contributors	Principal Civilian Police Contributors	Principal Civilian Staff Contributors	Civilian Police, Civilian Staff (Actual)	Total Deaths to Date/ in 2011 (due to hostilities, accidents, illness, other)
Temporary International Presence in Hebron (TIPH)	Hebron (Palestinian Territories)	Hebron Protocol (17 January 1997) and the Agreement on the Temporary International Presence in Hebron (21 January 1997)[15]	February 1997	—	—	Denmark, Italy, Norway, Turkey (7)	Denmark, Norway (15), Sweden (12), Switzerland	Civilian Police: 28 Civilian Staff: 39	2/–

15. TIPH 2 was established by the Protocol Concerning the Redeployment in Hebron (17 January 1997) and the Agreement on the Temporary International Peace Presence in Hebron (21 January 1997). It is mandated to provide by its presence, a secure and stable environment and to monitor and report breaches of international humanitarian law. The mandate is renewed every six months pending approval from both the Palestinian and Israeli parties.

5.12 Cost of Non-UN-Commanded Military, Observer, Civilian Police, and Civilian Missions: 1 October 2010–30 September 2011

Name	Location	Cost ($US Millions)
Non-UN Military and Observer Missions		
African Union Mission in Somalia (AMISOM)	Somalia	152.0
Mission for the Consolidation of Peace in Central Africa (MICOPAX)	Central African Republic	27.2
Joint Control Commission Peacekeeping Force (JCC)	Moldova-Transdniestria	—[1]
EU Military Operation in Bosnia and Herzegovina (EUFOR Althea)	Bosnia and Herzegovina	29.9
EU Naval Force Against Piracy (EU NAVFOR Somalia)	Somalia (Gulf of Aden)	11.3
EU Training Mission in Somalia (EUTM)	Uganda	5.8
NATO Kosovo Force (KFOR)	Kosovo	—[2]
International Security Assistance Mission (ISAF)	Afghanistan	292.0[3]
NATO Training Mission in Iraq (NTM-I)	Iraq	—[4]
Operation Unified Protector (OUP)	Libya	7.0
Multinational Force and Observers (MFO)	Sinai (Egypt)	78.3
Operation Licorne	Côte d'Ivoire	100.3[5]
Regional Assistance Mission to Solomon Islands (RAMSI)	Solomon Islands	42.5[6]
International Security Forces (ISF)	Timor-Leste	184.6[7]
International Monitoring Team (IMT)	Philippines	—[8]
Non-UN Civilian Police and Civilian Missions		
EU Police Mission in Bosnia and Herzegovina (EUPM)	Bosnia and Herzegovina	24.5
EU Advisory and Assistance Mission for DRC Security Reform (EUSEC RD Congo)	Democratic Republic of the Congo	17.6
EU Border Assistance Mission for the Rafah Crossing Point (EU BAM Rafah)	Rafah Crossing Point	2.0
EU Police Mission for the Palestinian Territories (EUPOL COPPS)	Palestinian Territories	11.0
EU Police Mission in Afghanistan (EUPOL Afghanistan)	Afghanistan	68.4
EU Police Mission in the Democratic Republic of the Congo (EUPOL RD Congo)	Democratic Republic of the Congo	8.9
EU Rule of Law Mission in Kosovo (EULEX Kosovo)	Kosovo	230.0
EU Monitoring Mission in Georgia (EUMM)	Georgia	37.1
OSCE Mission to Moldova	Moldova	2.9
OSCE Mission to Bosnia and Herzegovina	Bosnia and Herzegovina	20.8
OSCE Mission in Kosovo (OMIK)	Kosovo	31.5
Temporary International Presence in Hebron (TIPH)	Hebron (Palestinian territories)	—[9]

1. There is no designated budget for this mission. Contributing countries bear the cost of sending military and civilian personnel.
2. Budget data is not available for this mission.
3. This figure covers the period January 2011–December 2011.
4. Budget data is not available for this mission.
5. This figure covers the period January 2010–December 2010.
6. This figure only reflects the cost borne by Australia.
7. This figure is the sum of contributions from Australia and New Zealand, who are the principal contributors to this mission. The figure for Australia's contribution covers the period July 2010–June 2011. The figure for New Zealand is for October 2010–September 2011.
8. Budget data is not available for this mission.
9. For the period January 2011–December 2011, Sweden contributed $US3.4 million, which covers the operating costs and the cost of sending the personnel.

5.13 Heads and Force Commanders of Non-UN-Commanded Military, Observer, Civilian Police, and Civilian Missions: 30 September 2011

Name	Location	Head of Mission
Non-UN-Commanded Military and Observer Missions		
African Union Mission in Somalia (AMISOM)	Somalia	Special Representative of the Chairperson of the AU Commission: Ambassador Boubacar Gaoussou Diarra (Mali) Force Commander: Major-General Fred Mugisha (Uganda)
Mission for the Consolidation of Peace in Central Africa (MICOPAX)	Central African Republic	Special Representative: Ambassador Albert Akendengue (Gabon) Force Commander: Brigade-General Prosper Nabiolwa (Democratic Republic of the Congo)
Joint Control Commission Peacekeeping Force (JCC)	Moldova-Transdniestria	Chief of Staff, Joint Headquarters: Colonel Aleksei Tumashev (Russia)
EU Military Operation in Bosnia and Herzegovina (EUFOR Althea)	Bosnia and Herzegovina	Operation Commander: General Sir Richard Shirreff (UK) Force Commander: Major-General Bernhard Bair (Austria)
EU Naval Force against Piracy (EU NAVFOR Somalia)	Somalia (Gulf of Aden)	Operation Commander: Rear Admiral Duncan L. Potts (Malta) Force Commander: Rear Admiral Thomas E. P. Jugel (Germany)
NATO Kosovo Force (KFOR)	Kosovo	Major-General Erhard Drews (Germany)
International Security Assistance Mission (ISAF)	Afghanistan	General John R. Allen (USA)
NATO Training Mission in Iraq (NTM-I)	Iraq	Lieutenant-General Michael Ferriter (USA)
Operation Unified Protector	Libya	Vice Admiral Rinaldo Veri (Italy)
Multinational Force and Observers (MFO)	Sinai (Egypt)	Ambassador David M. Satterfield (USA) Force Commander: Major-General Warren J. Whiting (New Zealand)
Operation Licorne	Côte d'Ivoire	Colonel Daniel Jaunin (France)
Regional Assistance Mission to Solomon Islands (RAMSI)	Solomon Islands	Special Coordinator: Nicholas Coppel (Australia) Force Commander: Lieutenant Colonel Campbell Smith (Australia)
International Security Forces (ISF)	Timor-Leste	Colonel Luke Foster (Australia)
International Monitoring Team (IMT)	Philippines	Major General Mahdi Yusof (Malaysia)

continues

5.13 Continued

Name	Location	Head of Mission
Non-UN Civilian Police and Civilian Missions		
EU Police Mission in Bosnia and Herzegovina (EUPM)	Bosnia and Herzegovina	Brigadier-General Stefan Feller (Germany)
EU Advisory and Assistance Mission for DRC Security Reform (EUSEC RD Congo)	Democratic Republic of the Congo	General António Martin (Portugal)
EU Border Assistance Mission for the Rafah Crossing Point (EU BAM Rafah)	Rafah Crossing Point	Colonel Alain Faugeras (France)
EU Police Mission for the Palestinian Territories (EUPOL COPPS)	Palestinian Territories	Commissioner Henrik Malmquist (Sweden)
EU Police Mission in Afghanistan (EUPOL Afghanistan)	Afghanistan	Brigadier General Jukka Savolainen (Finland)
EU Police Mission in the Democratic Republic of the Congo (EUPOL RD Congo)	Democratic Republic of the Congo	Commissioner Jean Paul Rikir (Belgium)
EU Rule of Law Mission in Kosovo (EULEX Kosovo)	Kosovo	Xavier Bout de Marnhac (France)
EU Monitoring Mission in Georgia (EUMM)	Georgia	Mr Andrzej Tyszkiewicz (Poland)
EU Training Mission in Somalia (EUTM)	Uganda	Colonel Michael Beary (Ireland)
OSCE Mission to Moldova	Moldova	Ambassador Philip N. Remler (USA)
OSCE Mission to Bosnia and Herzegovina	Bosnia and Herzegovina	Ambassador Fletcher M. Burton (USA)
OSCE Mission in Kosovo (OMIK)	Kosovo	Ambassador Werner Almhofer (Austria)
Temporary International Presence in Hebron (TIPH)	Hebron (Palestinian Territories)	Brigadier-General Einar Johnsen (Norway)

6 UN Mission-by-Mission Statistics

This chapter contains data on all current missions of the UN Department of Peacekeeping Operations (DPKO) and the UN Department of Field Support (DFS).[1] It is based on public UN documents and sources, combined with data provided by DPKO and DFS, and in some cases by the UN Department of Management (DM) and the United Nations Volunteer (UNV) Programme in Bonn.

Variations in types of data sources and reporting dates between missions are often a result of differences in the structure, reporting, and funding mechanisms for different types of UN peace operations:

- Peacekeeping missions funded by the General Assembly on the basis of a financial period running from 1 July to 30 June of the following year.
- Peacekeeping missions funded by the biennial UN budget, which runs from January in even years to December of odd years (UNMOGIP and UNTSO).

The features of our dataset are outlined below.

Key Facts
Notes on mandates and key personnel.

Personnel:
July 2010–September 2011
These graphs cover personnel trends through the last UN peacekeeping financial year and through the first quarter of the 2010–2011 financial year on a month-by-month basis. Authorized military and police personnel strengths are based on *authorized* strengths in Security Council resolutions, relevant budgetary documentation, or were provided directly by the DPKO Force Generation Service (FGS) and the DPKO Police Division (PD). Actual military and personnel strengths were provided by the FGS and PD. Actual and authorized strengths for international staff and national staff were provided by the DFS Field Personnel Division (FPD). UNV actual and authorized strengths (based on exchange of letters and mission-specific agreements between the UNV Programme and DFS) were provided by the UNV Programme in Bonn.

Personnel: Since 2000
These graphs show average annual number of personnel and average annual number of authorized personnel since 2000 (up to June 2011 for missions funded by the peacekeeping budget and through September 2011 for other missions). For the July 2006–September 2011 periods, actual military and police personnel figures were calculated based on information provided by the DPKO FGS or PD. Authorized military and police personnel figures were derived from Security Council resolutions or obtained from the DPKO FGS and PD in cases where Security Council resolutions did not specify authorized strengths. International and national civilian staff actual and authorized strengths were calculated based on information provided by the DFS FPD. UNV actual and authorized figures were provided by the UNV Programme.

Average actual and authorized figures for the January–June 2006 period were obtained from official budgetary and financial performance reports covering that year or from data collected directly from the relevant UN Departments for past editions of the *Review*. Exceptions include UNMOGIP and UNTSO, for which historical and actual personnel figures were derived from the UN's Proposed Programme Budget for the Biennium.

Military and Police Contributors: 30 September 2011

These data show all contributors to the mission on 30 September 2011 and were provided by the DPKO FGS and PD. The categories "Troops" and "Military Observers" are used to classify military staff where: "Troops" refer to both Troops and Staff Officers and "Military Observers" refer to Military Observers, Military Liaison Officers, and Military Advisors unless otherwise noted.

Military Units: 30 September 2011

These data show units in the field on 30 September 2011 by their type and country of origin, based on information provided by the DPKO FGS. Military staff are not formed into traditional units in observer missions, political missions, and in the observer elements of larger missions, therefore, these personnel are not recorded in this section. The categories "Troops" and "Military Observers" are used to classify military staff where: "Troops" refer to both Troops and Staff Officers and "Military Observers" refer to Military Observers, Military Liaison Officers, and Military Advisors unless otherwise noted.

International Civilian Personnel Occupations: 30 September 2011

These data, provided by the DFS FPD, break down international civilian staff into occupational groups, as provided by the DFS FPD.

Gender Statistics: 30 September 2011

These data show the total number of male and female troops, military observers, police, international staff, and national staff as of that date. Military data were provided by the DPKO FGS, police data were provided by the

DPKO PD, and international and national staff data were provided by the DFS FPD. Data for UNVs were not available. The categories "Troops" and "Military Observers" are used to classify military staff where: "Troops" refer to both Troops and Staff Officers and "Military Observers" refer to Military Observers, Military Liaison Officers, and Military Advisors unless otherwise noted.

Fatalities: Inception–September 2011

These data were provided by the DPKO Situation Centre. Differences may exist between the historical data shown here and fatality data shown in last year's edition of the *Review* due to investigations and reviews of fatality reports undertaken by the Situation Centre over the course of the year. Fatality incident types previously categorized as "hostile act" and "criminal act" have henceforth been combined into a single category—"malicious act." Fatality incident types previously categorized as "self-inflicted" have henceforth been combined into the "other" category. The categories "Military" and "Military Observers" are used to classify military staff where: "Military" refer to both Troops and Staff Officers and "Military Observers" refer to Military Observers, Military Liaison Officers, and Military Advisors unless otherwise noted.

Vehicles: 30 September 2011

These data cover both UN-owned vehicles and those vehicles owned by national contingents serving in the field under a Memorandum of Agreement and for which usage is reimbursed by the UN. Data on contingent-owned vehicles were obtained from a database managed by the DFS Contingent Owned Equipment and Management Section; data for UN-owned vehicles were provided by the DFS Surface Transport Section. The following missions do not have Contingent Owned Equipment vehicles: MINURSO, UNMIK, UNMOGIP, and UNTSO. All data for UNISFA and UNMISS under this section are preliminary and subject to change.

Aircraft: 30 September 2011

These data have been provided by the DFS Air Transport Section and identify aircraft by their type (transport fixed-wing, transport helicopter, or attack helicopter) and supplier (contractor or government). The following missions do not have aircraft: UNDOF, UNISFA, UNMIK, UNMOGIP, and UNTSO.

Budget and Expenditures: 2010–2012

All 2010–2012 data were obtained from official budgetary and financial performance reports covering that year, or provided by the DFS Field Budget and Finance Division (FBFD).

Peacekeeping missions funded by the peacekeeping budget show the budget and expenditures for the 2009/10 financial year as well as the budget for the 2010/11 financial year.

Peacekeeping missions funded from the regular biennial budget (UNTSO and UNMOGIP): these data show appropriations for the January 2012–December 2013 period.

Mission Expenditures: 2000–2010

Covering the financial years since 2000, this overview of expenditures has been derived from mission financing reports, financial performance reports, and reports on mission budgets. Information on UNTSO and UN-MOGIP has been provided by DFS FBFD. Some discrepancies may appear between the 2004–2005 data provided here, which is derived from official performance reports on the budget, and those data provided in last year's edition of the *Review,* which were provided by the DFS FBFD prior to the publication of official performance reports. The mission expenditure tables for peacekeeping missions funded by the peacekeeping budget are broken down into the three following categories (although there was some variation in subcategories in 2000–2001[2]):

1. *Military and police personnel.* Includes missions' subsistence allowance, travel on emplacement, rotation and repatriation, death and disability compensation, and rations and clothing allowances for military observers and police. This section also includes expenditures on major contingent-owned equipment and freight, and deployment of contingent-owned equipment.

2. *Civilian personnel.* Covers salaries, staff assessment, common staff costs, hazardous duty stations allowances, and overtime for international and national staff, as well as covers costs associated with United Nations Volunteers.

3. *Operational requirements.* Covers costs associated with general temporary assistance (salaries, common staff costs, staff assessment), government-provided personnel and civilian electoral observers (allowances and travel), consultants, official travel of civilian personnel, facilities and infrastructure, as well as self-sustainment costs of contingent-owned equipment. Also included are costs associated with ground, air, and naval transportation in mission, communications, IT, medical, special equipment, other supplies, services and equipment, and quick impact projects.

Expenditures on Contingent Owned Equipment: July 2010–June 2011

These data, provided by DFS FBFD and derived from mission budget reports, cover contingents' expenditures on major equipment for which they can be reimbursed by the UN, as well as self-sustainment (rations, etc.) for those missions financed by the peacekeeping budget. UNTSO does not have Contingent Owned Equipment.

Voluntary Contributions: July 2010–June 2011

These data cover those countries and organizations providing financial support to missions other than through assessed contributions. They are provided by the UN Department of

Management's Office of Programme Planning, Budget and Accounts (OPPBA). The following missions do not have voluntary contributions: MINUSTAH, UNAMID, UNDOF, UNIFIL, UNISFA, UNMIK, UNMISS, UNMIT, UNMOGIP, UNOCI, and UNTSO.

Notes

1. Data regarding the UNLB and DFS support to AMISOM and UNSOA is not included.

2. Prior to the July 2001–June 2002 financial year, "Staff Assessment" was reported as an additional line item in "Gross Expenditures" for each mission. Since then, staff assessment has been included as part of the "Civilian Personnel" line item. For the sake of consistency, figures for the 2000–2001 financial years are shown using the current financial reporting method and include staff assessment expenditures as part of the civilian personnel expenditures. For those years, civilian personnel expenditures will thus appear to be higher than in the official UN financial reports.

6.1 MINURSO (UN Mission for the Referendum in Western Sahara)

MINURSO Key Facts	
Latest Key Resolution	27 April 2011 (date of issue and effect) UNSC Res. 1979 (twelve month duration)
First Mandate	29 April 1991 (date of issue); 6 September 1991 (date of effect) UNSC Res. 690 (no determined duration)
SRSG	Hany Abdel-Aziz (Egypt) SG letter of appointment 6 October 2009
First SRSG	Johannes Manz (Switzerland)
Force Commander	Major-General Abdul Hafiz (Bangladesh) SG letter of appointment 22 July 2011
First Force Commander	Major-General Armand Roy (Canada)

MINURSO Personnel: July 2010–September 2011

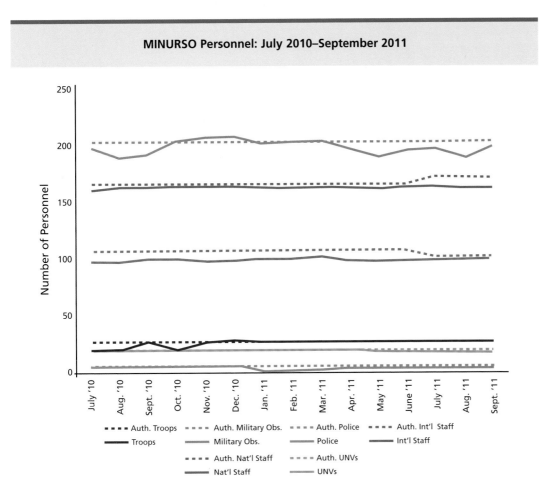

Sources: DFS FPD; DPKO FGS; DPKO PD; UNV Programme.

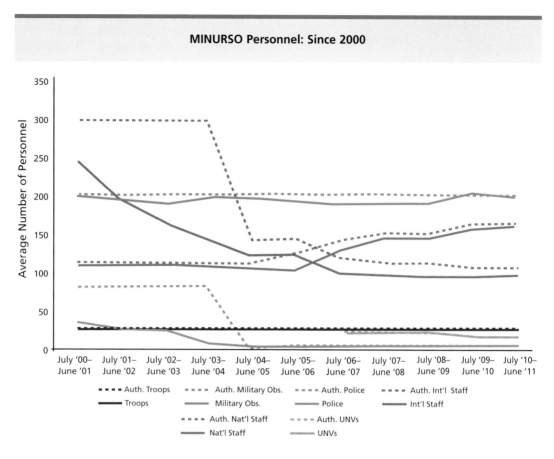

MINURSO Personnel: Since 2000

Sources: UN Documents A/56/818, A/57/674, A/58/642, A/59/619, A/60/634, and A/61/683; DFS FPD; DPKO FGS; DPKO PD; UNV Programme.

MINURSO Military and Police Contributors: 30 September 2011

Contributing Country	Troops	Military Observers	Police	Total	Contributing Country	Troops	Military Observers	Police	Total
Bangladesh	20	10	—	30	Italy	—	5	—	5
Egypt	—	21	2	23	Paraguay	—	5	—	5
Russia	—	21	—	21	El Salvador	—	3	1	4
Ghana	7	8	—	15	Mongolia	—	4	—	4
France	—	13	—	13	Nepal	—	4	—	4
Honduras	—	12	—	12	Republic of Korea	—	4	—	4
Brazil	—	11	—	11	Argentina	—	3	—	3
Pakistan	—	11	—	11	Ireland	—	3	—	3
China	—	10	—	10	Austria	—	2	—	2
Malaysia	—	10	—	10	Sri Lanka	—	2	—	2
Yemen	—	8	—	8	Djibouti	—	1	—	1
Croatia	—	7	—	7	Jordan	—	—	1	1
Hungary	—	7	—	7	Poland	—	1	—	1
Guinea	—	6	—	6	Uruguay	—	1	—	1
Nigeria	—	6	—	6	**Total**	**27**	**199**	**4**	**230**

Source: DPKO FGS.

MINURSO Military Units: 30 September 2011

Number	Unit Type	Country
1	Advanced Level I Medical Unit	Bangladesh

Source: DPKO FGS.

MINURSO International Civilian Personnel Occupations: 30 September 2011

Occupation	International Staff	Percentage International Staff
Administration	11	10.9%
Aviation	5	5.0%
Civil Affairs	—	—
Economic Affairs	—	—
Electoral Affairs	—	—
Engineering	11	10.9%
Finance	6	5.9%
Human Resources	5	5.0%
Human Rights	—	—
Humanitarian Affairs	—	—
Information Management	1	1.0%
Information Systems and Technology	13	12.9%
Legal Affairs	1	1.0%
Logistics	13	12.9%
Management and Programme Analysis	—	—
Medical Services	—	—
Political Affairs	7	6.9%
Procurement	2	2.0%
Programme Management	—	—
Public Information	1	1.0%
Rule of Law	1	1.0%
Security	10	9.9%
Social Affairs	—	—
Transport	14	13.9%
Total	**101**	

Source: DFS FPD.

MINURSO Personnel Gender Statistics: 30 September 2011

Personnel Type	Male	Female	Percentage Male	Percentage Female
Troops	25	2	92.6%	7.4%
Military Observers	194	5	97.5%	2.5%
Police	3	1	75.0%	25.0%
International Civilian Staff	82	19	81.2%	18.8%
National Civilian Staff	132	30	81.5%	18.5%
Total	**436**	**57**	**88.4%**	**11.6%**

Sources: DFS FPD; DPKO FGS; DPKO PD.

MINURSO Fatalities: Inception–September 2011

Time Period	Personnel Type						
	Troops	Military Obs.	Police	Int'l. Staff	National Staff	Other[a]	Total
1992–1999	5	1	1	2	2	—	11
2000	—	—	—	—	—	—	—
2001	—	—	—	—	1	—	1
2002	—	—	—	—	—	—	—
2003	—	—	—	—	—	—	—
2004	—	—	—	—	1	—	1
2005	—	—	—	—	1	—	1
2006	—	—	—	—	—	—	—
2007	—	—	—	1	—	—	1
2008	—	—	—	—	—	—	—
2009	—	—	—	—	—	—	—
2010	—	—	—	—	—	—	—
2011 (Jan.-Sept.)	—	—	—	—	—	—	—
January-March	—	—	—	—	—	—	—
April-June	—	—	—	—	—	—	—
July-September	—	—	—	—	—	—	—
Total Fatalities	**5**	**1**	**1**	**3**	**5**	**—**	**15**

Time Period	Incident Type				
	Malicious Act	Illness	Accident	Other[b]	Total
1992–1999	—	3	8	—	11
2000	—	—	—	—	—
2001	—	—	—	1	1
2002	—	—	—	—	—
2003	—	—	—	—	—
2004	—	—	1	—	1
2005	—	—	1	—	1
2006	—	—	—	—	—
2007	—	1	—	—	1
2008	—	—	—	—	—
2009	—	—	—	—	—
2010	—	—	—	—	—
2011 (Jan.-Sept.)	—	—	—	—	—
January-March	—	—	—	—	—
April-June	—	—	—	—	—
July-September	—	—	—	—	—
Total Fatalities	**—**	**4**	**10**	**1**	**15**

Source: DPKO Situation Centre.
Notes: a. Other refers to consultants, UNVs, etc.
b. Incident type is unknown, uncertain, or under investigation. Other includes what were previously qualified as self-inflicted.

MINURSO Vehicles: 30 September 2011

UN Owned Vehicles

Vehicle Type	Quantity
4x4 Vehicles	373
Airfield Support Equipment	9
Ambulances	4
Automobiles	4
Buses	21
Engineering Vehicles	20
Material Handling Equipment	20
Trucks	37
Total	**492**

Source: DFS Surface Transport Section.

MINURSO Aircraft: 30 September 2011

	Transport Fixed Wing	Transport Helicopter	Attack Helicopter
Commercial	3	2	—
Contingent Owned	—	—	—
Total	**3**	**2**	**—**

Source: DFS Air Transport Section.

MINURSO Budget and Expenditures (in thousands of US dollars)

Category	Budgeted July '10–June '11	Expenditures July '10–June '11	Budgeted July '11–June '12
Military Observers	5,855.5	5,804.2	5,743.7
Military Contingents	796.6	952.0	757.9
Civilian Police	—	—	165.5
Formed Police Units	—	—	—
United Nations Police	164.6	127.1	—
International Staff	15,649.4	15,751.2	17,649.6
National Staff	3,495.2	3,672.5	4,052.9
United Nations Volunteers	784.4	757.9	809.5
General Temporary Assistance	—	35.9	47.0
Government-provided Personnel	39.4	40.0	39.4
Civilian Electoral Observers	—	—	—
Consultants	15.0	15.0	15.0
Official Travel	690.0	488.6	704.5
Facilities and Infrastructure	3,918.6	3,168.7	4,467.8
Ground Transportation	3,897.8	3,009.3	3,609.3
Air Transportation	16,487.6	18,501.9	17,046.7
Naval Transportation	—	—	—
Communications and IT	2,430.3	2,310.1	2,507.9
Supplies, Services and Equipment	2,906.1	2,495.3	3,782.7
Quick-impact Projects	—	—	50.0
Gross Requirements	**57,130.5**	**57,129.6**	**61,449.4**
Staff Assessment Income	2,408.1	2,408.5	2,761.3
Net Requirements	**54,722.4**	**54,721.1**	**58,688.1**
Voluntary Contributions in Kind (budgeted)	2,908.0	2,908.0	1,769.9
Total Requirements	**60,038.5**	**60,037.6**	**63,219.3**

Sources: UN Documents A/65/743/Add.5 and A/C.5/65/19; DFS FBFD.
Notes: 2010–2011 expenditures are preliminary and subject to change. Discrepancies in expenditures from July 2010–June 2011 may be the result of figure estimations.

MINURSO Voluntary Contributions: July 2010–June 2011 (in thousands of US dollars)

Contributor	Contributions in Kind (budgeted)	Contributions in Kind (non-budgeted)	Contributions in Cash (budgeted)	Total
Morocco	2,191.0	—	—	2,191.0
Algeria	324.0	—	—	324.0
Frente Polisario	36.0	—	—	36.0
Total	**2,551.0**	**—**	**—**	**2,551.0**

Source: DM OPPBA.

MINURSO Expenditures on Contingent Owned Equipment: July 2010–June 2011 (in thousands of US dollars)

Military Contingents	85.1
Facilities and Infrastructure	1.6
Medical	59.1
Total	**145.8**

Sources: UN Document A/66/573; DFS FBFD.

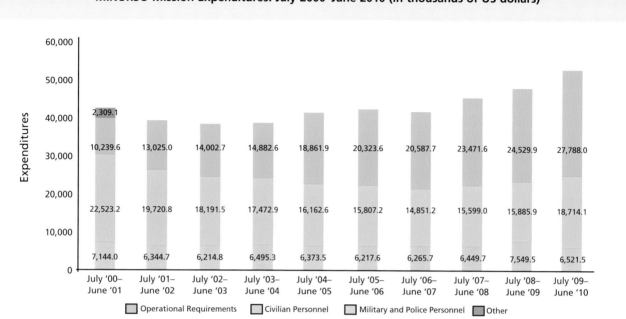

MINURSO Mission Expenditures: July 2000–June 2010 (in thousands of US dollars)

Category	July '00–June '01	Jul '01–June '02	July '02–June '03	July '03–June '04	July '04–June '05	July '05–June '06	July '06–June '07	July '07–June '08	July '08–June '09	July '09–June '10
Military and Police Personnel	7,144.0	6,344.7	6,214.8	6,495.3	6,373.5	6,217.6	6,265.7	6,449.7	7,549.5	6,321.5
Civilian Personnel	22,523.2	19,720.8	18,191.5	17,472.9	16,162.6	15,807.2	14,851.2	15,599.0	15,885.9	18,714.1
Operational Requirements	10,239.6	13,025.0	14,002.7	14,882.6	18,861.9	20,323.6	20,585.7	23,471.6	24,529.9	27,788.0
Other	2,309.1	—	—	—	—	—	—	—	—	—
Gross Requirements	**42,215.9**	**39,090.5**	**38,409.0**	**38,850.8**	**41,398.0**	**42,348.4**	**41,702.6**	**45,520.3**	**47,965.2**	**52,823.6**
Staff Assessment Income	3,773.4	2,751.3	2,636.2	2,442.8	2,311.9	2,191.5	1,860.7	2,017.0	—	2,188.7
Net Requirements	**38,442.5**	**36,339.2**	**35,772.8**	**36,408.0**	**39,086.1**	**40,156.9**	**39,841.9**	**43,503.3**	**47,965.2**	**50,634.9**
Voluntary Contributions in Kind (budgeted)	3,670.7	1,806.1	2,567.4	3,084.0	3,885.2	3,761.3	2,775.9	2,945.2	—	3,048.9
Total Requirements	**45,886.6**	**40,896.6**	**40,976.4**	**41,934.8**	**45,283.2**	**46,109.7**	**44,478.5**	**48,465.5**	**47,965.2**	**55,872.5**

Sources: UN Documents A/56/818, A/57/674, A/58/642, A/59/619, A/60/634, A/61/683, A/62/679, A/63/608, A/C.5/63/26, and A/64/660/Add.2; DFS FBFD.

6.2 MINUSTAH (UN Stabilization Mission in Haiti)

MINUSTAH Key Facts	
Latest Key Resolution	14 October 2011 (date of issue); 15 October 2011 (date of effect) UNSC Res. 2012 (twelve month duration and adjustment of the mission's overall force levels)
First Mandate	30 April 2004 (date of issue), 1 June 2004 (date of effect) UNSC Res. 1542 (six month duration)
SRSG	Mariano Fernández (Chile) SG letter of appointment 12 May 2011
First SRSG	Juan Gabriel Valdés (Chile)
Force Commander	Major-General Luiz Eduardo Ramos Pereira (Brazil) SG letter of appointment 23 March 2011
First Force Commander	Lieutenant-General Augusto Heleno Ribeiro Pereira (Brazil)
Police Commissioner	Marc Tardif (Canada)

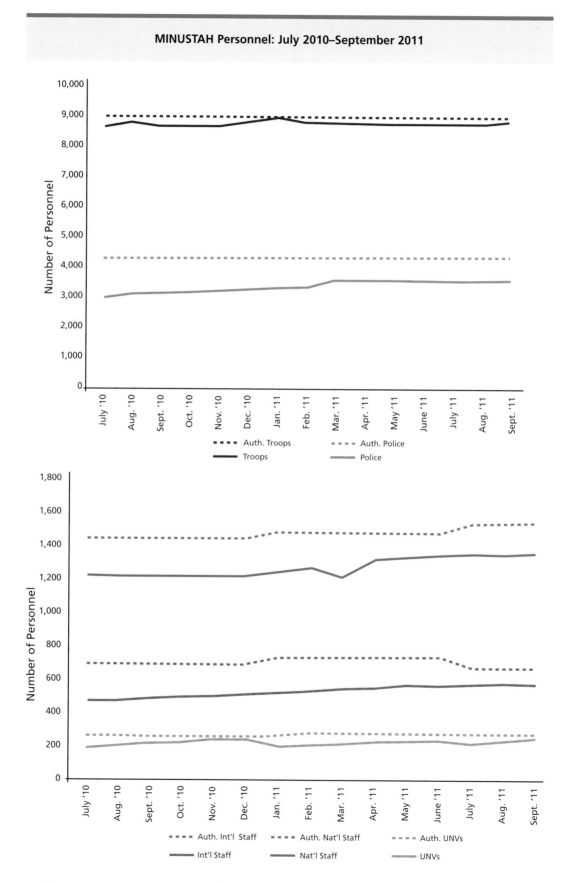

MINUSTAH Personnel: July 2010–September 2011

Sources: DFS FPD; DPKO FGS; DPKO PD; UNV Programme.

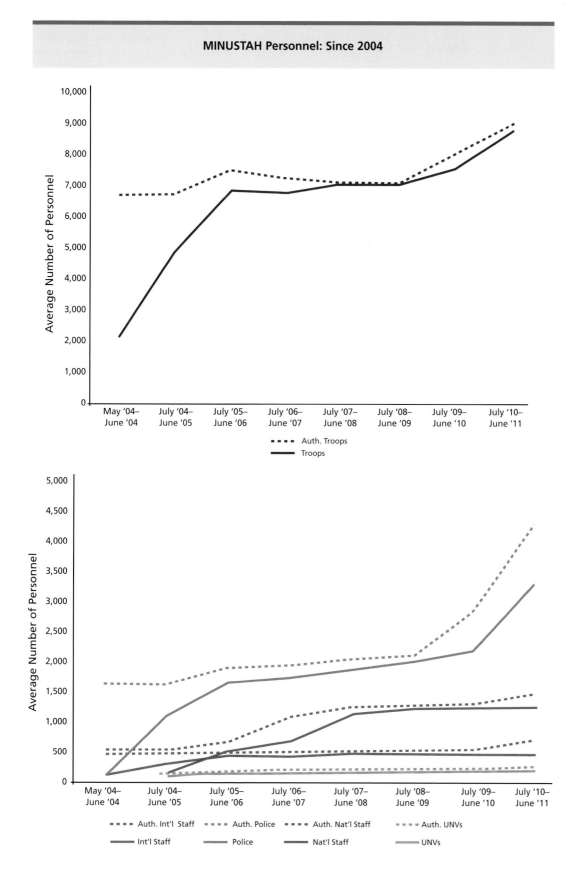

MINUSTAH Personnel: Since 2004

Sources: UN Documents S/RES/1542, S/RES/1608, S/RES/1702, A/60/646, A/61/741, S/RES/1702, and S/RES/1780; DFS FPD; DPKO FGS; DPKO PD; UNV Programme.

MINUSTAH Military and Police Contributors: 30 September 2011

Contributing Country	Troops	Military Observers	Police	Total	Contributing Country	Troops	Military Observers	Police	Total
Brazil	2,188	—	4	2,192	Paraguay	131	—	—	131
Nepal	1,075	—	168	1,243	Burkina Faso	—	—	63	63
Jordan	612	—	513	1,125	Turkey	—	—	40	40
Uruguay	1,090	—	8	1,098	Indonesia	20	—	10	30
Sri Lanka	960	—	15	975	China	—	—	29	29
Argentina	721	—	14	735	Spain	—	—	28	28
Chile	500	—	14	514	Egypt	—	—	26	26
India	—	—	456	456	Madagascar	—	—	26	26
Peru	372	—	—	372	Cameroon	—	—	25	25
Bangladesh	—	—	483	483	Yemen	—	—	25	25
Pakistan	—	—	298	298	Romania	—	—	24	24
Republic of Korea	242	—	—	242	Chad	—	—	23	23
Japan	225	—	—	225	Colombia	—	—	16	16
Bolivia	207	—	—	207	El Salvador	—	—	16	16
Philippines	173	—	31	204	Burundi	—	—	15	15
Rwanda	—	—	189	189	Central African Republic	—	—	15	15
Senegal	—	—	174	174	Thailand	—	—	10	10
Guatemala	148	—	—	148	Croatia	—	—	5	5
Nigeria	—	—	148	148	Norway	—	—	5	5
Canada	11	—	136	147	Russia	—	—	5	5
Côte d'Ivoire	—	—	113	113	Serbia	—	—	5	5
United States	8	—	82	90	Jamaica	—	—	4	4
Niger	—	—	82	82	Sierra Leone	—	—	4	4
Ecuador	67	—	—	67	Grenada	—	—	3	3
Mali	—	—	59	59	Sweden	—	—	3	3
France	2	—	49	51	Kyrgyzstan	—	—	2	2
Benin	—	—	43	43	Lithuania	—	—	2	2
Guinea	—	—	32	32	Togo	—	—	2	2
					Total	**8,752**	**—**	**3,542**	**12,294**

Source: DPKO FGS.

MINUSTAH Military Units: 30 September 2011

Number	Unit Type	Country
2	Aviation Units	Argentina, Chile
6	Engineering Companies	Brazil, Chile-Ecuador Composite, Indonesia, Japan, Korea, Paraguay
1	Headquarters Company	Philippines
10	Infantry Battalions	Argentina, Brazil (2), Chile, Jordan, Nepal (2), Sri Lanka, Uruguay (2)
2	Infantry Companies	Bolivia, Peru
1	Level II Hospital	Argentina
1	Maritime Unit	Uruguay
1	Military Police Company	Guatemala
1	Platoon	Paraguay

Source: DPKO FGS.
Note: Military Field Headquarters Staff Officers not included.

MINUSTAH International Civilian Personnel Occupations: 30 September 2011

Occupation	International Staff	Percentage International Staff
Administration	68	11.9%
Aviation	14	2.4%
Civil Affairs	31	5.4%
Economic Affairs	—	—
Electoral Affairs	5	0.9%
Engineering	33	5.8%
Finance	27	4.7%
Human Resources	34	5.9%
Human Rights	17	3.0%
Humanitarian Affairs	6	1.0%
Information Management	1	0.2%
Information Systems and Technology	28	4.9%
Legal Affairs	6	1.0%
Logistics	101	17.6%
Management and Programme Analysis	—	—
Medical Services	5	0.9%
Political Affairs	33	5.8%
Procurement	14	2.4%
Programme Management	9	1.6%
Public Information	18	3.1%
Rule of Law	29	5.1%
Security	67	11.7%
Social Affairs	5	0.9%
Transport	22	3.8%
Total	**573**	

Source: DFS FPD.

MINUSTAH Personnel Gender Statistics: 30 September 2011

Personnel Type	Male	Female	Percentage Male	Percentage Female
Troops	8,587	165	98.1%	1.9%
Military Observers	—	—	—	—
Police	3,228	314	91.1%	8.9%
International Civilian Staff	384	189	67.0%	33.0%
National Civilian Staff	1,070	281	79.2%	20.8%
Total	**13,269**	**949**	**93.3%**	**6.7%**

Sources: DFS FPD; DPKO FGS; DPKO PD.

MINUSTAH Fatalities: Inception–September 2011

Personnel Type

Time Period	Troops	Military Obs.	Police	Int'l. Staff	National Staff	Other[a]	Total
2004	—	—	—	—	—	—	—
2005	9	—	3	1	—	—	13
2006	6	—	—	3	3	—	12
2007	5	—	1	3	—	—	9
2008	2	—	3	—	—	—	5
2009	15	—	2	1	2	—	20
2010	26	—	18	32	21	4	101
January-March	25	—	18	32	17	4	96
April-June	1	—	—	—	2	—	3
July-September	—	—	—	—	1	—	1
October-December	—	—	—	—	1	—	1
2011 (Jan.-Sept.)	3	—	1	2	—	—	6
January-March	3	—	—	—	—	—	3
April-June	—	—	—	1	—	—	1
July-September	—	—	1	1	—	—	2
Total Fatalities	**66**	**—**	**28**	**42**	**26**	**4**	**166**

Incident Type

Time Period	Malicious Act	Illness	Accident	Other[b]	Total
2004	—	—	—	—	—
2005	6	3	3	1	13
2006	5	4	2	1	12
2007	—	6	3	—	9
2008	1	2	2	—	5
2009	1	4	13	2	20
2010	—	—	100	1	101
January-March	—	—	96	—	96
April-June	—	—	2	1	3
July-September	—	—	1	—	1
October-December	—	—	1	—	1
2011 (Jan.-Sept.)	—	2	2	2	6
January-March	—	—	2	1	3
April-June	—	1	—	—	1
July-September	—	1	—	1	2
Total Fatalities	**13**	**21**	**125**	**7**	**166**

Source: DPKO Situation Centre.
Notes: a. Other refers to consultants, UNVs, etc.
b. Incident type is unknown, uncertain, or under investigation. Other includes what were previously qualified as self-inflicted.

MINUSTAH Vehicles: 30 September 2011

Contingent Owned Vehicles		UN Owned Vehicles	
Vehicle Type	Quantity	Vehicle Type	Quantity
Aircraft/Airfield Support Equipment	17	4x4 Vehicles	1,363
Combat Vehicles	264	Aircraft/Airfield Support Equipment	13
Engineering Vehicles	243	Ambulances	9
Material Handling Equipment	47	Buses	80
Naval Vessels	24	Engineering Vehicles	13
Support Vehicles (Commerical Pattern)	828	Material Handling Equipment	44
Support Vehicles (Military Pattern)	876	Trucks	104
Total	**2,299**	Vans	11
		Total	**1,637**

Sources: DFS Contingent Owned Equipment and Property Management Section; DFS Surface Transport Section.

MINUSTAH Aircraft: 30 September 2011

	Transport Fixed Wing	Transport Helicopter	Attack Helicopter
Commercial	2	4	—
Contingent Owned	—	6 (2 Argentina, 4 Chile)	—
Total	**2**	**10**	—

Source: DFS Air Transport Section.

MINUSTAH Budget and Expenditures (in thousands of US dollars)

Category	Budgeted July '10–June '11	Expenditures July '10–June '11	Budgeted July '11–June '12
Military Observers	122,968.6	—	—
Military Contingents	36,751.5	239,193.5	233,522.3
Civilian Police	—	—	80,685.1
Formed Police Units	—	53,140.4	63,770.5
United Nations Police	31,368.4	74,556.8	—
International Staff	44,422.0	92,186.3	95,264.1
National Staff	15,386.5	32,397.0	34,838.3
United Nations Volunteers	17,202.3	11,903.6	12,571.2
General Temporary Assistance	—	9,357.8	27,674.7
Government-provided Personnel	725.6	2,686.1	4,635.0
Civilian Electoral Observers	—	—	—
Consultants	107.5	613.3	626.4
Official Travel	914.6	8,472.2	7,745.3
Facilities and Infrastructure	52,120.9	148,400.9	121,037.6
Ground Transportation	6,423.6	44,166.4	12,796.5
Air Transportation	15,121.6	31,821.3	26,767.2
Naval Transportation	658.2	781.8	964.5
Communications and IT	17,018.1	55,028.6	36,521.5
Supplies, Services and Equipment	13,790.6	38,102.2	26,596.8
Quick-impact Projects	5,000.0	7,500.0	7,500.0
Gross Requirements	**380,000.0**	**850,308.2**	**793,517.1**
Staff Assessment Income	8,219.9	16,002.6	18,070.0
Net Requirements	**371,780.1**	**834,305.6**	**775,447.1**
Voluntary Contributions in Kind (budgeted)	—	—	—
Total Requirements	**380,000.0**	**850,308.2**	**793,517.1**

Sources: UN Documents A/65/743/Add.15 and A/C.5/65/19; DFS FBFD.
Notes: 2010–2011 expenditures are preliminary and subject to change. Discrepancies in budgeted costs from July 2011–June 2012 may be the result of figure estimations.

MINUSTAH Expenditures on Contingent Owned Equipment: July 2010–June 2011 (in thousands of US dollars)

Military Contingents	44,524.4
Formed Police Units	12,858.0
Facilities and Infrastructure	28,423.0
Communications	10,848.5
Medical	6,720.9
Special Equipment	4,700.4
Total	**108,075.2**

Source: UN Document A/65/535.
Note: 2010–2011 expenditures are preliminary and subject to change.

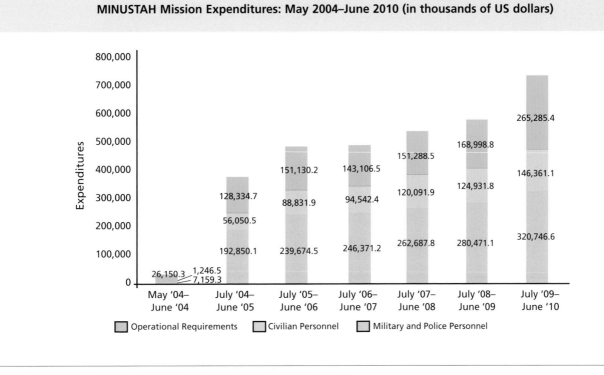

MINUSTAH Mission Expenditures: May 2004–June 2010 (in thousands of US dollars)

Category	May '04–June '04	July '04–June '05	July '05–June '06	July '06–June '07	July '07–June '08	July '08–June '09	July '09–June '10
Military and Police Personnel	7,159.3	192,850.1	239,674.5	246,371.2	262,687.8	280,471.1	320,746.6
Civilian Personnel	1,246.5	56,050.5	88,831.9	94,542.4	120,091.9	124,931.8	146,361.1
Operational Requirements	26,150.3	128,334.7	151,130.2	143,106.5	151,288.5	168,998.8	265,285.4
Other	—	—	—	—	—	—	—
Gross Requirements	**34,556.1**	**377,235.3**	**479,636.6**	**484,020.1**	**534,068.2**	**574,401.7**	**732,393.0**
Staff Assessment Income	60.7	5,347.3	8,664.8	9,313.5	12,171.2	—	—
Net Requirements	**34,495.4**	**371,888.0**	**470,971.8**	**474,706.6**	**521,897.0**	**574,401.7**	**732,393.0**
Voluntary Contributions in Kind (budgeted)	—	—	—	—	—	—	—
Total Requirements	**34,556.1**	**377,235.3**	**479,636.6**	**484,020.1**	**534,068.2**	**574,401.7**	**732,393.0**

Sources: UN Documents A/59/745, A/60/646, A/61/741, A/62/720, A/63/549/Corr.1, and A/C.5/63/26.
Note: Discrepancies in estimated expenditures from July 2009–June 2010 may be the result of figure estimations.

6.3 MONUSCO (UN Organization Stabilization Mission in the Democratic Republic of Congo)

MONUSCO Key Facts	
Latest Key Resolution	28 June 2011 (date of issue and effect) UNSC Res. 1991 (twelve month duration)
First Mandate	28 May 2010 (date of issue); 1 July 2010 (date of effect) UNSC Res. 1925 (one month duration of MONUC and decision to change title effective 1 July 2010 to "United Nations Organization Stabilization Mission in the Democratic Republic of the Congo (MONUSCO)" for twelve month duration)
SRSG	Roger Meece (United States) SG letter of appointment 7 June 2010 Entry on duty 1 July 2010
First SRSG	Kamel Morjane (Tunisia)
Force Commander	Lieutenant General Chander Prakash (India) SG letter of appointment 6 July 2010
Police Commissioner	Abdallah Wafy (Niger)

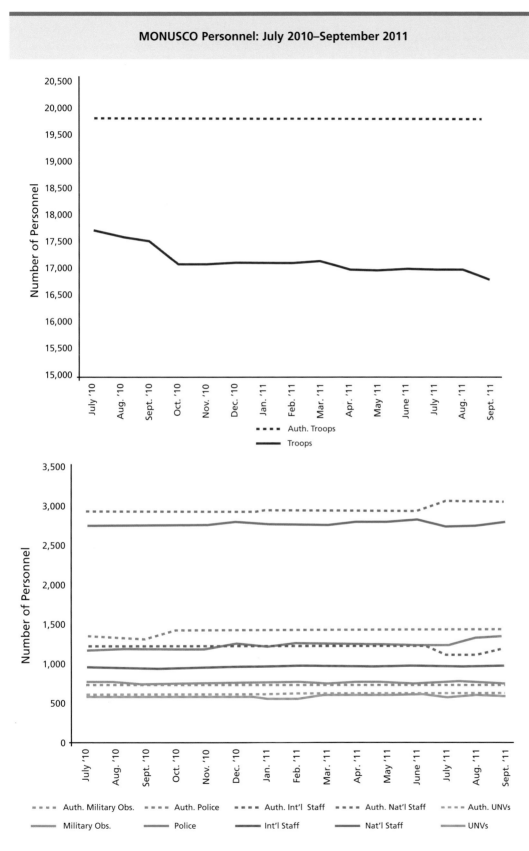

MONUSCO Personnel: July 2010–September 2011

Sources: DFS FPD; DPKO FGS; DPKO PD; UNV Programme.

MONUSCO Military and Police Contributors: 30 September 2011

Contributing Country	Troops	Military Observers	Police	Total	Contributing Country	Troops	Military Observers	Police	Total
India	3,707	60	255	4,022	Malawi	—	17	—	17
Pakistan	3,562	57	—	3,619	Paraguay	—	17	—	17
Bangladesh	2,523	30	387	2,940	Ukraine	—	13	4	17
Uruguay	1,248	45	2	1,295	Yemen	—	6	10	16
South Africa	1,202	12	—	1,214	Malaysia	—	15	—	15
Egypt	1,000	24	144	1,168	Central African Republic	—	—	14	14
Nepal	1,026	25	—	1,051	France	—	5	9	14
Morocco	848	5	—	853	Canada	—	8	4	12
Ghana	462	27	—	489	Turkey	—	—	11	11
Benin	450	14	21	485	Bolivia	—	10	—	10
Senegal	—	20	270	290	Sweden	—	6	4	10
Jordan	220	25	9	254	Serbia	6	2	—	8
China	218	16	—	234	Peru	—	7	—	7
Indonesia	175	17	—	192	Algeria	—	5	—	5
Guatemala	150	8	—	158	Bosnia and Herzegovina	—	5	—	5
Mali	—	19	27	46	Togo	—	—	5	5
Niger	—	15	30	45	United Kingdom	—	5	—	5
Romania	—	22	14	36	Sri Lanka	—	4	—	4
Côte d'Ivoire	—	—	35	35	Czech Republic	—	3	—	3
Russia	—	30	1	31	Ireland	—	3	—	3
Tunisia	—	31	—	31	Poland	—	3	—	3
Belgium	22	5	1	28	Switzerland	—	3	—	3
Burkina Faso	—	9	18	27	Denmark	—	2	—	2
Nigeria	—	26	1	27	Mongolia	—	2	—	2
Cameroon	—	5	19	24	Spain	—	2	—	2
Kenya	—	24	—	24	Tanzania	—	2	—	2
Guinea	—	—	22	22	United States	—	2	—	2
Zambia	—	21	—	21	Mozambique	—	1	—	1
Chad	—	—	20	20	Norway	—	1	—	1
Madagascar	—	—	17	17	**Total**	**16,819**	**741**	**1,354**	**18,914**

Source: DPKO FGS.

MONUSCO Military Units: 30 September 2011

Number	Unit Type	Country
4	Air Medical Evacuation Teams	Morocco, Pakistan, South Africa, Serbia
1	Airfield Crash Rescue Unit	South Africa
1	Airfield Service Unit	Bangladesh
1	Airfield Support Unit	Uruguay
2	Aviation Units	South Africa, Uruguay
2	Brigade Headquarters and Training Teams	India, Pakistan
2	C-130 Aviation Units	Bangladesh, Belgium
1	Cargo Handling Unit	South Africa
1	Engineering Company	Bangladesh
5	Engineering Units	China, Indonesia, Nepal, South Africa, Uruguay
1	Headquarters Support and Signal Company	Bangladesh
16	Infantry Battalions	Bangladesh (2), Benin, Egypt, India (4), Morocco, Nepal, Pakistan (4), South Africa, Uruguay
1	Infantry Mechanized Unit	Ghana
3	Level II Hospitals	China, Jordan, Morocco
1	Levell III Hospital	India
2	Military Police Units	Bangladesh, South Africa
1	Observation Aviation Unit	India
1	Riverine Unit	Uruguay
3	Special Forces Companies	Egypt, Guatemala, Jordan
1	Utility Aviation Unit	Bangladesh
1	Water Treatment Plant	Uruguay

Source: DPKO FGS.

MONUSCO International Civilian Personnel Occupations: 30 September 2011

Occupation	International Staff	Percentage International Staff
Administration	126	12.8%
Aviation	59	6.0%
Civil Affairs	21	2.1%
Economic Affairs	—	—
Electoral Affairs	32	3.3%
Engineering	53	5.4%
Finance	41	4.2%
Human Resources	37	3.8%
Human Rights	28	2.8%
Humanitarian Affairs	—	—
Information Management	4	0.4%
Information Systems and Technology	85	8.6%
Legal Affairs	5	0.5%
Logistics	168	17.1%
Management and Programme Analysis	1	0.1%
Medical Services	15	1.5%
Political Affairs	60	6.1%
Procurement	22	2.2%
Programme Management	36	3.7%
Public Information	36	3.7%
Rule of Law	23	2.3%
Security	92	9.4%
Social Affairs	15	1.5%
Transport	24	2.4%
Total	**983**	

Source: DFS FPD.

MONUSCO Gender Statistics: 30 September 2011

Personnel Type	Male	Female	Percentage Male	Percentage Female
Troops	16,445	374	97.8%	2.2%
Military Observers	715	26	96.5%	3.5%
Police	1,308	46	96.6%	3.4%
International Civilian Staff	692	291	70.4%	29.6%
National Civilian Staff	2,419	401	85.8%	14.2%
Total	**21,579**	**1,138**	**95.0%**	**5.0%**

Sources: DFS FPD; DPKO FGS; DPKO PD.

MONUSCO Fatalities: Inception–September 2011

Personnel Type

Time Period	Troops	Military Obs.	Police	Int'l. Staff	National Staff	Other[a]	Total
2010 (Jul.-Dec.)	8	—	—	1	1	—	10
July-September	4	—	—	1	1	—	6
October-December	4	—	—	—	—	—	4
2011 (Jan.-Sept.)	6	—	2	8	5	—	21
January-March	1	—	—	1	—	—	2
April-June	3	—	1	7	4	—	15
July-September	2	—	1	—	1	—	4
Total Fatalities	**14**	**—**	**2**	**9**	**6**	**—**	**31**

Incident Type

Time Period	Malicious Act	Illness	Accident	Other[b]	Total
2010 (Jul.-Dec.)	3	6	1	—	10
July-September	3	3	—	—	6
October-December	—	3	1	—	4
2011 (Jan.-Sept.)	—	6	15	—	21
January-March	—	1	1	—	2
April-June	—	2	13	—	15
July-September	—	3	1	—	4
Total Fatalities	**3**	**12**	**16**	**—**	**31**

Source: DPKO Situation Centre.
Notes: a. Other refers to consultants, UNVs, etc.
b. Incident type is unknown, uncertain, or under investigation. Other includes what were previously qualified as self-inflicted.

MONUSCO Vehicles: 30 September 2011

Contingent Owned Vehicles		UN Owned Vehicles	
Vehicle Type	Quantity	Vehicle Type	Quantity
Aircraft/Airfield Support Equipment	89	4x4 Vehicles	1,897
Combat Vehicles	541	Aircraft/Airfield Support Equipment	81
Communications Vehicles	9	Ambulances	34
Engineering Vehicles	257	Automobiles	2
Material Handling Equipment	74	Boats	3
Naval Vessels	47	Buses	263
Support Vehicles		Engineering Vehicles	34
(Commercial Pattern)	645	Material Handling Equipment	128
Support Vehicles (Military Pattern)	2,187	Trucks	320
Total	**3,849**	Vans	21
		Total	**2,783**

Sources: DFS Contingent Owned Equipment and Property Management Section; DFS Surface Transport Section.

MONUSCO Aircraft: 30 September 2011

	Transport Fixed Wing	Transport Helicopter	Attack Helicopter
Commercial	18	23	—
Contingent Owned	2 (Bangladesh, Belgium)	14 (6 Bangladesh, 4 India, 2 South Africa, 2 Uruguay)	—
Total	**20**	**37**	—

Source: DFS Air Transport Section.

MONUSCO Budget and Expenditures (in thousands of US dollars)

Category	Budgeted July '10–June '11	Expenditures July '10–June '11	Budgeted July '11–June '12
Military Observers	47,742.3	48,993.4	48,473.5
Military Contingents	476,268.8	440,342.9	437,930.4
Civilian Police	—	—	22,217.1
Formed Police Units	27,043.2	23,444.3	22,440.1
United Nations Police	20,795.0	21,935.0	—
International Staff	179,324.5	170,319.6	202,503.3
National Staff	64,742.6	65,965.4	69,752.5
United Nations Volunteers	32,944.8	33,029.2	30,369.7
General Temporary Assistance	—	6,526.1	11,579.7
Government-provided Personnel	2,560.5	1,841.7	4,776.8
Civilian Electoral Observers	—	—	—
Consultants	189.8	26.7	236.8
Official Travel	9,064.3	9,543.9	10,408.4
Facilities and Infrastructure	125,179.4	125,892.1	131,421.3
Ground Transportation	37,696.9	33,324.7	37,493.9
Air Transportation	238,443.3	286,227.1	339,278.3
Naval Transportation	1,719.6	1,905.2	1,868.6
Communications and IT	51,827.6	53,175.7	55,485.4
Supplies, Services and Equipment	47,957.4	41,095.3	63,750.3
Quick-impact Projects	1,500.0	1,500.0	1,500.0
Gross Requirements	**1,365,000.0**	**1,365,088.3**	**1,491,486.1**
Staff Assessment Income	30,456.1	26,404.5	31,980.5
Net Requirements	**1,334,543.9**	**1,338,683.8**	**1,459,505.6**
Voluntary Contributions in Kind (budgeted)	4,000.0	4,000.0	2,904.4
Total Requirements	**1,369,000.0**	**1,369,088.3**	**1,494,390.5**

Sources: UN Documents A/65/743/Add.8, A/C.5/65/19 and A/66/375; DFS FBFD.
Note: 2010–2011 expenditures are preliminary and subject to change.

MONUC Expenditures on Contingent Owned Equipment: July 2010–June 2011 (in thousands of US dollars)

Military Contingents	82,422.8
Formed Police Units	5,089.8
Facilities and Infrastructure	49,152.8
Communications	19,887.3
Medical	14,835.6
Special Equipment	8,848.1
Total	**180,236.4**

Source: UN Document A/64/670.
Notes: 2010–2011 expenditures are preliminary and subject to change. Effective July 2010, the UN Organization Mission in the Democratic Republic of Congo (MONUC) was renamed the UN Organization Stabilization Mission in the Democratic Republic of Congo (MONUSCO). Expenditures reflect the transition and drawdown of MONUC following the inception of MONUSCO.

MONUSCO Voluntary Contributions: July 2010–June 2011 (in thousands of US dollars)

Contributor	Contributions in Kind (budgeted)	Contributions in Kind (non-budgeted)	Contributions in Cash (budgeted)	Total
Foundation Hirondelle	2,667.0	—	—	2,667.0
Total	**2,667.0**	**—**	**—**	**2,667.0**

Source: DM OPPBA.

6.4 UNAMID (UN-AU Hybrid Mission in Darfur)

UNAMID Key Facts	
Latest Key Resolution	29 July 2011 (date of issue); 31 July 2011 (date of effect) UNSC Res. 2003 (twelve month duration and decision to maintain the mission under its current mandate and troop levels)
First Mandate	31 July 2007 (date of issue); Implement mandated tasks no later than 31 December 2007 UNSC Res. 1769 (twelve month duration)
Joint AU/UN Special Representative	Ibrahim Gambari (Nigeria) Date of effect 1 January 2010
First Joint AU/UN Special Representative	Rodolphe Adada (Republic of the Congo)
Force Commander	Lieutenant-General Patrick Nyamvumba (Rwanda) SG letter of appointment 22 July 2009
First Force Commander	General Martin Luther Agwai (Nigeria)
Police Commissioner	James Oppong-Boanuh (Ghana)

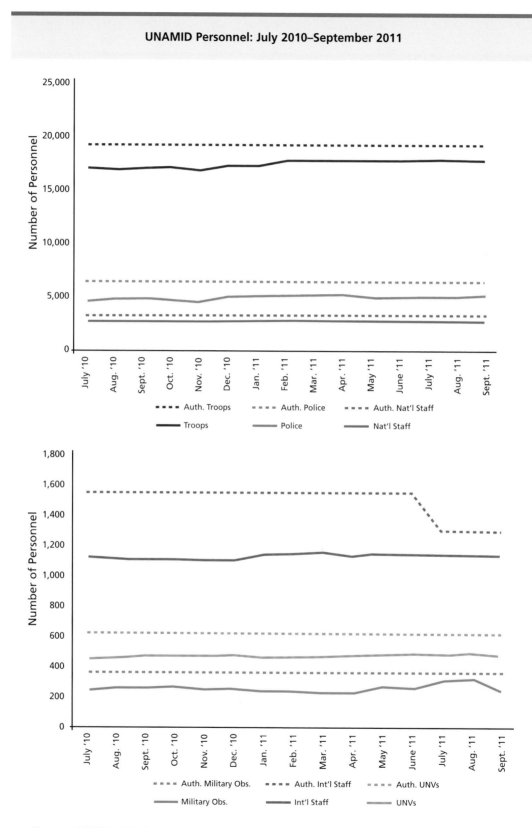

UNAMID Personnel: July 2010–September 2011

Sources: DFS FPD; DPKO FGS; DPKO PD; UNV Programme.

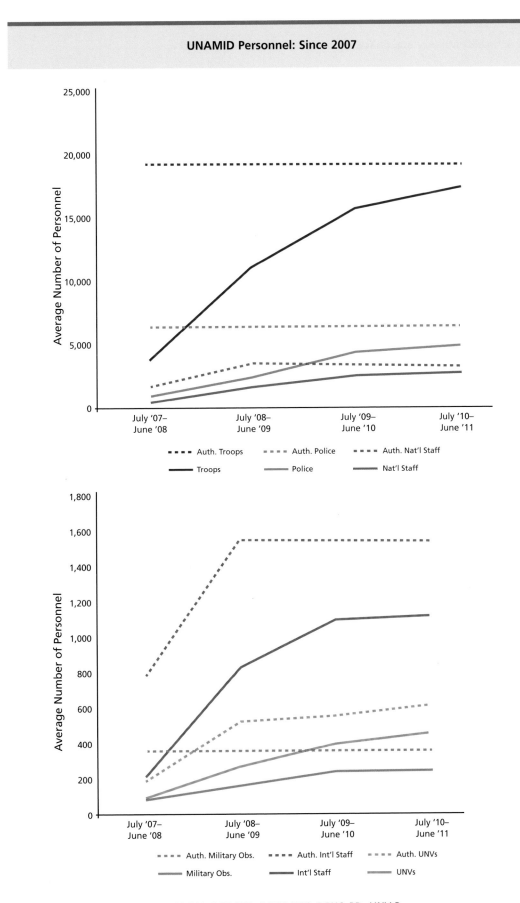

UNAMID Personnel: Since 2007

Sources: UN Document S/RES/1769; DFS FPD; DPKO FGS; DPKO PD; UNV Programme.

UNAMID Military and Police Contributors: 30 September 2011

Contributing Country	Troops	Military Observers	Police	Total	Contributing Country	Troops	Military Observers	Police	Total
Nigeria	3,317	17	359	3,693	Malaysia	13	3	42	58
Rwanda	3,237	10	198	3,445	Namibia	3	5	36	44
Egypt	2,398	21	250	2,669	Malawi	2	4	32	38
Ethiopia	2,386	14	—	2,400	Cameroon	—	3	32	35
Senegal	1,026	12	292	1,330	Niger	—	—	19	19
Bangladesh	395	12	684	1,091	Jamaica	—	—	15	15
Tanzania	892	12	186	1,090	Fiji	—	—	12	12
Burkina Faso	803	7	160	970	Tajikistan	—	—	11	11
South Africa	782	3	131	916	Turkey	—	—	11	11
Thailand	820	10	—	830	Germany	4	—	5	9
Pakistan	500	6	218	724	Mali	—	9	—	9
Jordan	7	4	686	697	Canada	4	—	2	6
Nepal	346	8	330	684	Côte d'Ivoire	—	—	6	6
Sierra Leone	135	8	218	361	Madagascar	—	—	6	6
Gambia	196	—	145	341	Kyrgyzstan	—	—	5	5
China	322	—	—	322	Norway	—	—	5	5
Ghana	7	5	305	317	Zimbabwe	1	4	—	5
Zambia	6	14	186	206	Guatemala	—	2	—	2
Yemen	5	24	161	190	Ecuador	—	1	—	1
Togo	—	8	139	147	Italy	1	—	—	1
Indonesia	1	5	140	146	Lesotho	—	1	—	1
Kenya	79	5	—	84	Netherlands	1	—	—	1
Mongolia	70	—	—	70	Palau	—	—	1	1
Philippines	—	—	70	70	Uganda	—	1	—	1
Burundi	4	2	61	67	**Total**	**17,763**	**240**	**5,159**	**23,162**

Source: DPKO FGS.

	UNAMID Military Units: 30 September 2011	
Number	Unit Type	Country
1	Headquarters Company	Gambia
1	Heavy Transport Company	Egypt
17	Infantry Battalions	Burkina Faso, Egypt (2), Ethiopia (2), Nigeria (4), Rwanda (4), Senegal (2), South Africa, Tanzania, Thailand
2	Level II Hospitals	Mongolia, Nigeria
1	Level III Hospital	Pakistan
1	Light Tactical Helicopter Unit	Ethiopia
1	Medical Transport Company	Ethiopia
1	Military Police Company	Kenya
3	Multi-Role Engineering Companies	China, Egypt, Pakistan
2	Multi-Role Logistics Companies	Bangladesh, Ethiopia
2	Sector Reconnaissance Companies	Ethiopia, Sierra Leone
2	Sector Reserve Infantry Companies	Bangladesh, Nepal
1	Signals Unit	Egypt
1	Special Forces Company	Nepal

Source: DPKO FGS.

UNAMID International Civilian Personnel Occupations: 30 September 2011

Occupation	International Staff	Percentage International Staff
Administration	126	11.1%
Aviation	39	3.4%
Civil Affairs	27	2.4%
Economic Affairs	1	0.1%
Electoral Affairs	—	—
Engineering	89	7.9%
Finance	35	3.1%
Human Resources	66	5.8%
Human Rights	36	3.2%
Humanitarian Affairs	16	1.4%
Information Management	23	2.0%
Information Systems and Technology	129	11.4%
Legal Affairs	11	1.0%
Logistics	166	14.7%
Management and Programme Analysis	—	—
Medical Services	27	2.4%
Political Affairs	58	5.1%
Procurement	16	1.4%
Programme Management	20	1.8%
Public Information	17	1.5%
Rule of Law	32	2.8%
Security	124	11.0%
Social Affairs	12	1.1%
Transport	61	5.4%
Total	**1,131**	

Source: DFS FPD.

UNAMID Personnel Gender Statistics: 30 September 2011

Personnel Type	Male	Female	Percentage Male	Percentage Female
Troops	17,293	470	97.4%	2.6%
Military Observers	228	12	95.0%	5.0%
Police	4,557	602	88.3%	11.7%
International Civilian Staff	820	311	72.5%	27.5%
National Civilian Staff	2,533	383	86.9%	13.1%
Total	**25,431**	**1,778**	**93.5%**	**6.5%**

Sources: DFS FPD; DPKO FGS; DPKO PD.

UNAMID Fatalities: Inception–September 2011

Personnel Type

Time Period	Troops	Military Obs.	Police	Int'l. Staff	National Staff	Other[a]	Total
2008	16	1	9	—	3	—	29
2009	17	—	2	2	6	—	27
2010	18	—	4	1	—	—	23
January–March	4	—	—	—	—	—	4
April–June	6	—	—	—	—	—	6
July–September	7	—	1	1	—	—	9
October–December	1	—	3	—	—	—	4
2011 (Jan.–Sept.)	11	—	4	—	1	—	16
January–March	5	—	2	—	1	—	8
April–June	1	—	2	—	—	—	3
July–September	5	—	—	—	—	—	5
Total Fatalities	**62**	**1**	**19**	**3**	**10**	**—**	**95**

Incident Type

Time Period	Malicious Act	Illness	Accident	Other[b]	Total
2008	11	11	5	2	29
2009	9	16	1	1	27
2010	5	9	9	—	23
January–March	—	3	1	—	4
April–June	5	—	1	—	6
July–September	—	3	6	—	9
October–December	—	3	1	—	4
2011 (Jan.–Sept.)	3	6	1	6	16
January–March	—	4	—	4	8
April–June	2	—	—	1	3
July–September	1	2	1	1	5
Total Fatalities	**28**	**42**	**16**	**9**	**95**

Source: DPKO Situation Centre.
Notes: a. Other refers to consultants, UNVs, etc.
b. Incident type is unknown, uncertain, or under investigation. Other includes what were previously qualified as self-inflicted.

UNAMID Vehicles: 30 September 2011

Contingent Owned Vehicles		UN Owned Vehicles	
Vehicle Type	Quantity	Vehicle Type	Quantity
Aircraft/Airfield Support Equipment	6	4x4 Vehicles	2,018
Combat Vehicles	611	Airfield Support Equipment	48
Engineering Vehicles	235	Ambulances	17
Material Handling Equipment	106	Automobiles	4
Support Vehicles		Buses	340
(Commercial Pattern)	851	Engineering Vehicles	115
Support Vehicles (Military Pattern)	1,818	Material Handling Equipment	89
Total	**3,627**	Trucks	294
		Vans	4
		Total	**2,929**

Sources: DFS Contingent Owned Equipment and Property Management Section; DFS Surface Transport Section.

UNAMID Aircraft: 30 September 2011

	Transport Fixed Wing	Transport Helicopter	Attack Helicopter
Commercial	9	27	—
Contingent Owned	—	—	5 (Ethiopia)
Total	9	27	5

Source: DFS Air Transport Section.

UNAMID Budget and Expenditures (in thousands of US dollars)

Category	Budgeted July '10–June '11	Expenditures July '10–June '11	Budgeted July '11–June '12
Military Observers	11,396.4	11,395.7	12,610.0
Military Contingents	520,581.1	513,550.5	528,255.3
Civilian Police	—	—	167,220.0
Formed Police Units	74,124.4	73,606.6	72,656.0
United Nations Police	168,188.5	164,332.3	—
International Staff	261,836.5	216,533.7	205,045.9
National Staff	65,731.7	64,788.2	49,501.1
United Nations Volunteers	29,155.3	23,306.5	28,327.6
General Temporary Assistance	—	4,371.9	5,386.4
Government-provided Personnel	279.9	277.6	266.3
Civilian Electoral Observers	—	—	—
Consultants	203.7	1,149.6	184.5
Official Travel	4,486.1	9,999.7	4,684.9
Facilities and Infrastructure	223,259.0	261,279.0	177,140.7
Ground Transportation	32,302.9	32,242.7	24,371.9
Air Transportation	261,957.4	257,995.2	263,105.6
Naval Transportation	—	—	—
Communications and IT	77,331.2	77,210.8	70,582.4
Supplies, Services and Equipment	73,293.4	76,013.8	75,967.4
Quick-impact Projects	4,000.0	4,000.0	4,000.0
Gross Requirements	**1,808,127.5**	**1,792,053.8**	**1,689,306.0**
Staff Assessment Income	31,972.2	25,502.7	28,161.8
Net Requirements	**1,776,155.3**	**1,766,551.1**	**1,661,144.2**
Voluntary Contributions in Kind (budgeted)	—	—	—
Total Requirements	**1,808,127.5**	**1,792,053.8**	**1,689,306.0**

Sources: UN Documents A/65/743/Add.13 and A/C.5/64/19; DFS FBFD.
Note: July 2010–2011 expenditures are preliminary and subject to change.

UNAMID Expenditures on Contingent Owned Equipment: July 2010–June 2011 (in thousands of US dollars)

Military Contingents	105,587.1
Formed Police Units	21,227.0
Facilities and Infrastructure	57,717.7
Communications	17,991.8
Medical	19,502.7
Special Equipment	8,109.9
Total	**230,136.2**

Source: UN Document A/64/685.
Note: 2010–2011 expenditures are preliminary and subject to change.

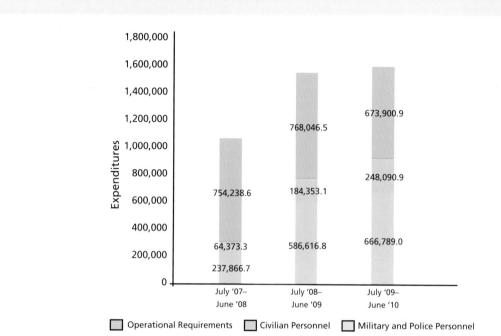

UNAMID Mission Expenditures: July 2007–June 2010 (in thousands of US dollars)

Category	July '07–June '08	July '08–June '09	July '09–June '10
Military and Police Personnel	237,866.7	586,616.8	666,789.0
Civilian Personnel	64,373.3	184,353.1	248,090.9
Operational Requirements	754,238.6	768,046.5	673,900.9
Other	—	—	—
Gross Requirements	**1,056,478.6**	**1,539,016.4**	**1,588,780.8**
Staff Assessment Income	6,692.3	—	—
Net Requirements	**1,049,786.3**	**1,539,016.4**	**1,588,780.8**
Voluntary Contributions in Kind (budgeted)	—	—	—
Total Requirements	**1,056,478.6**	**1,539,016.4**	**1,588,780.8**

Sources: UN Documents A/63/535, A/C.5/63/26, and A/64/660/Add.13; DFS FBFD.

6.5 UNDOF (UN Disengagement Observer Force)

UNDOF Key Facts	
Latest Key Resolution	21 December 2011 (date of issue); 1 January 2012 (date of effect) UNSC Res. 2028 (six month duration)
First Mandate	31 May 1974 (date of issue and effect) UNSC Res. 350 (six month duration)
Force Commander	Major-General Natalio C. Ecarma (Philippines) SG letter of appointment 28 January 2010
First Force Commander	Brigadier-General Gonzalo Briceno Zevallos (Peru)

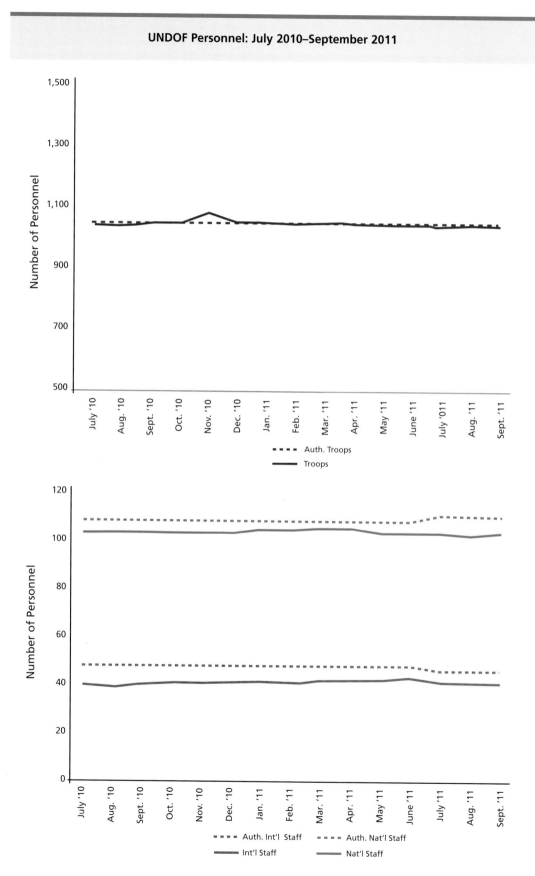

UNDOF Personnel: July 2010–September 2011

Sources: DFS FPD; DPKO FGS.

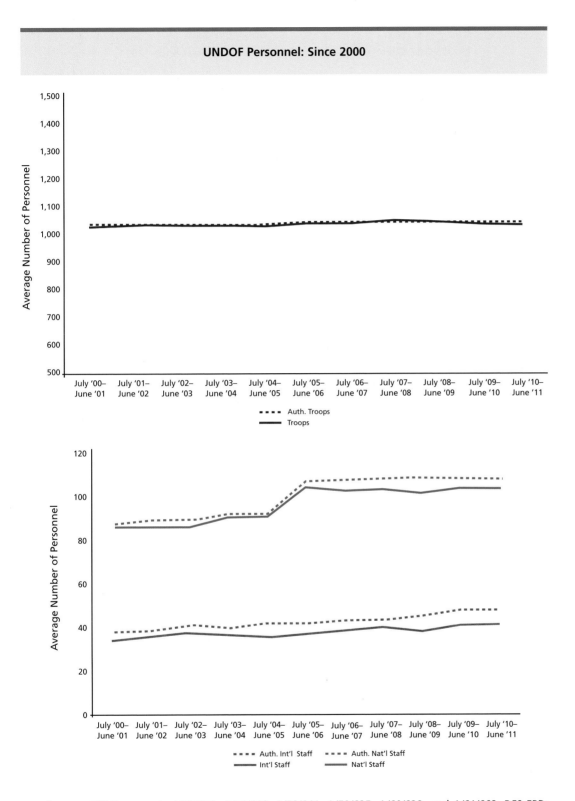

UNDOF Personnel: Since 2000

Sources: UN Documents A/56/813, A/57/668, A/58/641, A/59/625, A/60/628, and A/61/662; DFS FPD; DPKO FGS.

UNDOF Military and Police Contributors: 30 September 2011

Contributing Country	Troops	Military Observers	Police	Total
Austria	374	—	—	374
Philippines	343	—	—	343
India	192	—	—	192
Croatia	95	—	—	95
Japan	31	—	—	31
Canada	3	—	—	3
Total	**1,038**	**—**	**—**	**1,038**

Source: DPKO FGS.

UNDOF Military Units: 30 September 2011

Number	Unit Type	Country
2	Infantry Battalions	Australia, Philippines
1	Infantry Company	Croatia
1	Logistics Battalion	India
1	Transport Company	Japan

Source: DPKO FGS.
Note: Military Field Headquarters Staff Officers not included.

UNDOF International Civilian Personnel Occupations: 30 September 2011

Occupation	International Staff	Percentage International Staff
Administration	7	17.1%
Aviation	—	—
Civil Affairs	1	2.4%
Economic Affairs	—	—
Electoral Affairs	—	—
Engineering	4	9.8%
Finance	2	4.9%
Human Resources	2	4.9%
Human Rights	—	—
Humanitarian Affairs	—	—
Information Management	1	2.4%
Information Systems and Technology	10	24.4%
Legal Affairs	1	2.4%
Logistics	4	9.8%
Management and Programme Analysis	—	—
Medical Services	—	—
Political Affairs	—	—
Procurement	2	4.9%
Programme Management	—	—
Public Information	—	—
Rule of Law	1	2.4%
Security	2	4.9%
Social Affairs	—	—
Transport	4	9.8%
Total	**41**	

Source: DFS FPD.

UNDOF Personnel Gender Statistics: 30 September 2011

Personnel Type	Male	Female	Percentage Male	Percentage Female
Troops	997	41	96.1%	3.9%
Military Observers	—	—	—	—
Police	—	—	—	—
International Civilian Staff	29	12	70.7%	29.3%
National Civilian Staff	79	24	76.7%	23.3%
Total	**1,105**	**77**	**93.5%**	**6.5%**

Sources: DFS FPD; DPKO FGS.

UNDOF Fatalities: Inception–September 2011

Personnel Type

Time Period	Troops	Military Obs.	Police	Int'l. Staff	National Staff	Other[a]	Total
1974–1999	38	—	—	1	—	—	39
2000	—	—	—	—	—	—	—
2001	—	—	—	—	—	—	—
2002	—	—	—	—	—	—	—
2003	—	—	—	—	—	—	—
2004	—	—	—	—	—	—	—
2005	2	—	—	—	—	—	2
2006	1	—	—	—	—	—	1
2007	—	—	—	—	—	—	—
2008	1	—	—	—	—	—	1
2009	—	—	—	—	—	—	—
2010	—	—	—	—	—	—	—
2011 (Jan.-Sept.)	—	—	—	—	—	—	—
January-March	—	—	—	—	—	—	—
April-June	—	—	—	—	—	—	—
July-September	—	—	—	—	—	—	—
Total Fatalities	**42**	**—**	**—**	**1**	**—**	**—**	**43**

Incident Type

Time Period	Malicious Act	Illness	Accident	Other[b]	Total
1974–1999	7	6	19	7	39
2000	—	—	—	—	—
2001	—	—	—	—	—
2002	—	—	—	—	—
2003	—	—	—	—	—
2004	—	—	—	—	—
2005	—	—	—	2	2
2006	—	—	—	1	1
2007	—	—	—	—	—
2008	—	—	—	1	1
2009	—	—	—	—	—
2010	—	—	—	—	—
2011 (Jan.-Sept.)	—	—	—	—	—
January-March	—	—	—	—	—
April-June	—	—	—	—	—
July-September	—	—	—	—	—
Total Fatalities	**7**	**6**	**19**	**11**	**43**

Source: DPKO Situation Centre.
Notes: a. Other refers to consultants, UNVs, etc.
 b. Incident type is unknown, uncertain, or under investigation. Other includes what were previously qualified as self-inflicted.

UNDOF Vehicles: 30 September 2011

Contingent Owned Vehicles

Vehicle Type	Quantity
Engineering Vehicles	2
Material Handling Equipment	1
Support Vehicles (Commercial Pattern)	5
Support Vehicles (Military Pattern)	5
Total	**13**

UN Owned Vehicles

Vehicle Type	Quantity
4x4 Vehicles	221
Ambulances	9
Armoured Personnel Carriers	18
Automobiles	2
Buses	59
Engineering Vehicles	23
Material Handling Equipment	11
Trucks	75
Vans	3
Total	**421**

Sources: DFS Contingent Owned Equipment and Property Management Section; DFS Surface Transport Section.

UNDOF Budget and Expenditures (in thousands of US dollars)

Category	Budgeted July '10–June '11	Expenditures July '10–June '11	Budgeted July '11–June '12
Military Observers	—	—	—
Military Contingents	23,778.3	23,635.3	24,862.8
Civilian Police	—	—	—
Formed Police Units	—	—	—
United Nations Police	—	—	—
International Staff	7,608.4	7,714.0	8,071.0
National Staff	2,824.5	3,239.7	3,567.4
United Nations Volunteers	40.0	—	—
General Temporary Assistance	—	33.4	41.0
Government-provided Personnel	—	—	—
Civilian Electoral Observers	—	—	—
Consultants	21.2	5.6	20.5
Official Travel	407.4	307.4	458.8
Facilities and Infrastructure	6,057.4	6,012.3	6,198.0
Ground Transportation	3,681.9	3,697.7	3,798.1
Air Transportation	—	—	—
Naval Transportation	—	—	—
Communications and IT	2,051.6	1,976.6	2,189.6
Supplies, Services and Equipment	1,336.2	1,184.9	1,318.9
Quick-impact Projects	—	—	—
Gross Requirements	**47,806.9**	**47,806.9**	**50,526.1**
Staff Assessment Income	1,393.0	1,451.1	1,526.7
Net Requirements	**46,413.9**	**46,355.8**	**48,999.4**
Voluntary Contributions in Kind (budgeted)	—	—	—
Total Requirements	**47,806.9**	**47,806.9**	**50,526.1**

Sources: UN Documents A/65/743/Add.3 and A/C.5/65/19; DFS FBFD.
Note: 2010–2011 expenditures are preliminary and subject to change.

UNDOF Expenditures on Contingent Owned Equipment: July 2010–June 2011 (in thousands of US dollars)

Military Contingents	339.6
Facilities and Infrastructure	248.7
Medical	143.6
Special Equipment	4.4
Total	**736.3**

Sources: UN Document A/66/556; DFS FPD.

UNDOF Mission Expenditures: July 2000–June 2010 (in thousands of US dollars)

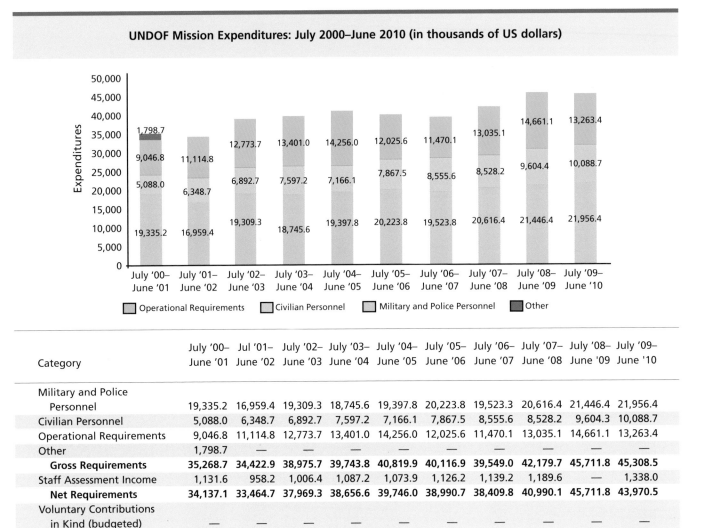

Category	July '00– June '01	Jul '01– June '02	July '02– June '03	July '03– June '04	July '04– June '05	July '05– June '06	July '06– June '07	July '07– June '08	July '08– June '09	July '09– June '10
Military and Police Personnel	19,335.2	16,959.4	19,309.3	18,745.6	19,397.8	20,223.8	19,523.3	20,616.4	21,446.4	21,956.4
Civilian Personnel	5,088.0	6,348.7	6,892.7	7,597.2	7,166.1	7,867.5	8,555.6	8,528.2	9,604.3	10,088.7
Operational Requirements	9,046.8	11,114.8	12,773.7	13,401.0	14,256.0	12,025.6	11,470.1	13,035.1	14,661.1	13,263.4
Other	1,798.7	—	—	—	—	—	—	—	—	—
Gross Requirements	**35,268.7**	**34,422.9**	**38,975.7**	**39,743.8**	**40,819.9**	**40,116.9**	**39,549.0**	**42,179.7**	**45,711.8**	**45,308.5**
Staff Assessment Income	1,131.6	958.2	1,006.4	1,087.2	1,073.9	1,126.2	1,139.2	1,189.6	—	1,338.0
Net Requirements	**34,137.1**	**33,464.7**	**37,969.3**	**38,656.6**	**39,746.0**	**38,990.7**	**38,409.8**	**40,990.1**	**45,711.8**	**43,970.5**
Voluntary Contributions in Kind (budgeted)	—	—	—	—	—	—	—	—	—	—
Total Requirements	**35,268.7**	**34,422.9**	**38,975.7**	**39,743.8**	**40,819.9**	**40,116.9**	**39,549.0**	**42,179.7**	**45,711.8**	**45,308.5**

Sources: UN Documents A/56/813, A/57/668, A/58/641, A/59/625, A/60/628, A/61/662, A/62/719, A/63/521, A/C.5/63/26, and A/64/660/Add.4.

6.6 UNFICYP (UN Peacekeeping Force in Cyprus)

UNFICYP Key Facts	
Latest Key Resolution	14 December 2011 (date of issue); 19 December 2011 (date of effect) UNSC Res. 2026 (three month duration)
First Mandate	4 March 1964 (date of issue and effect) UNSC Res. 186 (three month duration)
SRSG	Lisa Buttenheim (United States) SG letter of appointment 27 May 2010
First SRSG	Galo Plaza Lasso (appointed as mediator, Ecuador)
Force Commander	Major General Chao Liu (China) SG letter of appointment 10 January 2011
First Force Commander	Lieutenant General P.S. Gyani (India)

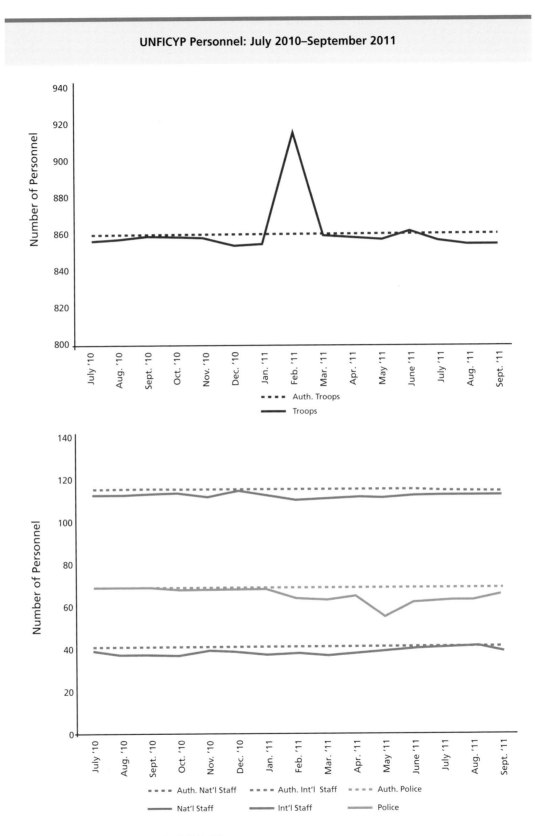

UNFICYP Personnel: July 2010–September 2011

Sources: DFS FPD; DPKO FGS; DPKO PD.

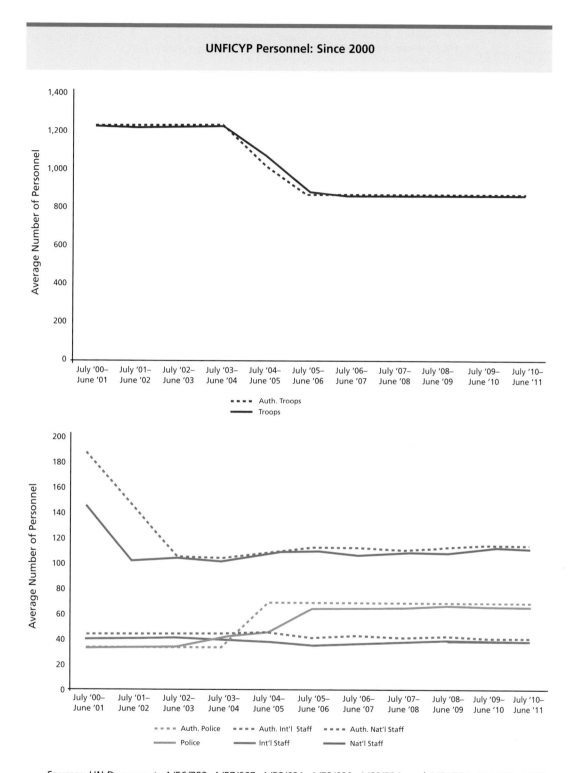

UNFICYP Personnel: Since 2000

Sources: UN Documents A/56/782, A/57/667, A/58/631, A/59/620, A/60/584, and A/61/724; DFS FPD; DPKO FGS; DPKO PD.

UNFICYP Military and Police Contributors: 30 September 2011

Contributing Country	Troops	Military Observers	Police	Total
United Kingdom	271	—	—	271
Argentina	264	—	—	264
Slovakia	159	—	—	159
Hungary	77	—	—	77
Serbia	45			45
Ireland	—	—	18	18
Chile	15	—	—	15
Paraguay	14	—	—	14
Australia	—	—	14	14
Bosnia and Herzegovina	—	—	8	8
Croatia	2	—	4	6
India	—	—	6	6
Ukraine	—	—	6	6
Austria	4	—	—	4
Italy	—	—	4	4
El Salvador	—	—	3	3
Montenegro	—	—	3	3
China	2	—	—	2
Brazil	1	—	—	1
Canada	1	—	—	1
Total	**855**	**—**	**66**	**921**

Source: DPKO FGS.

UNFICYP Military Units: 30 September 2011

Number	Unit Type	Country
1	Aviation Unit	Argentina
1	Force Engineers Platoon	Slovakia
1	Force Medical Unit	Argentina
1	Force Military Police Unit	Argentina-Hungary-Slovakia-United Kingdom Composite
3	Infantry Units	Argentina, Slovakia-Hungary-Serbia Composite, United Kingdom
1	Mobile Force Reserve Unit	Argentina-Hungary-Slovakia-United Kingdom Composite

Source: DPKO FGS.

UNFICYP International Civilian Personnel Occupations: 30 September 2011

Occupation	International Staff	Percentage International Staff
Administration	10	25.6%
Aviation	—	—
Civil Affairs	2	5.1%
Economic Affairs	—	—
Electoral Affairs	—	—
Engineering	2	5.1%
Finance	2	5.1%
Human Resources	1	2.6%
Human Rights	—	—
Humanitarian Affairs	—	—
Information Management	1	2.6%
Information Systems and Technology	5	12.8%
Legal Affairs	1	2.6%
Logistics	2	5.1%
Management and Programme Analysis	—	—
Medical Services	—	—
Political Affairs	5	12.8%
Procurement	2	5.1%
Programme Management	—	—
Public Information	2	5.1%
Rule of Law	2	5.1%
Security	2	5.1%
Social Affairs	—	—
Transport	—	—
Total	**39**	

Source: DFS FPD.

UNFICYP Personnel Gender Statistics: 30 September 2011

Personnel Type	Male	Female	Percentage Male	Percentage Female
Troops	790	65	92.4%	7.6%
Military Observers	—	—	—	—
Police	56	10	84.8%	15.2%
International Civilian Staff	28	11	71.8%	28.2%
National Civilian Staff	71	41	63.4%	36.6%
Total	**945**	**127**	**88.2%**	**11.8%**

Sources: DFS FPD; DPKO FGS; DPKO PD.

UNFICYP Fatalities: Inception–September 2011

Personnel Type

Time Period	Troops	Military Obs.	Police	Int'l. Staff	National Staff	Other[a]	Total
1963–1999	163	—	3	3	—	—	169
2000	1	—	—	—	—	—	1
2001	—	—	—	—	—	—	—
2002	—	—	—	—	—	—	—
2003	2	—	—	—	—	—	2
2004	1	—	—	—	1	—	2
2005	—	—	—	1	—	—	1
2006	—	—	—	—	1	—	1
2007	1	—	—	—	—	—	1
2008	1	—	—	1	—	—	2
2009	1	—	—	—	—	—	1
2010	—	—	—	—	—	—	—
2011 (Jan.-Sept.)	1	—	—	—	—	—	1
January-March	—	—	—	—	—	—	—
April-June	1	—	—	—	—	—	1
July-September	—	—	—	—	—	—	—
Total Fatalities	**171**	**—**	**3**	**5**	**2**	**—**	**181**

Incident Type

Time Period	Malicious Act	Illness	Accident	Other[b]	Total
1963–1999	15	41	91	22	169
2000	—	—	—	1	1
2001	—	—	—	—	—
2002	—	—	—	—	—
2003	—	—	2	—	2
2004	—	—	2	—	2
2005	—	1	—	—	1
2006	—	1	—	—	1
2007	—	—	1	—	1
2008	—	1	1	—	2
2009	—	—	1	—	1
2010	—	—	—	—	—
2011 (Jan.-Sept.)	—	—	—	1	1
January-March	—	—	—	—	—
April-June	—	—	—	1	1
July-September	—	—	—	—	—
Total Fatalities	**15**	**44**	**98**	**24**	**181**

Source: DPKO Situation Centre.
Notes: a. Other refers to consultants, UNVs, etc.
b. Incident type is unknown, uncertain, or under investigation. Other includes what were previously qualified as self-inflicted.

UNFICYP Vehicles: 30 September 2011

Contingent Owned Vehicles		UN Owned Vehicles	
Vehicle Type	Quantity	Vehicle Type	Quantity
Aircraft/Airfield Support Equipment	1	4x4 Vehicles	29
Combat Vehicles	9	Airfield Support Equipment	2
Engineering Vehicles	4	Ambulances	2
Material Handling Equipment	1	Buses	11
Support Vehicles		Engineering Vehicles	15
(Commercial Pattern)	6	Material Handling Equipment	7
Support Vehicles (Military Pattern)	14	Trucks	26
Total	**35**	**Total**	**92**

Sources: DFS Contingent Owned Equipment and Property Management Section; DFS Surface Transport Section.

UNFICYP Aircraft: 30 September 2011

	Transport Fixed Wing	Transport Helicopter	Attack Helicopter
Commercial	—	—	—
Contingent Owned	—	3 (Argentina)	—
Total	—	**3**	—

Source: DFS Air Transport Section.

UNFICYP Budget and Expenditures (in thousands of US dollars)

Category	Budgeted July '10–June '11	Expenditures July '10–June '11	Budgeted July '11–June '12
Military Observers	—	—	—
Military Contingents	21,072.6	20,484.0	21,540.2
Civilian Police	—	—	3,096.6
Formed Police Units	—	—	—
United Nations Police	3,176.6	3,034.0	—
International Staff	6,795.9	6,683.0	6,624.5
National Staff	8,694.7	8,759.0	7,969.8
United Nations Volunteers	192.0	—	—
General Temporary Assistance	—	200.0	192.0
Government-provided Personnel	—	—	—
Civilian Electoral Observers	—	—	—
Consultants	—	—	19.1
Official Travel	425.2	281.0	388.7
Facilities and Infrastructure	8,195.5	8,309.0	8,616.9
Ground Transportation	3,338.7	4,269.0	3,583.2
Air Transportation	1,836.4	1,848.0	1,960.1
Naval Transportation	—	—	—
Communications and IT	1,632.4	1,540.0	1,607.6
Supplies, Services and Equipment	—	909.0	913.3
Quick-impact Projects	965.7	—	—
Gross Requirements	**56,325.7**	**56,314.5**	**56,512.0**
Staff Assessment Income	2,555.7	1,465.0	2,404.2
Net Requirements	**53,770.0**	**54,849.1**	**54,107.8**
Voluntary Contributions in Kind (budgeted)	1,830.6	150.0	1,692.2
Total Requirements	**58,156.3**	**56,464.7**	**58,204.2**

Sources: UN Documents A/65/743/Add.2 and A/C.5/65/19; DFS FBFD.
Notes: 2010–2011 expenditures are preliminary and subject to change. Discrepancies in expenditures from July 2010–June 2011 may be the result of figure estimations.

UNFICYP Expenditures on Contingent Owned Equipment: July 2010–June 2011 (in thousands of US dollars)

Military Contingents	1,205.6
Facilities and Infrastructure	164.2
Total	**1,369.8**

Sources: UN Document A/66/568; DFS FBFD.

UNFICYP Voluntary Contributions: July 2010–June 2011 (in thousands of US dollars)

Contributor	Contributions in Kind (budgeted)	Contributions in Kind (non-budgeted)	Contributions in Cash (budgeted)	Total
Cyprus	1,562.0	—	18,956.0	20,518.0
Greece	—	—	6,500.0	6,500.0
Total	**1,562.0**	**—**	**25,456.0**	**27,018.0**

Source: DM OPPBA.

UNFICYP Mission Expenditures: July 2000–June 2010 (in thousands of US dollars)

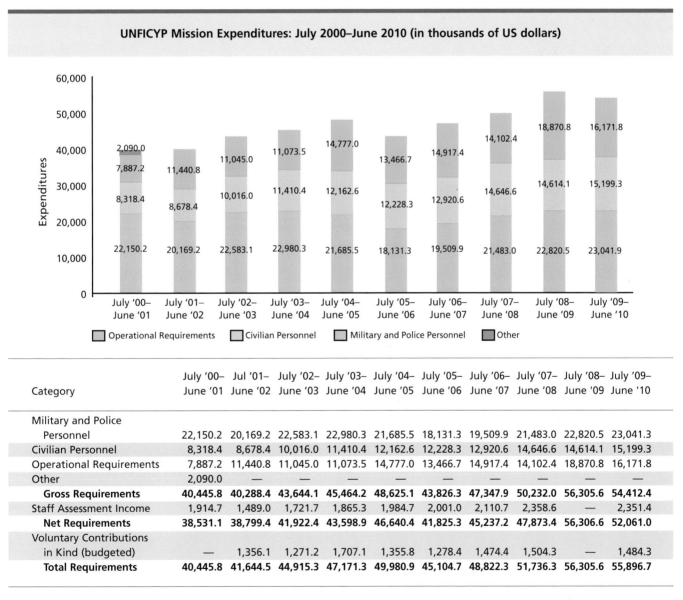

Category	July '00– June '01	Jul '01– June '02	July '02– June '03	July '03– June '04	July '04– June '05	July '05– June '06	July '06– June '07	July '07– June '08	July '08– June '09	July '09– June '10
Military and Police Personnel	22,150.2	20,169.2	22,583.1	22,980.3	21,685.5	18,131.3	19,509.9	21,483.0	22,820.5	23,041.3
Civilian Personnel	8,318.4	8,678.4	10,016.0	11,410.4	12,162.6	12,228.3	12,920.6	14,646.6	14,614.1	15,199.3
Operational Requirements	7,887.2	11,440.8	11,045.0	11,073.5	14,777.0	13,466.7	14,917.4	14,102.4	18,870.8	16,171.8
Other	2,090.0	—	—	—	—	—	—	—	—	—
Gross Requirements	**40,445.8**	**40,288.4**	**43,644.1**	**45,464.2**	**48,625.1**	**43,826.3**	**47,347.9**	**50,232.0**	**56,305.6**	**54,412.4**
Staff Assessment Income	1,914.7	1,489.0	1,721.7	1,865.3	1,984.7	2,001.0	2,110.7	2,358.6	—	2,351.4
Net Requirements	**38,531.1**	**38,799.4**	**41,922.4**	**43,598.9**	**46,640.4**	**41,825.3**	**45,237.2**	**47,873.4**	**56,306.6**	**52,061.0**
Voluntary Contributions in Kind (budgeted)	—	1,356.1	1,271.2	1,707.1	1,355.8	1,278.4	1,474.4	1,504.3	—	1,484.3
Total Requirements	**40,445.8**	**41,644.5**	**44,915.3**	**47,171.3**	**49,980.9**	**45,104.7**	**48,822.3**	**51,736.3**	**56,305.6**	**55,896.7**

Sources: UN Documents A/56/782, A/57/667, A/58/631, A/59/620, A/60/584, A/61/724, A/62/718, A/63/536, A/C.5/63/26, and A/64/660/Add.5.

6.7 UNIFIL (UN Interim Force in Lebanon)

UNIFIL Key Facts	
Latest Key Resolution	30 August 2011 (date of issue); 31 August 2011 (date of effect) UNSC Res. 2004 (twelve month duration)
First Mandate	19 March 1978 (date of issue and effect) UNSC Res. 425/426 (six month duration)
Force Commander	Major General Alberto Asarta Cuevas (Spain)
First Force Commander	Lieutenant-General Emmanuel A. Erskine (Ghana)

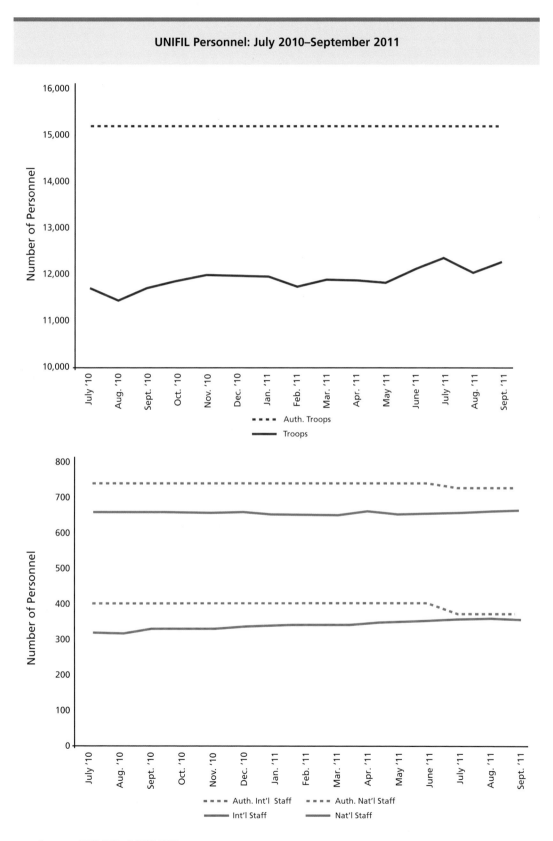

UNIFIL Personnel: July 2010–September 2011

Sources: DFS FPD; DPKO FGS.

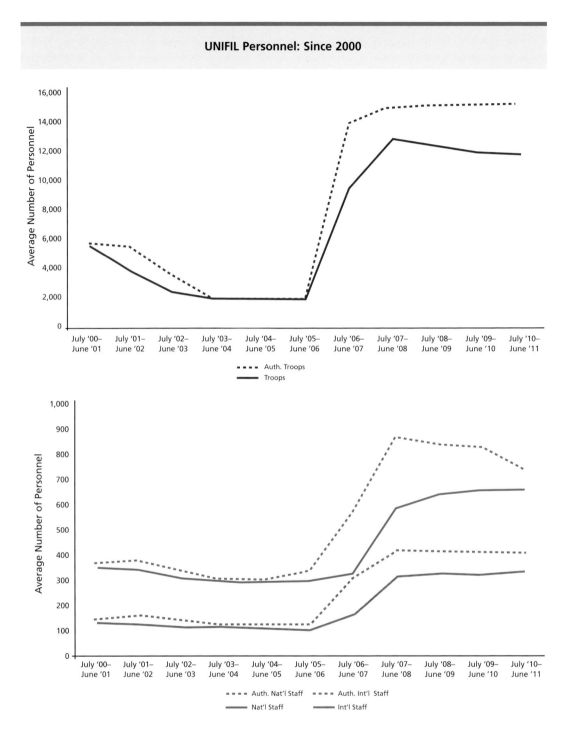

Sources: UN Documents A/56/822, A/57/662, A/58/637, A/59/626, A/60/629, and A/61/829; DFS FPD; DPKO FGS.

UNIFIL Military and Police Contributors: 30 September 2011

Contributing Country	Troops	Military Observers	Police	Total	Contributing Country	Troops	Military Observers	Police	Total
Italy	1,686	—	—	1,686	Portugal	150	—	—	150
France	1,439	—	—	1,439	Belgium	99	—	—	99
Indonesia	1,356	—	—	1,356	El Salvador	52	—	—	52
Spain	1,069	—	—	1,069	Greece	52	—	—	52
Nepal	1,019	—	—	1,019	Brunei	30	—	—	30
India	896	—	—	896	Slovenia	14	—	—	14
Ghana	876	—	—	876	Brazil	11	—	—	11
Malaysia	780	—	—	780	Serbia	5	—	—	5
Ireland	445	—	—	445	Hungary	4	—	—	4
Republic of Korea	369	—	—	369	Belarus	3	—	—	3
Turkey	357	—	—	357	Guatemala	3	—	—	3
China	344	—	—	344	Luxembourg	3	—	—	3
Bangladesh	326	—	—	326	Qatar	3	—	—	3
Germany	232	—	—	232	Sierra Leone	3	—	—	3
Cambodia	217	—	—	217	Cyprus	2	—	—	2
Tanzania	154	—	—	154	Croatia	1	—	—	1
Denmark	151	—	—	151	FYR of Macedonia	1	—	—	1
Sri Lanka	151	—	—	151	Nigeria	1	—	—	1
					Total	**12,304**	**—**	**—**	**12,304**

Source: DPKO FGS.

UNIFIL Military Units: 30 September 2011

Number	Unit Type	Country
2	Aviation Units	France, Italy
1	Civil Military Cooperation Unit	Italy
4	Combat Support Service Units	France, Germany, Italy, Spain
3	Combined Task Forces	Bangladesh, Germany, Indonesia
3	Corvettes	Spain, Turkey (2)
3	Engineering Companies	France, Italy, Portugal
7	Fast Patrol Boats	Germany (2), Greece (3) Turkey (2)
1	Field Artillery Unit	France
1	Fire Brigade	Denmark
3	Force Protection Companies	Indonesia, Italy, Sri Lanka
1	Force Support Unit	Germany
2	Frigates	Belgium, Germany
1	Headquarters Company	Indonesia
1	Helicopter Unit	Spain
20	Infantry Battalions	Bangladesh (2), Cambodia, China, El Salvador, France, Ghana, India, Indonesia, Ireland, Italy (2), Korea, Malaysia-Brunei Composite (3), Nepal, Serbia, Spain, Turkey
2	Information, Surveillance and Reconnaissance Companies	Italy, Spain
3	Level II Hospitals	Belarus, China, India
1	Maintenance Platoon	Denmark
1	Medical Unit	Indonesia
1	Military Community Outreach Unit	Italy
6	Military Police Units	Belgium, Denmark, Indonesia, Italy, Tanzania (2)
1	Mine Counter Measure Vessel	Germany
2	Multi-Role Engineering Companies	Belgium (2)
2	Naval Units	Germany, Indonesia
1	Operation Cell	Denmark
1	Quick Reaction Force	France
1	Reconnaissance Detachment	Slovenia
12	Sector Headquarters Companies	El Salvador, Ghana, India, Indonesia, Ireland, Italy, Korea, Malaysia-Brunei Composite, Nepal, Serbia, Slovenia, Spain
2	Signal Companies	Italy, Spain
1	Transport Platoon	Denmark

Source: DPKO FGS.
Note: Military headquarters and national support elements staff and staff officers not included.

UNIFIL International Civilian Personnel Occupations: 30 September 2011

Occupation	International Staff	Percentage International Staff
Administration	55	15.5%
Aviation	4	1.1%
Civil Affairs	6	1.7%
Economic Affairs	—	—
Electoral Affairs	—	—
Engineering	28	7.9%
Finance	13	3.7%
Human Resources	23	6.5%
Human Rights	—	—
Humanitarian Affairs	—	—
Information Management	2	0.6%
Information Systems and Technology	55	15.5%
Legal Affairs	2	0.6%
Logistics	64	18.0%
Management and Programme Analysis	1	0.3%
Medical Services	4	1.1%
Political Affairs	16	4.5%
Procurement	10	2.8%
Programme Management	—	—
Public Information	5	1.4%
Rule of Law	3	0.8%
Security	42	11.8%
Social Affairs	1	0.3%
Transport	21	5.9%
Total	**355**	

Source: DFS FPD.

UNIFIL Personnel Gender Statistics: 30 September 2011

Personnel Type	Male	Female	Percentage Male	Percentage Female
Troops	11,731	573	95.3%	4.7%
Military Observers	—	—	—	—
Police	—	—	—	—
International Civilian Staff	254	101	71.5%	28.5%
National Civilian Staff	493	173	74.0%	26.0%
Total	**12,478**	**847**	**93.6%**	**6.4%**

Sources: DFS FPD; DPKO FGS.

UNIFIL Fatalities: Inception–September 2011

Personnel Type

Time Period	Troops	Military Obs.	Police	Int'l. Staff	National Staff	Other[a]	Total
1978–1999	233	1	—	2	1	—	237
2000	6	—	—	—	—	—	6
2001	3	1	—	—	—	—	4
2002	3	—	—	—	3	—	6
2003	1	—	—	—	—	—	1
2004	3	—	—	—	—	—	3
2005	—	—	—	—	—	—	—
2006	—	—	—	1	—	—	1
2007	11	—	—	1	—	—	12
2008	6	—	—	1	2	—	9
2009	2	—	—	1	—	—	3
2010	6	—	—	2	—	—	8
January-March	3	—	—	—	—	—	3
April-June	1	—	—	2	—	—	3
July-September	2	—	—	—	—	—	2
October-December	—	—	—	—	—	—	—
2011 (Jan.-Sept.)	3	—	—	—	—	—	3
January-March	2	—	—	—	—	—	2
April-June	1	—	—	—	—	—	1
July-September	—	—	—	—	—	—	—
Total Fatalities	**277**	**2**	**—**	**8**	**6**	**—**	**293**

Incident Type

Time Period	Malicious Act	Illness	Accident	Other[b]	Total
1978–1999	84	46	95	12	237
2000	1	—	5	—	6
2001	—	2	2	—	4
2002	—	3	3	—	6
2003	—	1	—	—	1
2004	—	—	3	—	3
2005	—	—	—	—	—
2006	1	—	—	—	1
2007	6	1	5	—	12
2008	—	5	4	—	9
2009	—	1	1	1	3
2010	—	2	6	—	8
January-March	—	—	3	—	3
April-June	—	2	1	—	3
July-September	—	—	2	—	2
October-December	—	—	—	—	—
2011 (Jan.-Sept.)	—	1	1	1	3
January-March	—	1	—	1	2
April-June	—	—	1	—	1
July-September	—	—	—	—	—
Total Fatalities	**92**	**62**	**125**	**14**	**293**

Source: DPKO Situation Centre.
Notes: a. Other refers to consultants, UNVs, etc.
b. Incident type is unknown, uncertain, or under investigation. Other includes what were previously qualified as self-inflicted.

UNIFIL Vehicles: 30 September 2011

Contingent Owned Vehicles		UN Owned Vehicles	
Vehicle Type	Quantity	Vehicle Type	Quantity
Aircraft/Airfield Support Equipment	11	4x4 Vehicles	576
Combat Vehicles	606	Airfield Support Equipment	3
Communications Vehicles	48	Ambulances	23
Engineering Vehicles	186	Armoured Personnel Carriers	37
Material Handling Equipment	47	Automobiles	1
Support Vehicles		Buses	66
(Commercial Pattern)	328	Engineering Vehicles	89
Support Vehicles (Military Pattern)	1,320	Material Handling Equipment	40
Total	**2,546**	Trucks	120
		Vans	20
		Total	**975**

Sources: DFS Contingent Owned Equipment and Property Management Section; DFS Surface Transport Section.

UNIFIL Aircraft: 30 September 2011

	Transport Fixed Wing	Transport Helicopter	Attack Helicopter
Commercial	—	1	—
Contingent Owned	—	6	—
		(4 Italy, 2 Spain)	
Total	—	7	—

Source: DFS Air Transport Section.

UNIFIL Budget and Expenditures (in thousands of US dollars)

Category	Budgeted July '10–June '11	Expenditures July '10–June '11	Budgeted July '11–June '12
Military Observers	—	—	—
Military Contingents	295,615.1	289,438.4	312,578.4
Civilian Police	—	—	—
Formed Police Units	—	—	—
United Nations Police	—	—	—
International Staff	56,887.0	57,569.0	61,518.3
National Staff	33,527.7	37,919.0	36,569.7
United Nations Volunteers	549.1	—	—
General Temporary Assistance	—	405.8	567.6
Government-provided Personnel	—	—	—
Civilian Electoral Observers	—	—	—
Consultants	282.0	282.0	136.2
Official Travel	1,148.7	1,120.2	1,291.8
Facilities and Infrastructure	49,742.3	49,913.2	51,753.5
Ground Transportation	8,594.3	9,154.6	8,422.0
Air Transportation	7,753.1	7,774.0	8,487.9
Naval Transportation	30,456.7	32,498.0	31,905.8
Communications and IT	20,441.7	20,144.3	18,654.0
Supplies, Services and Equipment	13,212.5	11,921.4	13,085.4
Quick-impact Projects	500.0	500.0	500.0
Gross Requirements	**518,710.2**	**518,639.8**	**545,470.6**
Staff Assessment Income	10,996.5	13,091.7	12,287.4
Net Requirements	**507,713.7**	**505,548.2**	**533,183.2**
Voluntary Contributions in Kind (budgeted)	—	—	—
Total Requirements	**518,710.2**	**518,639.8**	**545,470.6**

Sources: UN Documents A/65/743/Add.9 and A/C.5/65/19; DFS FBFD.

Notes: 2010–2011 expenditures are preliminary and subject to change. Discrepancies in expenditures from July 2010–June 2011 may be the result of figure estimations.

UNIFIL Expenditures on Contingent Owned Equipment: July 2010–June 2011 (in thousands of US dollars)

Military Contingents	78,915.5
Facilities and Infrastructure	26,511.5
Communications	9,204.3
Medical	3,658.9
Special Equipment	5,445.3
Total	**123,735.5**

Source: UN Document A/64/641.

Note: 2010–2011 expenditures are preliminary and subject to change.

UNIFIL Mission Expenditures: July 2000–June 2010 (in thousands of US dollars)

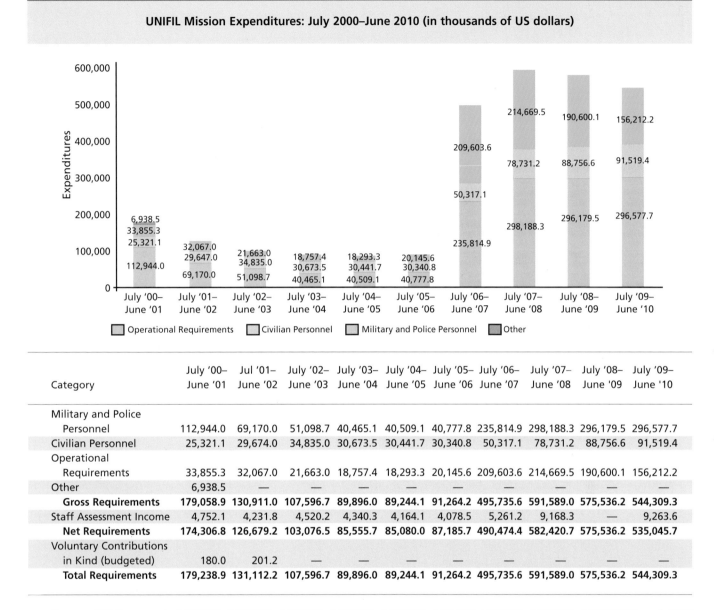

Category	July '00–June '01	Jul '01–June '02	July '02–June '03	July '03–June '04	July '04–June '05	July '05–June '06	July '06–June '07	July '07–June '08	July '08–June '09	July '09–June '10
Military and Police Personnel	112,944.0	69,170.0	51,098.7	40,465.1	40,509.1	40,777.8	235,814.9	298,188.3	296,179.5	296,577.7
Civilian Personnel	25,321.1	29,674.0	34,835.0	30,673.5	30,441.7	30,340.8	50,317.1	78,731.2	88,756.6	91,519.4
Operational Requirements	33,855.3	32,067.0	21,663.0	18,757.4	18,293.3	20,145.6	209,603.6	214,669.5	190,600.1	156,212.2
Other	6,938.5	—	—	—	—	—	—	—	—	—
Gross Requirements	179,058.9	130,911.0	107,596.7	89,896.0	89,244.1	91,264.2	495,735.6	591,589.0	575,536.2	544,309.3
Staff Assessment Income	4,752.1	4,231.8	4,520.2	4,340.3	4,164.1	4,078.5	5,261.2	9,168.3	—	9,263.6
Net Requirements	174,306.8	126,679.2	103,076.5	85,555.7	85,080.0	87,185.7	490,474.4	582,420.7	575,536.2	535,045.7
Voluntary Contributions in Kind (budgeted)	180.0	201.2	—	—	—	—	—	—	—	—
Total Requirements	179,238.9	131,112.2	107,596.7	89,896.0	89,244.1	91,264.2	495,735.6	591,589.0	575,536.2	544,309.3

Sources: UN Documents A/56/763, A/57/678, A/58/634, A/59/623, A/60/637, A/61/675 A/62/687, A/63/569, A/C.5/63/26, and A/64/660/Add.14.

6.8 UNISFA (UN Interim Security Force for Abyei)

UNISFA Key Facts	
Latest Key Resolution	22 December 2011 (date of issue); 27 December 2011 (date of effect) UNSC Res. 2032 (five month duration)
First Mandate	27 June 2011 (date of issue and effect) UNSC Res. 1990 (six month duration)
Force Commander	Lieutenant-General Tadesse Werede Tesfay (Ethiopia) SG letter of appointment 22 July 2011

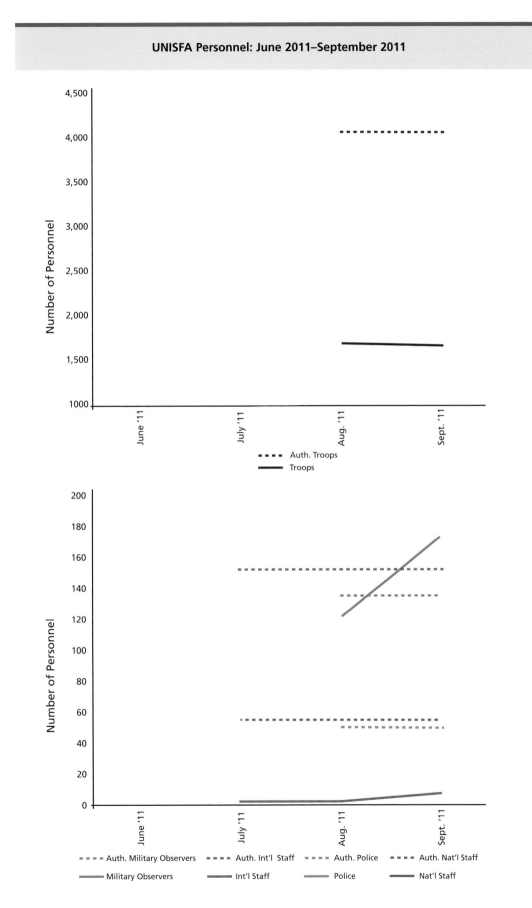

UNISFA Personnel: June 2011–September 2011

Sources: UN Document A/66/526; DFS FPD; DPKO FGS; DPKO PD; UNV Programme.

UNISFA Military and Police Contributors: 30 September 2011

Contributing Country	Troops	Military Observers	Police	Total	Contributing Country	Troops	Military Observers	Police	Total
Ethiopia	1,645	135	—	1,780	China	—	1	—	1
Egypt	11	4	—	15	Guatemala	—	1	—	1
Zambia	12	2	—	14	Namibia	—	1	—	1
India	—	5	—	5	Nigeria	—	1	—	1
Brazil	—	3	—	3	Pakistan	—	1	—	1
Jordan	—	3	—	3	Republic of Korea	—	1	—	1
Rwanda	—	3	—	3	Russia	—	1	—	1
Burkina Faso	—	2	—	2	Sierra Leone	—	1	—	1
Guinea	—	2	—	2	Sri Lanka	—	1	—	1
United Kingdom	—	2	—	2	Sweden	—	1	—	1
Yemen	—	2	—	2	**Total**	**1,668**	**174**	**—**	**1,842**
Bangladesh	—	1	—	1					

Source: DPKO FGS.

UNISFA Military Units: 30 September 2011

Number	Unit Type	Country
2	Artillery Companies	Ethiopia (2)
1	Demining Company	Ethiopia
1	Infantry Battalion	Ethiopia
1	Level II Hospital	Ethiopia
1	Light Field Engineering Company	Ethiopia
1	Multi-Role Logistics Company	Ethiopia
1	Signals Unit	Ethiopia
1	Tank Company	Ethiopia

Source: DPKO FGS.
Note: Military headquarters staff and military observers not included.

UNISFA International Civilian Personnel Occupations: 30 September 2011

Occupation	International Staff	Percentage International Staff
Administration	1	14.3%
Aviation	—	—
Civil Affairs	—	—
Economic Affairs	—	—
Electoral Affairs	—	—
Engineering	—	—
Finance	1	14.3%
Human Resources	1	14.3%
Human Rights	—	—
Humanitarian Affairs	—	—
Information Management	—	—
Information Systems and Technology	—	—
Legal Affairs	—	—
Logistics	—	—
Management and Programme Analysis	—	—
Medical Services	—	—
Political Affairs	—	—
Procurement	—	—
Programme Management	—	—
Public Information	—	—
Rule of Law	3	42.9%
Security	—	—
Social Affairs	—	—
Transport	1	14.3%
Total	**7**	

Source: DFS FPD.

UNISFA Personnel Gender Statistics: 30 September 2011

Personnel Type	Male	Female	Percentage Male	Percentage Female
Troops	1,568	100	94.0%	6.0%
Military Observers	169	5	97.1%	2.9%
Police	—	—	—	—
International Civilian Staff	6	1	85.7%	14.3%
National Civilian Staff	—	—	—	—
Total	**1,743**	**106**	**94.3%**	**5.7%**

Sources: DFS FPD; DPKO FGS; DPKO PD.

UNISFA Fatalities: Inception–September 2011

Time Period	Personnel Type						
	Troops	Military Obs.	Police	Int'l. Staff	National Staff	Other[a]	Total
2011 (June-Sept.)	5	—	—	—	—	—	5
June	—	—	—	—	—	—	—
July-September	5	—	—	—	—	—	5
Total Fatalities	**5**	**—**	**—**	**—**	**—**	**—**	**5**

Time Period	Incident Type				
	Malicious Act	Illness	Accident	Other[b]	Total
2011 (June-Sept.)	—	1	4	—	5
June	—	—	—	—	—
July-September	—	1	4	—	5
Total Fatalities	**—**	**1**	**4**	**—**	**5**

Source: DPKO Situation Centre.
Notes: a. Other refers to consultants, UNVs, etc.
b. Incident type is unknown, uncertain, or under investigation. Other includes what were previously qualified as self-inflicted.

UNISFA Vehicles: 30 September 2011

Contingent Owned Vehicles		UN Owned Vehicles	
Vehicle Type	Quantity	Vehicle Type	Quantity
Combat Vehicles	19	4x4 Vehicles	28
Engineering Vehicles	4	Ambulances	1
Support Vehicles		Buses	1
(Commerical Pattern)	8	Engineering Equipment	18
Support Vehicles (Military Pattern)	94	Material Handling Equipment	6
Total	**125**	Trucks	16
		Total	**70**

Sources: DFS Contingent Owned Equipment and Property Management Section; DFS Surface Transport Section.

Note: All contingent owned vehicles are preliminary and subject to change.

UNISFA Budget and Expenditures (in thousands of US dollars)

Category	Budgeted July '11–June '12
Military Observers	3,364.8
Military Contingents	80,512.3
Civilian Police	1,600.0
Formed Police Units	—
United Nations Police	—
International Staff	12,577.2
National Staff	693.2
United Nations Volunteers	600.7
General Temporary Assistance	—
Government-provided Personnel	—
Civilian Electoral Observers	—
Consultants	—
Official Travel	212.3
Facilities and Infrastructure	31,080.2
Ground Transportation	5,397.3
Air Transportation	22,856.6
Naval Transportation	—
Communications and IT	7,397.3
Supplies, Services and Equipment	14,250.0
Quick-impact Projects	150.0
Gross Requirements	**180,691.9**
Staff Assessment Income	1,363.8
Net Requirements	**179,328.1**
Voluntary Contributions in Kind (budgeted)	—
Total Requirements	**180,691.9**

Source: UN Documents A/66/526; DFS FBFD.

6.9 UNMIK (UN Interim Administration in Kosovo)

UNMIK Key Facts	
First Mandate	10 June 1999 (date of issue and effect) UNSC Res. 1244 (paragraph 19 of the Resolution states that international civil and security presences are established for an initial period of twelve months, to continue thereafter unless the Security Council decides otherwise.)
SRSG	Farid Zarif (Afghanistan) SG letter of appointment 7 October 2011
First SRSG	Bernard Kouchner (France)

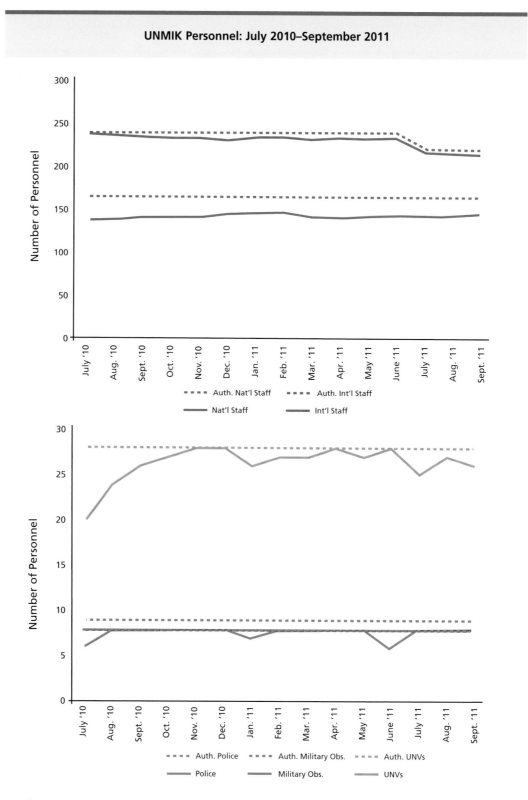

UNMIK Personnel: July 2010–September 2011

Sources: DFS FPD; DPKO FGS; DPKO PD; UNV Programme.

UNMIK Personnel: Since 2000

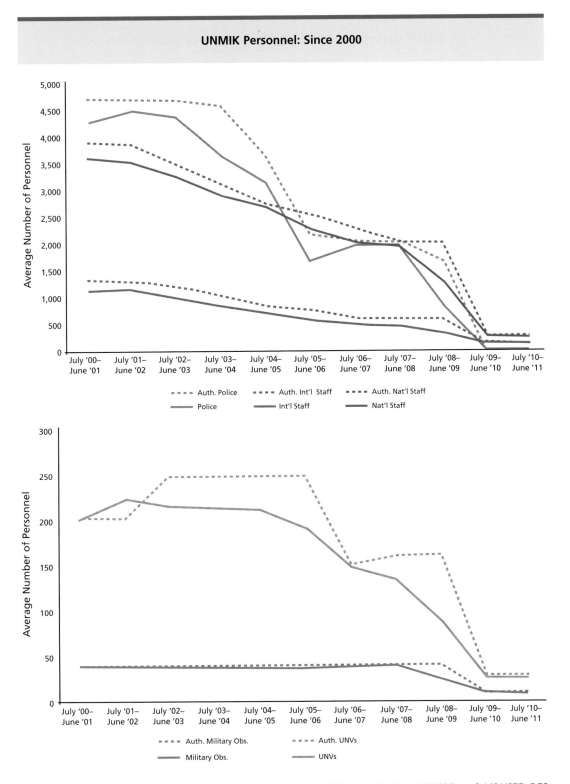

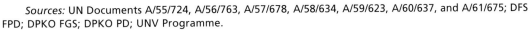

Sources: UN Documents A/55/724, A/56/763, A/57/678, A/58/634, A/59/623, A/60/637, and A/61/675; DFS FPD; DPKO FGS; DPKO PD; UNV Programme.

UNMIK Military and Police Contributors: 30 September 2011

Contributing Country	Troops	Military Observers	Police	Total
Ukraine	—	2	1	3
Romania	—	1	1	2
Czech Republic	—	1	—	1
Denmark	—	1	—	1
Germany	—	—	1	1
Ghana	—	—	1	1
Italy	—	—	1	1
Norway	—	1	—	1
Pakistan	—	—	1	1
Poland	—	1	—	1
Russia	—	—	1	1
Spain	—	1	—	1
Turkey	—	—	1	1
Total	**—**	**8**	**8**	**16**

Source: DPKO FGS.

UNMIK International Civilian Personnel Occupations: 30 September 2011

Occupation	International Staff	Percentage International Staff
Administration	19	13.0%
Aviation	—	—
Civil Affairs	12	8.2%
Economic Affairs	1	0.7%
Electoral Affairs	—	—
Engineering	3	2.1%
Finance	5	3.4%
Human Resources	6	4.1%
Human Rights	—	—
Humanitarian Affairs	—	—
Information Management	1	0.7%
Information Systems and Technology	11	7.5%
Legal Affairs	14	9.6%
Logistics	9	6.2%
Management and Programme Analysis	—	—
Medical Services	3	2.1%
Political Affairs	18	12.3%
Procurement	4	2.7%
Programme Management	2	1.4%
Public Information	2	1.4%
Rule of Law	5	3.4%
Security	28	19.2%
Social Affairs	—	—
Transport	3	2.1%
Total	**146**	

Source: DFS FPD.

UNMIK Personnel Gender Statistics: 30 September 2011

Personnel Type	Male	Female	Percentage Male	Percentage Female
Troops	—	—	—	—
Military Observers	8	—	100.0%	—
Police	7	1	87.5%	12.5%
International Civilian Staff	96	50	65.8%	34.2%
National Civilian Staff	132	83	61.4%	38.6%
Total	**243**	**134**	**64.5%**	**35.5%**

Sources: DFS FPD; DPKO FGS; DPKO PD.

UNMIK Fatalities: Inception–September 2011

Personnel Type

Time Period	Troops	Military Obs.	Police	Int'l. Staff	National Staff	Other[a]	Total
1999	—	—	5	2	—	1	8
2000	—	—	2	1	3	1	7
2001	—	—	1	1	—	—	2
2002	—	—	3	—	4	—	7
2003	—	—	4	1	2	—	7
2004	—	—	5	1	2	—	8
2005	—	—	4	—	2	—	6
2006	—	—	—	—	1	—	1
2007	—	—	1	—	2	—	3
2008	—	1	1	1	2	—	5
2009	—	—	—	—	—	—	—
2010	—	—	—	—	—	—	—
2011 (Jan.-Sept.)	—	—	—	—	—	—	—
January-March	—	—	—	—	—	—	—
April-June	—	—	—	—	—	—	—
July-September	—	—	—	—	—	—	—
Total Fatalities	—	1	26	7	18	2	54

Incident Type

Time Period	Malicious Act	Illness	Accident	Other[b]	Total
1999	1	—	7	—	8
2000	1	4	1	1	7
2001	—	2	—	—	2
2002	1	3	—	3	7
2003	3	3	—	1	7
2004	4	2	1	1	8
2005	1	3	1	1	6
2006	—	1	—	—	1
2007	—	3	—	—	3
2008	1	2	1	1	5
2009	—	—	—	—	—
2010	—	—	—	—	—
2011 (Jan.-Sept.)	—	—	—	—	—
January-March	—	—	—	—	—
April-June	—	—	—	—	—
July-September	—	—	—	—	—
Total Fatalities	12	23	11	8	54

Source: DPKO Situation Centre.
Notes: a. Other refers to consultants, UNVs, etc.
b. Incident type is unknown, uncertain, or under investigation. Other includes what were previously qualified as self-inflicted.

UNMIK Vehicles: 30 September 2011

UN Owned Vehicles

Vehicle Type	Quantity
4x4 Vehicles	177
Ambulances	4
Automobiles	5
Buses	8
Engineering Vehicles	2
Material Handling Equipment	8
Trucks	12
Vans	5
Total	**221**

Source: DFS Surface Transport Section.

UNMIK Budgets and Expenditures (in thousands of US dollars)

Category	Budgeted July '10–June '11	Expenditures July '10–June '11	Budgeted July '11–June '12
Military Observers	404.5	368.0	361.7
Military Contingents	—	—	—
Civilian Police	400.2	—	369.6
Formed Police Units	—	—	—
United Nations Police	—	347.0	—
International Staff	27,335.9	25,137.0	27,515.1
National Staff	7,216.7	7,495.0	6,504.5
United Nations Volunteers	1,098.1	1,059.0	1,140.6
General Temporary Assistance	—	31.0	28.8
Government-provided Personnel	—	—	—
Civilian Electoral Observers	—	—	—
Consultants	217.5	237.0	283.3
Official Travel	629.1	763.0	627.6
Facilities and Infrastructure	4,407.4	4,459.0	4,083.8
Ground Transportation	1,764.6	1,808.0	706.2
Air Transportation	—	—	—
Naval Transportation	—	—	—
Communications and IT	3,566.5	3,427.0	2,777.4
Supplies, Services and Equipment	833.9	1,235.0	516.2
Quick-impact Projects	—	—	—
Gross Requirements	**47,874.4**	**46,366.0**	**44,914.8**
Staff Assessment Income	4,558.1	4,558.0	4,381.3
Net Requirements	**43,316.3**	**41,808.0**	**40,533.5**
Voluntary Contributions in Kind (budgeted)	—	—	—
Total Requirements	**47,874.4**	**46,366.0**	**44,914.8**

Sources: UN Documents A/65/743/Add.4 and A/C.5/65/19; DFS FBFD.
Note: 2010–2011 expenditures are preliminary and subject to change.

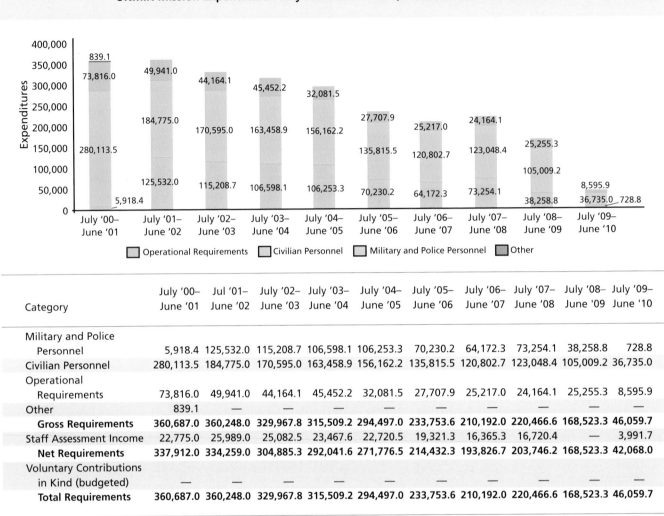

UNMIK Mission Expenditures: July 2000–June 2010 (in thousands of US dollars)

Category	July '00–June '01	Jul '01–June '02	July '02–June '03	July '03–June '04	July '04–June '05	July '05–June '06	July '06–June '07	July '07–June '08	July '08–June '09	July '09–June '10
Military and Police Personnel	5,918.4	125,532.0	115,208.7	106,598.1	106,253.3	70,230.2	64,172.3	73,254.1	38,258.8	728.8
Civilian Personnel	280,113.5	184,775.0	170,595.0	163,458.9	156,162.2	135,815.5	120,802.7	123,048.4	105,009.2	36,735.0
Operational Requirements	73,816.0	49,941.0	44,164.1	45,452.2	32,081.5	27,707.9	25,217.0	24,164.1	25,255.3	8,595.9
Other	839.1	—	—	—	—	—	—	—	—	—
Gross Requirements	**360,687.0**	**360,248.0**	**329,967.8**	**315,509.2**	**294,497.0**	**233,753.6**	**210,192.0**	**220,466.6**	**168,523.3**	**46,059.7**
Staff Assessment Income	22,775.0	25,989.0	25,082.5	23,467.6	22,720.5	19,321.3	16,365.3	16,720.4	—	3,991.7
Net Requirements	**337,912.0**	**334,259.0**	**304,885.3**	**292,041.6**	**271,776.5**	**214,432.3**	**193,826.7**	**203,746.2**	**168,523.3**	**42,068.0**
Voluntary Contributions in Kind (budgeted)	—	—	—	—	—	—	—	—	—	—
Total Requirements	**360,687.0**	**360,248.0**	**329,967.8**	**315,509.2**	**294,497.0**	**233,753.6**	**210,192.0**	**220,466.6**	**168,523.3**	**46,059.7**

Sources: UN Documents A/56/763, A/57/678, A/58/634, A/59/623, A/60/637, A/61/675, A/62/687, A/63/569, A/C.5/63/26, and A/64/660/Add.6.

6.10 UNMIL (UN Mission in Liberia)

UNMIL Key Facts	
Latest Key Resolution	16 September 2011 (date of issue and effect) UNSC Res. 2008 (twelve month duration)
First Mandate	19 September 2003 (date of issue and effect) UNSC Res. 1509 (twelve month duration)
SRSG	Ellen Margrethe Løj (Denmark) SG letter of appointment 17 October 2007
First SRSG	Jacques Klein (United States)
Force Commander	Major General Muhammad Khalid (Pakistan) SG letter of appointment 11 October 2010
First Force Commander	Lieutenant-General Daniel Ishmael Opande (Kenya)
Police Commissioner	Gautam Sawang (India)

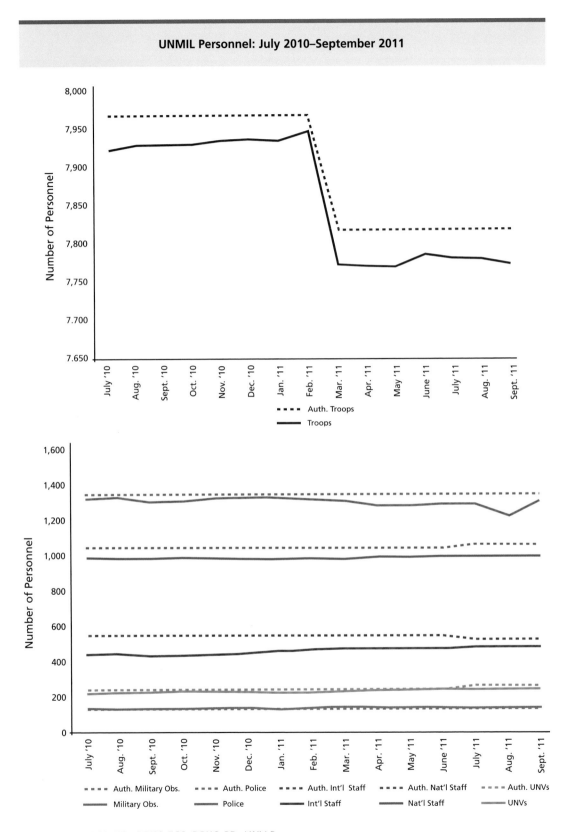

Sources: DFS FPD; DPKO FGS; DPKO PD; UNV Programme.

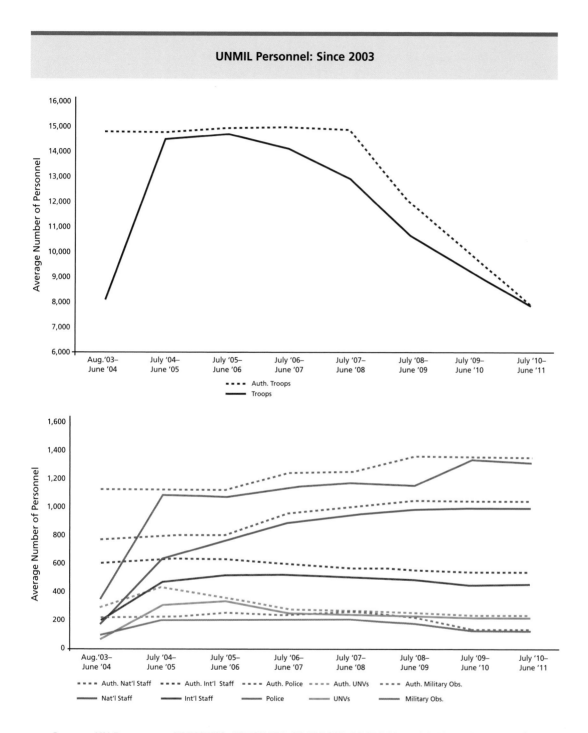

UNMIL Personnel: Since 2003

Sources: UN Documents S/RES/1509, S/RES/1626, S/RES/1667, S/RES/1694, A/59/624, A/60/645, and A/61/715; DFS FPD; DPKO FGS; DPKO PD; UNV Programme.

UNMIL Military and Police Contributors: 30 September 2011

Contributing Country	Troops	Military Observers	Police	Total	Contributing Country	Troops	Military Observers	Police	Total
Pakistan	2,958	7	23	2,988	Malaysia	—	6	—	6
Nigeria	1,548	14	138	1,700	Denmark	2	3	—	5
Bangladesh	1,437	13	21	1,471	Germany	—	—	5	5
Ghana	706	9	20	735	Brazil	2	2	—	4
China	564	2	17	583	Peru	2	2	—	4
Jordan	120	4	248	372	Poland	—	1	3	4
Ukraine	277	2	17	296	Benin	1	2	—	3
Nepal	18	2	252	272	Bolivia	1	2	—	3
India	—	—	248	248	Czech Republic	—	—	3	3
Philippines	115	2	36	153	Ecuador	1	2	—	3
Zimbabwe	—	2	37	39	El Salvador	—	2	1	3
Turkey	—	—	32	32	Paraguay	1	2	—	3
Fiji	—	—	28	28	Senegal	2	1	—	3
Zambia	—	3	24	27	Togo	1	2	—	3
Gambia	—	2	21	23	Bulgaria	—	2	—	2
United States	5	4	12	21	Croatia	2	—	—	2
Kenya	—	—	17	17	Finland	2	—	—	2
Sweden	—	—	14	14	Moldova	—	2	—	2
Ethiopia	4	9	—	13	Montenegro	—	2	—	2
Russia	—	4	9	13	Niger	—	2	—	2
Sri Lanka	—	—	13	13	Republic of Korea	1	1	—	2
Uganda	—	—	13	13	Romania	—	2	—	2
Egypt	—	7	4	11	Switzerland	—	—	2	2
Bosnia and Herzegovina	—	—	10	10	France	1	—	—	1
Norway	—	—	10	10	Indonesia	—	1	—	1
Serbia	—	4	6	10	Jamaica	—	—	1	1
Namibia	3	1	5	9	Mali	—	1	—	1
Argentina	—	—	7	7	Rwanda	—	—	1	1
Yemen	1	—	6	7	**Total**	**7,775**	**133**	**1,308**	**9,216**
Kyrgyzstan	—	2	4	6					

Source: DPKO FGS.

UNMIL Military Units: 30 September 2011

Number	Unit Type	Country
1	Aviation Unit	Ukraine
1	Communications Squadron	Nigeria
5	Engineering Companies	Bangladesh (2), China, Pakistan (2)
1	Quick Reaction Force	Pakistan
3	Heaquarters Companies	Bangladesh, Nigeria, Philippines
6	Infantry Battalions	Bangladesh, Ghana, Nigeria (2), Pakistan (2)
3	Level II Hospitals	Bangladesh, China, Pakistan
1	Level III Hospital	Jordan
1	Logistics Company	Bangladesh
2	Military Police Units	Bangladesh, Nepal
1	Road and Airfield Maintanence Unit	Pakistan
1	Signal Company	Bangladesh
1	Transport Company	China

Source: : DPKO FGS.

UNMIL International Civilian Personnel Occupations: 30 September 2011

Occupation	International Staff	Percentage International Staff
Administration	78	16.2%
Aviation	12	2.5%
Civil Affairs	30	6.2%
Economic Affairs	—	—
Electoral Affairs	—	—
Engineering	20	4.2%
Finance	21	4.4%
Human Resources	16	3.3%
Human Rights	18	3.7%
Humanitarian Affairs	—	—
Information Management	3	0.6%
Information Systems and Technology	28	5.8%
Legal Affairs	6	1.2%
Logistics	75	15.6%
Management and Programme Analysis	—	—
Medical Services	4	0.8%
Political Affairs	31	6.4%
Procurement	15	3.1%
Programme Management	8	1.7%
Public Information	13	2.7%
Rule of Law	11	2.3%
Security	71	14.8%
Social Affairs	2	0.4%
Transport	19	4.0%
Total	**481**	

Source: DFS FPD.

UNMIL Personnel Gender Statistics: 30 September 2011

Personnel Type	Male	Female	Percentage Male	Percentage Female
Troops	7,571	204	97.4%	2.6%
Military Observers	130	3	97.7%	2.3%
Police	1,110	198	84.9%	15.1%
International Civilian Staff	318	163	66.1%	33.9%
National Civilian Staff	806	187	81.2%	18.8%
Total	**9,935**	**755**	**92.9%**	**7.1%**

Sources: DFS FPD; DPKO FGS; DPKO PD.

UNMIL Fatalities: Inception–September 2011

Personnel Type

Time Period	Troops	Military Obs.	Police	Int'l. Staff	National Staff	Other[a]	Total
2003	5	—	—	—	—	—	5
2004	23	1	3	1	1	—	29
2005	26	—	3	3	4	—	36
2006	13	—	2	1	2	—	18
2007	9	—	2	—	3	—	14
2008	12	—	5	1	3	—	21
2009	14	—	1	1	4	—	20
2010	7	—	1	—	1	—	9
January-March	1	—	—	—	—	—	1
April-June	1	—	1	—	—	—	2
July-September	—	—	—	—	1	—	1
October-December	5	—	—	—	—	—	5
2011 (Jan.-Sept.)	6	—	1	—	2	—	9
January-March	1	—	1	—	2	—	4
April-June	4	—	—	—	—	—	4
July-September	1	—	—	—	—	—	1
Total Fatalities	**115**	**1**	**18**	**7**	**20**	**—**	**161**

Incident Type

Time Period	Malicious Act	Illness	Accident	Other[b]	Total
2003	—	1	4	—	5
2004	—	22	6	1	29
2005	—	28	7	1	36
2006	—	16	1	1	18
2007	—	13	1	—	14
2008	—	16	5	—	21
2009	—	10	6	4	20
2010	1	4	4	—	9
January-March	—	1	—	—	1
April-June	1	—	1	—	2
July-September	—	1	—	—	1
October-December	—	2	3	—	5
2011 (Jan.-Sept.)	1	4	3	1	9
January-March	—	3	—	1	4
April-June	1	1	2	—	4
July-September	—	—	1	—	1
Total Fatalities	**2**	**114**	**37**	**8**	**161**

Source: DPKO Situation Centre.
Notes: a. Other refers to consultants, UNVs, etc.
    b. Incident type is unknown, uncertain, or under investigation. Other includes what were previously qualified as self-inflicted.

UNMIL Vehicles: 30 September 2011

Contingent Owned Vehicles		UN Owned Vehicles	
Vehicle Type	Quantity	Vehicle Type	Quantity
Aircraft/Airfield Support Equipment	5	4x4 Vehicles	1,204
Combat Vehicles	132	Aircraft/Airfield Support Equipment	21
Communications Vehicles	2	Ambulances	14
Engineering Vehicles	138	Automobiles	2
Material Handling Equipment	24	Buses	106
Support Vehicles		Engineering Vehicles	8
(Commercial Pattern)	413	Material Handling Equipment	48
Support Vehicles (Military Pattern)	791	Trucks	170
Total	**1,505**	Vans	4
		Total	**1,577**

Sources: DFS Contingent Owned Equipment and Property Management Section; DFS Surface Transport Section.

UNMIL Aircraft: 30 September 2011

	Transport Fixed Wing	Transport Helicopter	Attack Helicopter
Commercial	3	7	—
Contingent Owned	—	8 (Ukraine)	3 (Ukraine)
Total	**3**	**15**	**3**

Source: DFS Air Transport Section.

UNMIL Budget and Expenditures (in thousands of US dollars)

Category	Budgeted July '10–June '11	Expenditures July '10–June '11	Budgeted July '11–June '12
Military Observers	6,996.7	7,467.0	7,256.8
Military Contingents	186,241.6	182,896.7	182,586.0
Civilian Police	—	—	26,236.4
Formed Police Units	19,379.8	18,796.1	19,886.3
United Nations Police	26,295.2	26,783.8	—
International Staff	92,674.6	86,812.6	91,091.8
National Staff	18,381.5	16,336.5	16,148.7
United Nations Volunteers	12,740.5	10,809.0	12,234.0
General Temporary Assistance	—	463.4	881.5
Government-provided Personnel	1,663.1	1,607.5	1,561.6
Civilian Electoral Observers	—	—	—
Consultants	1,295.0	1,295.0	1,042.2
Official Travel	2,709.2	2,714.6	2,848.3
Facilities and Infrastructure	46,350.6	47,625.9	54,339.0
Ground Transportation	11,037.5	11,967.5	9,708.0
Air Transportation	60,236.5	64,960.6	65,325.1
Naval Transportation	3,075.0	3,077.5	3,115.1
Communications and IT	17,860.3	16,081.5	16,702.5
Supplies, Services and Equipment	16,062.9	13,790.1	13,596.6
Quick-impact Projects	1,000.0	1,000.0	1,000.0
Gross Requirements	**524,000.0**	**514,485.3**	**525,559.9**
Staff Assessment Income	12,805.2	11,751.3	12,316.3
Net Requirements	**511,194.8**	**502,734.0**	**513,243.6**
Voluntary Contributions in Kind (budgeted)	52.8	52.8	52.8
Total Requirements	**524,052.8**	**514,538.1**	**525,612.7**

Sources: UN Documents A/65/743/Add.7 and A/C.5/65/19; DFS FBFD.
Note: 2010–2011 expenditures are preliminary and subject to change.

UNMIL Expenditures on Contingent Owned Equipment: July 2010–June 2011 (in thousands of US dollars)

Military Contingents	33,090.0
Formed Police Units	4,138.9
Facilities and Infrastructure	19,809.0
Communications	8,337.4
Medical	9,571.3
Special Equipment	2,209.4
Total	**77,156.0**

Source: UN Document A/64/647.
Note: 2010–2011 expenditures are preliminary and subject to change.

UNMIL Voluntary Contributions: July 2010–June 2011 (in thousands of US dollars)

Contributor	Contributions in Kind (budgeted)	Contributions in Kind (non-budgeted)	Contributions in Cash (budgeted)	Total
Germany	53.0	—	—	53.0
Total	**53.0**	**—**	**—**	**53.0**

Source: DM OPPBA.

UNMIL Mission Expenditures: August 2003–June 2010 (in thousands of US dollars)

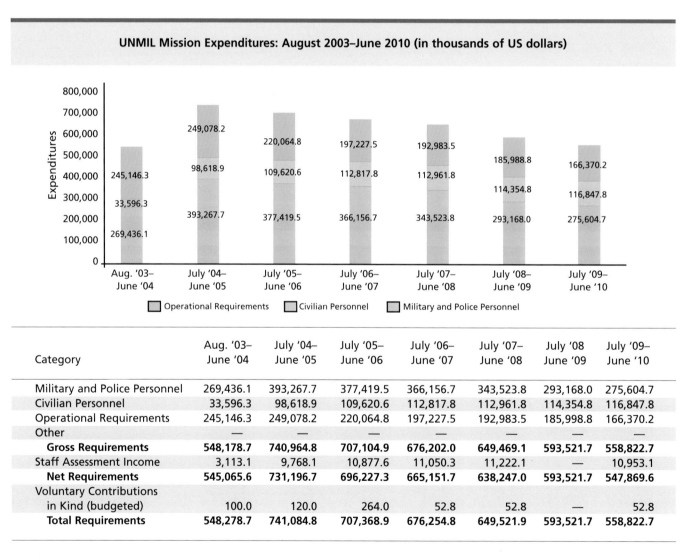

Category	Aug. '03– June '04	July '04– June '05	July '05– June '06	July '06– June '07	July '07– June '08	July '08 June '09	July '09– June '10
Military and Police Personnel	269,436.1	393,267.7	377,419.5	366,156.7	343,523.8	293,168.0	275,604.7
Civilian Personnel	33,596.3	98,618.9	109,620.6	112,817.8	112,961.8	114,354.8	116,847.8
Operational Requirements	245,146.3	249,078.2	220,064.8	197,227.5	192,983.5	185,998.8	166,370.2
Other	—	—	—	—	—	—	—
Gross Requirements	**548,178.7**	**740,964.8**	**707,104.9**	**676,202.0**	**649,469.1**	**593,521.7**	**558,822.7**
Staff Assessment Income	3,113.1	9,768.1	10,877.6	11,050.3	11,222.1	—	10,953.1
Net Requirements	**545,065.6**	**731,196.7**	**696,227.3**	**665,151.7**	**638,247.0**	**593,521.7**	**547,869.6**
Voluntary Contributions in Kind (budgeted)	100.0	120.0	264.0	52.8	52.8	—	52.8
Total Requirements	**548,278.7**	**741,084.8**	**707,368.9**	**676,254.8**	**649,521.9**	**593,521.7**	**558,822.7**

Sources: UN Documents A/59/624, A/60/645, A/61/715, A/62/764, A/63/588, A/C.5/63/26, and A/64/660/Add.9.

6.11 UNMISS (UN Mission in South Sudan)/ UNMIS (UN Mission in Sudan)

UNMISS Key Facts	
First Mandate	8 July 2011 (date of issue) 9 July 2011 (date of effect) UNSC Res. 1996 (decision to transfer appropriate functions performed by UNMIS to UNMISS, effective 9 July 2011, for twelve month duration)
SRSG	Hilde Johnson (Norway) SG letter of appointment 15 June 2011
Force Commander	Major-General Moses Bisong Obi (Nigeria) SG letter of appointment 8 June 2010

UNMIS Key Facts	
First Mandate	24 March 2005 (date of issue and effect) UNSC Res. 1590 (six month duration)
SRSG	Haile Menkerios (South Africa) SG letter of appointment 29 January 2010
First SRSG	Jan Pronk (Netherlands)
Force Commander	Major-General Moses Bisong Obi (Nigeria) SG letter of appointment 8 June 2010
First Force Commander	Major-General Fazle Elahi Akbar (Bangladesh)
Acting Police Commissioner	Klaus-Dieter Tietz (Germany)
First Police Commissioner	Kai Vittrup (Denmark)

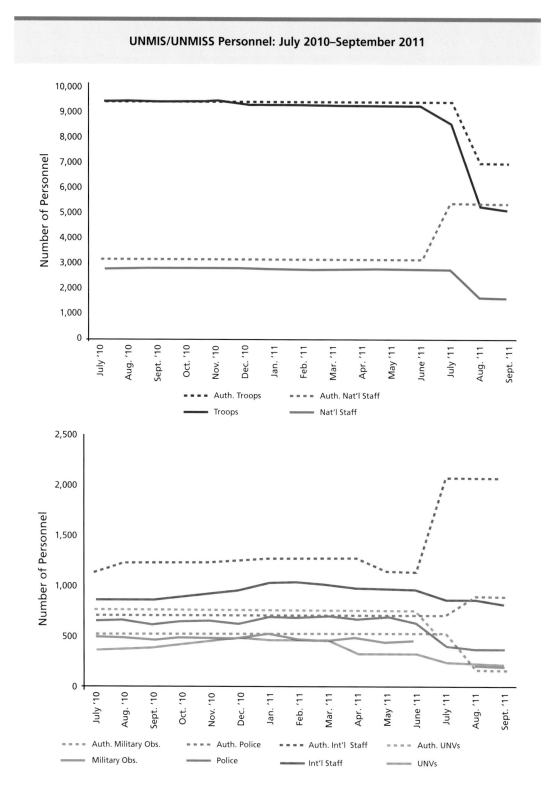

UNMIS/UNMISS Personnel: July 2010–September 2011

Sources: DFS FPD; DPKO FGS; DPKO PD; UNV Programme.

Note: In accordance with S/RES/1996 of 8 July 2011, the appropriate functions of UNMIS were transferred to UNMISS effective 9 July 2011.

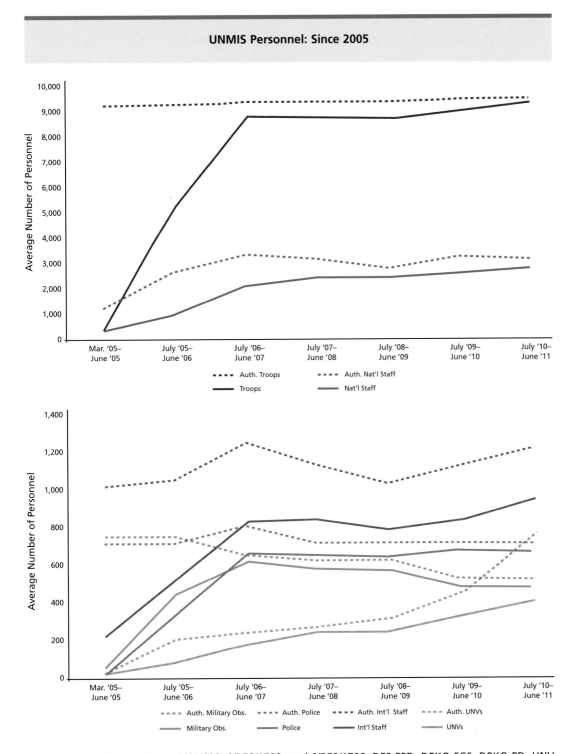

UNMIS Personnel: Since 2005

Sources: UN Documents A/61/689, S/RES/1590, and S/RES/1706; DFS FPD; DPKO FGS; DPKO PD; UNV Programme.

Note: In accordance with S/RES/1996 of 8 July 2011, the appropriate functions of UNMIS were transferred to UNMISS effective 9 July 2011.

UNMISS Military and Police Contributors: 30 September 2011

Contributing Country	Troops	Military Observers	Police	Total	Contributing Country	Troops	Military Observers	Police	Total
India	2,303	12	24	2,339	Indonesia	—	—	6	6
Bangladesh	1,563	7	13	1,583	Korea	—	6	—	6
Kenya	691	5	2	698	El Salvador	—	4	1	5
China	367	10	6	383	Argentina	—	—	4	4
Russia	135	6	—	141	Guatemala	—	4	—	4
Nigeria	3	8	36	47	Kyrgystan	—	4	—	4
Zambia	3	6	35	44	Peru	—	4	—	4
Zimbabwe	—	—	35	35	Sierra Leone	—	4	—	4
Ukraine	—	10	23	33	Uganda	—	1	3	4
Rwanda	3	3	25	31	United States	—	—	4	4
Gambia	—	—	24	24	Benin	—	3	—	3
Australia	8	6	9	23	Cambodia	1	2	—	3
Germany	5	8	7	20	New Zealand	1	2	—	3
Philippines	—	3	16	19	Paraguay	—	3	—	3
Sri Lanka	—	3	16	19	Tanzania	—	3	—	3
Canada	3	5	9	17	Jordan	2	—	—	2
Ghana	—	—	17	17	Mali	—	2	—	2
Nepal	1	6	9	16	Mongolia	—	2	—	2
Egypt	8	7	—	15	Poland	—	2	—	2
Turkey	—	—	13	13	Romania	—	2	—	2
Namibia	—	3	9	12	United Kingdom	2	—	—	2
Norway	3	5	3	11	Burkina Faso	—	1	—	1
Sweden	3	2	5	10	Denmark	—	1	—	1
Bosnia and Herzegovina	—	—	9	9	Ethiopia	—	—	1	1
Brazil	2	6	—	8	Greece	—	1	—	1
Ecuador	—	8	—	8	Guinea	—	1	—	1
Fiji	—	5	3	8	Jamaica	—	—	1	1
Yemen	2	6	—	8	Samoa	—	—	1	1
Malaysia	—	2	5	7	**Total**	**5,109**	**194**	**374**	**5,677**

Source: DPKO FGS.

UNMISS Military Units: 30 September 2011

Number	Unit Type	Country
1	Aviation Unit	Russia
3	Engineering Companies	Bangladesh, China, India
4	Infantry Battalions	Bangladesh, India (2), Kenya
3	Level II Hospitals	Bangladesh, China, India
1	Military Police Company	Bangladesh
1	Petroleum Platoon	Bangladesh
1	Signal Company	India

Source: DPKO FGS.

UNMISS International Civilian Personnel Occupations: 30 September 2011

Occupation	International Staff	Percentage International Staff
Administration	68	9.6%
Aviation	30	4.2%
Civil Affairs	24	3.4%
Economic Affairs	—	—
Electoral Affairs	—	0.0%
Engineering	51	7.2%
Finance	29	4.1%
Human Resources	43	6.1%
Human Rights	21	3.0%
Humanitarian Affairs	—	—
Information Management	8	1.1%
Information Systems and Technology	61	8.6%
Legal Affairs	3	0.4%
Logistics	91	12.9%
Management and Programme Analysis	—	—
Medical Services	6	0.8%
Political Affairs	39	5.5%
Procurement	11	1.6%
Programme Management	55	7.8%
Public Information	16	2.3%
Rule of Law	16	2.3%
Security	94	13.3%
Social Affairs	9	1.3%
Transport	31	4.4%
Total	**706**	

Source: DFS FPD.

UNMISS Personnel Gender Statistics: 30 September 2011

Personnel Type	Male	Female	Percentage Male	Percentage Female
Troops	5,035	74	98.6%	1.4%
Military Observers	187	7	96.4%	3.6%
Police	310	64	82.9%	17.1%
International Civilian Staff	507	199	71.8%	28.2%
National Civilian Staff	883	173	83.6%	16.4%
Total	**6,922**	**517**	**93.1%**	**6.9%**

Sources: DFS FPD; DPKO FGS; DPKO PD.

UNMIS/UNMISS Fatalities: Inception–September 2011

Personnel Type

Time Period	Troops	Military Obs.	Police	Int'l. Staff	National Staff	Other[a]	Total
2005	1	—	—	—	1	—	2
2006	5	1	1	4	4	—	15
2007	3	2	1	1	8	—	15
2008	4	—	—	2	4	—	10
2009	5	—	1	—	3	1	10
2010	2	—	—	1	1	—	4
January-March	—	—	—	—	1	—	1
April-June	1	—	—	—	—	—	1
July-September	—	—	—	—	—	—	—
October-December	1	—	—	1	—	—	2
2011 (Jan.-Sept.)	3	—	—	—	1	—	4
January-March	2	—	—	—	1	—	3
April-June	1	—	—	—	—	—	1
July-September	—	—	—	—	—	—	—
Total Fatalities	**23**	**3**	**3**	**8**	**22**	**1**	**60**

Incident Type

Time Period	Malicious Act	Illness	Accident	Other[b]	Total
2005	—	1	1	—	2
2006	1	13	1	—	15
2007	2	9	2	2	15
2008	—	7	3	—	10
2009	1	5	3	1	10
2010	—	3	—	1	4
January-March	—	1	—	—	1
April-June	—	—	—	1	1
July-September	—	—	—	—	—
October-December	—	2	—	—	2
2011 (Jan.-Sept.)	1	2	1	—	4
January-March	—	2	1	—	3
April-June	1	—	—	—	1
July-September	—	—	—	—	—
Total Fatalities	**5**	**40**	**11**	**4**	**60**

Source: DPKO Situation Centre.
Notes: In accordance with S/RES/1996 of 8 July 2011, the appropriate functions of UNMIS were transferred to UNMISS effective 9 July 2011.
a. Other refers to consultants, UNVs, etc.
b. Incident type is unknown, uncertain, or under investigation. Other includes what were previously qualified as self-inflicted.

UNMISS Vehicles: 30 September 2011

Contingent Owned Vehicles		UN Owned Vehicles	
Vehicle Type	Quantity	Vehicle Type	Quantity
Combat Vehicles	102	4x4 Vehicles	873
Engineering Vehicles	136	Aircraft/Airfield Support Equipment	19
Material Handling Equipment	19	Ambulances	7
Support Vehicles		Buses	54
(Commercial Pattern)	166	Engineering Vehicles	61
Support Vehicles (Military Pattern)	1,061	Material Handling Equipment	61
Total	**1,484**	Trucks	163
		Vans	8
		Total	**1,246**

Sources: DFS Contingent Owned Equipment and Property Management Section; DFS Surface Transport Section.

Note: All contingent owned vehicles are preliminary and subject to change.

UNMISS Aircraft: 30 September 2011

	Transport Fixed Wing	Transport Helicopter	Attack Helicopter
Commercial	8	16	—
Contingent Owned	—	8 (Russia)	—
Total	**8**	**24**	—

Source: DFS Air Transport Section.

UNMIS/UNMISS Budget and Expenditures (in thousands of US dollars)

Category	Budgeted July '10–June '11	Expenditures July '10–June '11	Budgeted July '11–June '12	Proposed Costs for UNMIS Liquidation July '11–June '12
Military Observers	26,483.7	26,582.0	5,578.3	2,813.2
Military Contingents	258,181.0	256,182.6	198,922.3	42,590.6
Civilian Police	—	—	—	3,954.1
Formed Police Units	—	—	27,128.7	—
United Nations Police	36,983.8	35,361.0	15,379.8	—
International Staff	142,713.5	155,448.0	66,104.2	26,490.9
National Staff	67,887.4	62,848.6	22,814.5	18,378.8
United Nations Volunteers	19,246.7	18,433.1	2,755.6	1,858.1
General Temporary Assistance	—	12,076.5	—	534.6
Government-provided Personnel	1,779.7	1,374.3	—	122.8
Civilian Electoral Observers	—	—	—	—
Consultants	472.0	571.1	168.7	—
Official Travel	5,160.9	6,625.5	1,498.9	1,165.5
Facilities and Infrastructure	85,246.0	91,137.9	123,487.6	8,918.9
Ground Transportation	19,482.8	18,292.0	60,262.8	1,671.9
Air Transportation	152,706.1	187,786.2	142,001.5	15,562.6
Naval Transportation	101.7	101.7	—	8.9
Communications and IT	34,527.0	41,530.1	46,868.7	2,309.2
Supplies, Services and Equipment	86,027.7	92,281.8	24,394.9	11,152.2
Quick-impact Projects	1,000.0	1,000.0	900.0	—
Gross Requirements	**938,000.0**	**1,007,632.3**	**738,266.5**	**137,532.0**
Staff Assessment Income	25,325.9	—	10,302.0	3,477.7
Net Requirements	**912,674.1**	**1,007,632.3**	**727,964.5**	**134,054.3**
Voluntary Contributions in Kind (budgeted)	—	—	—	—
Total Requirements	**938,000.0**	**1,007,632.3**	**738,266.5**	**137,532.0**

Sources: UN Documents A/64/660/Add.3, A/C.5/64/19, A/66/519, and A/66/532; DFS FBFD.
Notes: 2010–2011 expenditures are preliminary and subject to change. Discrepancies in proposed costs for the liquidation of UNMIS may be the result of figure estimations. In accordance with S/RES/1996 of 8 July 2011, the appropriate functions of UNMIS were transferred to UNMISS effective 9 July 2011.

UNMIS Expenditures on Contingent Owned Equipment: July 2010–June 2011 (in thousands of US dollars)

Military Contingents	51,926.4
Facilities and Infrastructure	20,723.5
Communications	9,337.8
Medical	8,578.5
Special Equipment	3,253.5
Total	**93,819.7**

Source: UN Document A/64/632.
Note: 2010–2011 expenditures are preliminary and subject to change.

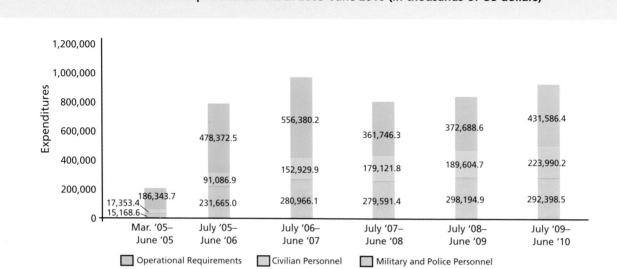

UNMIS Mission Expenditures: March 2005–June 2010 (in thousands of US dollars)

Category	Mar '05–June '05	July '05–June '06	July '06–June '07	July '07–June '08	July '08–June '09	July '09–June '10
Military and Police Personnel	15,168.6	231,665.0	280,966.1	279,591.4	298,194.9	292,398.5
Civilian Personnel	17,353.4	91,086.9	152,929.9	179,121.8	189,604.7	223,990.2
Operational Requirements	186,343.7	478,372.5	556,380.2	361,746.3	372,688.6	431,586.4
Other	—	—	—	—	—	—
Gross Requirements	**218,865.7**	**801,124.4**	**990,276.2**	**820,459.5**	**860,488.1**	**947,975.1**
Staff Assessment Income	2,090.2	10,968.4	18,593.6	20,399.0	—	17,872.6
Net Requirements	**216,775.5**	**790,156.0**	**971,682.6**	**800,060.5**	**860,488.1**	**930,102.5**
Voluntary Contributions in Kind (budgeted)	—	—	—	—	—	—
Total Requirements	**218,865.7**	**801,124.4**	**990,276.2**	**820,459.5**	**860,488.1**	**947,975.1**

Sources: UN Documents A/60/626, A/61/689, A/62/785, A/63/604, A/C.5/63/26, and A/64/660/Add.3.

6.12 UNMIT (UN Integrated Mission in Timor-Leste)

UNMIT Key Facts	
Latest Key Resolution	24 February 2011 (date of issue and effect) UNSC Res. 1969 (twelve month duration and decision to maintain current authorized levels)
First Mandate	25 August 2006 (date of issue and effect) UNSC Res. 1704 (six month duration)
SRSG	Ameerah Haq (Bangladesh) SG letter of appointment 25 November 2009
First SRSG	Sukehiro Hasegawa (Japan)
Police Commissioner	Luis Miguel Carrilho (Portugal) Entry on duty 23 February 2009
First Police Commissioner	Rodolfo Aser Tor (Philippines)

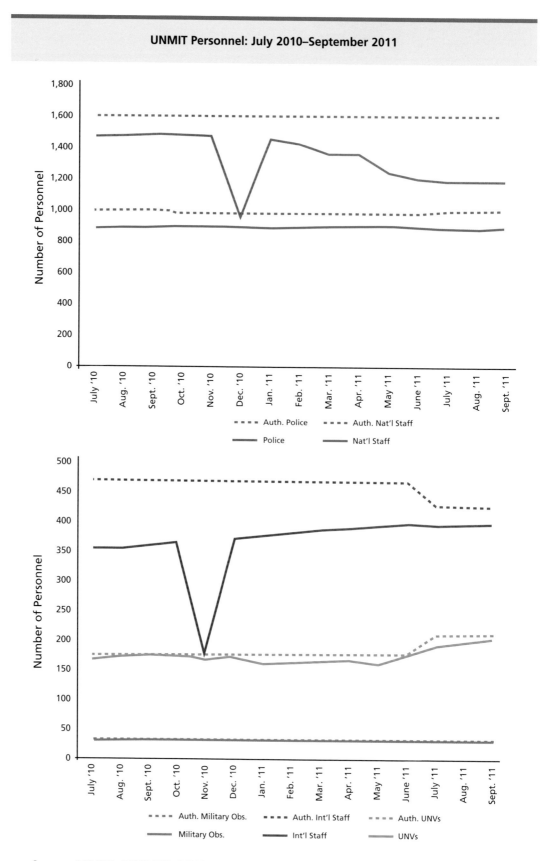

UNMIT Personnel: July 2010–September 2011

Sources: DFS FPD; DPKO FGS; DPKO PD; UNV Programme.

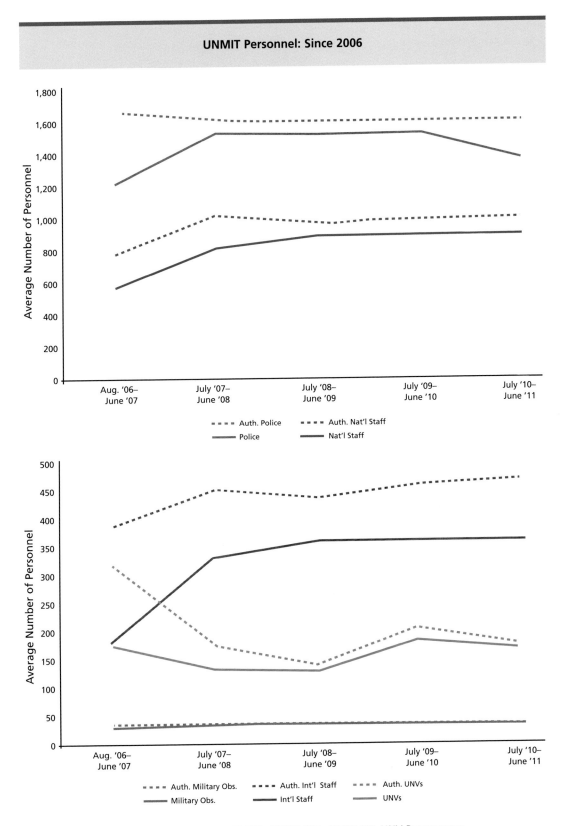

Sources: UN Document S/RES/1704; DFS FPD; DPKO FGS; DPKO PD; UNV Programme.

UNMIT Military and Police Contributors: 30 September 2011

Contributing Country	Troops	Military Observers	Police	Total	Contributing Country	Troops	Military Observers	Police	Total
Malaysia	—	2	215	217	Yemen	—	—	13	13
Portugal	—	3	181	184	Spain	—	—	10	10
Bangladesh	—	3	140	143	Thailand	—	—	10	10
Pakistan	—	4	121	125	Ukraine	—	—	9	9
Philippines	—	3	89	92	Namibia	—	—	8	8
Australia	—	4	50	54	Romania	—	—	8	8
Nigeria	—	—	37	37	Senegal	—	—	7	7
Nepal	—	1	35	36	El Salvador	—	—	6	6
Sri Lanka	—	—	34	34	New Zealand	—	1	5	6
China	—	2	23	25	Croatia	—	—	4	4
Zimbabwe	—	—	25	25	Republic of Korea	—	—	4	4
Gambia	—	—	21	21	Russia	—	—	4	4
India	—	1	19	20	Samoa	—	—	4	4
Jordan	—	—	19	19	Uruguay	—	—	3	3
Singapore	—	2	16	18	Japan	—	2	—	2
Turkey	—	—	16	16	Fiji	—	1	—	1
Brazil	—	3	12	15	Jamaica	—	—	1	1
Uganda	—	—	14	14	Kyrgyzstan	—	—	1	1
Zambia	—	—	14	14	Sierra Leone	—	1	—	1
Egypt	—	—	13	13	**Total**	—	33	1,191	1,224

Source: DPKO FGS.

UNMIT International Civilian Personnel Occupations: 30 September 2011

Occupation	International Staff	Percentage International Staff
Administration	66	16.7%
Aviation	9	2.3%
Civil Affairs	11	2.8%
Economic Affairs	1	0.3%
Electoral Affairs	—	—
Engineering	21	5.3%
Finance	16	4.0%
Human Resources	19	4.8%
Human Rights	14	3.5%
Humanitarian Affairs	2	0.5%
Information Management	4	1.0%
Information Systems and Technology	24	6.1%
Legal Affairs	8	2.0%
Logistics	38	9.6%
Management and Programme Analysis	1	0.3%
Medical Services	10	2.5%
Political Affairs	20	5.1%
Procurement	9	2.3%
Programme Management	20	5.1%
Public Information	11	2.8%
Rule of Law	25	6.3%
Security	52	13.1%
Social Affairs	4	1.0%
Transport	11	2.8%
Total	**396**	

Source: DFS FPD.

UNMIT Personnel Gender Statistics: 30 September 2011

Personnel Type	Male	Female	Percentage Male	Percentage Female
Troops	—	—	—	—
Military Observers	31	2	93.9%	6.1%
Police	1,112	79	93.4%	6.6%
International Civilian Staff	249	147	62.9%	37.1%
National Civilian Staff	716	171	80.7%	19.3%
Total	**2,108**	**399**	**84.1%**	**15.9%**

Sources: DFS FPD; DPKO FGS; DPKO PD.

UNMIT Fatalities: Inception–September 2011

Personnel Type

Time Period	Troops	Military Obs.	Police	Int'l. Staff	National Staff	Other[a]	Total
2006	—	—	—	—	1	—	1
2007	—	—	1	—	—	—	1
2008	—	—	1	1	1	—	3
2009	—	—	2	—	—	—	2
2010	—	—	1	1	—	—	2
January-March	—	—	—	1	—	—	1
April-June	—	—	1	—	—	—	1
July-September	—	—	—	—	—	—	—
October-December	—	—	—	—	—	—	—
2011 (Jan.-Sept.)	—	—	1	1	—	—	2
January-March	—	—	—	1	—	—	1
April-June	—	—	—	—	—	—	—
July-September	—	—	1	—	—	—	1
Total Fatalilties	**—**	**—**	**6**	**3**	**2**	**—**	**11**

Incident Type

Time Period	Malicious Act	Illness	Accident	Other[b]	Total
2006	1	—	—	—	1
2007	—	1	—	—	1
2008	—	2	1	—	3
2009	—	—	1	1	2
2010	—	1	1	—	2
January-March	—	1	—	—	1
April-June	—	—	1	—	1
July-September	—	—	—	—	—
October-December	—	—	—	—	—
2011 (Jan.-Sept.)	—	1	1	—	2
January-March	—	1	—	—	1
April-June	—	—	—	—	—
July-September	—	—	1	—	1
Total Fatalilties	**1**	**5**	**4**	**1**	**11**

Source: DPKO Situation Centre.
Notes: a. Other refers to consultants, UNVs, etc.
b. Incident type is unknown, uncertain, or under investigation. Other includes what were previously qualified as self-inflicted.

UNMIT Vehicles: 30 September 2011

Contingent Owned Vehicles		UN Owned Vehicles	
Vehicle Type	Quantity	Vehicle Type	Quantity
Combat Vehicles	18	4x4 Vehicles	726
Communications Vehicles	2	Aircraft/Airfield Support Equipment	1
Material Handling Equipment	3	Ambulances	7
Support Vehicles		Automobiles	2
(Commercial Pattern)	86	Boats	3
Support Vehicles (Military Pattern)	42	Buses	69
Total	**151**	Engineering Vehicles	3
		Material Handling Equipment	19
		Trucks	30
		Vans	8
		Total	**868**

Sources: DFS Contingent Owned Equipment and Property Management Section; DFS Surface Transport Section.

UNMIT Aircraft: 30 September 2011

	Transport Fixed Wing	Transport Helicopter	Attack Helicopter
Commercial	—	4	—
Contingent Owned	—	—	—
Total	—	**4**	—

Source: DFS Air Transport Section.

UNMIT Budget and Expenditures (in thousands of US dollars)

Category	Budgeted July '10–June '11	Expenditures July '10–June '11	Budgeted July '11–June '12
Military Observers	1,680.2	1,602.8	1,670.3
Military Contingents	—	—	—
Civilian Police	—	—	38,499.6
Formed Police Units	16,817.8	15,550.8	15,679.5
United Nations Police	46,202.5	42,418.3	—
International Staff	68,601.7	65,106.3	68,262.6
National Staff	9,674.1	9,971.5	9,899.0
United Nations Volunteers	9,445.2	7,534.6	10,262.4
General Temporary Assistance	—	614.6	1,838.1
Government-provided Personnel	—	—	—
Civilian Electoral Observers	—	—	—
Consultants	140.5	139.8	383.3
Official Travel	4,274.1	3,452.1	4,803.7
Facilities and Infrastructure	13,684.8	12,483.5	11,402.8
Ground Transportation	2,536.4	2,819.4	2,178.8
Air Transportation	17,509.5	17,855.2	20,452.4
Naval Transportation	—	—	—
Communications and IT	10,949.8	8,833.6	6,837.8
Supplies, Services and Equipment	4,795.0	4,167.2	3,907.2
Quick-impact Projects	—	—	—
Gross Requirements	**206,311.6**	**192,549.7**	**196,077.5**
Staff Assessment Income	9,474.6	8,986.4	9,174.0
Net Requirements	**196,837.0**	**183,563.3**	**186,903.5**
Voluntary Contributions in Kind (budgeted)	—	—	—
Total Requirements	**206,311.6**	**192,549.7**	**196,077.5**

Sources: UN Documents A/65/743/Add.6 and A/C.5/65/19; DFS FBFD.

Notes: 2010–2011 expenditures are preliminary and subject to change. Discrepancies in expenditures from July 2010–June 2011 may be the result of figure estimations.

UNMIT Expenditures on Contingent Owned Equipment: July 2010–June 2011 (in thousands of US dollars)

Formed Police Units	3,376.3
Facilities and Infrastructure	1,154.4
Communications	496.7
Medical	159.3
Special Equipment	394.2
Total	**5,580.9**

Source: UN Document A/64/686.

Note: 2010–2011 expenditures are preliminary and subject to change.

UNMIT Mission Expenditures: August 2006–June 2010 (in thousands of US dollars)

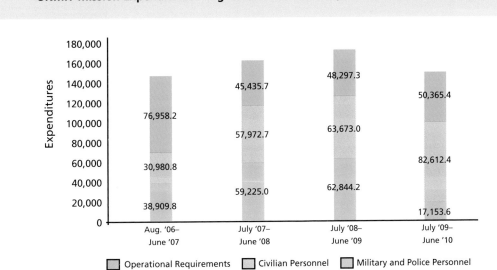

Category	Aug. '06–June '07	July '07–June '08	July '08–June '09	July '09–June '10
Military and Police Personnel	38,909.8	59,225.0	62,844.2	17,153.6
Civilian Personnel	30,980.8	57,972.7	63,673.0	82,612.4
Operational Requirements	76,958.2	45,435.7	46,297.3	50,365.4
Other	—	—	—	—
Gross Requirements	**146,848.8**	**162,633.4**	**172,814.5**	**150,131.4**
Staff Assessment Income	3,009.2	6,729.7	—	—
Net Requirements	**143,839.6**	**155,903.7**	**172,814.5**	**150,131.4**
Voluntary Contributions in Kind (budgeted)	—	—	—	—
Total Requirements	**146,848.8**	**162,633.4**	**172,814.5**	**150,131.4**

Source: UN Documents A/62/753, A/63/607, A/C.5/63/26, and A/64/660/Add.11.

6.13 UNMOGIP (UN Military Observer Group in India and Pakistan)

UNMOGIP Key Facts	
Latest Key Resolution	21 December 1971 (date of issue and effect) UNSC Res. 307 (to continue thereafter until the Security Council decides otherwise)
First Mandate	21 April 1948 (date of issue); 1 January 1949 (date of effect) UNSC Res. 47 (no determined duration)
Chief Military Observer	Major-General Raul Gloodtdofsky Fernandez (Uruguay) SG letter of appointment 15 December 2010
First Chief Military Observer	Brigadier H.H. Angle (Canada)

UNMOGIP Personnel: July 2010–September 2011

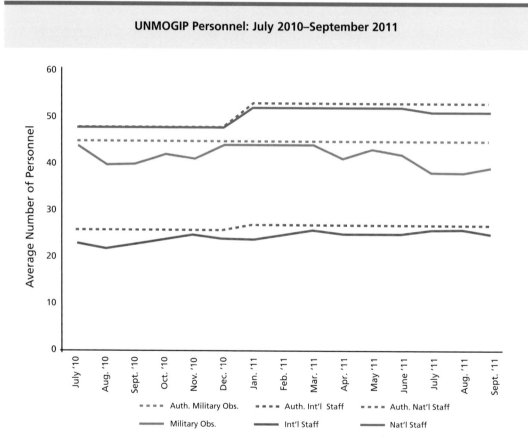

Sources: DFS FPD; DPKO FGS.

UNMOGIP Personnel: Since 2000

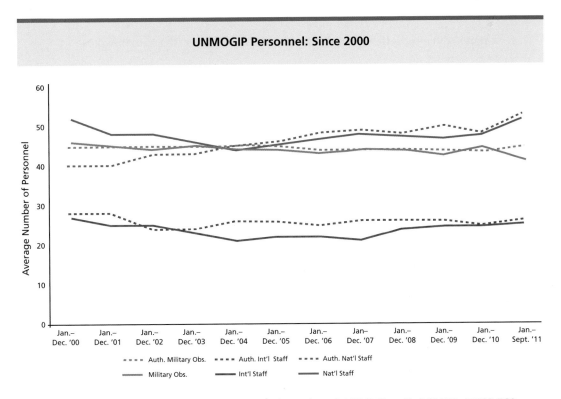

Sources: UN Documents A/56/6 (Sect.5), A/58/6 (Sect.5), and A/60/6 (Sect.5); DFS FPD; DPKO FGS.

UNMOGIP Military and Police Contributors: 30 September 2011

Contributing Country	Troops	Military Observers	Police	Total
Croatia	—	9	—	9
Republic of Korea	—	8	—	8
Sweden	—	6	—	6
Finland	—	5	—	5
Italy	—	4	—	4
Philippines	—	3	—	3
Chile	—	2	—	2
Uruguay	—	2	—	2
Total	—	39	—	39

Source: DPKO FGS.

UNMOGIP International Civilian Personnel Occupations: 30 September 2011

Occupation	International Staff	Percentage International Staff
Administration	3	12.0%
Aviation	—	—
Civil Affairs	—	—
Economic Affairs	—	—
Electoral Affairs	—	—
Engineering	2	8.0%
Finance	2	8.0%
Human Resources	2	8.0%
Human Rights	—	—
Humanitarian Affairs	—	—
Information Management	1	4.0%
Information Systems and Technology	8	32.0%
Legal Affairs	—	—
Logistics	—	—
Management and Programme Analysis	—	—
Medical Services	—	—
Political Affairs	—	—
Procurement	2	8.0%
Programme Management	—	—
Public Information	—	—
Rule of Law	1	4.0%
Security	3	12.0%
Social Affairs	—	—
Transport	1	4.0%
Total	**25**	

Source: DFS FPD.

UNMOGIP Personnel Gender Statistics: 30 September 2011

Personnel Type	Male	Female	Percentage Male	Percentage Female
Troops	—	—	—	—
Military Observers	36	3	92.3%	7.7%
Police	—	—	—	—
International Civilian Staff	20	5	80.0%	20.0%
National Civilian Staff	46	5	90.2%	9.8%
Total	**102**	**13**	**88.7%**	**11.3%**

Sources: DFS FPD; DPKO FGS.

UNMOGIP Fatalities: Inception–September 2011

Personnel Type

Time Period	Troops	Military Obs.	Police	Int'l. Staff	National Staff	Other[a]	Total
1949–1999	5	1	—	1	2	—	9
2000	—	—	—	—	—	—	—
2001	—	—	—	—	—	—	—
2002	—	—	—	—	1	—	1
2003	—	—	—	—	—	—	—
2004	—	—	—	—	—	—	—
2005	—	—	—	1	—	—	1
2006	—	—	—	—	—	—	—
2007	—	—	—	—	—	—	—
2008	—	—	—	—	—	—	—
2009	—	—	—	—	—	—	—
2010	—	—	—	—	—	—	—
2011 (Jan.-Sept.)	—	—	—	—	—	—	—
January-March	—	—	—	—	—	—	—
April-June	—	—	—	—	—	—	—
July-September	—	—	—	—	—	—	—
Total Fatalities	**5**	**1**	**—**	**2**	**3**	**—**	**11**

Incident Type

Time Period	Malicious Act	Illness	Accident	Other[b]	Total
1949–1999	—	1	8	—	9
2000	—	—	—	—	—
2001	—	—	—	—	—
2002	—	1	—	—	1
2003	—	—	—	—	—
2004	—	—	—	—	—
2005	—	—	1	—	1
2006	—	—	—	—	—
2007	—	—	—	—	—
2008	—	—	—	—	—
2009	—	—	—	—	—
2010	—	—	—	—	—
2011 (Jan.-Sept.)	—	—	—	—	—
January-March	—	—	—	—	—
April-June	—	—	—	—	—
July-September	—	—	—	—	—
Total Fatalities	**—**	**2**	**9**	**—**	**11**

Source: DPKO Situation Centre.
Notes: a. Other refers to consultants, UNVs, etc.
b. Incident type is unknown, uncertain, or under investigation. Other includes what were previously qualified as self-inflicted.

UNMOGIP Vehicles: 30 September 2011

UN Owned Vehicles

Vehicle Type	Quantity
4x4 Vehicles	47
Ambulance	1
Automobiles	3
Buses	12
Trucks	2
Total	**65**

Source: DFS Surface Transport Section.

UNMOGIP Budget and Expenditure (in thousands of US dollars)

Category	Appropriation Jan '12–Dec '13
Post	10,762.0
Non-post	10,448.0
Total	**21,210.0**

Sources: UN Document A/66/6(Sect. 5); DFS FBFD.

Category	Jan. '00–Dec. '01	Jan. '02–Dec. '03	Jan. '04–Dec. '05	Jan. '06–Dec. '07	Jan. '08–Dec. '09	Jan. '10–Dec. '11
UNMOGIP Mission Expenditures: January 2000–December 2010 (in thousands of US dollars)						
Posts	5,574.1	6,370.9	6,482.6	4,293.4	9,193.4	10,752.0
Non-posts	—	—	—	—	—	11,667.0
Other Staff Costs	1,593.5	1,983.8	2,038.7	5,504.9	3,300.8	—
Travel of Staff	865.9	1,247.5	1,309.6	193.2	—	—
Contractual Services	—	38.9	21.5	—	—	—
General Operating Expenses	1,772.6	1,174.3	1,995.9	3,435.2	—	—
Hospitality	2.3	2.5	2.3	2.4	2.9	—
Supplies and Materials	1,022.4	800.1	355.7	769.5	—	—
Furniture and Equipment	1,332.0	1,107.6	2,527.5	1,023.3	—	—
Other Expenditures	—	—	—	0.0	5,116.2	—
Total Requirements	**12,162.8**	**12,725.6**	**14,733.8**	**15,221.9**	**17,613.3**	**22,418.0**

Sources: UN Documents A/64/6(Sect.5) and A/66/6(Sect. 5); DFS FBFD.

Notes: 2008–2009 expenditures are preliminary and subject to change. Discrepancies in expenditures from January 2010–December 2011 may be the result of figure estimations.

6.14 UNOCI (UN Operation in Côte d'Ivoire)

UNOCI Key Facts	
Latest Key Resolution	27 July 2011 (date of issue and effect) UNSC Res. 1933 (twelve month duration)
First Mandate	27 February 2004 (date of issue); 4 April 2004 (date of effect) UNSC Res. 1528 (twelve month duration)
SRSG	Albert Gerard Koenders (Netherlands) SG letter of appointment 26 July 2011
First SRSG	Albert Tevoedjre (Benin)
Force Commander	Major-General Gnakoudè Béréna (Togo) SG letter of appointment 11 March 2011
First Force Commander	Major-General Abdoulaye Fall (Senegal)
Police Commissioner	Major-General Jean Marie Bourry (France)
First Police Commander	Yves Bouchard (Canada)

UNOCI Personnel: July 2010–September 2011

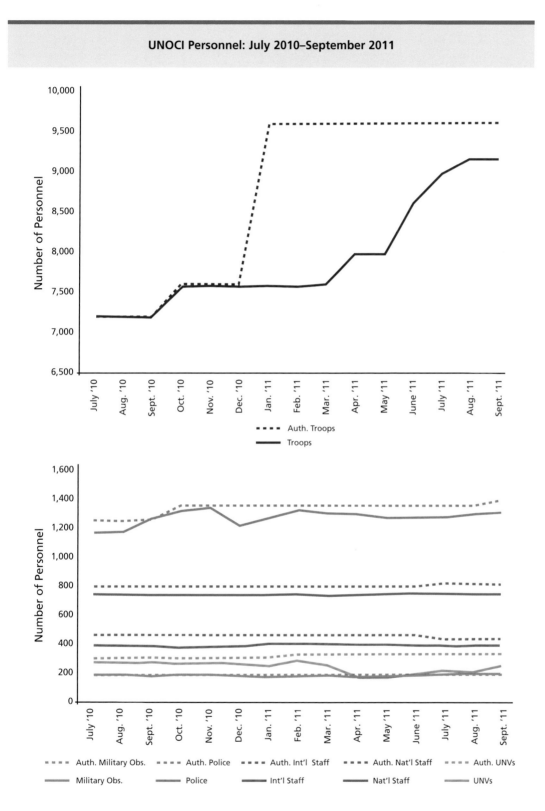

Sources: DFS FPD; DPKO FGS; DPKO PD; UNV Programme.

Note: The increase of 65 authorized police of September 2011 is due to a reallocation of personnel from the mission's military.

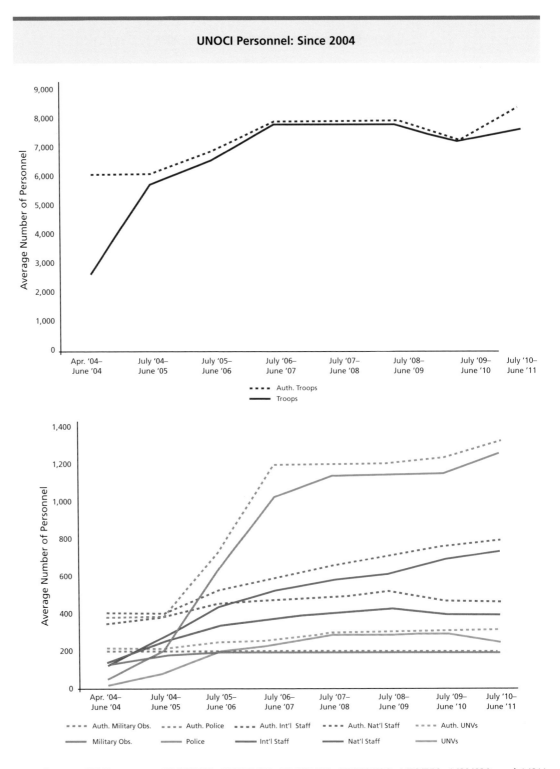

Sources: UN Documents S/RES/1528, S/RES/1609, S/RES/1682, S/RES/1739, A/59/750, A/60/630, and A/61/673; DFS FPD; DPKO FGS; DPKO PD; UNV Programme.

UNOCI Military and Police Contributors: 30 September 2011

Contributing Country	Troops	Military Observers	Police	Total	Contributing Country	Troops	Military Observers	Police	Total
Bangladesh	2,170	13	358	2,541	Philippines	3	4	—	7
Jordan	1,068	8	461	1,537	Ukraine	—	—	7	7
Pakistan	1,187	11	150	1,348	China	—	6	—	6
Niger	934	7	34	975	Romania	—	6	—	6
Malawi	853	3	—	856	Uganda	1	5	—	6
Morocco	726	—	—	726	Guatemala	—	5	—	5
Senegal	527	13	13	553	Canada	—	—	4	4
Ghana	535	6	—	541	Moldova	—	4	—	4
Togo	524	7	7	538	Nepal	1	3	—	4
Benin	426	8	42	476	Bolivia	—	3	—	3
Egypt	176	—	2	178	El Salvador	—	3	—	3
Burundi	—	—	40	40	Gambia	—	3	—	3
Djibouti	—	—	40	40	Guinea	—	3	—	3
Republic of Congo	—	—	30	30	Peru	—	3	—	3
Cameroon	—	—	27	27	Poland	—	3	—	3
Chad	1	3	23	27	Serbia	—	3	—	3
Yemen	1	7	18	26	Tanzania	2	1	—	3
France	6	—	13	19	Zimbabwe	—	3	—	3
Central African Republic	—	—	17	17	Ireland	—	2	—	2
Turkey	—	—	15	15	Namibia	—	2	—	2
Russia	—	11	—	11	Republic of Korea	—	2	—	2
Paraguay	2	7	—	9	Uruguay	—	2	—	2
India	—	8	—	8	Zambia	—	2	—	2
Tunisia	3	5	—	8	Ecuador	—	1	—	1
Brazil	3	4	—	7	Ethiopia	—	1	—	1
Nigeria	1	6	—	7	**Total**	**9,150**	**197**	**1,301**	**10,648**

Source: DPKO FGS.

UNOCI Military Units: 30 September 2011

Number	Unit Type	Country
2	Aviation Units	Bangladesh, Ghana
1	Communications Company	Bangladesh
3	Engineering Companies	Bangladesh, Egypt, Pakistan
1	Guard and Administration Company	Bangladesh
1	Gendarme Security Company	Benin-Ghana-Niger-Senegal-Togo Composite
11	Infantry Battalions	Bangladesh (2), Benin, Ghana, Jordan, Malawi, Morocco, Niger, Pakistan, Senegal, Togo
2	Level II Hospitals	Bangladesh, Ghana
1	Special Forces Company	Jordan
1	Transport Company	Pakistan

Source: DPKO FGS.
Note: Military headquarters staff and military observers not included.

UNOCI International Civilian Personnel Occupations: 30 September 2011

Occupation	International Staff	Percentage International Staff
Administration	41	10.5%
Aviation	12	3.1%
Civil Affairs	4	1.0%
Economic Affairs	—	—
Electoral Affairs	16	4.1%
Engineering	14	3.6%
Finance	15	3.8%
Human Resources	16	4.1%
Human Rights	12	3.1%
Humanitarian Affairs	—	—
Information Management	1	0.3%
Information Systems and Technology	40	10.2%
Legal Affairs	1	0.3%
Logistics	66	16.8%
Management and Programme Analysis	—	—
Medical Services	3	0.8%
Political Affairs	22	5.6%
Procurement	9	2.3%
Programme Management	8	2.0%
Public Information	15	3.8%
Rule of Law	11	2.8%
Security	64	16.3%
Social Affairs	3	0.8%
Transport	19	4.8%
Total	**392**	

Source: DFS FPD.

UNOCI Personnel Gender Statistics: 30 September 2011

Personnel Type	Male	Female	Percentage Male	Percentage Female
Troops	9,047	103	98.9%	1.1%
Military Observers	189	8	95.9%	4.1%
Police	1,276	25	98.1%	1.9%
International Civilian Staff	277	115	70.7%	29.3%
National Civilian Staff	570	171	76.9%	23.1%
Total	**11,359**	**422**	**96.4%**	**3.6%**

Sources: DFS FPD; DPKO FGS; DPKO PD.

UNOCI Fatalities: Inception–September 2011

Personnel Type

Time Period	Troops	Military Obs.	Police	Int'l. Staff	National Staff	Other[a]	Total
2004	—	—	—	—	—	—	—
2005	10	1	1	1	2	—	15
2006	11	—	1	—	1	—	13
2007	4	—	2	2	—	—	8
2008	13	—	2	1	2	—	18
2009	8	—	1	—	1	—	10
2010	7	—	—	—	—	—	7
January-March	2	—	—	—	—	—	2
April-June	1	—	—	—	—	—	1
July-September	4	—	—	—	—	—	4
October-December	—	—	—	—	—	—	—
2011 (Jan.-Sept.)	5	—	5	—	1	—	11
January-March	1	—	—	—	—	—	1
April-June	3	—	2	—	—	—	5
July-September	1	—	3	—	1	—	5
Total Fatalities	**58**	**1**	**12**	**4**	**7**	**—**	**82**

Incident Type

Time Period	Malicious Act	Illness	Accident	Other[b]	Total
2004	—	—	—	—	—
2005	1	10	3	1	15
2006	—	5	8	—	13
2007	1	3	4	—	8
2008	—	6	11	1	18
2009	—	5	3	2	10
2010	—	6	1	—	7
January-March	—	2	—	—	2
April-June	—	—	1	—	1
July-September	—	4	—	—	4
October-December	—	—	—	—	—
2011 (Jan.-Sept.)	—	7	3	1	11
January-March	—	—	1	—	1
April-June	—	4	1	—	5
July-September	—	3	1	1	5
Total Fatalities	**2**	**42**	**33**	**5**	**82**

Source: DPKO Situation Centre.
Notes: a. Other refers to consultants, UNVs, etc.
b. Incident type is unknown, uncertain, or under investigation. Other includes what were previously qualified as self-inflicted.

UNOCI Vehicles: 30 September 2011

Contingent Owned Vehicles		UN Owned Vehicles	
Vehicle Type	Quantity	Vehicle Type	Quantity
Aircraft/Airfield Support Equipment	9	4x4 Vehicles	895
Combat Vehicles	212	Aircraft/Airfield Support Equipment	20
Engineering Vehicles	75	Ambulances	13
Material Handling Equipment	22	Automobiles	5
Naval Vessels	4	Buses	68
Support Vehicles		Engineering Vehicles	10
(Commercial Pattern)	392	Material Handling Equipment	20
Support Vehicles (Military Pattern)	1,025	Trucks	90
Total	**1,739**	Vans	9
		Total	**1,130**

Sources: DFS Contingent Owned Equipment and Property Management Section; DFS Surface Transport Section.

UNOCI Aircraft: 30 September 2011

	Transport Fixed Wing	Transport Helicopter	Attack Helicopter
Commercial	3	5	—
Contingent Owned	—	6 (3 Bangladesh, 3 Ghana)	—
Total	**3**	**11**	—

Source: DFS Air Transport Section.

UNOCI Budget and Expenditures (in thousands of US dollars)

Category	Budgeted July '10–June '11	Expenditures July '10–June '11	Budgeted July '11–June '12
Military Observers	10,732.4	9,756.9	10,687.2
Military Contingents	178,496.2	208,698.6	181,665.1
Civilian Police	—	—	23,026.3
Formed Police Units	18,860.5	24,744.1	19,510.4
United Nations Police	22,902.1	19,553.1	—
International Staff	69,201.1	69,510.7	67,804.1
National Staff	18,983.1	23,549.2	20,048.7
United Nations Volunteers	10,869.1	13,509.3	7,949.3
General Temporary Assistance	—	5,457.5	3,371.3
Government-provided Personnel	440.8	607.2	877.1
Civilian Electoral Observers	—	—	—
Consultants	180.9	242.4	181.7
Official Travel	4,368.6	5,027.6	3,526.9
Facilities and Infrastructure	45,992.3	63,635.5	46,843.4
Ground Transportation	13,265.9	14,637.4	11,953.2
Air Transportation	51,835.4	67,332.8	52,806.8
Naval Transportation	19.0	19.0	15.5
Communications and IT	22,358.8	21,559.8	20,302.8
Supplies, Services and Equipment	15,572.0	21,494.4	15,156.6
Quick-impact Projects	1,000.0	1,000.0	1,000.0
Gross Requirements	**485,078.2**	**570,335.5**	**486,726.4**
Staff Assessment Income	10,800.2	10,961.7	10,723.4
Net Requirements	**474,278.0**	**559,373.8**	**476,003.0**
Voluntary Contributions in Kind (budgeted)	—	—	—
Total Requirements	**485,078.2**	**570,335.5**	**486,726.4**

Sources: UN Document A/65/743/Add.14 and A/C.5/65/19; DFS FBFD.
Note: 2010–2011 expenditures are preliminary and subject to change.

UNOCI Expenditures on Contingent Owned Equipment: July 2010–June 2011 (in thousands of US dollars)

Military Contingents	35,138.2
Formed Police Units	5,076.2
Facilities and Infrastructure	15,341.5
Communications	7,240.2
Medical	4,677.3
Special Equipment	3,500.3
Total	**70,973.7**

Source: UN Document A/64/673.
Note: 2010–2011 expenditures are preliminary and subject to change.

UNOCI Mission Expenditures: April 2004–June 2010 (in thousands of US dollars)

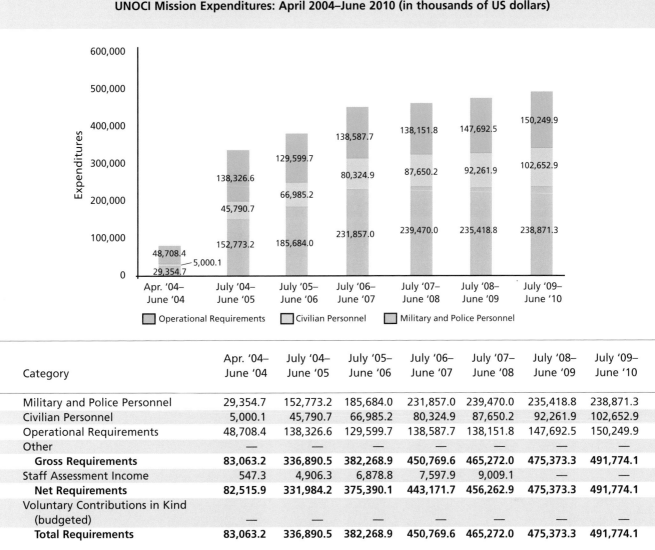

Category	Apr. '04–June '04	July '04–June '05	July '05–June '06	July '06–June '07	July '07–June '08	July '08–June '09	July '09–June '10
Military and Police Personnel	29,354.7	152,773.2	185,684.0	231,857.0	239,470.0	235,418.8	238,871.3
Civilian Personnel	5,000.1	45,790.7	66,985.2	80,324.9	87,650.2	92,261.9	102,652.9
Operational Requirements	48,708.4	138,326.6	129,599.7	138,587.7	138,151.8	147,692.5	150,249.9
Other	—	—	—	—	—	—	—
Gross Requirements	**83,063.2**	**336,890.5**	**382,268.9**	**450,769.6**	**465,272.0**	**475,373.3**	**491,774.1**
Staff Assessment Income	547.3	4,906.3	6,878.8	7,597.9	9,009.1	—	—
Net Requirements	**82,515.9**	**331,984.2**	**375,390.1**	**443,171.7**	**456,262.9**	**475,373.3**	**491,774.1**
Voluntary Contributions in Kind (budgeted)	—	—	—	—	—	—	—
Total Requirements	**83,063.2**	**336,890.5**	**382,268.9**	**450,769.6**	**465,272.0**	**475,373.3**	**491,774.1**

Sources: UN Documents A/59/750, A/60/643, A/61/673, A/62/750, A/63/610, A/C.5/63/26, and A/64/660/Add.7.

6.15 UNTSO (UN Truce Supervision Organization)

UNTSO Key Facts	
Latest Key Resolution	23 October 1973 (date of issue and effect) UNSC Res. 339 (to continue thereafter, until the Security Council decides otherwise)
First Mandate	29 May 1948 (date of issue and effect) UNSC Res. 50 (no duration determined)
Chief of Staff	Major General Juha Kilpia (Finland) SG letter of appointment 23 March 2011
First Chief of Staff	Colonel Count Thord Bonde (Sweden)

UNTSO Personnel: July 2010–September 2011

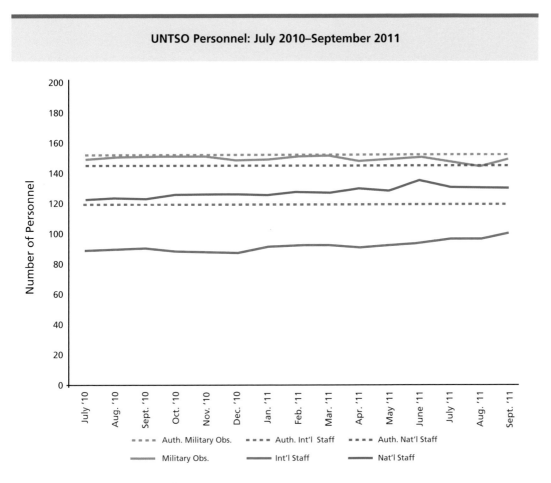

Sources: DFS FPD; DPKO FGS.

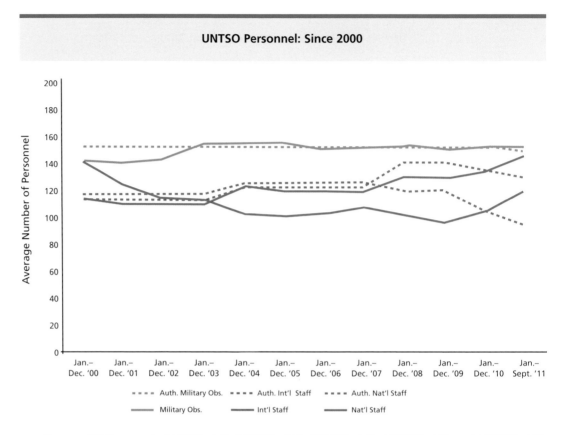

UNTSO Personnel: Since 2000

Sources: UN Documents A/54/6(Sect.5), A/56/6(Sect.5), A/58/6(Sect.5), A/60/6(Sect.5), and A/60/9(Sect.5); DFS FPD; DPKO FGS.

UNTSO Military and Police Contributors: 30 September 2011

Contributing Country	Troops	Military Observers	Police	Total	Contributing Country	Troops	Military Observers	Police	Total
Finland	—	14	—	14	China	—	4	—	4
Australia	—	12	—	12	Russia	—	4	—	4
Ireland	—	12	—	12	Argentina	—	3	—	3
Netherlands	—	12	—	12	France	—	3	—	3
Norway	—	12	—	12	Nepal	—	3	—	3
Denmark	—	11	—	11	Slovakia	—	3	—	3
Switzerland	—	11	—	11	Slovenia	—	3	—	3
Italy	—	8	—	8	Belgium	—	2	—	2
Austria	—	7	—	7	Chile	—	2	—	2
Canada	—	7	—	7	Estonia	—	2	—	2
New Zealand	—	7	—	7	Malawi	—	1	—	1
Sweden	—	6	—	6	United States	—	1	—	1
					Total	—	**150**	—	**150**

Source: DPKO FGS.

UNTSO International Civilian Personnel Occupations: 30 September 2011

Occupation	International Staff	Percentage International Staff
Administration	16	15.8%
Aviation	—	—
Civil Affairs	—	—
Economic Affairs	—	—
Electoral Affairs	—	—
Engineering	4	4.0%
Finance	6	5.9%
Human Resources	7	6.9%
Human Rights	—	—
Humanitarian Affairs	—	—
Information Management	2	2.0%
Information Systems and Technology	15	14.9%
Legal Affairs	1	1.0%
Logistics	8	7.9%
Management and Programme Analysis	—	—
Medical Services	2	2.0%
Political Affairs	2	2.0%
Procurement	2	2.0%
Programme Management	—	—
Public Information	—	—
Rule of Law	2	2.0%
Security	24	23.8%
Social Affairs	—	—
Transport	10	9.9%
Total	**101**	

Source: DFS FPD.

UNTSO Personnel Gender Statistics: 30 September 2011

Personnel Type	Male	Female	Percentage Male	Percentage Female
Troops	—	—	—	—
Military Observers	138	12	92.0%	8.0%
Police	—	—	—	—
International Civilian Staff	78	23	77.2%	22.8%
National Civilian Staff	110	21	84.0%	16.0%
Total	**326**	**56**	**85.3%**	**14.7%**

Sources: DFS FPD; DPKO FGS.

UNTSO Fatalities: Inception–September 2011

Personnel Type

Time Period	Troops	Military Obs.	Police	Int'l. Staff	National Staff	Other[a]	Total
1948–1999	18	12	—	6	3	—	39
2000	—	—	—	—	—	—	—
2001	—	—	—	—	—	—	—
2002	—	—	—	—	—	—	—
2003	—	—	—	—	1	—	1
2004	—	1	—	1	—	—	2
2005	—	1	—	1	—	—	2
2006	—	4	—	—	—	—	4
2007	—	—	—	—	1	—	1
2008	—	—	—	—	—	—	—
2009	—	—	—	—	1	—	1
2010	—	—	—	—	—	—	—
2011 (Jan.-Sept.)	—	—	—	—	—	—	—
January-March	—	—	—	—	—	—	—
April-June	—	—	—	—	—	—	—
July-September	—	—	—	—	—	—	—
Total Fatalities	**18**	**18**	**—**	**8**	**6**	**—**	**50**

Incident Type

Time Period	Malicious Act	Illness	Accident	Other[b]	Total
1948–1999	25	5	8	1	39
2000	—	—	—	—	—
2001	—	—	—	—	—
2002	—	—	—	—	—
2003	—	1	—	—	1
2004	—	1	1	—	2
2005	1	1	—	—	2
2006	—	—	4	—	4
2007	—	—	1	—	1
2008	—	—	—	—	—
2009	—	—	—	1	1
2010	—	—	—	—	—
2011 (Jan.-Sept.)	—	—	—	—	—
January-March	—	—	—	—	—
April-June	—	—	—	—	—
July-September	—	—	—	—	—
Total Fatalities	**26**	**8**	**14**	**2**	**50**

Source: DPKO Situation Centre.
Notes: a. Other refers to consultants, UNVs, etc.
  b. Incident type is unknown, uncertain, or under investigation. Other includes what were previously qualified as self-inflicted.

UNTSO Vehicles: 30 September 2011

UN Owned Vehicles

Vehicle Type	Quantity
4x4 Vehicles	156
Automobiles	6
Buses	16
Engineering Equipment	3
Material Handling Equipment	3
Trucks	17
Vans	4
Total	**205**

Source: DFS Surface Transport Section.

UNTSO Budget and Expenditure (in thousands of US dollars)

Category	Appropriation Jan '12–Dec '13
Post	45,940.0
Non-post	23,733.0
Total	**69,672.0**

Sources: UN Document A/66/6(Sect.5); DFS FBFD.
Note: Discrepancies in appropriations from January 2012–December 2013 may be the result of figure estimations.

UNTSO Mission Expenditures: January 2000–December 2010 (in thousands of US dollars)

Category	Jan. '00–Dec. '01	Jan. '02–Dec. '03	Jan. '04–Dec. '05	Jan. '06–Dec. '07	Jan. '08–Dec. '09	Jan. '10–Dec. '11
Posts	30,532.2	31,679.1	33,215.7	21,993.1	41,833.9	47,832.0
Non-posts	—	—	—	—	—	21,087.0
Other Staff Costs	8,547.1	9,588.0	10,443.2	26,726.5	12,103.3	—
Hospitality	—	7.8	7.6	9.5	12.5	—
Travel of Staff	1,793.3	2,658.2	2,763.5	234.5	—	—
Contractual Services	—	49.5	39.7	12.9	—	—
General Operating Expenses	2,538.2	3,422.8	5,010.0	6,433.8	—	—
Supplies and Materials	1,117.1	982.0	1,035.3	1,447.4	—	—
Furniture and Equipment	1,614.5	1,498.4	3,214.7	2,362.1	—	—
Other Expenditures	—	—	—	—	10,186.7	—
Total Requirements	**46,142.4**	**49,885.8**	**55,729.7**	**59,219.8**	**64,136.3**	**68,919.0**

Sources: UN Documents A/58/6(Sect.5), A/60/6(Sect.5), A/64/6(Sect.5), and A/66/6(Sect.5); DFS FBFD.

Index

Abdel-Aziz, Hany, 123
Abidjan, Côte d'Ivoire, 38, 39, 40, 41, 42
Abkhazia, 87, 88, 89
ABLs (administrative boundary lines), 88
Abobo district, 41
Abyei area, 7, 69, 72, 75–77. *See also* UN
    Interim Security Force for Abyei
ADF (Ugandan Allied Democratic Front), 49
Administrative boundary lines (ABLs), 88
Afghan National Army (ANA), 18, 33
Afghan National Police (ANP), 18, 24, 31, 33
Afghan National Security Forces (ANSF), 31,
    33, 34
Afghanistan: assassinations in, 33–34;
    EUPOL Afghanistan and, 29;
    extending/restoring state authority in, 9, 17,
    34; fatalities in, 28, 35, 72; Kabul, 28, 29,
    30, 31, 33, 34; Karzai, H., and, 20, 28, 30,
    31, 33, 34; LOTFA and, 24; map of, 28;
    military surge for, 17, 30, 33; mission
    review for, 28–35; NATO and, 5, 17, 18,
    28, 29, 30, 31, 64; political settlement and,
    30–31; security issues and, 33, 72; Taliban
    and, 17, 28, 29, 30–31, 33–34; UNAMA in,
    21, 24, 29, 30, 33; women's governmental
    participation and, 85. *See also* International
    Security Assistance Force
Afghanistan Compact, 29–30
AFL (Armed Forces of Liberia), 66
Africa: elections in, 40; peacekeeping
    missions in, 37. *See also specific countries*
African Great Lakes region, 47, 49
African Union (AU), 1, 6, 8, 17, 38, 49, 63,
    69, 99, 107, 115, 116, 123. *See also* UN-
    AU Hybrid Mission in Darfur
Ahmed, Sharif Sheikh, 111, 112
Aidid, Mohamed Farrah, 110

Akendengue, Albert, 48
Alawites, 101
Albanians, 91, 92, 94
Algeria, 96, 123, 124, 125
Ali, Abdiweli Mohamed, 112
Allen, John R., 29, 31
Allied Democratic Front, Ugandan, 49
Almhofer, Werner, 92
AMISOM (AU Mission in Somalia), 6, 10,
    17, 109–116
ANA. *See* Afghan National Army
Angola, 45, 49, 50
ANP. *See* Afghan National Police
ANSF. *See* Afghan National Security Forces
Anti-Corruption Commission, 65
Aquino, Benigno, III, 120
Arab Spring, 96, 102
Arab-Israeli conflict, 96
Arbonite River, 54, 60
Aristide, Jean Bertrand, 53, 54, 55
Armed Forces of Liberia (AFL), 66
ARMM (Autonomous Region of Muslim
    Mindanao), 120
ASEAN (Association of Southeast Asian
    Nations), 107
Assad, Bashar al-, 96, 101
Assassinations, 29, 31, 33–34, 35
Association of Southeast Asian Nations
    (ASEAN), 107
AU. *See* African Union
AU Mission in Somalia (AMISOM), 6, 10,
    17, 109–116
Autonomous Region of Muslim Mindanao
    (ARMM), 120

Bahrain, 96, 98
Baidoa, 113

Bair, Bernhard, 80
Balkans, 16, 94
Bamyan, 33
Banny, Charles Konan, 43
Barre, Siad, 109
Bashir, Omar al-, 76
Battle of Sirte, 99
Bekaa, 98
Bel Air, 57
Belgrade, 91, 94
Bélizaire, Arnel, 56
Ben Ali regime, 96
Benghazi, 99
Béréna, Gnakoudè, 38
BiH. *See* Bosnia and Herzegovina
Bin Laden, Osama, 33
BINUCA (UN Integrated Peacebuilding
    Office in the Central African Republic), 48
"Blackhawk down" incident, 110
Blue helmets, 14, 40, 111
Blue Line, 97, 98, 100, 101
Blue Nile State, 7, 69, 70, 71, 73, 74, 77
Bonn Agreement, 29
Bosnia and Herzegovina (BiH), 80–82
Bourry, Jean Marie, 38
Bozizé, François, 48
Brunei, 120
Buala, Isabel province, 108
Buehler, Erhard, 94
Bureau of Immigration and Naturalization, 67
Burton, Fletcher M., 81
Burundi, 6, 45, 49, 113, 116
Burundian Forces Nationals de Libération
    (FNL), 49
Bush, George H. W., 110
Buttenheim, Lisa, 83, 84

Cambodia, 98, 107, 116
Campaign for Innocent Victims in Conflict,
    113
Capstone Doctrine, 12
CAR. *See* Central African Republic
Caribbean Community (CARICOM), 55
Carrilho, Luis Miguel, 118, 119
Carter Center, 51, 63, 66, 71
Cease-Fire Political Commission, 73
CEEAC. *See* Economic Community of
    Central African States

Célestin, Jude, 55
CENI. *See* Conseil Electoral National
    Independent
Central African Republic (CAR), 48, 49
Cholera epidemic, 8, 53, 54–55, 57, 59
Christofias, Dimitris, 84
CIS (Commonwealth of Independent States),
    82, 87
Cité Soleil, 13, 15, 57
Civilian capacities, 16
Civilian Capacity in the Aftermath of
    Conflict, 16
Clinton, Bill, 56, 58
Clinton, Hillary, 30
CNDP. *See* Congrès National pour la Défense
    du Peuple
Collective Security Treaty Organization
    (CSTO), 107
Commonwealth of Independent States (CIS),
    82, 87
Comprehensive Peace Agreement (CPA):
    Liberia and, 62; MICOPAX and, 48;
    Sudan/South Sudan and, 69, 70–71
Congrès National pour la Défense du Peuple
    (CNDP), 14, 47, 49
Conille, Garry, 55, 56
Conseil Electoral National Independent
    (CENI), 46, 50, 51
Contact Group on Piracy off the Coast of
    Somalia, 115
Convention of Patriots for Justice and Peace, 48
Convention on the Safety of United Nations
    and Associated Personnel, 72
Coppel, Nicholas, 106
Côte d'Ivoire: Abidjan, 38, 39, 40, 41, 42;
    elections in, 43–44; electoral violence in,
    36, 38–42, 61; extending/restoring state
    authority in, 9, 15–16; Gbagbo and, 9, 15,
    36, 38, 39, 40, 41, 42, 43, 44, 64, 65;
    justice/reconciliation in, 42–43; key
    developments in, 39–41; Liberian
    mercenaries in, 9, 39, 41, 61, 65; map of,
    36; mission review for, 36–44; Ouattara
    and, 9, 15, 36, 38, 39, 40, 41, 42, 43, 44;
    refugees and, 9, 43, 65; security in, 41–42.
    See also UN Operation in Côte d'Ivoire
Counterinsurgency campaign, 9, 17, 28, 31,
    33, 113

Counterterrorism campaign, 9, 28, 31–33, 112

CPA. *See* Comprehensive Peace Agreement

Criminal gangs, 13, 14, 18, 54, 57, 106

CSTO (Collective Security Treaty Organization), 107

Cuevas, Alberto Asarta, 96

Customs stamp issue, 91, 94

Cyprus, 83–86

Cyprus National Guard, 83

Damascus, 102

Darfur: conflict in, 70, 73, 77; Côte d'Ivoire and, 116; helicopters and, 64; UNAMID and, 4, 8, 64, 70, 71, 76, 77; women and, 85

Darfur Agreement, 71

Daud, Mohammed Daud, 34

Dayton Accords, 80, 81

DDR (disarmament, demobilization, and reintegration), 41, 42, 48, 62

DDRRR (disarmament, demobilization, repatriation, resettlement, and reintegration) programs, 46, 47

de Marnhac, Xavier Bout, 90, 93

Democratic Republic of Congo (DRC): electoral violence and, 40, 45, 50–52; EUPOL RD Congo and, 46, 47; EUSEC RD Congo and, 46, 47; extending/restoring state authority in, 8, 14; FARDC and, 13, 14, 18, 19, 20, 46–47, 48, 49; Kabila and, 40, 45, 46, 49, 50, 51, 52; key developments in, 47–52; map of, 45; mission review for, 45–52; women's governmental participation and, 85. *See also* UN Organization Stabilization in the Democratic Republic of Congo

Department of Field Support (DFS), 85

Department of Peacekeeping Operations (DPKO), 12, 23, 24, 25, 85, 93

Department of Political Affairs, 85

DFS (Department of Field Support), 85

Diamond mining, 18, 48

Diaspora, 43, 52, 111, 112

Dieter-Tietz, Klaus, 70

Dili, 119, 120

Disarmament, demobilization, and reintegration (DDR), 41, 42, 48, 62

Disarmament, demobilization, repatriation, resettlement, and reintegration (DDRRR) programs, 46, 47

Djibouti, 6, 111, 113, 115

Djinnit, Said, 38

Doha negotiations, 77

DPKO. *See* Department of Peacekeeping Operations

DRC. *See* Democratic Republic of Congo

DRC Catholic Church, 51

Drews, Erhard, 92

Drogba, Didier, 43

Drought, 109

Drug trafficking, 33, 57, 65

Duvalier, François "Papa Doc," 55

Duvalier, Jean-Claude "Baby Doc," 55, 58

Earthquake, 6, 8, 13, 15, 22, 53, 54, 56, 57, 58, 59

East Timor, 16, 117, 119

Ecarma, Natalio C., 102

Economic Community of Central African States (CEEAC), 48

Economic Community of West African States (ECOWAS), 38, 39, 62, 63, 65, 66

Egypt, 6, 96, 102, 103, 104

El Salvador, 116

Elections: Africa, 40; Côte d'Ivoire, 43–44; Haiti, 55–56; Kosovo, 92; Liberia, 61, 62–65, 68; MONUSCO and, 50–52; Timor-Leste, 118–119; women's governmental participation and, 85

Electoral violence, 40; in Côte d'Ivoire, 36, 38–42, 61; in Democratic Republic of Congo, 40, 45, 50–52; in Haiti, 40, 55; peace operations and, 40

Eroglu, Dervis, 85

Estonian cyclists, 98

Ethiopia, 7, 10, 23, 45, 64, 71, 109, 110, 111, 112

Ethiopian Defense Force, 76

EU. *See* European Union

EU Advisory and Assistance Mission for Security Reform in the Democratic Republic of Congo (EUSEC RD Congo), 46, 47

EU Border Assistance Mission at Rafah (EUBAM Rafah), 103

EU Coordinating Office for Palestinian Police Support (EUPOL COPPS), 103

EU Force in Bosnia and Herzegovina (EUFOR Althea), 80, 81, 82

EU Naval Force (EU NAVFOR), 114

EU Police Mission in Bosnia and Herzegovina (EUPM), 80, 81, 82

EU Police Mission in the Democratic Republic of Congo (EUPOL RD Congo), 46, 47

EU Rule of Law Mission in Kosovo (EULEX), 90, 91, 92–94

EU Training Mission in Somalia, 114

EUBAM Rafah (EU Border Assistance Mission at Rafah), 103

EUFOR Althea (EU Force in Bosnia and Herzegovina), 80, 81, 82

EUFOR Libya, 99

EULEX (EU Rule of Law Mission in Kosovo), 90, 91, 92–94

EUMM (EU Monitoring Mission in Georgia), 87–89

EUPM (EU Police Mission in Bosnia and Herzegovina), 80, 81, 82

EUPOL Afghanistan (EU Police Mission in Afghanistan), 29

EUPOL COPPS (EU Coordinating Office for Palestinian Police Support), 103

EUPOL RD Congo. *See* EU Police Mission in the Democratic Republic of Congo

European Commission, 86

European Union (EU): Gbagbo administration and, 38; IMT and, 120; MICOPAX and, 48; NATO and, 89; regional stability and, 107

EUSEC RD Congo (EU Advisory and Assistance Mission for Security Reform in the Democratic Republic of Congo), 46, 47

Extending/restoring state authority, 7–10, 12–13; Afghanistan, 9, 17, 34; Côte d'Ivoire, 9, 15–16; Democratic Republic of Congo, 8, 14; force and, 17–18; Haiti, 8, 14–15, 22, 53; lessons for, 17–22; Libya, 4, 5, 12, 24, 99; national security forces and, 18; operational challenges for, 22–24; peacekeepers' posture and, 21; in practice, 13; realistic expectations and, 21–22; Sierra Leone, 13–14; Somalia, 9–10, 17; South Sudan, 7–8, 16–17; state presence and, 18–20; Sudan, 7–8

Failed state, 109

FANCI. *See* Forces Armées Nationales de Côte d'Ivoire

FARDC. *See* Forces Armées du République Démocratique du Congo

Faugeras, Alain, 103

FDLR. *See* Forces Démocratiques de la Libération du Rwanda

FDS. *See* Forces de Défense et de Sécurité

Fefeh, 63

Feller, Stefan, 81

Fernández, Mariano, 53, 54

Fernandez, Raul Gloodtdofsky, 32

Ferriter, Michael, 104

Financial crisis, global, 4, 5, 10, 23, 56

FN. *See* Forces Nouvelles

FNL (Burundian Forces Nationals de Libération), 49

Food for sex allegations, 42

Force, extension of state authority and, 17–18

Forces Armées du République Démocratique du Congo (FARDC), 13, 14, 18, 19, 20, 46–47, 48, 49

Forces Armées Nationales de Côte d'Ivoire (FANCI), 42

Forces de Défense et de Sécurité (FDS), 39

Forces Démocratiques de la Libération du Rwanda (FDLR), 14, 46, 47, 49

Forces Nouvelles (FN), 39, 43

Forces Républicaines de Côte d'Ivoire (FRCI), 39, 41, 42, 44

Former Yugoslavia, International Criminal Tribunal for, 80

Foster, Luke, 118

France: Côte d'Ivoire and, 42; MONUSCO and, 50; Operation Licorne and, 5, 9, 12, 13, 18, 36, 38, 40–41, 44, 64; Operation Unified Protector and, 99; Sarkozy and, 33, 100

Frattini, Franco, 100, 105

FRCI. *See* Forces Républicaines de Côte d'Ivoire

Frente Popular para la Liberación de Saguia el-Hamra y de Río de Oro. *See* POLISARIO

Fromayan, James, 63
Front Populaire Ivoirien, 43

Gambari, Ibrahim, 76
Gangs, criminal, 13, 14, 18, 54, 57, 106
Gaza, 103, 104
Gbagbo, Laurent, 9, 15, 36, 38, 39, 40, 41, 42, 43, 44, 64, 65
Gbarnga, 68
Gbowee, Leymah, 65
Gender equality, in government, 85
General Assembly, UN, 56, 89, 93, 99
Georgia, 87–89
Global financial crisis, 4, 5, 10, 23, 56
Golan, 101, 102
Golf Hotel, 38, 40
Gonaïves, 54
Great Lakes region, 47, 49
Greek Cypriots, 84, 86
Guale ethnic group, 106
Guéhenno, Jean-Marie, 16
Guéhenno Report, 16
Guinea, 65, 115
Gulf of Aden, 114, 115
Gusmão, Kay Rala Xanana, 118, 119

Hafiz, Abdul, 123, 124
The Hague, 43
Haiti: cholera epidemic in, 8, 53, 54–55, 57, 59; earthquake in, 6, 8, 13, 15, 22, 53, 54, 56, 57, 58, 59; electoral violence and, 40, 55; extending/restoring state authority in, 8, 14–15, 22, 53; gang violence and, 13, 14, 18, 54, 57; key developments in, 55–59; map of, 53; Martelly and, 8, 21, 40, 53, 55, 56, 57, 58, 59; military surge and, 6, 53, 59; mission review for, 53–60; political developments in, 55–56; Port-au-Prince, 15, 54, 55, 57, 59; post-earthquake recovery in, 58–59; prisons in, 56, 57, 58; rule of law/justice in, 57–58; teenager rape in, 8, 53, 59; women's governmental participation and, 85. *See also* UN Stabilization Mission in Haiti
Haitian National Police (HNP), 14, 18, 54, 57, 58, 59
Haitian Provisional Electoral Council, 55, 56
Haq, Ameerah, 118

Hariri, Saad, 98
Haroun, Ahmed, 73
Hebron, 104
Helicopters: AMISOM and, 113, 114; Angola and, 50; MONUSCO and, 8, 46, 64; Operation Licorne and, 44; in peacekeeping operations, 64; shortage of, 40, 49; Sudan and, 72; UNOCI and, 9, 38, 39, 41, 64, 65
Helmand, 29
Herat, 33
Herzegovina. *See* Bosnia and Herzegovina
Hezbollah, 98, 100, 101, 102, 105
High Representative for Bosnia and Herzegovina, 81
High Representative in Sarajevo, 81
High-Level Implementation Panel, AU, 71
Hilu, Abdul Aziz al-, 73
HIV/AIDS, peacekeeping and, 93
HNP. *See* Haitian National Police
Host nations, troop contributors and, 116
Huffman, Gary E., 81
Human rights violations, 14, 20, 42, 46, 47, 49, 50, 124
Human Rights Watch, 24, 42, 50
Human trafficking, 65

Ibrahim, Khalil, 76, 77
ICU. *See* Islamic Courts Union
IDF. *See* Israeli Defense Forces
IDPs. *See* Internally displaced persons
IEC. *See* Independent Election Commission
IGAD (Inter-Governmental Authority on Development), 110, 112
IHRC (Interim Haiti Reconstruction Commission), 58–59
IMT (International Monitoring Team), 120
Incident Prevention and Response Mechanism (IPRM), 88
Independent Election Commission (IEC), 31, 38, 43
India, 28, 32
Indian Ocean, 115
Indonesia, 107, 117, 120, 121
Integrated strategic framework (ISF), 58
Inter-Governmental Authority on Development (IGAD), 110, 112
Interim Haiti Reconstruction Commission (IHRC), 58–59

Internally displaced persons (IDPs), 57, 58, 59, 89
International civilian capacities, 16
International Court of Justice, 107
International Criminal Court, 43, 99
International Criminal Tribunal for the Former Yugoslavia, 80
International Monitoring Team (IMT), 120
International Organization for Migration, 99
International Security and Stabilization Support Strategy, 46
International Security Assistance Force (ISAF): costs of, 56; counterinsurgency campaign of, 9, 17, 28, 31, 33; counterterrorism campaign of, 9, 28, 31–33; drawdown of, 28–29, 30, 31–33; governance/security handover and, 9, 17, 18, 28, 33; statistical information on, 29
International Security Forces (ISF), 117, 118, 121
Internecine conflict, Liberia, 62
Inzko, Valentin, 81
IPRM (Incident Prevention and Response Mechanism), 88
Iran, 101
Iraq, 31, 35, 96, 104
Isabel province, 108
ISAF. *See* International Security Assistance Force
ISF. *See* Integrated strategic framework; International Security Forces
Islamic Courts Union (ICU), 110
Islamic Liberation Front, Moro, 120
Islamic Maghreb, 126
Islamist extremist groups, 110
Islamist rebels, 32
Israeli Defense Forces (IDF), 100, 101, 102
Israeli-Arab conflict, 96
Israeli-Lebanese conflict, 96–98, 102
Israeli-Palestinian agreement, 103, 104
Israeli-Palestinian impasse, 102
Israel-Syria disengagement agreement, 102

Jahjaga, Atifete, 92
Jalil, Mustafa Abdel, 99
Jammu-Kashmir, 28, 32
Japan, 40, 120
Jaunin, Daniel, 38

JCC (Joint Control Commission Peacekeeping Force), 82
JEM. *See* Justice and Equality Movement
Johnsen, Einar, 104
Johnson, Hilde, 70
Johnson, Prince Yormie, 67
Joint Control Commission Peacekeeping Force (JCC), 82
Joint Coordination and Monitoring Board, 30
Joint Political and Security Mechanism, 72
Joint UN Programme on HIV/AIDS, 93
Jonglei, 74
Jordan, 6, 7, 96
Juba, 69
Justice: in Côte d'Ivoire, 42–43; in Haiti, 57–58; in Liberia, 67–68; in Timor-Leste, 121–122
Justice and Equality Movement (JEM), 77
Justice and Security Trust Fund, 67

Kabila, Joseph, 40, 45, 46, 49, 50, 51, 52
Kabila, Laurent, 45
Kabul, Afghanistan, 28, 29, 30, 31, 33, 34
Kamerhe, Vital, 51
Kampala Accords, 112
Kandahar, 29
Kandahar Provincial Council, 34
Karachi Agreement, 32
Karzai, Ahmed Wali, 34
Karzai, Hamid, 20, 28, 30, 31, 33, 34
Kasai province, 51
Kashmir, 28, 32
Katanga province, 47, 51
Kenya, 10, 23, 109, 111, 112, 113, 114
KFOR (NATO Kosovo Force), 90, 91–92, 93, 94
Khalid, Muhammad, 61
Khan, Jan Mohammed, 34
Khan, Matiullah, 34
Khartoum, 69, 72, 73, 76, 77
Khatib, Abdel-Elah al-, 99
Kidnappings, 56, 77, 98, 111, 115, 126
Kiir, Salva, 75, 76
Kilpia, Juha, 103
Ki-moon, Ban, 39
Kinshasa tabulation center, 51
Kismayo, 109
Kivus, 46, 47, 49

Koenders, Albert Gerard, 38, 43–44
Kosovo: EULEX and, 90, 91, 92–94; mission notes for, 90–95; OMIK and, 90, 91, 92, 94; peace operations in, 92–94; UNMIK and, 90, 91, 92, 94
Kosovo Force (KFOR), 90, 91–92, 93, 94
Kosovo Liberation Army, 90
Kwa Na Kwa, 48
Kyrgyzstan, 107

Laayoune, 123, 125
LAF. *See* Lebanese Armed Forces
Lakshar Gah, 33
Lamamra, Ramtane, 8
Land Commission, 65
Landmines, 72, 84, 100, 124, 125
Law and Order Trust Fund for Afghanistan (LOTFA), 24
Law Reform Commission, 65, 67
Le Roy, Alain, 8
Lebanese Armed Forces (LAF), 98, 100, 101
Lebanon: Hezbollah and, 98, 100, 101, 102, 105; Israeli-Lebanese conflict, 96–98, 102; STL and, 98, 101; UNIFIL and, 24, 96–98, 100, 101, 102, 105, 116, 121
Legal Training Center, 122
"Legitimate force," 39
Liberation and Justice Movement, 77
Liberia: CPA and, 62; elections in, 61, 62–65, 68; internecine conflict in, 62; justice and, 67–68; key developments in, 62–68; map of, 61; mercenaries, in Côte d'Ivoire, 9, 39, 41, 61, 65; Ministry of Internal Affairs, 19; mission review for, 61–68; political developments in, 62–65; refugees and, 9, 43; security in, 65–67; Sirleaf and, 8, 61, 62, 63, 64, 65, 67; women's governmental participation and, 85. *See also* UN Mission in Liberia
"Liberia Rising 2030," 65
Liberian Ministry of Justice and Law Reform, 67
Liberian National Police (LNP), 63, 64, 65, 66, 67
Liberians United for Reconciliation and Democracy (LURD), 62
Libya: extending/restoring state authority in, 4, 5, 12, 24, 99; Ibrahim and, 76, 77; IMT and, 120; NATO and, 4, 99; Operation Unified Protector in, 99; Qaddafi and, 4, 77, 99; UNSMIL and, 4, 12, 24, 99
Linas-Marcoussis Accords, 36
Line of control (LOC), 32
Lisbon conference, 28, 30
Litani River, 98, 100
Liu, Chao, 83, 84
LNP. *See* Liberian National Police
LOC (line of control), 32
Løj, Ellen Margrethe, 61
Lord's Resistance Army (LRA), 46, 47, 48, 49
LOTFA (Law and Order Trust Fund for Afghanistan), 24
LRA. *See* Lord's Resistance Army
LURD (Liberians United for Reconciliation and Democracy), 62
Lusaka Agreement, 45, 46

Macedonia, 94
Malatians, 106
Malaysia, 120
Malcorra, Susana, 16
Malemba-Nkulu tabulation center, 51
Malmquist, Henrik, 103
Manigat, Mirlande, 55
Mano River Union, 65
Maronites, 84
Maroun ar-Ras, 100
Martelly, Michel, 8, 21, 40, 53, 55, 56, 57, 58, 59
Martin, Ian, 99
Martins, Antonio, 47
Martissant, 57
Mauritania, 123, 125
Mayi-Mayi militias, 47, 49
Mazar-i-Sharif, 33
Meece, Roger, 45, 51
Menkerios, Haile, 70, 72, 73
Mercenaries, 9, 39, 41, 61, 65
MFO Sinai (Multinational Force and Observers in Sinai), 104
MICOPAX (Mission for the Consolidation of Peace in the Central African Republic), 48
Middle East: background information, 96–98; map of, 97; mission notes for, 96–105; political/regional dynamics, 100–102; security in, 96

MIF (multinational interim force), 54
Mikati, Najib, 98, 100, 101
MILF. *See* Moro Islamic Liberation Front
Military peacekeepers, deployment of, 4–5, 9
Military surge, 6, 17, 30, 33, 53, 59
Milosevic, Slobodan, 90
Mindanao, Philippines, 120
Mine Action Coordination Centre, 125
Mining, diamond, 18, 48
Ministry of Internal Affairs, Liberia, 19
MINURSO. *See* UN Mission for the Referendum in Western Sahara
MINUSTAH. *See* UN Stabilization Mission in Haiti
Mission for the Consolidation of Peace in the Central African Republic (MICOPAX), 48
Mission notes: Bosnia and Herzegovina, 80–82; Cyprus, 83–86; Georgia, 87–89; Kosovo, 90–95; Middle East, 96–105; Solomon Islands, 106–108; Somalia, 109–116; Timor-Leste, 117–122; Western Sahara, 123–126. *See also* Peacekeeping missions
Mission reviews: Afghanistan, 28–35; Côte d'Ivoire, 36–44; Democratic Republic of Congo, 45–52; Haiti, 53–60; Liberia, 61–68; South Sudan, 69–78; Sudan, 69–78. *See also* Peacekeeping missions
Mitrovica, 93
Mladic, Ratko, 94
MNLF. *See* Moro National Liberation Front
Mobutu Sese Seko, 45
MODEL (Movement for Democracy in Liberia), 62
Mogadishu, 9, 17, 109, 110, 111, 113, 114
Mohamed, Mohamed Abdullahi, 112
Moldova, Transdniestria and, 82
Monrovia, 65, 66, 67, 68
Montenegro, 94
MONUC. *See* UN Organization Mission in the Democratic Republic of Congo
MONUSCO. *See* UN Organization Stabilization Mission in the Democratic Republic of Congo
Moro Islamic Liberation Front (MILF), 120
Moro National Liberation Front (MNLF), 120
Morocco, 96, 123, 124, 125, 126
Moscow, 89

Mouvement de Libération du Congo, 50
Movement for Democracy in Liberia (MODEL), 62
Mubarak, Hosni, 96, 104
Mugisha, Fred, 110
Mujica, José, 57
Mulet, Edmond, 53, 57, 60
Mullen, Michael, 34
Multinational Battalion, 82
Multinational Force and Observers in Sinai (MFO Sinai), 104
Multinational interim force (MIF), 54
Mumbai, 32
Munene, Faustin, 50

Nabiolwa, Prosper, 48
Nairobi, 110, 112
Nakba Day, 100, 102
Naksa Day, 100, 102
Nasrallah, Hassan, 98
National Congress Party (NCP), 71, 73, 74
National Patriotic Front of Liberia (NPFL), 61
National security forces, extending state authority and, 18
National Transition Council (NTC), 99
NATO: Afghanistan and, 5, 17, 18, 28, 29, 30, 31, 64; Bosnia and, 80; deployment increases and, 6; EU and, 89; Georgia and, 89; KFOR and, 90, 91–92, 93, 94; Libya and, 4, 99; North Atlantic Council of, 104; NTM-I and, 104; Operation Ocean Shield and, 115; Operation Unified Protector and, 99
NATO Headquarters Sarajevo, 81
NATO Kosovo Force (KFOR), 90, 91–92, 93, 94
NATO Training Mission in Iraq (NTM-I), 104
NCP. *See* National Congress Party
Nelson, Elizabeth J., 63
Nepal, 7, 54, 55
New Zealand, 104, 107, 108
Nicosia, 83, 84
9/11 terrorist attacks, 29
Non-UN-commanded missions, global statistics: in Africa, deployment, 175, 177; contributors of police, 168, 170; contributors of troops, 168–169, 171; costs of missions,

189; deployment of military by region, 172; deployment of police, 173–174; in Europe, troop deployment, 176; heads of missions, 190–191; military and observer missions, 178–183; police and civilian missions, 184–188. *See also individual countries*

North Atlantic Council, NATO, 104

Northern Cyprus, 84, 86

NPFL (National Patriotic Front of Liberia), 61

NTC. *See* National Transition Council

NTM-I (NATO Training Mission in Iraq), 104

Nyamvumba, Patrick, 76

OAS (Organization of American States), 55

Obama, Barack, 31, 33

Obi, Moses Bisong, 70

OCHA. *See* Office for the Coordination of Humanitarian Affairs

OEF. *See* Operation Enduring Freedom

Office for the Coordination of Humanitarian Affairs (OCHA), 21, 99

Office of the High Commissioner for Human Rights (OHCHR), 49

OMIK (OSCE Mission in Kosovo), 90, 91, 92, 94

Operation Atalanta, 114, 115

Operation Enduring Freedom (OEF), 29

Operation Hope, 57

Operation Licorne, 5, 9, 12, 13, 18, 36, 38, 40–41, 44, 64

Operation Ocean Shield, 115

Operation Phoenix, 15, 57

Operation Unified Protector, 99

Oppong-Boanuh, James, 76

Organ trafficking, 92

Organization for Security and Cooperation in Europe (OSCE), 81, 82, 87, 88, 90, 92, 107

Organization of American States (OAS), 55

Orientale province, 49

OSCE. *See* Organization for Security and Cooperation in Europe

OSCE Mission in Kosovo (OMIK), 90, 91, 92, 94

Ouagadougou Agreement, 36

Ouattara, Alassane, 9, 15, 36, 38, 39, 40, 41, 42, 43, 44

Pacific Islands Forum, 106

Pakistan, 28, 29, 31, 32, 34

Palava Hut program, 67

Palestine Liberation Organization, 96

Palestinian demonstrations, 100

Palestinian issue, 96

Palestinian Police Support, EU Coordinating Office for, 103

Palestinian refugees, 100

Palestinian-Israeli agreement, 103, 104

Palestinian-Israeli impasse, 102

Panjshir, 33

Payams, 74, 75

Peace and Reconciliation Initiative, 65

Peace operations: default model for, 4, 10; deployment of military peacekeepers, 4–5, 9; DPKO and, 12, 23, 24, 25, 85, 93; electoral violence and, 40; global financial crisis and, 4, 5, 10, 23, 56; helicopters in, 64; in Kosovo, 92–94; regional organizations and, 107; in Somalia, 113–114; troop-contributing countries and, 7

Peacebuilding Commission, UN, 62

Peacebuilding Fund, UN, 62, 98

Peacebuilding Support Office, UN, 23, 62

Peacekeeping missions: in Africa, 37; blue helmets and, 14, 40, 111; extending state authority and, 7–10, 12; HIV/AIDS and, 93; host nations and, 116; resolutions for, 13; staff, security/safety of, 72; women's governmental participation and, 85; year in numbers for, 6–7. *See also* Extending/restoring state authority; Mission notes; Mission reviews

Peacekeeping troop reimbursement, 56

People's Party for Reconstruction and Democracy, 40

Pereira, Luiz Eduardo Ramos, 54

Petraeus, David, 31

Philip, Danny, 106

Philippines, 102, 120

Piracy, Somalia and, 114, 115

PNTL (Polícia Nacional de Timor-Leste), 119, 120, 121

Police deployments, 6, 9

Police handover, Timor-Leste and, 119–121

Police Support Unit, LNP, 66, 67

Polícia Nacional de Timor-Leste (PNTL), 119, 120, 121

POLISARIO (Frente Popular para la Liberación de Saguia el-Hamra y de Río de Oro), 123, 124, 125, 126
Popular Consultations, 73
Port-au-Prince, Haiti, 15, 54, 55, 57, 59
Portuguese contingent, 116, 121
Prakash, Chander, 45
Preah Vihear temple, 107
Pretrial Detention Task Force, 67
Préval, René, 54, 55, 56
Prisons, Haitian, 56, 57, 58
Pristina, 90, 91, 94
Provisional Electoral Council, Haitian, 55, 56

Qaddafi, Muammar, 4, 77, 99
Al-Qaida, 29, 30, 112, 125–126

Rabbani, Burhanuddin, 29, 31, 34, 35
Rafah, 103
Ramos-Horta, José, 118
RAMSI (Regional Assistance Mission in the Solomon Islands), 106–108
Rapes, 8, 43, 47, 53, 56, 59, 66
Realistic expectations, for extending state authority, 21–22
Red Cross, 84
Refugees: Côte d'Ivoire and, 9, 43, 65; Liberia and, 9, 43; Palestinian, 100; Sahrawi, 123, 126; and South Sudan refugee camp bombing, 70, 73; UNHCR and, 50, 84, 124
Regional Assistance Mission in the Solomon Islands (RAMSI), 106–108
Regional organizations, 107
Reimbursement, troop, 56
Reintegration. *See* Disarmament, demobilization, and reintegration
Republic of Cyprus, 84, 86
Republika Srpska, 80, 81
Resolutions: 425, 24, 96; 426, 96; 1244, 90, 91; 1308, 93; 1313, 13, 14; 1325, 85; 1386, 29; 1401, 29; 1509, 13, 61, 62; 1528, 13, 15, 38; 1542, 13, 25, 54; 1545, 13; 1590, 70; 1652, 38; 1701, 98, 100, 101, 105; 1856, 13; 1925, 13, 45, 46; 1942, 36, 39; 1962, 38; 1967, 39; 1968, 39; 1970, 99; 1973, 99; 1975, 15, 39; 1976, 115; 1990, 75, 76; 1991, 46; 1992, 41; 1996, 13, 45,
70, 74; 2000, 41; 2009, 99; 2015, 115; 2016, 99; for peacekeeping missions, 13; for UNOCI, 13, 15, 36–37, 38–39, 41
Resource constraints, 5, 24, 40, 57, 67
Review of International Civilian Capacities, 7, 16, 23
Rikir, Jean Paul, 47
Ross, Christopher, 125
Royal Solomon Islands Police Force, 107–108
Rule of law, 57–58, 67–68
Russia, 82, 87, 88, 89
Rwanda: Democratic Republic of Congo and, 14, 49; FDLR and, 14, 46, 47, 49; troop contributions and, 7; UNAMIR and, 116

Saakashvili, Mikhail, 87, 89
SAF. *See* Sudan Armed Forces
Sahrawi Arab Democratic Republic, 123
Sahrawi people, 123, 124, 125, 126
Saleh, Ali Abdullah, 96
Sarajevo, 81
Sarkozy, Nicolas, 33, 100
Satterfield, David M., 104
Saudi Arabia, 120
Savolainen, Jukka, 29
Sawang, Gautam, 61
Security: Afghanistan, 33, 72; Côte d'Ivoire, 41–42; extending state authority and, 18; Haiti, 56–57; Liberia, 65–67; Middle East, 96; for peacekeeping mission personnel, 72; Somalia, 111–112; South Sudan, 75; Timor-Leste, 121–122; women's governmental participation and, 85
Sekaggya, Margaret, 32
Senate Armed Services Committee, 34
Serbia-Kosovo relations, 90–94. *See also* Kosovo
Al-Shabaab, 9–10, 17, 21, 109, 110, 111–112, 113, 114
Shared Awareness and Deconfliction, 115
Shirreff, Richard, 80
Sierra Leone: AMISOM and, 113; civil war, 13, 67; extending/restoring state authority in, 13–14; UNAMSIL and, 13, 14, 18, 21
Sikua, Derek, 106
Simla Agreement, 32
Sinai, 104

SIPRI. *See* Stockholm International Peace Research Institute
Sirleaf, Ellen Johnson, 8, 61, 62, 63, 64, 65, 67
Sirte, Battle of, 99
Six-Point Plan, 91
Smith, Campbell, 106
SMS communications, 50
Solomon Islands, 106–108
Somalia: AMISOM and, 6, 10, 17, 109–116; background information, 109–111; drought in, 109; EU Training Mission in, 114; extending/restoring state authority in, 9–10, 17; map of, 109; mission notes for, 109–116; Mogadishu, 9, 17, 109, 110, 111, 113, 114; peace operations in, 113–114; peacekeeping fatalities in, 72; piracy and, 114, 115; security developments, 111–112; Al-Shabaab and, 9–10, 17, 21, 109, 110, 111–112, 113, 114; TFG and, 17, 21, 110, 111, 112, 113, 114
Soro, Guillame, 39, 43
South Ossetia, 87, 88, 89
South Sudan: CPA and, 69, 70–71; extending/restoring state authority in, 7–8, 16–17; independence of, 69, 71; map of, 69; mission review for, 69–78; refugee camp bombing in, 70, 73; security challenges in, 75. *See also* Sudan; UN Mission in South Sudan
South Sudan Police Service (SSPS), 75
Southern Kordofan State, 7, 69, 70, 71, 73, 74, 77
Southern Sudan Referendum Commission, 71
Soviet Union, 87
Special Envoy: AU, 49; Haiti, 56, 58; Khatib, 99; South Sudan, 72; Sudan, 72
Special Rapporteur for Human Rights, UN, 32
Special Representative of the Secretary-General (SRSG): Côte d'Ivoire elections and, 43; Fernández, 53, 54; Koenders, 38, 43–44; Mulet, 53, 57, 60; RRP officers and, 16; Young-Jin, 15, 38, 43
Special Tribunal for Lebanon (STL), 98, 101
SPLA. *See* Sudan People's Liberation Army
SPLM. *See* Sudan People's Liberation Movement
Srinagar, 32

SRSG. *See* Special Representative of the Secretary-General
SSPS. *See* South Sudan Police Service
Stabilization and Reconstruction Plan, 46
Stamp issue, 91, 94
State presence, state authority *v.,* 18–20. *See also* Extending/restoring state authority
STL (Special Tribunal for Lebanon), 98, 101
Stockholm International Peace Research Institute (SIPRI), 166
Sudan: Blue Nile State, 7, 69, 70, 71, 73, 74, 77; CPA and, 69, 70–71; extending/restoring state authority in, 7–8; map of, 69; mission review for, 69–78; peacekeeping fatalities in, 72; Southern Kordofan State, 7, 69, 70, 71, 73, 74, 77; women's governmental participation and, 85. *See also* South Sudan; UN Interim Security Force for Abyei; UN Mission in Sudan
Sudan Armed Forces (SAF), 69, 70, 76
Sudan People's Liberation Army (SPLA), 8, 69, 70, 73, 74, 75, 76, 77
Sudan People's Liberation Movement (SPLM), 70, 73, 74, 76, 77
Sudanese Revolutionary Front, 77
Suicide bombings, 34, 111, 112, 113, 126
Surveillance drones, 112
Syria: crisis in, 101; demonstrations in, 96, 100; Hezbollah and, 98, 100, 101, 102, 105; Israel-Syria disengagement agreement, 102; Lebanon and, 96, 97, 98, 101

Taif Accords, 98
Taliban, 17, 28, 29, 30–31, 33–34
Tardif, Marc, 54
Taylor, Charles, 61, 62, 67
Tbilisi, 87, 88, 89
Teenager rape, Haitian, 8, 53, 59
Temporary International Presence in Hebron (TIPH), 104
Tesfay, Tadesse Werede, 75
TFG. *See* Transitional Federal Government
Thailand, 107
Timor-Leste: background information, 117–118; elections in, 118–119; extending/restoring state authority in, 8–9; International Security Forces and, 117, 118,

121; map of, 117; mission notes for, 117–122; PNTL and, 119, 120, 121; police handover and, 119–120; political developments in, 118–119; security and, 121–122; transition planning and, 119; UNMIT and, 6, 116, 117, 118, 119, 120, 121, 122; women's governmental participation and, 85

Tindouf, 123, 126

TIPH (Temporary International Presence in Hebron), 104

Torture, 33

Trafficking: drug, 33, 57, 65; human, 65; organ, 92

Transdniestria, Moldova and, 82

Transitional Federal Government (TFG), 17, 21, 110, 111, 112, 113, 114

Tripoli, 99

Tripoli Peace Agreement, 120

Troop reimbursement, 56, 116

Troop-contributing countries, 7, 116

Truth, Reconciliation and Dialogue Commission, 42–43

Tshisekedi, Etienne, 45, 51, 52

Tubman, Winston, 63, 64

Tunisia, 96

Turkey, 86, 104

Turkish Cypriot military forces, 83, 84

Tyszkiewicz, Andrzej, 87

Udjani, Mangbama Lebesse, 50

Uganda, 6, 23, 45, 49, 110, 111, 112, 113, 114

Ugandan Allied Democratic Front (ADF), 49

Ugandan People's Defense Force (UPDF), 48

Ukraine, 82

UN Assistance Mission in Afghanistan (UNAMA), 21, 24, 29, 30, 33

UN Assistance Mission in Rwanda (UNAMIR), 116

UN-AU Hybrid Mission in Darfur (UNAMID), 4, 8, 64, 70, 71, 76, 77; mission statistics, 225–234

UN-commanded missions, global statistics: in Africa, 130, 146, 147; budgets and financial contributions, 158–161; civilian personnel, 149, 151–154; fatalities, 156–157; gender statistics, 155; headquarters staff, 150, 152; total personnel, 155; mandate renewals, 162; in the Middle East, 148; military observers, 134–136; police, 137–141, 144–145; timeline, operations, 163; troops, 128, 131–133, 142–143. *See also individual countries and individual missions*

UN Country Team, 15, 16, 21, 43, 46, 68, 74

UN Development Assistance Framework, 58

UN Development Programme (UNDP), 14, 22, 23, 24, 71, 84, 116, 121, 122

UN Disengagement Observer Force (UNDOF), 96, 100, 102; mission statistics, 235–242

UN Educational, Scientific, and Cultural Organization (UNESCO), 107

UN Entity for Gender Equality and the Empowerment of Women, 85

UN General Assembly, 56, 89, 93, 99

UN High Commissioner for Refugees (UNHCR), 50, 84, 124

UN Integrated Mission in Timor-Leste (UNMIT), 6, 116, 117, 118, 119, 120, 121, 122; mission statistics, 297–305

UN Integrated Peacebuilding Office in the Central African Republic (BINUCA), 48

UN Integrated Referendum and Electoral Division, 71

UN Interim Administration Mission in Kosovo (UNMIK), 90, 91, 92, 94; mission statistics, 269–276

UN Interim Force in Lebanon (UNIFIL), 24, 96–98, 100, 101, 102, 105, 116, 121; mission statistics, 252–261

UN Interim Security Force for Abyei (UNISFA): Abyei area and, 7, 69, 72, 75–77; authorization of, 4; deployment of, 69; peacekeeper fatalities and, 72; statistical information for, 75, 262–268

UN Military Observer Group in India and Pakistan (UNMOGIP), 32; mission statistics, 306–311

UN Mine Action Centre in Cyprus, 84

UN Mission for the Referendum in Western Sahara (MINURSO), 123–126; mission statistics, 198–206

UN Mission in Liberia (UNMIL): background information, 61–62; drawdown, 6, 9, 61, 62, 67; Ministry of Internal Affairs and, 19;

rule of law/justice and, 67–68; security sector reform and, 66–67; statistical information for, 61, 277–286; UNOCI and, 9, 38, 39, 41, 65

UN Mission in Sierra Leone (UNAMSIL), 13, 14, 18, 21

UN Mission in South Sudan (UNMISS): authorization of, 4, 69; establishment of, 74–75; statistical information for, 70, 287–296; UNMIS *v.*, 16, 74

UN Mission in Sudan (UNMIS): authorizing resolution for, 70; closure of, 6, 69; statistical information for, 70, 287–296; UNMISS *v.*, 16, 74

UN Operation in Côte d'Ivoire (UNOCI), 5, 6; authorizing resolutions for, 13, 15, 36–37, 38–39, 41; background information, 36–39; food for sex allegations and, 42; FRCI and, 41, 42; helicopters and, 9, 38, 39, 41, 64, 65; Koenders and, 43–44; Operation Licorne and, 5, 9, 12, 13, 18, 36, 38, 40–41, 44, 64; statistical information for, 38, 312–321; troop increase in, 6; UN Country Team and, 43; UNMIL and, 9, 38, 39, 41, 65; Young-jin and, 15, 38, 43

UN Operation in Somalia (UNOSOM), 110

UN Organization Mission in the Democratic Republic of Congo (MONUC), 13, 14, 18, 46

UN Organization Stabilization Mission in the Democratic Republic of Congo (MONUSCO): authorizing resolution for, 13; background information, 45–47; developments in east and, 47–49; elections and, 50–52; electoral violence and, 40; FARDC and, 13; helicopters and, 8, 46, 64; MONUC and, 14, 18, 46; regional relations and, 49–50; statistical information on, 45, 216–224; struggling of, 5, 8, 45; UN Country Team and, 46

UN Peacebuilding Commission, 62

UN Peacebuilding Fund, 62, 98

UN Peacebuilding Support Office, 23, 62

UN Peacekeeping Force in Cyprus (UNFICYP), 83–84, 86; mission statistics, 243–251

UN Police (UNPOL), 14, 80, 119, 121

UN Political Office in Somalia (UNPOS), 110, 112, 114

UN Special Adviser on Genocide, 39

UN Special Adviser on Responsibility to Protect, 39

UN Special Rapporteur for Human Rights, 32

UN Stabilization Mission in Haiti (MINUSTAH): authorizing resolution for, 13; background information, 53–55; cholera epidemic and, 8, 53, 54–55, 57, 59; Department of Local Government and, 20; drawdown, 6, 8, 15, 21, 53, 54, 59; electoral violence and, 40; extending/restoring state authority and, 8, 14–15, 22, 53; HNP and, 14, 18, 54, 57, 58, 59; statistical information for, 54, 207–215; teenager rape and, 8, 53, 59

UN Support Office for AMISOM (UNSOA), 114

UN Transitional Administration in East Timor (UNTAET), 117

UN Truce Supervision Organization (UNTSO), 102–103; mission statistics, 322–328

UN Women, 85

UNAIDS, 93

UNAMA. *See* UN Assistance Mission in Afghanistan

UNAMID. *See* UN-AU Hybrid Mission in Darfur

UNAMIR (UN Assistance Mission in Rwanda), 116

UNAMSIL (UN Mission in Sierra Leone), 13, 14, 18, 21

UNDOF. *See* UN Disengagement Observer Force

UNDP. *See* UN Development Programme

UNESCO (UN Educational, Scientific, and Cultural Organization), 107

UNFICYP. *See* UN Peacekeeping Force in Cyprus

UNHCR. *See* UN High Commissioner for Refugees

UNIFIL. *See* UN Interim Force in Lebanon

Union for Democracy and Social Progress, 40

Union pour la Démocratie et le Progrès Social, 50

Union pour la Nation Congolaise, 50

UNISFA. *See* UN Interim Security Force for Abyei

UNITAF (US-led Unified Taskforce), 110

United States: Afghanistan and, 29–30; Gbagbo administration and, 38; OAS and, 55; Pakistan and, 34; UNITAF and, 110
UNMIK. *See* UN Interim Administration Mission in Kosovo
UNMIL. *See* UN Mission in Liberia
UNMIS. *See* UN Mission in Sudan
UNMISS. *See* UN Mission in South Sudan
UNMIT. *See* UN Integrated Mission in Timor-Leste
UNMOGIP. *See* UN Military Observer Group in India and Pakistan
UNOCI. *See* UN Operation in Côte d'Ivoire
UNOSOM (UN Operation in Somalia), 110
UNPOL (UN Police), 14, 80, 119, 121
UNPOS (UN Political Office in Somalia), 110, 112, 114
UN's Capstone Doctrine, 12
UNSMIL (UN Support Mission in Libya), 4, 12, 24, 99
UNSOA (UN Support Office for AMISOM), 114
UNTAET (UN Transitional Administration in East Timor), 117
UNTSO. *See* UN Truce Supervision Organization
UPDF (Ugandan People's Defense Force), 48
Uruzgan, 29
US-led Unified Taskforce (UNITAF), 110

VCCT (voluntary confidential counseling and testing), 93

Veri, Rinaldo, 99
Voluntary confidential counseling and testing (VCCT), 93

WACI (West Africa Coast Initiative), 65, 66
Wafy, Abdallah, 45
West Africa Coast Initiative (WACI), 65, 66
West Bank, 96, 103
Western Sahara, 123–126
Whiting, Warren J., 104
Williams, Michael, 101
Women, Peace, and Security (WPS) framework, 85
Women's governmental participation, 85
World Bank, 7, 8, 19, 22, 23, 38
World Development Report, 7, 8, 19, 22, 23
World Food Programme, 112, 114
World Health Organization, 39
World Heritage site, 107
WPS (Women, Peace, and Security) framework, 85

Yamoussoukro Airport, 39
Yemen, 96
Yida, 73
Yopougon district, 41
Young-jin, Choi, 15, 38, 43
Yusof, Mahdi, 120

Zarif, Farid, 90, 92
Zhao Jingmin, 124

About the Book

Unique in its breadth of coverage, the *Annual Review of Global Peace Operations* presents the most detailed collection of data on peace operations—those launched by the UN, by regional organizations, and by coalitions—that is available. Features of the 2012 volume include:

- a thematic focus on the role of peace operations in the extension of state authority
- a summary analysis of trends and developments in peace operations through 2011
- concise analyses of all peacekeeping missions on the ground in 2011
- in-depth explorations of key missions, focusing on those that faced significant challenges or underwent major developments in 2011
- extensive, full-color maps, figures, and photographs

The editorially independent *Annual Review* is a project of the **Center on International Cooperation** at New York University, with the support of both the Peacekeeping Best Practices Section of the UN Department of Peacekeeping Operations and the UN Department of Field Support.